Hannah Arendt (1906–1975) was a philosopher and political theorist of astonishing range and originality and one of the leading
thinkers of the twentieth century. A former student of Martin Heidegger and Karl Jaspers, she fled Nazi Germany to Paris in 1933, and
subsequently escaped from Vichy France to New York in 1941. The
Origins of Totalitarianism (1951) made her famous. After visiting profes-
sorships at Princeton, Berkeley, and the University of Chicago, she
took up a permanent position at the New School in 1967. Renowned
for The Human Condition, On Revolution, and The Life of the Mind, she is also
known for her brilliant but controversial reporting and analysis of
Adolf Eichmann's 1961 trial in Jerusalem—an experience that led
her to coin the phrase "the banality of evil."

In this outstanding introduction to Arendt's thought Dana Villa
begins with a helpful overview of Arendt's life and intellectual development, before examining and assessing the following important
topics:

• Arendt's analysis of the nature of political evil and the arguments
  of The Origins of Totalitarianism
• political freedom and political action and the arguments of On
  the Human Condition, especially Arendt's return to the ancient Greek
  polis and her critique of modernity
• modernity and revolution and Arendt's text On Revolution
• responsibility and judgment and her reporting of the Eichmann
  trial

- Arendt's view of contemplation and the fundamental faculties of mental life
- Arendt's rich legacy and influence, including her civic republican understanding of freedom and her influence on the Frankfurt School, communitarianism, and democratic theory.

Including a chronology, chapter summaries, and suggestions for further reading, this indispensable guide to Arendt's philosophy will also be useful to those in related disciplines such as politics, sociology, history, and economics.

Dana Villa is Packey J. Dee Professor of Political Theory at the University of Notre Dame, USA. An internationally known scholar of the political thought of Arendt, Villa's work has been translated into numerous languages, and he has received awards and fellowships from the National Endowment for the Humanities, the American Council of Learned Societies, the Institute for Advanced Study, and the American Academy in Berlin.

Routledge Philosophers
Edited by Brian Leiter

University of Chicago, USA

Routledge Philosophers is a major series of introductions to the great Western philosophers. Each book places a major philosopher or thinker in historical context, explains and assesses their key arguments, and considers their legacy. Additional features include a chronology of major dates and events, chapter summaries, annotated suggestions for further reading and a glossary of technical terms.

An ideal starting point for those new to philosophy, they are also essential reading for those interested in the subject at any level.

Also available:

For more information about this series, please visit: https://www.routledge.com/The-Routledge-Philosophers/book-series/ROUTPHIL

Dana Villa

Arendt

Routledge
Taylor & Francis Group

LONDON AND NEW YORK

First published 2021
by Routledge
2 Park Square, Milton Park, Abingdon, Oxon OX14 4RN

and by Routledge
52 Vanderbilt Avenue, New York, NY 10017

Routledge is an imprint of the Taylor & Francis Group, an informa business

British Library Cataloguing-in-Publication Data
A catalogue record for this book is available from the British Library

Library of Congress Cataloging-in-Publication Data
Names: Villa, Dana Richard, author.
Title: Arendt / Dana Villa.
Description: Abingdon, Oxon; New York, NY: Routledge, 2021. |
Series: The routledge philosophers | Includes bibliographical
references and index. |
Identifiers: LCCN 2020044622 (print) | LCCN 2020044623 (ebook) |
ISBN 9781138938991 (hbk) | ISBN 9781138939004 (pbk) |
ISBN 9780429424212 (ebk)
Subjects: LCSH: Arendt, Hannah, 1906–1975.
Classification: LCC B945.A694 V55 2021 (print) | LCC B945.A694 (ebook) |
DDC 320.5092—dc23
LC record available at https://lccn.loc.gov/2020044622
LC ebook record available at https://lccn.loc.gov/2020044623

ISBN: 978-1-138-93899-1 (hbk)
ISBN: 978-1-138-93900-4 (pbk)
ISBN: 978-0-429-42421-2 (ebk)

Typeset in Joanna
by codeMantra

To Ulrika and Noa Björk

Contents

Chronology

1906   Born in Hannover, Germany, the only child to a secular
                Jewish couple, Paul and Martha (Cohn) Arendt. They
                move to Königsberg, East Prussia, where the Cohn
                family has a successful tea importing business and
                where Paul's family, the Arendts, has deep roots.
1913   Father dies after a long and debilitating illness.
1914   Outbreak of WWI. Arendt and mother flee from
                Russian advance to relatives in Berlin. Returns to
                Königsberg ten weeks later.
1918–1919   Fall of the *Kaiserreich*. Socialist revolutions break out in
                Berlin and Munich.
1920   Arendt expelled from the *Luiseschule* for insubordination.
1922–1923   Studies classics and theology for a few semesters at
                the University in Berlin, as preparation for the *Abitur*
                university entrance exam.
1924   Enters Marburg University and studies philosophy
                with Heidegger.
1925   Enters into a relationship with the married Heidegger.
1926   Moves to Heidelberg to write her thesis with Karl
                Jaspers. Continues seeing Heidegger clandestinely.
1927   Meets the Zionist organizer Kurt Blumenfeld at
                Heidelberg lecture.
1929   Meets Gunther Stern, a Jewish philosophy student
                who will become her first husband. Her dissertation
                on Augustine's concept of love, *Der Liebesbegriffe bei
                Augustin*, is published by J. Springer later that year.

1930	Moves to Berlin with Stern.
1931–1932	Becomes involved with Zionist discussion groups in Berlin.
1933	The Reichstag fire (February 4). Nazi persecution of all communists and leftists. Stern flees Berlin for Paris. Arendt arrested for collecting anti-Semitic propaganda from the Prussian State Library at the behest of Blumenfeld. Questioned and released, she and her mother flee across the German border to Czechoslovakia. They then move to Geneva and (finally) Paris.
1934	Starts work for Agriculture et Artisinat, an organization that prepares young Jewish emigres for life in Palestine, the "Jewish Homeland." Later becomes director of Youth Aliyah in Paris, a Jewish organization with a similar mission. Befriends Walter Benjamin, another stateless refugee from Berlin.
1936	Meets Heinrich Blücher, a leftist German refugee who had taken part in the Spartacist uprising in Berlin led by Rosa Luxemburg.
1937	Divorces Stern.
1938	Youth Aliyah moves to London. Arendt begins work for the Jewish Agency in Paris.
1940	War declared between France and Germany. Arendt and her mother detained as "enemy aliens" in a French concentration camp at Gurs. Blücher interred at a similar camp for men at Villemalard. In the confusion after France's quick defeat, Arendt, her mother, and Blücher are able to escape to Montauban.
1941	Arendt and her husband escape to Vichy France, then to Lisbon where a brief relaxation of emigration policy allows them to board a ship to the United States. Arendt begins working for the German-Jewish paper *Aufbau* in New York.
1942	Arendt and Blücher learn of the Nazi death camps set up for the destruction of European Jewry. Arendt writes newspaper columns calling for the formation of a Jewish Army to fight alongside the Allies.

1944   Undertakes research work for the Commission on
            European Jewish Cultural Reconstruction, cataloging
            Jewish cultural treasures that were put at risk by the
            war and the Nazi's Jewish policy. Begins work on the
            manuscript that will become The Origins of Totalitarianism.
1946   Begins work as an editor at Schocken Books. Publishes
            the essay "What is Existenz Philosophy?" which is
            quite critical of Heidegger.
1948   Death of mother.
1949   Becomes Executive Director of Jewish Cultural
            Reconstruction and travels for six months to post-
            war Europe where she directs the recovery of over
            1.5 million volumes of Hebraica and Judaica, as
            well as scrolls of law. Meets with both Jaspers and
            Heidegger.
1950   Becomes a senior editor at Schocken Books.
1951   Publishes The Origins of Totalitarianism to great acclaim;
            becomes famous.
1952   Receives Guggenheim Fellowship for a project on
            "Totalitarian Elements in Marxism."
1953   Gives Gaus Seminars at Princeton University.
1955   Takes up duties as a visiting professor of political
            theory at Berkeley.
1956   Gives Walgreen Foundations Lectures, which will
            become The Human Condition, at the University of Chicago.
1958   Publishes The Human Condition.
1959   Publishes the essay "Reflections on Little Rock"
            which stokes controversy. Awarded the Lessing Prize
            by the city of Hamburg.
1961   Travels to Jerusalem to cover the Eichmann trial for
            The New Yorker. Publishes Between Past and Future.
1963   Publishes the five part article "A Reporter at Large:
            Eichmann in Jerusalem" which is revised and issued
            as a book the same year. Tremendous controversy
            over her portrayal of Eichmann as a non-fanatical
            "desk murderer." On Revolution also published. Begins
            teaching at the University of Chicago on a regular
            visiting basis.

1967	Takes a full-time position at the New School for Social Research in New York.
1968	Witness to student unrest at Columbia University. Publishes *Men in Dark Times*, a collection of portrait essays of various figures, including Walter Benjamin and Jaspers.
1969	Jaspers dies. Arendt publishes the essay "Reflections on Violence" and supports the student movement against the Vietnam War.
1970	Blücher dies. Arendt gives Kant seminar at the New School, the source of the posthumously published *Lectures on Kant's Political Philosophy*.
1971	"Thinking and Moral Considerations" published in *Social Research*.
1972	Attends conference in her honor at York University, Toronto, and publishes *Crises of the Republic*. The volume includes "Reflections on Violence" and the essays "Civil Disobedience" and "Lying in Politics."
1973	Gives the first series (on "Thinking") of her Gifford Lecture at Aberdeen University.
1974	Returns to Aberdeen to give second series of Gifford Lectures (on "Willing") but suffers a near fatal heart attack during her first lecture.
1975	Wins the Danish Sonning Prize for Contributions to European Civilization. Visits Heidegger one last time (he dies in 1976). Revises her Gifford lectures and (barely) begins the third and final part, "Judging," for *The Life of the Mind*. Dies suddenly of a heart attack on December 4.
1978	The two volumes of *The Life of the Mind* (edited by her friend, the novelist Mary McCarthy), published posthumously.

One
Life, influences, and central concerns

I From Europe to America, philosophy to politics

Hannah Arendt (1906–1975) has been justly acclaimed as one of the most original political thinkers of the twentieth century. She is the only woman to have been granted the coveted status of a "canonical" thinker in the Western tradition of political theory. A German-Jewish emigré to the United States she first achieved fame with the publication of The Origins of Totalitarianism in 1951. This fame grew with the publication of The Human Condition (1958), Between Past and Future (1961), and On Revolution (1963). It is in these three works that she most fully develops her political thinking. In 1963, the publication of Eichmann in Jerusalem added notoriety to her celebrity, largely because of the controversy it stirred among members of the American Jewish community. The controversy continues to this day.

After 1965, with the most vehement phase of the Eichmann controversy over, Arendt's reputation as a political thinker reasserted itself. She held visiting positions at major American universities—Princeton, Berkeley, and the University of Chicago among them—before finally negotiating a permanent position at the New School for Social Research in 1967. Arendt's disinclination to take on a full-time professorial position after The Origins of Totalitarianism made her famous was a function of three factors. First, there was her desire to spend as much time as possible in New York with her husband, native Berliner and former Spartacist radical (and, ultimately, Bard College professor) Heinrich Blücher. Second, she had an extreme and lingering distaste for the academic conformity and intellectual irresponsibility she encountered in Germany during the 1930s. Third, she confessed to a certain shyness and an inability to appear in public "four or five times a week." She was, nevertheless, a charismatic teacher and lecturer, albeit one who jealously preserved her time to think. Thinking, as she observed numerous times, is something we can do only in solitude, when we withdraw from the "world of appearances" and engage in a silent dialogue with ourselves.

In the second half of the 1960s and early part of the 1970s, Arendt was a widely recognized public intellectual, commenting on American political affairs (such as the Vietnam War and the Watergate scandal) as well as global issues (such as the possibility of nuclear war). The essays collected in Crises of the Republic (1972) provide a representative sampling and include the much-cited "Lying in Politics." Her last and unfinished work, The Life of the Mind, appeared posthumously in 1978, as did an edited collection of her writings on Jewish history and politics entitled The Jew as Pariah: Jewish Identity and Politics in the Modern Age. In the last years of her life, she received many honorary degrees (from Princeton, Dartmouth, and Fordham, among others) as well as such major awards as the Danish Sonning Prize for Contributions to European Civilization (1975). In 1973, she was invited to give the Gifford Lectures at the University of Aberdeen. The two sets of Gifford Lectures—on the mental activities of thinking and willing—constitute the body of the two-volume The Life of the Mind. Arendt had barely begun work on the second part of the second volume, on our faculty of judgment, when she died suddenly on December 4, 1975 at the age of sixty-nine.

This thumbnail sketch of Arendt's American career as a political thinker, author, lecturer, and professor makes no mention of her life in Germany from her birth (in 1906) and childhood in Königsberg, East Prussia to her flight from Nazi persecution in 1933. Nor does it address her intellectual context or the major influences on her thought. The latter include (most notably): ancient Greek philosophy, poetry and drama; early Christian theology; the German philosophical tradition from Kant to Nietzsche; the Western canon of political philosophy; and the work of her teachers Martin Heidegger (at Marburg) and Karl Jaspers (at Heidelberg). Heidegger and Jaspers were the leading lights of the new Existenz philosophy born during

Arendt's university years (1924–1929), the most stable period of the notoriously unstable Weimar Republic.

A strong influence of a different sort was that of Kurt Blumenfeld (1884–1964), the German-Jewish Zionist responsible for stimulating Arendt's latent interest in her Jewish identity and co-responsible (in tandem with the growth of the Nazi movement) for her political awakening in the early 1930s. It was Blumenfeld who commissioned Arendt, who was not a member of his or any other Zionist organization known to the Nazis, to surreptitiously collect anti-Semitic propaganda material in the Prussian State Library in order to raise awareness of the persecution of German Jewry both at home and abroad. This was a delicate and risky operation. Arendt was caught by the authorities and questioned by a (fortunately sympathetic) police detective who was new to the job of interrogating political "criminals." Miraculously, she was released. She immediately fled Germany with her mother, Martha Arendt, crossing the German-Czech border in 1933.

My sketch of Arendt's American career also makes no mention of the years she spent as a refugee in Paris (1933–1941) or of her intense work for a variety of Jewish aid and charitable organizations during this same period. She became director of the Paris Branch of Youth Aliyah, an organization devoted to preparing Jewish refugee children for emigration to, and life in, Palestine. Arendt herself helped to deliver one group of children to Palestine in 1935—her first trip to the region. Her refugee status continued after her escape, along with Blücher (whom she had met in Paris), to America in 1941. It only ended with her receipt of American citizenship in 1951. It was this experience that led her to focus on the plight of stateless people during the interwar period in the second part of *The Origins of Totalitarianism*.

In the years leading up to her receipt of American citizenship, Arendt worked as an editor for Schocken Books in New York. After the war, in 1948, the organization Jewish Cultural Reconstruction was established and she was appointed its executive director. It was in this capacity that Arendt returned to Europe for six months in 1949–1950, laying the groundwork for the eventual recovery of over 1.5 million volumes of Hebraica and Judaica, along with "thousands of ceremonial and artistic objects, and over a thousand scrolls of law."[1] During this early period of her American life, she became engaged with the extraordinary group of writers, artists, and editors that history has dubbed "the New York intellectuals." This group included Irving Howe and Nathan Glazer (originally Arendt's co-editors at Schocken), as well as the poet Randall Jarrell, the novelist Mary McCarthy, Philip Rahv (the founding editor of *Partisan Review*), and David Riesman (sociologist and author of *The Lonely Crowd*).

All of these items—her classical German education, the awakening of interest in her Jewish identity, the narrow escape from Germany, the eighteen years spent as a stateless person, her work for Jewish charitable and cultural organizations in both Paris and New York, her receipt of American citizenship, and her entry into the higher echelons of New York intellectual and cultural life—were formative for Arendt. They trace a peculiarly twentieth-century life—a life of flight, exile, refuge, intense intellectual achievement, and (ultimately) fame at home and abroad. Superficially at least, her life bears more resemblance to the threat-filled existence Plato and Aristotle faced during the final phases of the Athenian democracy than it does to the calmer professorial existence of, say, Kant or Hegel.

But while Plato and Aristotle's experience of politics led them to become harsh critics of Athenian democracy, Arendt did not share their longing to tame the political world and curb the freedom of what Plato called the "beast-like" *demos*. Quite the contrary. Once secure in her new American home, Arendt went on to *celebrate* the political life as lived by diverse, public-spirited, and democratic citizens. Coming on the heels of *The Origins of Totalitarianism*, *The Human Condition* began life as an examination of what Arendt termed "the proto-totalitarian elements in Marx's thought." It evolved, however, to become a quasi-Periclean riposte to those who would denigrate the *bios politikos* from the standpoint of either the *vita contemplativa* (such as Plato and Aristotle) or that of *homo economicus* (such as Adam Smith and Marx himself).

II Praising politics after totalitarianism

This fact points to one of the central interpretive dilemmas faced by any newcomer to Arendt's work. How is it that one of the premier analysts of Nazi and Soviet totalitarianism—of a form of government that appeared to politicize everything, inflating the State to massive proportions—came to celebrate politics and political action? How is it that Arendt, a refugee from a politics seemingly without limits, came to value the *positive* freedom of political participation over the *negative* freedom from interference (by the state or popular majorities) celebrated by such liberal thinkers as Benjamin Constant, John Stuart Mill, or her contemporary Isaiah Berlin? As Arendt rhetorically asks in her essay "What is Freedom?" (1961),

> Was not the liberal credo, 'The less politics, the more freedom,' right after all?...Is it not true, as we all somehow believe, that politics is compatible with freedom only because and insofar as it guarantees a possible freedom *from* politics?[2]

The short answer to this question is that she did not view totalitarianism as the product of an unbounded politics. In Arendt's view, it was, rather, a radical form of *anti-politics*, one devoted to the destruction of the elements she viewed as basic to—and constitutive of—all genuine political life: human plurality, public freedom, equal citizenship, and the human capacity for spontaneous (initiatory) action. The ancient Greeks, she thought, had invented *politics* (as distinct from domination or rule) based on these elements. Athenian democracy created the possibility of conducting common affairs by means of collective debate, deliberation, and decision. This was a possibility unknown not only to those ruled by "Asiatic despots" (such as the Persian emperors Darius and Xerxes), but also to Greek life itself prior to reforms instituted by Cleisthenes in sixth-century (BCE) Athens. Political life as it emerged in this period was based upon a high degree of citizen participation as well as adherence to law and constitutional government.

In contrast, totalitarianism destroyed not only the rule of law; it also destroyed all stable legal and institutional structures, including those of the state itself. The totalitarians did this, Arendt claimed, in order to make individual peoples and (ultimately) the world as a whole subject to "laws of movement" ostensibly dictated by Nature or History. For the Nazis, the law of Nature was one of perpetual racial struggle, a struggle destined to end with the "survival of the fittest" and the Aryan or master race dominating all others. For the Bolsheviks, the law of History was one of ceaseless struggle between

social classes. It was destined to produce the dictatorship of the proletariat and, ultimately, the creation of a classless utopia.

The popular image of totalitarian government as rule of a mammoth and monolithic "total State" thus gets it wrong. Arendt viewed
totalitarian government not as a static structure of domination but
rather as endlessly and destructively dynamic. The regimes of Hitler
and Stalin attempted to create a condition of more or less permanent revolution, one designed to facilitate the execution of the
all-determining laws of Nature or History supposedly discovered by
their respective ideologies. Politics—understood as the creation and
preservation of relatively permanent legal-institutional structures
within which the activities of public deliberation and persuasion
can take place—thus gave way to a uniquely violent and destructive
form of anti-politics. That is, it gave way to the attempt to destroy all
obstacles to the acceleration of the "laws of movement" the totalitarians thought inherent in historical or natural evolution.

Viewed from this angle, the link between the historical analysis
of The Origins of Totalitarianism and the more abstract theoretical themes
of The Human Condition comes into clearer focus. It is not as if Arendt
somehow forgot the monumental catastrophes to which politics can
lead. The deep and abiding shock she and her husband experienced
in 1943 when they learned that the darkest rumors about the fate of
European Jewry were true made that an impossibility. Rather, she devoted the bulk of her post-Origins writing to reminding her audience
of the nature and promise of politics and the dignity of leading a political
life, one grounded in civic responsibility and the imperative of caring
for our shared (institutionally articulated) public world. In Arendt's
view, it was precisely the selfishness, cynicism, and lack of concern
for the public world characteristic of European politics during the
Imperialist era (1884–1914) that—together with the resentment,
traumas, and tribal nationalism of the interwar period—helped to
make the unprecedented phenomenon of totalitarianism possible. She
was convinced that, whenever citizens abandon their shared responsibility for the legal-institutional structure of the public world, there
totalitarianism—or something like it—became possible.

Arendt's quasi-Periclean celebration of political action in The Human Condition thus aims at making us see that, no matter how low
our contemporary public life may have sunk, the life of the engaged

citizen—the *bios politikos*—is not just an honorable one but a distinctively human one as well. It is distinctively human because it through the words and deeds performed by citizens upon a public stage that our freedom—our human capacity to rise above biological, economic, and even technological determinism—is most palpably manifest. As she puts it in her essay "What is Freedom?":

> The field where freedom has always been known, not as a [philosophical] problem, to be sure, but as a fact of everyday life, is the political realm. And even today, whether we know it or not, the question of politics and the fact that man is endowed with the gift of action must always be present to our mind when we speak of the problem of freedom; for action and politics, among all the capabilities and potentialities of human life, are the only things of which we could not even conceive without at least assuming that freedom exists, and we can hardly touch upon a single political issue without, implicitly or explicitly, touching upon an issue of man's liberty. Freedom, moreover, is not only one of the many problems and phenomena of the political realm, properly speaking, such as justice, or power, or equality; freedom, which only seldom–in times of crisis or revolution–becomes the direct aim of political action, is actually the reason why men live together in political organization at all. Without it, political life as such would be meaningless. The *raison d'être* of politics is freedom, and its field of experience is action.[3]

Arendt thinks our distinctively human freedom—the capacity to begin, to initiate, to start something new—is undeniably on display in the public realm, the realm of *political* action. This fact endows political freedom and political action with what might be called their "existential supremacy."[4] Of course, Arendt does not discount the freedom from interference—the freedom to be left alone—protected by all forms of limited or constitutional government. However, she thinks that this "negative" liberty is, so to speak, incomplete. The individual's "pursuit of happiness" needs to be matched or complemented by the "pursuit of public happiness" if human freedom is to reach its fullest—that is, its most tangible and worldly—expression.

III Locating Arendt in the political and philosophical landscape

Arendt's claim may appear outlandish to those of us who have been taught to understand free activity in primarily economic or individually expressive terms. Things aren't helped much when, a little further in the same essay, Arendt claims that "men are free—as distinguished from their possessing the gift for freedom—so long as they act, neither before nor after; for to be free and to act are the same."[5] This claim, combined with Arendt's insistence that "the performing arts…have indeed a strong affinity with politics," has led critics to charge her with having a "dramaturgical" or overtly theatrical notion of political action. If this charge were true, it would place Arendt in uncomfortable proximity to various neo-Nietzschean (and proto-fascist) intellectuals who wrote during the 1920s and 1930s. At the very least, it would place her well out of the mainstream of modern western, Enlightenment-inflected, political thought.

While Nietzsche's influence on Arendt can hardly be denied, his anti-Platonism had more impact on her thinking about the western philosophical tradition (and its "end" in the writings of Kierkegaard, Marx, and Nietzsche himself) than it did upon her political theorizing. Contrary to what her critics have suggested, Arendt's political thinking can be clearly located in the mainstream of the civic republican tradition. Along with liberalism, civic republicanism is one of the two great bodies of political thought that form the backdrop for virtually all modern Western political theory. The roots of the civic republican tradition can be traced back to Aristotle, Cicero, and the histories of the Rome written by Livy and Tacitus. It developed through a distinctively modern synthesis of Aristotelian and neo-Roman thought trains in the work of such Renaissance humanists as Piero Guicciardini and Niccolò Machiavelli. Both Guicciardini and Machiavelli stressed the importance of the *vivere civile* for living a fully human life, as well as for preserving freedom and self-government in republican city-states such as Venice and Florence.[6] Crucial to such preservation, they thought, was the presence of a strong civic ethos, one characterized by the priority citizens gave to the "public thing" (or *res publica*) over their own individual (or "selfish") interests.

Seventeenth-century English political thinkers such as James Harrington and Algernon Sydney appropriated the civic humanist and republican themes found in Guicciardini and Machiavelli, giving them new life during the tumultuous period stretching from the lead-up to the English Civil War to the Stuart Restoration. In France, Montesquieu's influential *Spirit of the Laws* (1748) identified civic virtue as the animating principle of all republican government, while Rousseau's *Social Contract* (1762) made the case that popular sovereignty was the only valid ground of *legitimate* political authority. It is no exaggeration to say that these English and French sources had a tremendous, albeit sometimes indirect, impact on the American founders. Thomas Jefferson's writings in particular are an expression of a distinctively republican political sensibility. He stressed the importance of the civic virtue possessed by the citizen-farmers of a largely agrarian republic and feared that commercial and banking interests would become sources of corruption and domination by "factions." In the first half of the nineteenth century, Alexis de Tocqueville's two-volume *Democracy in America* (1835 and 1840) analyzed how American democracy accomplished the seemingly impossible task of combining the republican emphasis on political freedom and civic participation with the liberal tradition's focus upon individual rights and the pursuit of private interests.

Arendt's thoughts on the centrality of political action and political freedom look markedly less exotic when placed in the context of the civic republican tradition. Of course, not all the writers I have mentioned *positively* influenced her (she was as critical of Rousseau's "general will" as was her liberal contemporary, Isaiah Berlin). However, any moderately attentive reader of her work, *On Revolution* in particular, must recognize that the writings of Aristotle, Machiavelli, Montesquieu, and Tocqueville are formative influences on her political thinking, her recurrent references to Homeric poetry, Periclean Athens, Nietzsche, and Heidegger notwithstanding.

This is not to deny the strong Greek influence on Arendt's thought. In the chapter on "Action" in *The Human Condition*, Arendt draws on both Homer's *Iliad* and Pericles' Funeral Oration in order to reveal a world in which appearing publicly before one's peers in political speech and deeds was, in a very real sense, the point of life. However, and again contrary to what many critics have suggested, she *does not* draw upon them in order to provide a normative model for democratic political association in the present. Her intent, rather, is to confront us with our own unthought prejudices about *what* politics is and the role political life can play in what Max Weber once referred to as "the total economy of human life." Similarly, she draws on Nietzsche and Heidegger *not* because she in any way admires their political views (she vehemently rejects Nietzsche's aristocratism and Heidegger's fatal attraction to the idea of a *Volksgemeinschaft*). Rather, she draws on them because they help us to see the desires (for power, domination, and revenge) and resentments (of human finitude and historical contingency) that underlie much of the Western metaphysical-theological tradition, which has a notably dim view of the activity of politics and the realm of human affairs.

Both Nietzsche and Heidegger thought that this tradition had, in a very important sense, come to an end in the late nineteenth century. While it was Hegel who first declared that "the sentiment underlying religion in the modern age [is] the sentiment: God is dead," it was Nietzsche, and later Heidegger, who drew out the implications of this for western culture and philosophy more generally. As Arendt notes in her "Introduction" to *The Life of the Mind*, the "death of God" is Nietzsche's metaphorical way of talking about the end of metaphysics—a phenomenon that would be of interest only to professional philosophers were it not for the fact that the distinction Plato drew between a fleeting, ever-changing sensible realm and an immutable, intelligible realm *beyond* the world of appearances came to structure *both* Western philosophical and theological thought, and (by extension) Western *political* thinking as well. The much commented upon "death of God" points not to the end of religious faith, but rather to the end of a particular way of thinking about the world and its ostensibly non-temporal ground or foundation. As Arendt writes:

> What has come to an end is the basic distinction between the sensory and the supersensory, together with the notion, at least as old as Parmenides, that whatever is not given to the senses–God, or Being, or the First Principles and Causes (*archai*) or the Ideas–is more real, more truthful, more meaningful than what appears, that it is not just *beyond* sense perception but *above* the world of the senses. What is "dead" is not only the localization of such "eternal truths" but also the distinction itself.[7]

This "death" is important because Arendt thinks Plato was driven to draw his original distinctions (in Books VI and VII of the *Republic*) for *political reasons*.[8] If particular, concrete, existing things are less real than the abstract, universal ideas they imperfectly instantiated, then it becomes possible to posit a set of ideal models or standards not just for things (like beds) but for human institutions and behavior as well. The contingency, relativity, and impermanence of the realm of human affairs then makes way for that which is necessary, absolute, and eternal—that "other" world, whether it be that of the Forms or God's commands. In this manner, the plural *opinions* of a body of diverse and equal citizens (such as we find in democratic Athens and in all authentic republics and democracies) can be set aside as clearly inferior to the eternal truths given by God, Nature, or the order of the cosmos. The debate, deliberation, and persuasion that constituted the political realm according to the original Greek understanding gives way to a metaphysically grounded *authority*, one that splits what had been a body of diverse equals into *rulers* (philosopher-kings, priests, aristocrats by nature, divinely appointed monarchs) and *ruled* (everybody else).

Viewed from *this* angle, a good deal of the western tradition of philosophical and political thought may be justly characterized as *authoritarian* in nature. Appealing to a distinction between a "true" and an "apparent" world—between *nature* and *convention*, *essence* and *existence*, genuine *knowledge* and "mere" *opinion*—Western political thinkers have generally sought to subject the political realm to something higher and outside itself. As Arendt writes in her essay "What is Authority?," the "source of authority in authoritarian government is always a force external and superior to its own power; it is always this source, this external force which transcends the political realm, from which the authorities derive their 'authority'..."[9]

The Ideas, God's commandments, or the "laws of nature" thus endow the laws and enactments of philosopher-kings, divinely appointed monarchs, or nature's aristocrats with a trans-political legitimacy. One important consequence of this is that wherever *some* form of the distinction between the "true" world and the "apparent" one is generally accepted, there a hierarchical relationship between rulers and ruled will be viewed not just as *legitimate* but as virtually *unquestionable*.

IV Praxis, political thinking, and the role of the Ancient Greeks

This fact gives the rather abstract topics of the "death of God" and the "end of metaphysics" a decidedly *political* spin. If, in western culture broadly considered, secularization has brought us to a point where not just "eternal truths" but the very distinctions upon which such truths are grounded are no longer convincing; if, in some as yet to be determined sense, our tradition of moral and political thought has played out the various iterations these distinctions made possible (metaphysical or divine hierarchies; natural law; natural rights, etc.), *then* we confront not so much the end of our tradition, as a very real *break* in it. Arendt suggests in numerous places that this fact not only creates the possibility of a wide-ranging crisis of legitimacy. More positively, it also creates the opportunity to look upon authentically *political* phenomena—human plurality, the public realm, political action, and political judgment—with new eyes. No longer blinded by the anti-political prejudices born of our philosophical and theological traditions, these phenomena can be recovered, described, and interpreted in a new way, one which invests the political realm with a dignity and integral meaning these traditions explicitly deny it.

This is the background for what the German philosopher and social theorist Jürgen Habermas once described as Arendt's "systematic renewal of the Aristotelian concept of *praxis*."[10] "*Praxis*" is the Greek word for action, which Aristotle carefully distinguished from *poiēsis* (production or fabrication) in his *Nicomachean Ethics*. As Aristotle pungently put it, "action is not production, nor production action" (Bk. VI, 1140a). Unlike making or fabrication, *praxis* has to do with deliberations and judgments performed in a public (ethical-political) context. For Aristotle, *praxis* involves *phronēsis*—the practical wisdom or prudence born of a combination of experience, foresight, and character. It does not aim, as does *poiēsis*, at an end—some finished product—outside itself. Rather, "good action is an end in itself" (1140b).

It is the entire realm of practical activity, in the broad Aristotelian sense, that Habermas views as increasingly absorbed by the technical, instrumental, and strategic modes of thinking and doing that have so dominated the modern age. This ubiquitous tendency—which devalues public debate and deliberation as much or more than Plato-like appeals to transcendent truth—leads Habermas to cast Arendt as a species of neo-Aristotelian, someone who fights the good fight for the sake of public dialogue and *communicative* (as opposed to instrumental or technical) action and rationality.

Habermas is hardly alone in viewing Arendt's project as one of renewal and recovery of Aristotelian conceptual resources. Doing so allows him and similarly disposed readers to pay Arendt a compliment—she performs the essential task of recovering *praxis* in our increasingly technocratic age—while simultaneously noting what they see as a serious debility. In *THC* and elsewhere, Habermas suggests, Arendt often appears trapped by the rigidity of her Aristotelian conceptual architecture. This fact, he argues, places severe limits on the contemporary relevance of her reflections on political action and the public realm, limits that his own theory of communicative action transcend.

Habermas' objection would be telling were it not for the fact that Arendt's theoretical project is far more ambitious, and far more radical, than the rhetoric of "recovery" or "renewal" suggests. In fact, Arendt's desire to restore dignity and inherent worth to the public-political realm—a desire born of her confrontation with both totalitarian anti-politics and the otherworldly biases of the Western philosophical and theological traditions—leads her to focus her theoretical ambitions along two fronts. First, she wants to highlight and describe such essentially political phenomena as action, speech, opinion, debate, deliberation, judgment, and the public realm, as well their fundamental preconditions (such as human plurality, equality, diversity, and worldliness). However, in order to accomplish this task, she must first reveal and critically examine the roots of our anti-political prejudices, prejudices we ultimately inherit from the tradition and which we habitually (and thoughtlessly) apply to the political realm. The first task is broadly phenomenological in nature and owes not a little to the approach Arendt learned from Heidegger and Jaspers, as well as from Edmund Husserl himself. The second task—the critical one—is more genealogical and "destructive," in the specific sense given these words by Nietzsche and Heidegger, respectively.

Another way of putting this is to say that one must first get beyond the encrusted prejudices that determine our view of something before the meaning (and unsuspected richness) of any given phenomenon—be it the fact of human plurality or the public realm itself—can be revealed. These phenomena have been distorted and covered over—first, by the 2,000-year dominance of a contemplative standpoint born of Greek philosophy and Christian theology; second, by the distinctively *modern* obsession with utility, instrumentality, and technical control (the standpoint of *homo faber*).

It is not enough, then, to remind us of some crucial Aristotelian distinctions. For while echoes of Greek political life resonate throughout the *Politics* and the *Nicomachean Ethics*, even Aristotle framed his distinctions from the standpoint of the *vita contemplativa*. Seen from *that* perspective, political participation—the life of the civic action and judgment—is but one (subsidiary and conditional) aspect of the good or virtuous life, a life that achieves its fullest happiness and perfection in the sustained activity of philosophical contemplation (NE 1177a-1178a). It is only when we turn to ancient Greek poetry, drama, and history and actively retrieve the non-philosophical evidence found there that we can begin to grasp the *bios politikos* in something like its own terms.

This way of putting it makes it sound as if Arendt thought of herself as a historian rather than as a philosopher. While it is certainly true that she was trained as a philosopher, she did not think of herself as one (even though many of her readers have felt otherwise). Neither, however, did she think of herself as a historian—a fact of some importance when it comes to understanding her extensive use of historical sources in such works as *The Human Condition* and *On Revolution*. She thought of herself, instead, as a *political theorist* or *political thinker*. Her deep knowledge of the Western tradition and its Greek and Christian sources led her to conclude that philosophers had harbored a certain enmity toward politics and the public realm—the realm of human plurality and free, unpredictable action—from the very beginning. In several places, she refers to this as a kind of *deformation professionnelle* typical of the class of "professional thinkers," a term she borrowed from Kant.

Political thinking, as Arendt understood it, begins with experience and has an irreducibly historical and interpretive dimension. *Historical* because history is the record of human words and deeds; *interpretive* because words and deeds are meaningful phenomena which, as such, demand interpretation. Interpretation must be *active* if it is to get behind inherited prejudices. And it must be *creative* if it is to breathe life back into sources and evidence that appear to provide no more than disjointed fragments or overly familiar, all-purpose concepts (such as freedom, authority, power, and justice).

Thus, in the Preface to *Between Past and Future*, Arendt describes the essays in that volume as *critical* and *experimental*. They are experimental for the simple reason that "there is an element of experiment in the critical interpretation of the past." The chief aim of critical interpretation is

> to discover the real origins of traditional concepts in order to distill from them anew their original spirit which has so sadly evaporated from the very key words of political language... leaving behind empty shells with which to settle almost all accounts, regardless of their underlying phenomenal reality.[11]

This critical and experimental task is both made possible and complicated by what Arendt calls "the break in our tradition." This break— which Arendt treats as an accomplished and undeniable fact—was the product, on the one hand, of catastrophic historical events (two world wars, the rise of totalitarianism, the Holocaust), and, on the other, by the playing out of various possibilities contained within the contemplative-philosophical tradition founded by Plato and Aristotle (the "death of God" alluded to above). Shattering historical experience and the dissolution of hallowed ethical and intellectual certainties inadequate to their comprehension deprive our tradition of its solidity and authority. Reduced to fragments, it can no longer serve as a reliable "transmission belt" for cultural, philosophical, and religious contents, ideals, and ethical norms. The result, as Alexis de Tocqueville observed long ago, is that the past no longer sheds its light on the present and "the mind of man wanders in obscurity."

However, what first appears to be an unmitigated disaster also opens the possibility of viewing the past with new eyes, unburdened by traditional (metaphysical or theological) prejudgments and habits of mind. This possibility can be redeemed only if one confronts the late modern situation with a high degree of intellectual integrity and dispenses with any attempt to "re-tie the broken thread of tradition." What is required is precisely the courage to be "critical and experimental" in our approach to the past. Such courage is born of the realization that, prior to the catastrophe, tradition had not only transmitted the contents of the past but had also deadened them, making them all-too-familiar and robbing them of the power to provoke thought and reflection.

These and related methodological considerations come to the fore in Arendt's essay on the work of her friend, the literary critic and cultural historian Walter Benjamin. Arendt's description of Benjamin's manner of thought and his approach to the past bears no small resemblance to her own:

> This thinking, fed by the present, works with the "thought fragments" it can wrest from the past and gather about itself. Like a pearl diver who descends to the bottom of the sea, not to excavate the bottom and bring it to light, but to pry loose the rich and the strange, the pearls and the coral in the depths and to carry them to the surface, this thinking delves into the depths of the past–but not in order to resuscitate it the way it was and to contribute to the renewal of extinct ages. What guides this thinking is the conviction that although the living is subject to the ruin of time, the process of decay is at the same time a process of crystallization, that in the depths of the sea, into which sinks and is dissolved what was once alive, some things "suffer a sea-change" and survive in new crystallized forms and shapes that remain immune to the elements, as though they waited only for the pearl diver who one day will come down to them and bring them up into the world of the living–as "thought fragments," as something "rich and strange," and perhaps ever-lasting Urphänomene.[12]

This passage provides some clues as to why and how Arendt approaches the ancient Greeks and the experience of the *polis*. As Arendt observes earlier in the same essay, "the Greek *polis* will continue to exist at the bottom of our political existence—that is, at the bottom of the sea—for as long as we use the word 'politics.'"[13]

The ancient Greeks thus play a central role in Arendt's project of rescuing the political life, political action, and the public realm from centuries of concerted cultural and philosophical devaluation. The Greeks can play this role not just because they *invented* politics (understood as debate and deliberation among diverse equals about matters of common concern), and not just because they invented the language and practices of democracy. Equally important is the fact that they practiced democratic politics for its own sake. That is, the democratic Athenians did not view political action and participation—the *bios politikos*—as subsidiary to, or derivative of, some allegedly higher activity. Affirming equality and human plurality as fundamental preconditions of political life, they embraced the contingency and seeming haphazardness that flowed from the participation of a large number of civic equals holding diverse opinions. They measured their individual and collective virtue not in terms of sovereign power, unanimous will, or masterly control of their environment, but rather in terms of the ability, foresight, courage, and public-spiritedness with which they met the opportunities, risks, and challenges of political life.

V The traditional substitution of making for acting—a link to totalitarianism?

While Athenian democracy hardly provides anything like a model or pattern for contemporary democracy, it *does* provide a glimpse at some of what Arendt considers to be the fundamental phenomena and conditions of an *authentic* politics. Any politics worthy of the name will embrace rather than reject human plurality, civic equality, diversity of opinion, and public debate and deliberation. In the contemporary world, liberal democracies can be said to endorse, officially at least, all of the items on this list, while what are effectively one-party systems (China and Russia, for example) or theocratic hybrids (the "republic" of Iran, the kingdom of Saudi Arabia) do not.

The latter go out of their way to monopolize public power, restrict public debate, and contain or curtail the unpredictability that flows from a plurality of political actors holding diverse opinions. In the unprecedented cases of Nazi Germany and Soviet Russia under Stalin, we witness the totalitarian attempt to not just *contain* the unpredictable effects of human plurality and spontaneity, but to eradicate their sources. Arendt thought totalitarian regimes aimed at the *elimination* of human spontaneity (our capacity to act in unpredictable ways) by means of a continuously applied and virtually never-ending terror. Totalitarian terror, in contrast to all previous forms, aimed at destroying the very space *between* individuals required for any action whatsoever. It aimed at creating "one Man of gigantic dimensions," a human species stripped of freedom and directly subject to what the totalitarians viewed as inflexible "laws" of natural or historical evolution.

I should add two important qualifications to these general observations. First, while Arendt hardly saw herself as engaged in the futile and fantastic attempt to resurrect Athenian direct democracy, she *was* critical of such apparently ineradicable features of contemporary liberal and parliamentary democracy as the party system, bureaucratic administration, and citizen over-reliance upon the "labor-saving" device of representative institutions. In Arendt's view, the latter tended to foster privatism and civic disengagement, giving rise to a politics defined by the clash of individual or group *interests* rather than debate between diverse opinions. The result is that public-spiritedness erodes and commitment to the "public thing" disappears.

The second point is that contemporary authoritarian regimes are far more cynical, and far less invested in any supposedly "transcendent" truth, than Arendt's description of what authority once *was* in the Western tradition might lead us to believe. The authoritarian regimes of the present overwhelmingly tend to view power as its own legitimation: might makes right. However, in marked contrast to such regimes, it is

> the monstrous yet seemingly unanswerable claim of totalitarian rule that, far from being 'lawless,' it goes to the sources of authority from which positive laws received their ultimate legitimation, that far from being arbitrary it is more obedient to these suprahuman forces than any government ever was before.[14]

This makes it sound as if, rather than constituting a definitive and undeniable *break* in our tradition, totalitarian ideology—whether in its Nazi or Bolshevik form—constitutes a kind of bastard fulfillment of it. True, in the case of totalitarianism, the animating and legitimating principles of authority are no longer "transcendent," as they were for Plato and Christianity. They have become unstoppable "laws of movement" immanently manifest in the very process of natural or historical development. This major difference notwithstanding, the casual reader of Arendt might well think that she is insinuating—à la Max Horkheimer and Theodor Adorno's *Dialectic of Enlightenment* or the later Heidegger's "history of Being"—that there is some kind of internal logic or tragic flaw that leads from the dawn of Western rationalism (in the pre-Socratics, Plato, and Aristotle) to the hell of the Gulag and extermination camps.

All the more reason to highlight a claim Arendt makes in a 1945 *Partisan Review* essay entitled "Approaches to the 'German Problem'." There Arendt insists that

> Nazism owes nothing to any part of the Western tradition, be it German or not, Catholic or Protestant, Christian, Greek or Roman. Whether we like Thomas Aquinas or Machiavelli or Luther or Kant or Hegel or Nietzsche... they have not the least responsibility for what is happening in the death camps.[15]

In making this claim, Arendt was responding not just to superficial intellectual histories (with titles like *From Luther to Hitler*), but also to the growing tendency among philosophers, theologians, and social critics to view this "gutter-born ideology" as somehow the predictable outgrowth of the "spiritual" (*geistlich*) inheritance of German or European culture. From Arendt's point of view, nothing could be further from the truth. Indeed, a good deal of the first and second parts of *The Origins of Totalitarianism* is devoted to tracing the decidedly non-highbrow sources of Nazi ideology and European racism and imperialism more generally.

However, there is a complicating factor. The sources Arendt uncovered and highlighted in her account in *Origins* had far more relevance to, and connection with, the Nazi case than to the Soviet-Bolshevik one. As many reviewers of *Origins* remarked, there was a notable imbalance in terms of depth of coverage when it came to Arendt's respective treatments of the two cases. This imbalance was due, in part, to the scarcity and inaccessibility of Soviet archival material during the Cold War period. But it was also due, as Arendt herself was painfully aware, to her failure to delve sufficiently into the historical sources of Bolshevik ideology, the thought of Karl Marx in particular. This fact led her, in 1951, to propose to the Guggenheim Foundation, a project on what she called the "Totalitarian Elements in Marxism."

Even Marxism's most ferocious critics would think twice before calling it a "gutter-born ideology," which it most certainly was not. Marx's social and economic theory derived from mainstream currents of the Western tradition: Enlightenment materialism, German Idealism, British political economy, and the political legacy of the French Revolution. Marx's intellectual achievement was undeniably towering and owed no small part of its power and originality to his deep knowledge of the Western philosophical tradition from the Greeks down to Hegel. Yet, the more Arendt studied Marx, the more she suspected that he might well be the "missing link between the unprecedentedness of our current situation and certain commonly accepted traditional categories of political thought." She came to this conclusion even though she rejected out of hand those who accused Marx himself of being a "totalitarian thinker." In her Gaus Lectures from 1953 she observes that "to accuse Marx of totalitarianism amounts to accusing the Western tradition itself of necessarily ending in the monstrosity of this novel form of government."[16] Arendt thought *that* was clearly absurd.

Arendt did not write her Marx book. Her investigations into the tradition led her to the much more ambitious (and theoretically more fruitful) project contained in The Human Condition (1958), which is a phenomenological-historical investigation of the three human activities—labor, work, and action—that together form what Arendt (following the tradition) refers to as the *vita activa*. She shifted her focus away from Marx, even though much of the material on Marx found its way into the book's chapter on labor. What takes center stage—beyond the phenomenological descriptions of the activities of labor, work, and action themselves—is the Western tradition's evolving conceptualization and understanding of these activities, as well as their shifting place within the hierarchy of the *vita activa*. What the Greeks viewed as the highest of all human activities—*action*, words and deeds in the public sphere—is displaced and demoted: first, in the early modern age, by *work* (the human activity of fabricating relatively permanent objects and structures that constitute the

artificial world standing between man and nature); subsequently by
labor (the activity that supplies us with the consumable goods needed
for daily subsistence and the reproduction of the species).

With this shift of focus, Arendt signals her move away from her
earlier suggestion that Marx, while hardly a "totalitarian thinker,"
might nevertheless be the "missing link" between the tradition and
"the unprecedentedness of our current situation." However, it is important to note that she does not revert to her previous position of
denying *any* connection whatsoever. Rather, the conceptual transformations and distortions implied by Marx's concept of *praxis* (which
manages to conflate labor, work, and action) led her to investigate
the roots of the persistent and long-lived view of political action as
a form of *making* or fabrication. What Arendt calls "the traditional
substitution of making for acting" is, in many respects, the primary
critical target of *The Human Condition*. In her reading, this substitution
begins with—is initiated by—Plato and Aristotle.

Looking to escape the "fragility, boundlessness, and unpredictability" that characterizes action performed in a democratic public
realm (a realm defined by a plurality of actors with diverse opinions), Plato and Aristotle fundamentally reinterpreted the nature and
character of political action. What had been previously understood
by democratic citizens as the "sharing of words and deeds" now became another form of making, one which required a craftsman-like
authority figure who remained in control of the process of political
action from start to finish. Thus, Plato's philosopher-kings appear
in the *Republic* as artificers of both justice and character, molding the
human "material" put in their charge so as to create an ordered hierarchy of classes within the state, as well as an ordered hierarchy of
reason, spirit, and appetite within the soul of the individual.

While critical of the idea that one can "make" a just state in quite
the way Plato imagined, Aristotle nevertheless saw the *polis* as a vehicle for the realization of man's end or perfection: the good or happy
life. In Aristotle's view, this is a life characterized by the exercise of
ethical and intellectual virtue. It can, but need not, include some
component of civic responsibility and political participation. The
role of the "statesman" in the Aristotelian conception is to enforce
those laws, customs, and norms that lead members of the political
association to a virtuous life.

Arendt's objection to this conception is not the standard liberal one, namely, that Aristotle sets up a "tutorial state," one which dramatically undercuts personal freedom in the name of pursuing virtue. It is, rather, that Aristotle sees the *polis* and political life as having no particular value in and of themselves. Whatever substantive value they possess derives from their contribution to the attainment of a "higher" end: the realization of man's supposedly singular end or perfection. The category most typical of the craftsman's mentality— that of *means and ends*—inserts itself into the very fabric of human relations, destroying both reciprocity and genuine civic equality in the process. The freedom and action born of the public sphere and human plurality give way to the project of "making men moral," as well as to a view of others as the means and material necessary for me to attain my ultimate happiness and "perfection."

The desire to escape the frailty, haphazardness, and unpredictability of action performed in the context of diverse equals is the motivation behind the Platonic-Aristotelian interpretation of action as a form of making. Disambiguated from the context of plural acting equals, the "action" of the craftsman-statesman is seen as consisting in the more or less skillful shaping of the human material at his disposal. As a result, the distinction between rulers and ruled—the "artists" and their ostensible material—becomes as central to the political realm as the means/end category itself. Arendt's fundamental thesis in this regard is that the Platonic and Aristotelian "escapes" from the contingency and relativity of the political realm lay the conceptual groundwork for most if not all the subsequent tradition:

> It has always been a great temptation, for men of action no less than men of thought, to find a substitute for action in the hope that the realm of human affairs may escape the haphazardness and moral irresponsibility inherent in a plurality of agents. The remarkable monotony of the proposed solutions throughout our recorded history testify to the elemental simplicity of the matter. Generally speaking, they always amount to seeking shelter from action's calamities in an activity where one man, isolated from all others, remains master of his doings from beginning to end. The attempt to replace action with making is manifest in the whole body of argument against "democracy," which,

the more consistently and better reasoned it is, will turn into
an argument against the essentials [plurality, equality, diversity]
of politics.[17]

This traditional way of viewing political action has a number of harmful effects. First and foremost, it creates a hierarchy between rulers and
ruled—between those who *have* political and moral knowledge and
those who don't—in a sphere previously composed of equals (citizens). Second, the substitution of making for acting frames those who
are ruled—ordinary people—as "material" which the artist-statesman
shapes into conformity with the "Idea" of justice, the teleological
order of nature, or the divine hierarchies created by God. As Arendt
points out, *making* something (whether it's a table, a chair, or a temple) always involves *doing violence* to the raw material—the wood or the
stone—out of which the product is fabricated.

In the *Republic* such violence is most immediately evident at the moment when Plato has Socrates (his mouthpiece in the dialogue) describe the first step the philosophic artificers of a just polity must take:

> They [the philosophical artists inspired by the divine Idea of
> justice] will take the city and the characters of men, as they
> might that of a tablet, and first wipe it clean–no easy task. But at
> any rate you know that this would be their first point of differ-
> ence from ordinary reformers, that they would refuse to take in
> hand either individual or state or to legislate before they either
> received a clean slate or themselves made it clean.
>
> (501a)

In the *Republic* this imperative leads to the banishment of citizens
over the age of ten. Some 2,300 years later, it led the totalitarians to
insist—in apparent but lethal conformity with "common sense"—
that "you can't make an omelette without breaking eggs."

A third fateful consequence of the substitution of making for acting is that we come to think of political action entirely in terms of
means and ends. This leads to a predictable reduction of the ethical questions attending political action to variations on cost/benefit
analysis or the question of "dirty hands." Max Weber framed the
central question of political ethics squarely: "does the end 'justify'

the means? Or does it not?"[18] Like Machiavelli, Weber thought the characteristic *means* of politics was "power backed up by violence" and that, as a result, any person who aspired to or became a "leading political actor" would invariably incur *some* degree of moral guilt, winding up with dirty—i.e. *bloody*—hands.

Of course, neither Weber nor Machiavelli endorse the "end justifies the means" view of typical power-hungry politicians, religious fanatics, or ideological true believers. Weber insists on the political actor taking personal responsibility for the foreseeable and (to a considerable degree) even the unforeseeable consequences of his or her actions and policies. Similarly, we find Machiavelli repeatedly insisting on the need for an economy of violence—that is, on the need to use precise dosages of power backed up by violence in order to stabilize the state and benefit the people at large.

Neither Weber nor Machiavelli come anywhere close to the Platonic ambition of "sculpting" the character of a people or the totalitarian ambition of "making" history as one makes an omelette. However, they *are* symptomatic of what we might call the "tyranny of the means–end category" when it comes to thinking about politics, ethics, and political action. What matters, we are repeatedly told, is the *cause* for which the political actor or actors commit their ethically dubious actions.

Thus, during the Cold War, the US sponsored the overthrow of democratically elected governments in Iran, the Congo, Guatemala, and Chile; the domestic persecution of government officials, artists, intellectuals, and émigrés who had, or were suspected of having, Communist sympathies or party memberships in their past; and the disastrous intervention in the civil war in Vietnam, an intervention that cost 58,000 American and an estimated two million Vietnamese lives—all in the name of the "cause" of freedom or democracy (more often than not equated with the "free enterprise system"). Where—for political, economic, religious, or cultural reasons—an absolute or "greatest" evil is stipulated, all manner of ostensibly lesser evils appear as completely and utterly justified. As Arendt put it in an unpublished address from about 1950,

> Democratic society as a living reality is threatened at the very
> moment that democracy becomes a 'cause' because then actions

are likely to be judged and opinions evaluated in terms of ultimate ends and not on their inherent merits. The democratic way
of life can be threatened only by people who see everything as
a means to an end….[19]

VI Alienation from the public world and the contemporary crisis

Originally motivated by the desire to escape the unpredictability,
haphazardness, and seeming moral irresponsibility inherent in
a democratic political realm, the "substitution of making for acting" thus inscribed *rulership* and an irreducibly *instrumental* attitude
toward political action at the heart of the Western tradition. Political
activity—the "discussions, the deliberations, and the making of decisions" by equal citizens—is deprived of any independent value.[20]
Over the course of Western history, politics is repeatedly degraded

> into a means to some allegedly 'higher' end–in antiquity the pro-
> tection of the good men [the few] from the rule of the bad [the
> many] in general…, in the Middle Ages the salvation of souls, in
> the modern age the productivity and progress of society.[21]

This deeply rooted attitude ("as old as the tradition of political philosophy itself," in Arendt's view) similarly permeates contemporary
culture and has a direct effect on our perception of the public-political
realm. One need only think of the low esteem in which politics,
politicians, and public institutions are held by many today. While
Arendt may have been overly broad in her criticisms of representative democracy, she was correct in holding that the representative
system is responsible, at least in part, for the origin, growth, and
apparent inescapability of interest group politics. This is a politics
that reduces our idea of the public good to that of an aggregation
of the dominant private interests of any given society. Self-interest
takes the place of public-spiritedness, and privatism—the tendency
to withdraw into the small circle of our family, friends, and business
or professional interests—undercuts attention to civic culture and
the health of our public institutions. At this stage, the "instruments"
of politics and political action no longer serve "allegedly *higher* ends."

Whatever positive value is accorded to politics is seen to derive almost solely from its potential contribution to economic growth and material prosperity.

Of course, such concerns predate Arendt. In the modern age they date back at least to the so-called "luxury debate" of the eighteenth century, a debate between proponents of civic virtue and an agrarian society (Rousseau and Adam Ferguson) and proponents of a commercial society with a vastly expanded division of labor (Adam Smith and David Hume). Such concerns also informed the liberal republican stance of thinkers like Constant and Tocqueville, with the latter pointing out that what American citizens of the early nineteenth century habitually referred to as their enlightened self-interest was, in fact, animated by energies that were often civic and even altruistic in nature. As Tocqueville was well aware, it was not such a limited and civically attuned notion of self-interest that triumphed in nineteenth-century France, but rather the more familiar bourgeois version in which the material self-interest perpetually trumps civic responsibilities. As we shall see in the next chapter, Arendt thought this bourgeois attitude evolved in the course of the nineteenth century from a studied disinterest in politics to an all-too-active desire to enlist the state in the imperialist project of expanding overseas markets and guaranteeing the safety of foreign investments.

Tocqueville, whose *Democracy in America* contributed importantly to Arendt's understanding of American politics, was adamant that "only [political] freedom can tear people away from the worship of Mammon and the petty daily concerns of their personal affairs and teach them to always see and feel the nation above and beside them."[22] Widespread political participation by citizens across classes was necessary if "the desire to enrich oneself at any price, the preference for business, the love of profit, the search for material pleasure and comfort" were not to "demoralize and degrade the entire nation."[23]

Tocqueville's language here strikes us as moralizing and more than a bit old fashioned. Moreover, the types of despotism he feared (the imperial dictatorships of Napoleon I and Napoleon III; the "democratic" despotism of the centralized bureaucratic state) pale in comparison with the totalitarian regimes of the twentieth century. Thus, while Arendt's attitude toward the bourgeoisie was, if anything, even more critical than Tocqueville's, it is not because she thought they were responsible for lowering the moral tone of society or frittering away traditional values. Rather, it is because she saw their imperialist ambitions destroying the relative stability of the territorially limited nation-state in pursuit of expansion for its own sake.

With the "political emancipation of the bourgeoisie" in the late nineteenth century, economic categories came to predominate the thinking of politicians and statesmen. During the imperialist epoch (1880–1914) the latter came to view their respective nations not as limited and institutionally articulated *political* entities, but rather as "fully armed business concerns" engaged in a world-wide competition for ever more territory and power. In Arendt's view this imperialist mind-set, together with the racist world-view it helped create and spread, provided one of the most crucial elements in the constellation of factors that later "crystallized" into totalitarianism in Europe.

Arendt's call for a revaluation of politics, political action, and the public realm is thus no neo-Aristotelian call to return "the good life" to the center of political discourse. The stakes are far too high to indulge in such ethical-philosophical nostalgia. What is at stake is not the possibility of a literal rebirth of totalitarianism, however worrying signs in the present may be. Rather, it is that the seemingly intractable nature of many of the problems we currently face— environmental degradation, a refugee crisis of immense proportions, expanding economic inequality, tensions between nuclear-armed nation-states, failure to integrate and protect minorities, and the supposed "failure" of liberal democratic institutions—may make totalitarian-type solutions appear increasingly attractive to many.

Arendt's prescience in this regard is undeniable. Today, it is not uncommon to find politicians and many ordinary citizens thinking (and acting) along the following lines: If there are more refugees and stateless people than we care to assimilate, why not deport them or confine them, more or less permanently, to displaced persons camps? If there are continuing tensions between ethnic-religious majorities and ethnic-religious minorities, why not create legal categories of first- and second-class citizenship? If diplomacy and/or economic sanctions fail to resolve disputes with rogue states who possess, or apparently possess, weapons of mass destruction, why not deploy one's own nuclear arsenal and be rid of the problem for good? And if a free press appears to undermine national solidarity by questioning governmental policy or legitimacy, why not accuse it of spreading "fake news" and attempt to muzzle it altogether?

These problems—and the dangerous and simplistic "solutions" often proposed for them—are, obviously, not a function of our failure to take the Aristotelian question of "the good life" seriously. Many of them are directly related to the alienation from public institutions currently felt by many citizens of Western liberal democracies, and to the undisguised antipathy to diversity of opinion, lifestyle, and belief found in authoritarian regimes around the world. On the one hand, we confront pervasive estrangement from the public world (what Arendt, in *The Human Condition*, refers to as "world alienation"). On the other, we face the quasi-totalitarian attempt to neutralize if not eradicate phenomena rooted in the fact of human plurality itself. In the former case, citizens turn away from political participation and their responsibility for the institutions of a shared public world. In the latter, the atomized individuals of contemporary mass societies are conditioned to affirm, or at the very least not challenge, existing power structures and reigning ideologies.

In this context, Arendt's attempt to retrieve the political life and political action from their philosophical, practical, and contemporary cultural devaluation retains a more than theoretical relevance. Across the globe, the public realm has been either abandoned by free but alienated citizens or forcibly monopolized by one-party dictatorships and strong-man regimes. In Western democracies, privatism and the pursuit of material comfort combined long ago with the rise of a permanent political class to create what Arendt, in *On Revolution*, referred to as a "de facto oligarchy." When representative institutions break down or fail to deliver the promised economic goods, citizens who have little choice but to place self-interest above all else become willing to endorse anyone or anything that promises to cut through all the "talk." Rarely if ever has public debate, deliberation, persuasion, and judgment led such a fugitive existence, and rarely have these activities had less status in the eyes of both leaders and ordinary citizens alike. These are the activities that Hannah Arendt places at the center of her political thought, reminding us that they—and not administration, rulership, the representation of interests, or even the "cultivation of virtue"—are the heart and soul of politics and the *bios politikos*.

****

In what follows I elaborate on these and other themes in Arendt's political thinking. I have devoted a chapter (and, in one case, two chapters) to each of the four major works—*The Origins of Totalitarianism*, *The Human Condition*, *On Revolution*, and *The Life of the Mind*—that form the core of her reputation as a political theorist and philosopher. I also look at selected essays as well as *Eichmann in Jerusalem* and the posthumously published *Lectures on Kant's Political Philosophy*. I do not examine Arendt's doctoral dissertation on Augustine's concept of love (1927), her biography of Berlin salon hostess Rahel Varnhagen (written largely in the 1930s), or her numerous journalistic and occasional pieces on Jewish history and politics (usefully collected by Jerome Kohn in the volume entitled *The Jewish Writings*). To have done so would have limited the space I could devote to considering the theoretical and philosophical arguments Arendt makes in her major works. It would also have resulted in a diffuse survey of her *oeuvre*, one unsuited to a series of this kind.

My consideration of Arendt's work proceeds in roughly chronological fashion, the better to give the reader a sense of how the essential themes of her political thinking took root and subsequently developed. I believe such an approach makes more sense in the case of a thinker like Arendt than would a strictly analytical or topical one.

Summary

Much of Arendt's fame derives from the attention—and controversy—generated by *Eichmann in Jerusalem: A Report on the Banality of Evil* (1963). Her role as an American public intellectual in the 1960s and 1970s has given way, in more recent years, to a fuller appreciation of the depth and originality of the political thinking found in such works as *The Origins of Totalitarianism* (1951), *The Human Condition* (1958), and *On Revolution* (1963). While she obtained a high degree of international recognition before her death in 1975, it is only in the last twenty years or so that her more theoretical work has earned her a place in the otherwise male-dominated Western canon of political philosophy.

Her originality as a political thinker flows, in part, from her unique background and experience. Born in 1906, she was the only child of a comfortably middle-class Jewish couple in Königsberg, East Prussia. She went on to study with Martin Heidegger at Marburg before writing her doctoral dissertation with Karl Jaspers in Heidelberg. Whatever ambitions she may have had as an academic philosopher were destroyed by the Nazi seizure of power, an event which politicized her and turned her into a Zionist fellow traveler for much of the 1930s and 1940s. Forced to flee by Nazi persecution, Arendt worked for a variety of Jewish aid organizations in Paris, before fleeing once again to America in 1941. Her eighteen years as a stateless person marked her indelibly, as did the confirmation (in 1943) of the Nazi extermination program aimed at European Jewry. From that experience arose her first great work, The Origins of Totalitarianism, which analyzed Nazism and Bolshevism as two iterations of an entirely novel form of government: totalitarianism.

Arendt's fame as an analyst of totalitarianism led many to be confused by her subsequent championing of the bios politikos, or political life. However, once we realize that she saw totalitarian regimes as the most extreme instance of anti-politics, the gap between Origins and her subsequent work closes significantly. Throughout her career as a political theorist, she focused her readers' attention on the phenomenological preconditions and experiential content of any genuine politics. The preconditions include the fact of human plurality, mortality, and worldliness, while the content includes initiatory action, debate, and deliberation among equals, as well as an institutionally articulated public realm distinct from both the economic and "household" spheres. Following in the footsteps of the civic republican tradition, she ranks political or public freedom—the freedom to be a "participator in public affairs"—as her foremost value. Her experience with totalitarian government did not lead her to dismiss the more familiar freedom from interference (or "negative liberty") championed by the liberal tradition. However, she remained convinced that only the "acting in concert" of diverse equals could preserve the public-political realm and the unique freedom it made possible.

Notes

1 Elisabeth Young-Bruehl, Hannah Arendt: For Love of the World (New Haven: Yale University Press, 1982), p. 188.
2 Hannah Arendt, Between Past and Future (New York: Penguin Books, 1977), p. 148. Hereafter cited as BPF.
3 Arendt, BPF, pp. 144–145.

4 See George Kateb, *Hannah Arendt: Politics, Conscience, Evil* (Totowa: Rowman & Allanheld, 1984), pp. 6–9.

5 Arendt, BPF, p. 151.

6 See J.G.A. Pocock, *The Machiavellian Moment* (Princeton: Princeton University Press, 1975).

7 Hannah Arendt, *The Life of the Mind* (New York: Harcourt, Inc., 1978), p. 10. Hereafter cited as LM.

8 Arendt, BPF, pp. 112–113.

9 Arendt, BPF, p. 97.

10 Jürgen Habermas, "On the Concept of Power: Hannah Arendt" in Habermas, *Political-Philosophical Profiles*, translated by Frederick Lawrence (Cambridge: MIT Press, 1983), pp. 171–188.

11 Arendt, BPF, p. 13.

12 Hannah Arendt, *Men in Dark Times* (New York: Harcourt Brace & Company, 1983), pp. 205–206. Hereafter cited as MDT.

13 Arendt, MDT, p. 204.

14 Hannah Arendt, *The Origins of Totalitarianism* (New York: Harcourt Inc., 1976), p. 461. Hereafter cited as OT.

15 Hannah Arendt, *Essays in Understanding, 1930–1954*, edited by Jerome Kohn (New York: Harcourt Brace & Company, 1994), p. 108. Hereafter cited as EU.

16 Hannah Arendt, "Karl Marx and the Tradition of Western Political Thought," cited in Margaret Canovan, *Hannah Arendt: A Reinterpretation of Her Political Thought* (New York: Cambridge University Press, 1992), p. 64.

17 Hannah Arendt, *The Human Condition* (Chicago: University of Chicago Press, 1958), p. 190. Hereafter cited as THC.

18 Max Weber, "Politics as a Vocation" in *From Max Weber: Essays in Sociology*, edited by C. Wright Mills and H. H. Gerth (New York: Oxford University Press, 1958), p. 151. Hereafter cited as FMW.

19 Arendt, EU, pp. 180–181.

20 Hannah Arendt, *On Revolution* (New York: Penguin Books, 2006), p. 110. Hereafter cited as OR.

21 Arendt, THC, p. 229.

22 Alexis de Tocqueville, *The Old Regime and the Revolution*, translated by Alan S. Kahan (Chicago: University of Chicago Press, 1998), p. 88. Hereafter cited as ORR.

23 Tocqueville, ORR, p. 87.

Further reading

R. H. King, *Arendt and America* (Chicago: University of Chicago Press, 2015). [Very good on context for various political debates and controversies.]

E. Young-Bruehl, *Hannah Arendt: For Love of the World* (New Haven: Yale University, 1982). [The standard and still unsurpassed biography.]

Two
Totalitarianism and political evil

I The relation of *Origins of Totalitarianism* to Arendt's later work

The Origins of Totalitarianism was almost universally hailed when it was first published in 1951. In this, her first major work, Arendt gave an account of the origins, development, and structural characteristics of both Nazi and Soviet totalitarianism, one which emphasized its *European* (rather than narrowly German or Russian) background and context. She tried to identify the events, experiences, attitudes, and practices in the period between 1888 (the start date of the European "Scramble for Africa") and 1953 (the year of Stalin's death) that made it possible for tens of millions to accept, and in many cases actively and energetically support, the elimination of political and personal freedom, the liquidation of entire populations at home and abroad, and the pursuit of world domination.

There can be little doubt that, biographically speaking, the seeds for this massive project were sown when, in 1943, Arendt and her husband Heinrich Blucher received confirmation that the darkest rumors from Europe were true: the systematic extermination of European Jewry was underway. While initially spurred by Arendt's need to understand how it was that the Jewish people had come to occupy the "storm center" of modern politics, *Origins* evolved into a much broader study. It examined not just the origins of anti-Semitism as a *political* ideology, but also the destructive legacy of European imperialism, the spread of racist ideas and policies across Europe, and the breakdown of the European nation-state system between the wars. Historically speaking, Arendt wanted to underline the utterly unprecedented quality of totalitarian domination as an *event*. Theoretically speaking, she wanted to show that totalitarianism was a novel and unprecedented form of government. It could not be accounted for in terms of the old catalog of regime forms (monarchy, aristocracy, and democracy) and it was radically distinct from the tyrannies, despotisms, and dictatorships of the past.

It is difficult to exaggerate the importance of *The Origins of Totalitarianism* in Arendt's *oeuvre*. This mammoth, wide-ranging work not only lays out Arendt's analysis of the nature, origins, and European context of totalitarianism; it also provides the essential background for her subsequent (more general and theoretical) work in books like *The Human Condition* and *On Revolution*. The latter have often been read by Arendt's critics as stand-alone works that contain morally dubious ideas—for example, Arendt's "Greek" theory of political action in THC or her ostensible endorsement of recurrent or continuous revolution in OR.

With respect to the first example, any reader of her earlier work knows that Arendt's enthusiasm for initiatory or "heroic" political action in THC is tempered by her emphasis in OT upon the importance of constitutional forms and legal-institutional structures that protect equal civil and political rights. The charge that she holds to an expressivist or "dramaturgical" theory of action, deaf to the claims of civil and political equality, is thus wildly off-base.[1] Similarly, given her stress upon the importance of preserving constitutional forms and institutional structures in the face of destructive economic, nationalistic, or proto-totalitarian political forces, the idea that Arendt would ever endorse anything like "permanent revolution" is simply ridiculous.

Recognizing that OT provides the backdrop for Arendt's later political thought is important not just because it helps us to avoid such obvious misinterpretations. The fact is that many readers of OT and THC have been mystified by the relationship between the two. Indeed, the first-time reader of Arendt will probably have the impression of massive discontinuity. There appear to be two Arendts. On the one hand, there is the historian and analyst of totalitarianism; on the other, the celebrator of Athenian democracy and the *bios politikos*. The fact that Arendt never *explains* how these two very different works hang together has often led readers to conclude that OT and THC are in tension, if not outright contradiction.

This underscores the need to be aware from the outset of just how frequently OT anticipates many of the central themes of Arendt's later thought. A few examples are in order here.

First, her analysis of the role state institutions and the rule of law played in creating and preserving civic equality in Western Europe after the French Revolution presages her later concern with the durability and viability of the public-political realm in modern times. Second, her analysis (in Part II of OT) of the reduction of politics to economics born of "the political emancipation of the bourgeoisie" anticipates her later controversial distinction between the *social* and the *political* in THC and OR—a distinction that must be read through the lens of her earlier discussion, lest it be grossly misunderstood. Third, Arendt's analysis of the susceptibility of traumatized European masses to totalitarianism's ideological fictions in the interwar period anticipates her later concern (in THC) with the *objective* character of a shared political realm.

Arendt viewed the public realm as largely constituted by a diversity of perspectives on the same "object"—that is, on a set of basic historical, political, and cultural *facts* on which all (or nearly all) can agree. Totalitarian fictions effaced the distinction between truth and falsehood, and with it the very objectivity of this common world. Where there are no facts—where ideology, propaganda, and media manipulation are free to create an alternative reality—plural perspectives are replaced by governmentally enforced fiction. The crucial distinction is between the *factual truths* that provide grounds for diverse opinions and the totalitarian-absolutist claim to possess a singular ideological-cum-metaphysical "Truth," one that liquidates all facts and opinions running counter to it.

Fourth, Arendt's focus in OT on the growing *rootlessness* and feeling of *superfluity* experienced by these same masses prefigures her later reflections on how a shared and relatively durable public-political world can provide a home—a place in the world—for its citizens. In this regard, Arendt's use of words like "rootlessness" and "homelessness" has led some to see her (wrongly) as a proponent of homey *Gemeinschaft* in an all-too-modern, secular world. In fact, her concern with homelessness arises from consideration of the desperate plight of millions of people rendered stateless by World War I (WWI), civil war, and the collapse of the Russian and Austro-Hungarian empires. Having a political "home" does not mean finding a place with like-minded others—people who share one's faith, language, ethnicity, or philosophy of life. It means possessing or being granted guaranteed civil and political rights, rights that make the expression of political opinion and dissent both possible and meaningful. Thus, what Arendt calls "the right to have rights" can be parsed, at the most basic level, as the moral imperative to create a world in which as many people as possible possess secure civic and legal membership in relatively stable political communities.

Here, we encounter a final albeit more general reason why familiarity with OT is essential if we are to understand Arendt's later political thought. In its analysis of terror as the *essence* of totalitarian regimes, its delineation of the "radical evil" perpetrated by them, and its focus upon the plight of the stateless and the "right to have rights," OT expresses a set of deeply felt moral concerns. It is easy to lose sight of these concerns when reading Arendt's later descriptions of the essence of such political phenomena as freedom, action, judgment, and authority. Nevertheless, it is imperative to remember that the moral concerns animating OT provide the backdrop to Arendt's later attempt to delineate a form of authentic or "pure" politics—one free of the proto-totalitarian distortions introduced by the tradition—in THC.

****

The regimes of Hitler and Stalin are usually viewed as particularly gruesome examples of familiar historical phenomena. Tyranny, despotism, and dictatorship have been present from the very beginning of Western political history and show no sign of disappearing anytime soon. As Socrates' remarks in the *Apology* about the rule of the Thirty in Athens indicate, Western political thought has long singled out terror as the crucial *means* by which such regimes gain and hold power. From Plato to Montesquieu, *fear* and *terror* have been regarded as the defining characteristics of such regimes.

As Arendt herself notes, terror as "a means of frightening people into submission" has taken "an extraordinary number" of forms through the ages. As a result, virtually all the modalities of totalitarian terror seem numbingly familiar:

> Many things that nowadays have become the specialty of totalitarian government are only too well known from the study of history. There have almost always been wars of aggression; the massacre of hostile populations after a victory went unchecked until the Romans mitigated it by introducing the *pacere subjectis*; through centuries the extermination of native peoples went hand in hand with the colonization of the Americas, Australia, and Africa; slavery is one of the oldest institutions of mankind and all empires of antiquity were based on the labor of state-owned slaves who erected their public buildings. Not even concentration camps are an invention of totalitarian movements. They emerge for the first time during the Boer War, at the beginning of the century....[2]

Such continuities place an exceptionally heavy burden on anyone who wants to argue, as Arendt does, that (a) totalitarian governments are an unprecedented form of political regime, and (b) that terror was not simply a *means* for these governments but their very *essence*. Their goal was not simply the monopolization of political power or expansion by conquest. Rather, their *raison d'être* was the use of terror to realize their guiding ideological fictions: a world organized completely along the lines of racial hierarchy (the Nazis) or one from which social class as well as divergent interests and opinions has been eliminated (the Bolsheviks).

According to Arendt, the totalitarians were aware that, in order to realize their ideological goals, it would be necessary to *change human nature*—to not merely repress, but to *eliminate* the characteristically human capacity for spontaneous (free) action. A new animal species, one whose behavior could be rendered completely predictable through the application of terror and the power of organization, would have to be produced. The totalitarians did not shy away from this task. Indeed, Arendt sees the concentration and extermination camps as experiments in total domination, experiments designed to facilitate the realization of this insane goal. Their utter uselessness from any recognizably strategic or utilitarian perspective testifies to the hubristic ambition to re-shape man and the world in accordance with the "Truth" of ideological fiction.

Unpacking Arendt's description of totalitarian government as a form of regime whose essence is terror allows us to appreciate more fully her claims about its "horrible originality." Precisely because it was so "unlike all forms of tyranny and despotism we know of," Arendt can claim that the *event* of totalitarianism in Europe not only "exploded our traditional categories of political thought" but our standards of moral and criminal judgment as well. In saying this, Arendt is hardly asserting that we are unable to judge or condemn totalitarian deeds and policies. Rather, she makes the claim because of the unprecedented nature and scale of the crimes committed by totalitarian regimes. The policies and practices embodied by Auschwitz and the Gulag are "very inadequately described as 'murder.'" Similarly, the perpetrators of totalitarian crimes "can hardly be punished [simply] as 'murderers'."[3]

Faced with the enormity of such crimes, our traditional standards of moral and legal judgment come up short. It is for this reason that Arendt thought that the Nuremberg trials, absolutely necessary though they were, ultimately failed in their primary task of meting out justice to the most highly placed of Nazi perpetrators. Murder and even "mass murder" reveal themselves to be pale and inadequate categories when confronted with phenomena such as concentration camps, the industrialized production of corpses, and the serial liquidation of entire categories of innocent individuals (be they Jews, "asocials," Roma, kulaks, or homosexuals). These phenomena confront us not only with evil but with what Arendt, following but also deviating from Kant, termed "radical evil."

Why *radical* evil rather than just "evil"? In Arendt's view, totalitarianism did not simply deprive enormous numbers of innocent people of rights, liberties, and (ultimately) life itself. Rather, the ideologically driven policies and practices of totalitarian regimes served as a kind of *practical demonstration* that there could be such a thing as a society in which human beings are superfluous *as* human beings. Totalitarian domination was thus not only an assault upon the rights, lives, and liberties of tens of millions. It was an assault upon human nature and upon the concept of humanity itself. Hence, the moral imperative of marking totalitarian evil as a form of *radical evil*.

Arendt attempted to convey the thinking behind this designation to her friend and former teacher Karl Jaspers in a letter dated March 4, 1951. With the advent of totalitarian domination, she wrote,

> Evil has proved to be more radical than expected. In objective terms, modern crimes are not provided for in the Ten Commandments. Or: the Western tradition is suffering from the preconception that the most evil things human beings can do arise from the vice of selfishness. Yet we know that the greatest evils or radical evil has nothing to do anymore with such humanly understandable, sinful motives. What radical evil really is I don't know, but it seems to me it somehow has to do with the following phenomenon: making human beings as human beings superfluous (not using them as means to an end, which leaves their essence as humans untouched and impinges only on their human dignity; rather, *making them superfluous as human beings*). This happens as soon as all unpredictability—which, in human beings, is the equivalent of spontaneity—is eliminated.[4]

This observation clarifies a statement Arendt makes toward the end of *The Origins of Totalitarianism*. There she states that "totalitarianism strives not toward despotic rule over men, but toward a system in which men are superfluous."[5] OT should thus be viewed as Arendt's attempt to understand how such an unprecedented and uniquely calamitous regime form—one predicated on systematic and literal dehumanization—came into being.

It is important to realize that the attempt to understand totalitarian evil is extraordinarily difficult *not* because Arendt thinks that this virtually incomprehensible or absolute evil traces back to a "correspondingly unfathomable depravity of [individual or human] nature."[6] Arendt's position in *Origins* is parallel, in one very important respect, to the quite different one she will take in *Eichmann in Jerusalem* (with its famous thesis about the "banality of evil"). She *never* thought that totalitarian evil was the result of some "unfathomable depravity" in the *character* of those who initiated, administered, or even carried out the liquidation of large numbers of innocent people. Her position from *Origins* to *Eichmann* is that "inhuman evil was…initiated and administered by human beings who were not inwardly unique."[7]

This applies as much to Hitler and Stalin as it does to a functionary like Eichmann. Totalitarian evil was committed not by devils and monsters, but by men—often, but not always, quite ordinary or unexceptional ones. How is it that millions of ordinary Europeans came to endorse—and, in many cases, carry out—policies that seem to us both mad and barbaric? OT attempts to provide an unblinking, unprejudiced, and decidedly non-chauvinist answer to this question, an answer that confronts us with the primary pathologies animating European politics and culture from the 1880s to World War II (WWII).

The title of OT leads one to expect a relatively straightforward work of historical investigation. Yet this expectation has led to serious misunderstandings of the book and the nature of Arendt's project. First, while reliant upon an enormous amount of historical and archival material, *Origins* is not primarily a work of historical reportage. Second, Arendt did not seek, as a historian or political scientist might, to reveal the *causes* of totalitarianism as either an event or as a form of government. Third, she did not see totalitarianism as a direct or natural *development* of pre-existing German, Russian, or even European factors. Finally, she did not view totalitarianism as the radical "other" of liberal capitalist modernity. She did not view it as the deformed outgrowth of Enlightenment rationality (as was suggested by Horkheimer and Adorno in their *Dialectic of* Enlightenment) nor as the result of a "spiritual crisis" generated by collapse of belief in the transcendent (as the neo-Platonist Eric Voegelin suggested).

In *The Origins of Totalitarianism*, Arendt devoted herself to teasing out the primary *events, practices, and attitudes* in late nineteenth and early twentieth-century Europe that made it possible for such a "horribly original" regime form to arise in the center of modern Western civilization. In a response to a critical 1953 review of OT by Voegelin in *The Review of Politics*, Arendt wrote:

> What I did [in *Origins*] was to discover the chief elements of totalitarianism and to analyze them in historical terms, tracing these elements back in history as far as I deemed proper and necessary. That is, I did not write a history of totalitarianism but an analysis in terms of history; I did not write a history of anti-Semitism or of imperialism, but analyzed the element of

Jew-hatred and the element of expansion insofar as these elements were still clearly' visible and played a decisive role in the totalitarian phenomenon itself. The book, therefore, does not really deal with the "origins" of totalitarianism—as its title unfortunately claims—but gives a *historical account of the elements which crystallized into totalitarianism*; this account is followed by an analysis of the elemental structure of totalitarian movements and domination itself.[8]

This clarifies matters to a degree, but what are the "chief elements" that "crystallized" into totalitarianism? Six years earlier, Arendt had sent an outline of the book to her publisher. There she noted that "full-fledged imperialism in its totalitarian form" was itself an "amalgam" of "certain elements which are present in all political conditions and problems of our time," including "anti-Semitism, decay of the national state, racism, expansion for expansion's sake, alliance between mob and capital."[9]

A glance at the Table of Contents of OT demonstrates that this early list of elements, while generally adhered to, turned out to be less than complete. For example, Arendt's original list contains no mention of the merging of racism and bureaucracy effected by British imperial rule in India and Egypt (a merging that helped create the paradigm of racialized government later copied by the Nazis). Nor does her early list mention the role played by tribal nationalism in the creation of an *intra*-European or "continental" form of imperialism, one distinct from the more familiar (economically driven) overseas variety.

The point here is less the number of elements Arendt ultimately chose to focus upon than the fact that they exemplify either pathological *attitudes* (racism, anti-Semitism, tribal nationalism) or *practices* (imperialism, administrative rule, government by the police), attitudes and practices that spread throughout Europe between the 1880s and the 1930s. They would later combine into the toxic and deadly "amalgam" of totalitarian politics and government.

I should stress that Arendt did not think that the "crystallization" of the elements she identified was in any way inevitable or predestined. Nor did she think of the elements she identified as the *causes* of totalitarianism. She thought that the category of causality—implying as it does a necessary connection between a specific set of causal factors and a predictable effect or result—was "an altogether alien and falsifying category in the historical sciences."[10] The crystallization of the events, practices, and attitudes Arendt analyzes in OT was contingent: there was no way the "horrible originality" of totalitarianism could have been predicted. Nevertheless, the totalitarian form of government did emerge, and it is the "burden of our times" to try to understand how specific European events, attitudes, and practices came together to make it a concrete possibility.

In what follows, I look at what Arendt considered the most important elements in the constellation that made totalitarianism possible. Section II focuses upon imperialist expansion and its relation to what she calls the "political emancipation of the bourgeoisie." Section III examines the role she assigns European racism (in theory and in practice) during the nineteenth and early twentieth centuries. Section IV looks at the intra-continental form of imperialism born of tribal nationalism's rise in Central and Eastern Europe after WWI. Section V traces the process by which the legal institutions of European states were transformed into instruments of the "nation" (or ethnic majority people) in response to the interwar refugee crisis. Section VI looks at the connection Arendt sees between the destruction of the European class system and the rise of totalitarian movements. Section VII examines anti-Semitism as a political ideology and the role it played in amalgamating a variety of proto-totalitarian attitudes and practices. Section VIII outlines Arendt's description of totalitarian regimes as a terror-driven form of party and police rule, one in which the seat of real power was ever-shifting. Finally, Section IX explains why Arendt saw the concentration, work, and extermination camps as the "central institutions" of the totalitarian form of government.

II Expansionism and the political emancipation of the Bourgeoisie

Arendt's most basic claim is that totalitarianism would not have arisen were it not for triumph of the imperialist idea that the supreme duty of any major European nation-state was to expand indefinitely, the better to excel in the competition for more wealth and power.

"Expansion as a permanent and supreme aim of politics," Arendt writes, is "the central idea of imperialism."[11] However, our historical familiarity with conquests and colonization blinds us to the fact that expansion is "an entirely new concept in the long history of political thought and action," one that "has its origin in the realm of business speculation where expansion meant the permanent broadening of industrial production and economic transactions...."[12] As such, it breaks definitively with the assumption that *political* associations are and must be territorially limited, institutionally articulated entities. This assumption had been central to virtually all western forms of political association, from the Greek *polis* to the modern European nation-state.

The question, then, is how did the essentially *economic* idea of un-limited expansion come to dominate the political imagination of the great majority of European statesmen, officials, and intellectuals in the last decades of the nineteenth century? How did unlimited expansion come to be viewed by so many as the natural goal and, indeed, the highest duty of the nation-state? The question is even more perplexing since, considered as a form of political organiza-tion, the nation-state appears to be uniquely *unsuited* to the pursuit of such a goal.

In Arendt's telling, the rise of industrial capitalism and mass pro-duction resulted in the saturation of markets and the plummeting of commodity prices. Indeed, economic crises of overproduction became a regular occurrence during this period.[13] "Superfluous money" in the form of the accumulation of excess capital pointed not just to the limits of available markets, but also to the limited nature of investment opportunities in the Western world. "Imperi-alism," Arendt writes, "was born when the ruling class in capital-ist production came up against national limitations to its economic expansion..."[14]

The business imperative of continual economic growth and ever-increasing capital accumulation helped foster the idea that un-limited *territorial* expansion was a legitimate and supremely impor-tant aim of all government and foreign policy. It is an irony of history that the nation-state—a form of political association whose identity rests upon territorial limitation and the notion that particular ethnic peoples had chosen to live together in distinct national-territorial homes—became the vehicle for this archetypally "bourgeois" idea. It is ironic because, prior to the imperialist period, the tension between the state and society—or, to use Hegelian language, between a politically and legally defined realm of "universal" concerns and an economically defined realm of individual or class-based interests— was precisely that, a tension. In the early part of the imperialist period, this internal tension gives way to outright conflict. Society, in the form of its dominant class, the politically emancipated and economically all-powerful bourgeoisie, gains ever increasing power over the state, ultimately transforming this guardian of the public (or "universal") interest into an instrument of a particular class' economic interests.

The accelerating competition for new investment opportunities overseas turned European attention to the previously undeveloped continent of Africa and ignited the so-called "scramble for Africa" of the 1880s. The initial violent land grabs on the "dark continent" were made possible by what Arendt terms the "alliance between capital and the mob"—that is, between bourgeois investors and the unemployed desiderata of the newly entrenched capitalist social order. However, the gangster/mercenary services rendered by these unprofessional "shock troops" of imperialist expansion were inadequate to the task of protecting the overseas investment of ever-larger portions of the national wealth. The power of the state, in the form of its military and police apparatus, was compelled to follow the advance of capitalist investment as it sought out ever more distant (and ever more risky) investment opportunities, such as those created by the Suez Canal and the discovery of gold and diamonds in South Africa.[15]

The deployment of state military and police power to protect overseas investments led European statesmen and politicians to increasingly identify the common good of the nation with the open-ended accumulation of wealth, territory, population, and power. It seemed equally clear to both governments and the bourgeoisie itself that "only the unlimited accumulation of power could bring about the unlimited accumulation of capital."[16] One result of this new attitude was that the precariously maintained balance of power among European nation-states was transformed into a competition between "fully armed business concerns"—imperial states—for

global political and economic hegemony.[17] A new political world
was created in which "all [stable and limited] political bodies appear
to be temporary obstacles" to the fundamental reality of "an eternal
stream of growing power."[18]

This destructive and unrealistic assumption of the new imperialist
order was to become one of the central "insights" of later totalitarian
movements and governments. While Arendt maintains a clear distinction between the accumulation of territory and power performed by
the overseas imperialism of the 1880–1914 period and the later continental form practiced by totalitarian regimes, she doesn't want us to
forget the crucial genealogical link back to bourgeois self-interest and
the worship of power that was ubiquitous in the upper echelons of
European society during the so-called *belle epoque*:

> Power became the essence of political action and the center of
> political thought when it was separated from the political com-
> munity [the territorially limited nation-state] which it should
> serve. This, it is true, was brought about by the economic factor.
> But the resulting introduction of power as the only content of
> politics, and of expansion as its only aim, would hardly have
> met with such universal applause, nor would the resulting dis-
> solution of the nation's body politic met with so little opposi-
> tion, had it not so perfectly answered the hidden desires and
> secret convictions of the economically and socially dominant
> classes. The bourgeoisie, so long excluded from government by
> the nation-state and by their lack of interest in public affairs,
> was politically emancipated by imperialism.[19]

Arendt's account of the genesis and significance of European imperialism in the late nineteenth century may well strike the reader as
broadly Marxist in character. In fact, while she drew upon the analyses of Rosa Luxemburg's *Accumulation of Capital* (1913), J. A. Hobson's
Imperialism (1902), and Rudolf Hilferding's *Finance Capital* (1910) for
her overall portrait of imperialism, her critique of bourgeois attitudes is more Tocquevillian-republican than Marxist-materialist in
inspiration.

Like Tocqueville and the republican tradition generally, Arendt is
adamant about the need to preserve a clear theoretical and practical

distinction between the economic and political spheres, that is, between *society* and the *state*. In contrast, Marx viewed such distinctions as ideological obfuscations from the first. In his view, both Hegel's political philosophy and the French revolutionary tradition were predicated on the idea that there was such a thing as an independent or relatively autonomous public sphere—the state or republic—when in fact the material interests of the dominant social class (in this case, the bourgeoisie) determined the institutional form and functions of the political realm.[20]

From the standpoint taken by Arendt in OT, Marx's unmasking of the distinction between state and society—between bourgeois and *citoyen*—is premature and wrong-headed. In her view, something like a relatively autonomous political sphere *had* existed from the French Revolution through the constitutional reforms pushed through in the wake of the largely unsuccessful revolutions of 1848. It was only in the last decades of the nineteenth century, with the exhaustion of domestic investment opportunities and the accelerating accumulation of surplus capital, that the bourgeoisie began to take a real interest in politics and conceived of deploying the "universal" power of the state in accordance with its overall class interests.

Thus, the bourgeoisie of Western Europe went from abdicating political responsibility and more or less docilely submitting to their political rulers (in the first half of the nineteenth century) to shaping foreign policy and effectively directing how the state would deploy its monopoly on "power backed up by violence" (Weber). The new constellation created by the political emancipation of the bourgeoisie made overseas profit-seeking and the accumulation of power, territory, and wealth virtually inseparable and all but indistinguishable. "Society" (in the form of the bourgeois class) had effectively taken over the state. But, contra Marx, this occurs well after the establishment of the industrial capitalist order in the first half of the nineteenth century.

However, Arendt doesn't leave it here, at what appears to be a temporally amended version of the basic Marxian story. In fact, she thinks the European imperialist project came fully into its own only when statesmen and politicians began to see the competition for power, territory, wealth, and global hegemony as the overriding purpose of the nation-state—indeed, its very *raison d'être*. This happened only after such essentially *economic* concepts as expansion, competition, and unlimited growth migrated from the economic to the political sphere. In the process, they took on a life and logic of their own. Once this happened, a new and destructive understanding of politics came to the fore in Europe, an understanding predicated on the *denial* of territorial boundedness and the idea that a given body of citizens were attached to a specific place in the world. The process of imperialist expansion that began with the "political emancipation of the bourgeoisie" comes to its climax when politicians and statesmen see the national interest as more or less identical with success in the global competition for empire. The self-interested profit motive of the bourgeoisie thus gives way to the expansion of power and territory *for its own sake*.

The most obvious example of this evolution—and the one Arendt focuses on—is the British Empire. What began as a commercial enterprise, underwritten by private investment and protected by state resources, is transfigured into a self-contained imperial project, one with an ethos, logic, and world-view of its own. The ethos of the most committed imperialists was far indeed from the self-interested one of the bourgeoisie. What the writer Rudyard Kipling dubbed the "great game"—the competition between the major European powers (Britain, France, Germany, and Russia) for global dominance—was not played by businessmen, but by statesmen, bureaucrats, soldiers, and secret agents. Many of the latter were motivated by a genuine idealism, albeit an idealism that looks completely perverse from a contemporary perspective.

As the British imperial project developed, the "worst"—the lumpenproletariat shock troops who had paved the way for capitalist investment overseas—were gradually supplemented, if not entirely supplanted, by the "best." The latter were educated and idealistic young men from Oxford and Cambridge who were responding to the call of imperial service and duty to the British Empire. Arendt cites T. E. Lawrence as a classic example of such a selfless, ideal- and duty-driven young man, one eager to take part in the world-historical drama of the "great game."

For Lawrence and others like him, the destiny of the globe seemed to hang in the balance. They viewed this destiny as shaped not by specific policies and decisions, but rather as determined by mysterious forces that dictated the course of the "great game" as well as the fate of the players. Their commitment was so intense that "these

secret and anonymous agents of the force of expansion felt no obli-
gation to man-made laws. The only 'law' they obeyed was the 'law'
of expansion, and the only proof of their 'lawfulness' was success
in expanding the empire."[21] We move from an imperialism driven
by selfishness to one characterized by the selfless devotion of young
men who willingly sacrifice themselves to the impenetrable logic
of the Great Game. Such self-sacrificing idealism in the service of
mysterious historical forces and hidden destinies was to have a long
career in the twentieth century, not least among the elite cadres of
Bolshevism and National Socialism striving to expand their respective empires and attain the goal of global domination.

III From race-thinking to racism in practice

Arendt thus sees the ideas, attitudes, and practices of European imperialism as fundamentally formative of the context in which totalitarianism became possible. To put the point baldly: the idea that
territorial expansion and the endless accumulation of power was
the primary business of the nation-state was not one invented by
either Hitler or Stalin. It had already become the "common sense"
of European business and political elites by the end of the nineteenth
century. Arendt cites Cecil Rhodes' pronouncement "I would annex
the planets if I could" as a quintessential expression of the European
imperialist mindset.

   Of course, pointing this out hardly establishes any dubious moral
equivalence between (say) the British Empire and the Third Reich
(although recent scholarly opinion is, if anything, more severely
critical of British imperialism than Arendt ever was). Rather, it
simply means that we must recognize, as Arendt forces us to, the
fact that totalitarian regimes did not arise in a historical-political
vacuum. The cultural-intellectual backdrop of the ruthless expansionism practiced by totalitarian regimes was not a specific (and
exceptionally wayward) national culture. It was, rather, the imperialist ideas, attitudes, and practices that had become ubiquitous—and,
indeed, hegemonic—in Europe half a century earlier.

   The second crucial element in the constellation of factors that
helped make totalitarianism possible was the spread of racist ideas
and attitudes during the imperialist epoch. Such ideas and attitudes

not only provided an ideological justification for imperialism; they also shaped many of its concrete, paternalistic yet exceedingly brutal, governing strategies and practices. If we follow Arendt in establishing a link between (a) the racist attitudes and practices underwriting overseas imperialism, and (b) the tribal nationalism and "continental" form of imperialism preached by the pan-German and pan-Slavic movements during the same period, we confront what can only be described as a massive and widespread redefinition of political membership and identity.

In different but parallel ways, both the overseas and continental imperialists dispensed with the old-fashioned idea that only a shared territory, representative institutions, and a stable legal structure could properly define a political people. In place of such "artificial" and seemingly external legal and political criteria, they defined political membership as something rooted in supposedly *inner* or *natural* characteristics. The ideas of German "blood" and the "Slavic soul" serve as examples of such inner criteria, while the assertion of the racial superiority of white northern Europeans (an assertion made by numerous British, French, and German authors) provides an example of the latter.

For the overseas imperialists, the confrontation with non-white, technologically less advanced ("primitive") peoples in Asia and Africa—peoples who submitted to the force of European arms and domination—led to the widespread presumption of inherent racial superiority. This attitude fully manifested itself in the idea of the "white man's burden" (or the French *mission civilisatrice*) as well as in the "survival of the fittest" ideology of Anglo-American social Darwinism. As Arendt points out, the latter did much to spread the idea of a "natural" racial hierarchy, one composed of masterly northern Europeans on top and lesser subordinate races (African, Asian, and Semitic) on the bottom.

The racist biologism we think of as the *sine qua non* of Nazi ideology and practice thus had *European*, and not merely Germanic, roots. Like the imperialist mindset, it was a pathology spread throughout the continent. In this regard, Arendt matter-of-factly observes that "Hitlerism exercised its strong international and inter-European appeal during the thirties because racism, although a state doctrine only in Germany, had been a powerful trend in public opinion everywhere."[22]

How did this cultural and intellectual shift away from a conception of political identity grounded on shared territory, representative institutions, and a stable legal-institutional structure toward one based on race, the "blood" of an ethnic group, or a pseudo-mystical essence ("soul") happen? According to Arendt, the beginnings of an answer can be found in the propagation of racist ideas by men like the Comte de Boulainvilliers in the eighteenth century and the Comte de Gobineau in the nineteenth century. Both offered analyses in which race and race struggle were presented as inescapable and determining factors in history.

Boulainvilliers viewed the emerging struggle between the French aristocracy and the rising Third Estate as tracing back to an original struggle between an invading Frankish-Germanic warrior race (who were the forebears of the French nobility) and native (more numerous and latinized) Gauls. Gobineau universalized Boulainvilliers' basic thought, offering race as the explanatory key not just to French, but to all human history. Gobineau saw northern Europeans (members of what he dubbed the "Aryan" race) engaged in an epoch-long losing battle against far more numerous and inferior sub-races.[23] Gobineau's *Essay on the Inequality of the Human Races* (1855)—in which he made his observations concerning the inherent superiority of the northern European race and issued dire warnings about its imperiled future—was a tremendously influential work, one that became virtually canonical by the end of the nineteenth century. Its elevated status helped to establish the basis for what would later come to be called "scientific racism."

The French writings of Boulainvilliers and Gobineau did much to stimulate the racist imagination in Europe. In Arendt's view, a more indirect yet nevertheless important contribution came from the German Romantics and Prussian patriots of the Napoleonic era. Hampered in their attempt to foment a national uprising against the French by the sheer diversity of German states and the lack of any common historical memories, Prussian patriots like the Catholic Joseph Göerres and liberals like Ernst Moritz Arndt and F. L. Jahn developed a naturalistic or "organic" appeal based on the idea of a common tribal origin and on the idea that "every race is a separate, complete whole" (Göerres). The romantics—Arendt mentions Novalis, Muller, and Haller—contributed the ideas of "innate personality" and "natural nobility," two qualities given by birth and independent of rank or social standing. Originally individualistic in character, the idea of an "innate personality" quickly came to be applied to Jews and Frenchmen as middle-class German thinkers sought to distinguish the purity and superiority of their national character from such "foreign" elements. Taken together, the ideas developed by the patriots and romantics "prepared the way for race-thinking in Germany."[24]

Another contribution to this overall intellectual trend was made by the Anglo-Irish writer and statesman Edmund Burke, who, in his *Reflections upon the Revolution in France* (1790), polemically juxtaposed the concrete and historical "rights of Englishmen" to the French "abstraction" of the Rights of Man. For Burke, the latter was a fanciful theoretical-ideological invention, while the former stood as the indubitable "entailed inheritance" of the English people. What Burke did, according to Arendt, was to take the feudal notion of liberty as the "sum total of privileges inherited together with title and land" and expand it beyond the aristocracy to include *all* Englishmen as the inheritors of a unique patrimony.

Thinking the rights and liberties of "free-born Englishmen" through the concept of inheritance became so engrained that, by the end of the nineteenth century, it was applied reflexively to the entire British "stock." It is not surprising that the English race-thinking "was almost obsessed with inheritance theories and their modern equivalent, eugenics," or that it fulsomely embraced Darwinism, which appeared to supply "the ideological weapons for race as well as class rule."[25] The Darwinian view that "man is an animal species like any other" prompted English writers and publicists to turn increasingly to biology and zoology for their explanations of, and justifications for, foreign policy goals.[26] The European competition for empire came to be viewed as a "struggle for existence" between biologically distinct peoples or "stocks," with the British Empire's evident success in the competitive struggle seen as proof of the superiority of peoples of "Saxon" descent.

The "national mission" of the British Empire and the domination of "lesser" races and peoples, then, were justified by an appeal to the ostensibly indubitable, scientifically established "facts" of human biology. It may be laughable now, but when evolutionist

John Davidson declared (in 1908) that "the Englishmen is the Over-
man and the history of England is the history of his evolution" many
in the British elite would have agreed with him. Forty years earlier Charles Dilke, a follower of Carlyle, wrote rapturously of "the
grandeur of our race already girdling the earth [Americans were
of "Saxon" descent as well]," a globe "it is destined, perhaps, to
overspread." This was the vision that guided Cecil Rhodes in his ambition to establish a British corridor from Cairo to the Cape, and to
ultimately create a class of Anglo-American philosopher-kings who
would oversee a global empire.[27]

As enlightening as Arendt's survey of European race-thinking
in the eighteenth and nineteenth centuries is, it has its limits. As
Arendt herself reminds us, "there is an abyss between the men of
brilliant and facile conceptions and men of brutal deeds and active
bestiality which no intellectual explanation is able to bridge."[28]
Any account of how Europeans were able to make the jump from
racist theory to racist practice—from "brilliant and facile conceptions" to a political and ideological program based on race and
"active bestiality"—demands the examination of "experiences
and political constellations which were still unknown and would
have been utterly strange even to such devoted defenders of 'race'
as Gobineau." Arendt suggests that, were it not for the fact that
"the scramble for Africa" and the rise of imperialism, it is "highly
probable that thinking in terms of race would have disappeared
in due time" from the European intellectual and political scene
rather than come to dominate it.[29]

What, then, were the experiences and political constellations ac-
companying these events that helped transform "facile ideas and
conceptions" into full-blown political ideologies and extraordinarily
brutal practice? For Arendt, the fundamental *experience* was the shock
Europeans felt when, in the course of the "scramble for Africa," they
encountered a "wild" continent full of hidden dangers and evidently
teeming with "savages." Before they could begin to effectively exploit their new holdings, the Europeans had first to makes sense of
this seeming chaos. They needed a form of understanding through
which they could orient themselves, thus facilitating the domination
of an "unreal" reality that seemed to defy the very possibility of organized domination.

The fundamental political *constellation* was the result of the British imperial officials realizing that they had to put an end to the ad hoc pillaging of colonial possessions if they were to facilitate a more systematic and efficient exploitation of the wealth and resources contained by these acquisitions. Such exploitation could be achieved only if an instrument for the government of large native populations could be found, one that avoided any suggestion of actually incorporating these populations into the British body politic. No one wanted the natives to think that they were somehow entitled to the inherited rights of "free-born Englishmen."

Both problems were solved, according to Arendt, by the "discovery" of two mechanisms that enabled the effective domination of African "savages" (on the one hand) and the organization and government of civilized yet "immature" native populations (on the other):

> Two new devices for political organization and rule over foreign peoples were discovered during the first decade of imperialism. One was *race* as a principle of the body politic and the other *bureaucracy* as a principle of foreign domination. Without race as a substitute for the *nation*, the scramble for Africa and investment fever might well have remained the purposeless "dance of death and trade" [Conrad] of all gold rushes. Without bureaucracy as a substitute for *government* the British possession of India might well have been left to the recklessness of the 'breakers of law' [Burke] without changing the political climate of an entire era.[30]

While discovered separately, these two "devices" turned out to be mutually reinforcing, with imperial bureaucracy giving forbidding institutional form to "ideological notions of racial difference."

The discovery of race as a "principle of the body politic" was made in South Africa. It was in South Africa that European fortune seekers, lured by the discovery of diamond fields (1867) and then gold (1884), encountered the race society created by the Boers, the almost forgotten descendants of eighteenth-century Dutch colonists. The racially organized society the Boers had established enabled the newly arrived Europeans to see "with their own eyes how peoples could be converted into races and how, simply by taking the initiative in this process, one might push one's own people into the position of the master race."[31]

In Arendt's view, the disorienting encounter of eighteenth-century Dutch immigrants with the native peoples of South Africa prefigured the experience European imperialists would have many decades later during the murderous, not to say genocidal, "scramble for Africa." The immigrants' response to that shock—the manner in which they and their descendants made sense of an experience they felt to be both baffling and terrifying—became paradigmatic for European imperialists in general:

> Race was the emergency explanation of human beings whom no European or civilized man could understand and whose humanity so frightened and humiliated the [Dutch] immigrants that they no longer cared to belong to the same human species. Race was the Boers' answer to the overwhelming monstrosity of Africa—a whole continent populated and overpopulated by savages—an explanation of the madness which grasped and illuminated them like "a flash of lightning in a serene sky: 'Exterminate all the brutes.'"[32]

For the Boers, "race" was the answer to the question of how these "monstrous" beings could be *human*—part of the same animal species—without sharing a common humanity with the Europeans. Viewed in this way, the natives appeared to the Boers to be little more than an example of the "raw material" Africa supplied in abundance.

The answer of race did not merely warrant the Boers' enslavement of the natives. As Arendt reminds us, it resulted in

> the most terrible massacres in recent history, the Boers' extermination of Hottentot tribes, the wild murdering by Carl Peters in German Southeast Africa, the decimation of the peaceful Congo population—from 20 to 40 million reduced to 8 million people; and finally and perhaps worst of all, it resulted in the triumphant introduction of such means of pacification into ordinary, respectable foreign policies.[33]

Arendt thinks the fact that the Boers (and subsequent Europeans) initially reacted to the natives not just with confusion and fear, but with disgust and murderous rage, rested on something quite distinct from observable physical differences:

> What made them [the natives] different from other human be-
> ings was not at all the color of their skin but the fact that they
> behaved like a part of nature, that they treated nature as their
> undisputed master, that they had not created a human world,
> a human reality, and that therefore nature had remained...the
> overwhelming reality—compared to which they appeared to be
> phantoms, unreal and ghostlike. They were, as it were, "natu-
> ral" human beings who lacked the specifically human charac-
> ter, the specifically human reality, so that when European men
> massacred them they somehow were not aware that they had
> committed murder.[34]

This is a disconcerting passage, and not just because it suggests that the disgust and contempt the Europeans had for black Africans was rooted in something other and deeper than the color of their skin. While Arendt's indictment of the Boers' treatment of the natives is as clear as her horror at the genocidal policies of later European im-perialists, some commentators have complained that she appears to share the view of the natives as more or less "natural" beings, lacking a civilization or "worldly artifice" of their own.

Warrant for this charge may be found in the emphasis she places (in The Human Condition) on the importance of building and preserving such an artifice, one that separates man from the tyranny of nature and the endless repetition of natural processes; one that makes both civilized life and political freedom possible. Moreover, in OT itself she asserts that the millions of refugees cre-ated by mass expulsions during the interwar period were effec-tively returned to a "peculiar state of nature," one in which they were not only stateless but rightless. She compares their condition to that of members of "savage tribes" who "inhabit an unchanged nature." These, she states, die "without leaving a trace" and fail to "contribute anything to a common world"—a fate awaiting the stateless as well.[35]

While it is safe to say that Arendt failed to appreciate the contributions and diversity of African cultures and civilization, we should not lose sight of the context of her remarks and the broader—indeed central—argument in OT. Whether discussing the Boers' response to the "monstrosity" of Africa or the odd "state of nature" in which stateless European refugees found themselves many decades later, Arendt's critical focus is on the role played by *the naturalizing gaze of the oppressors.* She wants to alert us to the rage and contempt Europeans felt entitled to express in the presence of those they perceived as "natural" beings, mere "specimens of the animal species mankind" who apparently lacked the marks of civilization. Her broader argument is that European politics and culture was propelled, for over fifty years, by the repudiation of the Enlightenment idea of a universal humanity and the vehement rejection of shared responsibility for creating and preserving a *human and humane* world.[36]

The totalitarian assault on the human status is thus the culmination of the naturalizing attitudes and practices that made it possible for Europeans to reduce large groups of human beings, whether abroad or at home, to the status of human *animals* fit only for exploitation, enslavement, expulsion, or extermination. The Boers' perception of the natives as "raw material" like any other anticipates the factory-like production of corpses in the death camps and the mass liquidations of the Stalinist purges. The "red thread" connecting them is the view that large groups of human beings are, *by their very nature,* superfluous or expendable. Under totalitarian regimes, with their positing of inescapable "laws" of History or Nature, this naturalizing perception is expanded to include virtually everyone.

But while totalitarian regimes may be indelibly associated with genocide and mass murder, it is important to remember that they were also *forms of government.* This fact leads Arendt to the consideration of bureaucratic rule, the second "device" discovered in the first decades of imperialism.

Arendt takes as her example Lord Cromer, secretary to the Viceroy of India, who, in 1894, declined the position of Viceroy and who—ten years later—also declined the position of Secretary of State for foreign affairs. Spurning these two high status positions, he chose instead to become and remain the "little publicized but all-powerful" British Consul General in Egypt from 1883 to 1907. He did so out of a profound sense of duty to the British Empire, and the conviction that "the Englishman straining far over to hold his loved India [has to] plant a firm foot on the banks of the Nile."[37] In economic terms, Egypt contributed relatively little to the British Empire. However, from the standpoint of the "great game," British rule of Egypt appeared as an absolutely necessary expansion "for the sake of the security of India," the real jewel in the crown of the Empire.[38] In this and other respects, Cromer and the British imperial mentality—so different from the "vulgar megalomania" of a Cecil Rhodes—can be seen as creating a paradigm in which the conquest or annexation of a nation of many millions for *purely instrumental reasons* is seen as a perfectly acceptable practice.

From Arendt's point of view, Cromer's exemplary significance far exceeds his willingness to treat entire nations as pawns in the "great game" in which rival empires contested the destiny of mankind. Since the British in Egypt had no interest in playing the paternalistic role they had assumed in India, a form of rule had to be created for a "lesser people" whose ultimate status or "maturity" was of no concern to the rulers. Cromer, in Arendt's telling, rose to the challenge by creating an "unprecedented hybrid form of government," a bureaucracy that ruled by decree, one whose higher reaches (including Cromer himself) operated entirely "behind the scenes," unanswerable not just to the people they governed, but also safe from the control of the British Parliament, the "English Departments" that oversaw imperial possessions, and the press.[39] If Rhodes had fantasized about a world in which the expansion of the "Nordic race," organized by a secret society of Anglo-American elites, would "establish a bureaucratic government over all the peoples of the earth," Cromer can be said to have brought that fantasy down to earth. In Egypt, he succeeded in creating an efficient form of bureaucratic rule, one that operated in secrecy and which was answerable to no one. As Consul General, he pulled all the strings.

It should be emphasized that Cromer's desire to be all-powerful and avoid oversight of any kind was not the result of any corrupt motivation. On the contrary, he embodied the sternest form of bureaucratic rectitude and imperial duty. His rule as Consul General of

Egypt was the polar opposite of corrupt and inefficient. It was correct, aloof, and indifferent. Indeed, it was this bureaucratic correctness and aloofness that guaranteed, in Cromer's mind, the integrity of his "hybrid form of government." However, as Arendt points out, it was this very aloofness that guaranteed this new form of government would achieve a qualitatively new level of inhumanity:

> Aloofness became the new attitude of all members of the British services; it was a more dangerous form of governing than despotism and arbitrariness because it did not even tolerate that last link between the despot and his subjects, which is formed by bribery and gifts. The very integrity of the British administration made despotic government more inhuman and inaccessible to its subjects than Asiatic rulers or reckless conquerors had ever been...In comparison, exploitation, oppression, and corruption look like safeguards of human dignity, because exploiter and exploited, oppressor and oppressed, conqueror and conquered, corruptor and corrupted still live in the same world...[40]

The two different worlds of all-powerful administrator and subject population were divided by culture and, more importantly, by race. While the Boers may have pioneered a racially organized society—the idea and practice of which was to migrate back to Europe as the "mob from the four corners of the earth" who had been lured to South Africa by the discovery of gold in Witwatersand and diamond fields in Kimberly returned home[41]—racialized bureaucratic rule was a British innovation. It was originally created by Cromer in Egypt and later applied to India (in addition to being copied by the French in Algeria). And, although Arendt is careful to note that Cromer "would no more have dreamed of combining administration with massacre ('administrative massacres' as Carthill bluntly put it forty years later), than the race fanatics of South Africa thought of organizing massacres for the purpose of establishing a circumscribed, rational political community (as the Nazis did in the extermination camps)," the fact remains that racialized bureaucratic rule became a paradigm for totalitarian regimes in mid-century.[42]

IV   Continental imperialism, tribal nationalism, and the pan-movements

"Of the two main political devices of imperialist rule," Arendt writes,

> race was discovered in South Africa and bureaucracy in Algeria, Egypt, and India; the former was the barely conscious reaction to tribes of whose humanity European man was ashamed and frightened, whereas the latter was a consequence of that administration by which Europeans had tried to rule foreign peoples who they felt were helplessly their inferiors and at the same time in need of their special protection.[43]

Mutually reinforcing, these two devices—and the attitudes and practices they gave rise to—would boomerang to Europe itself, with the rule of law established by constitutional republics or monarchies giving way to political entities increasingly organized by race, ethnicity, and administrative decree. The spread of *continental imperialism* among the nations of Central and Eastern Europe hugely facilitated this boomerang effect.

Continental imperialists felt "the same contempt for the narrow limits of the nation-state" as did their overseas imperialist peers. However, in their case, this contempt was animated less by the need for economic expansion than by what Arendt, following Emil Deckert, refers to as an "enlarged tribal consciousness," one which "was supposed to unite all people of similar folk origin, independent of history and no matter where they happened to live."[44] This consciousness found expression in the ideologies of Pan-Germanism and Pan-Slavism, two supra-nationalist off-shoots of Romanticism that would later crystallize into mass political movements demanding the erasure of the "artificial" political boundaries that separated them from others of German "blood" or from their Slavic "brothers." This happened, in part, as a response to the tremendously successful overseas expansion of the Western powers, a fact so massive that it convinced many in Central and Eastern Europe that they too had a "God-given right" to territorial expansion.

Arendt focuses on this relatively neglected chapter in the history of imperialism because she believes that "Nazism and Bolshevism owe more to Pan-Germanism and Pan-Slavism (respectively) than to any other ideology or political movement."[45] Both movements made nationalistic ideas of a "chosen people" central to their programs, and both were to utilize anti-Semitic ideology as a way to focus and direct the resentment of various ethnic minorities in Eastern and Southern Europe (Poles, Hungarians, Austrian Germans, Croatians, Serbs, the Baltic peoples) against the state structures of their imperial, Austro-Hungarian or Russian, overlords.

On a more theoretical level, Arendt draws our attention to the way these movements brought about a profound change in the way many millions of Europeans thought about political membership and their political identity. Her argument is that these movements expressed a specifically *tribal* form of nationalism, one that "had little in common with the nationalism of the fully developed Western nation-state." This was a form of nationalism that transformed established notions of political identity—based on such tangible and public things as shared laws, institutions, and historical accomplishments—into something essentially *private* and *intangible*, an inner essence or "soul."

As Arendt points out,

> the nation-state, with its claim to popular representation and national sovereignty, as it had developed since the French Revolution through the nineteenth century, was the result of the combination of two factors that were still separate in the eighteenth century and which remained separate in Russia and Austria-Hungary: nationality and state.

While the sense of *nationhood* was a relatively recent development in Western Europe, the structure of the *state* itself "was derived from centuries of monarchy and enlightened despotism." The modern state "inherited as its supreme function the protection of all inhabitants in its territory *no matter what their nationality* and was supposed to be the supreme legal institution."[46] The post-revolutionary European state, founded upon the abolition of feudal privilege, was above all a legal and institutional structure that treated all citizens alike—at least in principle.

The combination of the post-revolutionary state's civic-legal structure with an emerging sense of nationhood (born of the emancipation of the peasant class in Western Europe) gave rise to the nation-state as we know it. Yet, according to Arendt, the foundation of this new political form contained a "secret conflict" between nation and state. This conflict "came to light at the very birth of the modern nation-state" when the French Revolution included the demand for national sovereignty in its declaration of the Rights of Man. The result, Arendt observes, was that

> the same essential rights were at once claimed as the inaliena-ble heritage of all human beings *and* as the specific heritage of specific nations, the same nation was subject to laws, which supposedly would flow from the Rights of Man, *and* sovereign, that is, bound by no universal law and acknowledging nothing superior to itself.[47]

This contradiction was not merely a theoretical one. In practice, it meant that "from then on human rights were protected and enforced *only as national* rights." Arendt therefore views the nationalism that arose in Western Europe as "essentially an expression of this *perversion* of the state into an instrument of the nation and the identification of the citizen with the member of the nation." Its only saving grace was that "insofar as the state, even in its perverted form, remained a legal institution, nationalism was contained by some law…[and] limited by definite boundaries."[48]

The profile of the *tribal* nationalism that developed in Eastern and Southern Europe was quite different. In these parts of Europe, the borders between competing empires (Russian, Austro-Hungarian, and Ottoman) were constantly shifting, and this meant that the migratory movements of various ethnic peoples never really came to an end. Moreover, these populations were not just territorially "rootless." They were also un-emancipated, serfs rather than citizens. They lacked what Arendt viewed as the groundwork of the Western European nation-state, namely, the "trinity" of people-territory-state. Oppressed by distant governments in Vienna, Istanbul, or St. Petersburg, these groups were caught up in the nationalist fever that swept through Europe in the period leading up to the revolutions of 1848.

However, unlike their peers in the West, the ethnic minorities in Eastern and Southern Europe "had no country, no state, no historic achievements to show." If they wanted to match the national pride of the Western nations, they "could only point to themselves, and that meant, at best, to their language…at worst, to their Slavic, or German, or God-knows-what soul."[49] Their national identity appeared to be "much more a portable private matter, inherent in their very personality, rather than a matter of public concern and civilization."[50] The pan-movements were the first to articulate this rather inchoate sense of national identity in ideological terms. They organized politically rootless peoples who lacked not only a state and territory of their own, but also any traditions of public-spiritedness or civic responsibility.

German-speaking minorities in Czechoslovakia, the Austro-Hungarian Empire, and Poland may not have shared the same degree of territorial displacement, but they felt equally "not at home" and were, in this sense, "rootless" as well. Arendt maintains that tribal nationalism "grew out of this atmosphere of rootlessness." She sees rootlessness as "the true source of that 'enlarged tribal consciousness' which actually meant that members of these peoples had no definite home but felt at home wherever other members of their 'tribe' happened to live."[51] As the Georg Ritter von Schönerer, the founder of the Pan-German movement and one of Hitler's primary influences, was to put it, "It is our distinction that we do not gravitate towards Vienna but gravitate to whatever place Germans may live in."[52]

The significance of the pan-movements is not simply that they organized the tribal nationalism that had spread throughout Southern and Eastern Europe. Both the Russian Pan-Slavs and the Austrian Pan-Germans developed ideologies centered upon the idea of the divine chosenness of the Slavic or German people. Radically departing from the Judeo-Christian tradition's faith in the divine origin of Man, Pan-Slavism and Pan-Germanism insisted on the divine origin of one, and only one, people—the Slavic or Germanic people—and the non-divine origin of all the rest. The pan-movements thus created a form of nationalism that synthesized the imperialist claims to national superiority with racist claims (such as the Boers') to a singular divine origin:

> Nationalism and its concept of a "national mission" perverted
> the national concept of mankind as a family of nations into a

hierarchical structure where differences of history and organization were misinterpreted as differences between men, residing in natural origin. Racism, which denied the common origin of man and repudiated the common purpose of establishing humanity, introduced the concept of divine origin of one people as contrasted with all others, thereby covering the temporary and changeable product of human endeavor with a pseudomystical cloud of divine eternity and finality.[53]

The affinity of the pan-movements' tribal nationalism with racist concepts is unmistakable. Regardless of whether one thinks of one's people as chosen by God or Nature, the end result is the same: "... peoples are transformed into animal species so that a Russian appears as different from a German as a wolf is from a fox."[54] The people chosen by God or Nature thus become the "born persecutors" of weaker species or—alternatively—the martyr-like victim of all "stronger" species. Where one national people is viewed, in effect, as a different species from all the others, "only the rules of the animal kingdom can possibly apply to its political destinies."[55]

Expansionist ambitions and the resentments of linguistic and ethnic minorities aside, what accounts for the widespread appeal of such ideologies during this period? Arendt suggests that, beneath it all, they express an "instinctive feeling" against the Enlightenment idea of humanity and the shared responsibility for the world this idea implies. As she puts it, "tribalism and racism are very realistic, if very destructive, ways of escaping this predicament of common [human] responsibility."[56] The energy driving these distinctively modern and destructive forms of particularism is thus entirely reactive. They constitute a refusal to take up the burden of caring for a world we share with others who are at once different from, yet also the same as, ourselves. Equality and difference—the moral core of Arendt's notion of human plurality—are construed as mutually exclusive.

This destructive legacy of the pan-movements is joined to two others. The first is a deeply ingrained hostility to state institutions and the rule of law; the second, the idea that parliamentary politics—with its representative institutions, multiple parties, and conflicting interests—is farcical and ineffectual, incapable of expressing the people's will and satisfying their spiritual needs.

The hostility to legal and state institutions is understandable if one feels oppressed by them (as peoples in the central European "belt of mixed populations" certainly did). However, it becomes pathological where lack of political experience leads to a hostility toward state institutions and established legal orders as such. In the case of the Pan-Slavs, this hostility took the form of contempt for Western-style political parties and institutions, coupled with a superstitious worship of the Tsarist bureaucracy and "holy Russia." The opaque bureaucracy, ostensibly directed by the Tsar, ruled through decree rather than through any constricting legislative or constitutional channels. For the pan-Slavs, lawlessness and rule by decree thus became positive political ideals, the marks of an "organic" political entity composed of many impenetrable bureaucratic layers but one animated by one will, that of the Tsar, "God's representative on earth."

Antagonism toward parliamentary politics dates from the end of the nineteenth century, a period in which genuinely significant political developments in Europe increasingly took place outside the framework of the parliamentary party system. When the pan-movements came on the scene, they positioned themselves not so much as "above parties" as "above the state." This enabled them to claim "direct identification with the people."[57] In contrast to the Anglo-American two-party model, in which stable and (relatively) non-ideological parties alternated as government and opposition, parliamentary politics on the continent worked largely through the formation of multi-party coalitions, with the result that no single party ever felt *responsible* for policy. Moreover, the Continental parties were separate from the governing structures of the state and confined to a purely representative role.

Their class- and nation-centered rhetoric notwithstanding, the parties represented a relatively narrow set of particular interests (industry, agriculture, finance, labor). Ordinary people became increasingly skeptical about their less-than-honest ideological appeals and justifications. The result was that a system barely fifty years old came to be viewed with mounting scorn. Aggressive nationalist parties such as Mussolini's Fascists arose, but these merely sought to gain control of the state apparatus and establish one-party government. They appealed to popular dissatisfaction with the parliamentary system while never actually challenging the state structure that contained it. It was only the pan-movements—with their contempt for participation in the parliamentary "game" *and* their attacks on above-it-all state institutions—that seemed capable of expressing actual popular feeling and will. The movements channeled popular rage against the state, promising to tear down its obstructing institutions and laws and to replace them with popular energy and the dynamism of the movement itself.

This is an important precedent, since the pan-movements' "above the state" posturing and their anti-state politics foreshadow the strategy and tactics of both the National Socialist and Bolshevik movements (and, Arendt would add, all other totalitarian or proto-totalitarian movements and regimes). One of the great misconceptions about totalitarianism, whether as movement or regime, is that it represents the horrible fulfillment of what the philosopher Ernst Cassirer once called the "myth of the state." In fact, not only did totalitarian movements follow the pan-movements' precedent in campaigning *against* the state; they also made a point of either destroying the state institutions they inherited, or (at least) of depriving them of any real power.

Under totalitarian rule, real power is monopolized by the movement/party itself. It is directed in a way that creates a condition of perpetual revolution, one which keeps the movement moving and insures that the regime will not stabilize in recognizable and familiar state institutions. In stark contrast to Mussolini and the Italian Fascist party, Arendt argues, the goal of the totalitarians was not to seize the established institutional apparatus of the state, thereby establishing a one-party dictatorship. Rather, it was the far more radical goal of eliminating everything that stood in the way of accelerating the "laws of movement" dictated by Nature (in the form of the life and death struggle of the races postulated by the Nazis) or History (in the form of the equally violent class struggle postulated by the Bolsheviks).

V The decline of the nation-state: statelessness and the perplexities of the rights of man

The days before and the days after the first Word War are separated...like the days before and after an explosion. Yet, this figure of speech is as inaccurate as are all others, because the quiet of the sorrow which settles down after a catastrophe has never come to pass. The first explosion seems to have touched off a chain reaction in which we have been caught ever since and which nobody seems able to stop....Civil wars which ushered in and spread over the twenty years of uneasy peace were not only bloodier and more cruel than all their predecessors; they were followed by migrations of groups who...were welcomed nowhere and could be assimilated nowhere. Once they left their homeland, they remained homeless; once they had left their state, they became stateless; once they had been deprived of their human rights, they were rightless, the scum of the earth.[58]

This passage describes the situation of Europe between the wars, a period riven by violent revolution, civil war, economic crises and distinguished by a totally new phenomenon: the creation of a refugee population in the tens of millions. Expelled from their homelands with no prospect of returning, this mass of stateless individuals spread over Central and Western Europe. Their arrival strained a nation-state system whose comity (the mutual recognition of the legislative, executive, and juridical acts of other countries) had broken down, and whose ability to cope with the consequences of the mass denationalizations was extremely limited.

This situation was exacerbated by the creation, in Central and Eastern Europe, of "successor states" intended to cope with the collapse of the Russian, Austro-Hungarian, and Ottoman empires. Departing from the assumption that every national people deserved a nation-state of its own, the Peace Treaties attempted to achieve the impossible and unscramble the belt of mixed populations that stretched from the Baltic to the Balkans. Among other things, this effort led to the creation of the nation-states of Czechoslovakia and Yugoslavia, as well as the re-constitution of Poland as a sovereign state. In each case, a so-called "national people" supposedly shared power with a "partner" people (e.g. the "national" Czechs and the "partner" Slovaks), while observing special Treaty-created rights created for the protection of ethnic minorities (Jews, Hungarians, Germans) within their newly drawn borders.

The result was a situation in which the "national" peoples controlled the government and possessed first-class citizenship, while their "partners" enjoyed de facto second-class citizenship. The minorities had to make due with the "special rights" created by the Treaties and (supposedly) guaranteed by the League of Nations. Thus, in Arendt's words, the Treaties

> lumped together many peoples into single states, called some of them 'state people' and entrusted them with government, silently assumed others...were equal partners, which they were not, and with equal arbitrariness created out of the remnant a third group of nationalities called 'minorities' thereby adding to the burdens of the new states the trouble of observing special regulations for part of the population.[59]

It is not surprising that the Treaties were seen as "an arbitrary game in which rule was handed to some and servitude to others."

Committed to the creation of nation-states in places where the fundamental preconditions—homogeneity of population and root-edness in the soil—were missing, the Minority Treaties had the effect of instituting *degrees* of citizenship (with different legal statuses) among peoples who lived within a newly drawn set of borders. In Arendt's view, the Treaties had four primary results. First, they explicitly recognized the fact that many millions of people actually lived outside of normal legal protections. Second, they gave clear expression to the idea that "only nationals could be citizens" and (third) changed the state from being an "instrument of law" to an "instrument of the nation." Finally, they brought the flaw at the heart of the nation-state—the conflict between the inclusive legal principle of the state and the exclusive idea of membership inherent in the nation—front and center.[60]

The framers of the Minority Treaties thus contributed mightily to the creation of a Europe in which civic and political rights were functions of one's national origin and membership in a corresponding nation-state. Minorities within the nation-state were treated as exceptions to the rule that "only nationals can be citizens." However, the mechanism by which "special rights" were to be granted and protected completely broke down under the strain of the mass denationalizations and expulsions that occurred in the period after WWI—a phenomenon the framers of the Minority Treaties failed to imagine, let alone make any provision for.

In a situation oddly parallel to that of the present, the "successor states" of Central and Eastern Europe funneled increasing numbers of refugees to the nations of Western Europe, adding to the flood members of their own minority populations whom they had no will or desire to protect. Across Europe, the right to asylum was effectively abolished and a new maze of bureaucratic categories created. These were designed to distinguish legally national citizens from naturalized citizens, naturalized citizens from resident aliens, and resident aliens from the stateless person or *apatride*. Arendt is devastatingly clear about the consequences of this proliferation of legal statuses:

> The nation-state cannot exist once its principle of equality before the law has broken down. Without this legal equality, which was originally destined to replace the older laws and orders of feudal society, the nation dissolves into an anarchic mass of over- and underprivileged individuals. Laws that are not equal for all revert to rights and privileges, something contradictory to the very nature of nation-states. The clearer the proof of their inability to treat stateless people as legal persons and the greater the extension of arbitrary rule by police decree, the more difficult it is for states to resist the temptation to deprive all citizens of legal status and rule them with an omnipotent police.[61]

While previously a kind of "legal freak," the *apatride* quickly became the largest segment among the refugees. Faced with wave upon wave of Spanish, Russian, Jewish, and Armenian refugees, the countries of Western Europe proved constitutionally incapable of guaranteeing the human rights of the millions who had been deprived of whatever civic and political rights they had enjoyed in their home countries. The stateless were effectively rightless, and the whole ever-expanding problem was transferred by the government to the police, who indeed came to wield total power and discretion over the new arrivals. Camps for "displaced persons" sprang up all over Western Europe. The plight of the growing stateless population served as a "practical demonstration" of the cynical claim made by totalitarian movements that "no such thing as inalienable rights existed" and that the affirmations of the democracies to the contrary were "mere prejudice, hypocrisy, and cowardice."[62]

Undermined from the "outside" by imperialism and the pan-movements, the European nation-states faced a kind of "internal disintegration" resulting from the presence of ever-increasing numbers of stateless people within their borders. These, it was felt, were the first trickle of what would eventually become a flood, one that would swamp the normal processes of naturalization and assimilation. Recognized neither as citizens or nationals in their home countries and denied civil and political rights in their countries of refuge, the stateless wound up living outside the pale of any law whatsoever. The only status they continued to possess was their human one. As Arendt makes abundantly clear, this fact did not lead to any institutional recognition of their human dignity, nor did it lead to any attempt on the part of individual nation-states to enforce the supposedly inalienable Rights of Man on behalf of the stateless.

In a world where "only nationals can be citizens," losing one's national political home was thus equivalent to being thrust out of the protective legal and institutional structures of the "human artifice" altogether. The stateless occupied a zone—the permanent "outside" of the nation-state—where the category of rights simply did not reach. This explains Arendt's sad conclusion that

> the calamity of the right-less is not that they are deprived of life, liberty, and the pursuit of happiness, or of equality before the law and freedom of opinion—formulas designed to solve problems within given communities—but that they no longer belong to any community whatsoever.[63]

This lack of civic status rendered the stateless completely vulnerable to the machinations of an administrative and police apparatus whose primary objective was simply to dispose of the problem. Throughout the 1930s, European police forces repeatedly shoved large groups of stateless refugees across their borders, only to have them shoved back by the police of the neighboring nation-state. No one wanted these apparently "superfluous" people, individuals who had become—through no fault of their own—the "scum of the earth." Small wonder that internment camps became a regular feature of the European landscape, popping up in France, Holland, and elsewhere.

Such camps have recently reappeared all over Europe. As in the thirties, many have argued that the nation-state system has few alternatives in responding to the crisis. Administrative and juridical apparatuses are overwhelmed, and the "absorptive" capacity of the nation is (supposedly) strained beyond limit. Arendt was familiar with such justifications. However, against them she argues that the response to the refugee crisis in the interwar period was hardly as ad hoc and situationally determined as such justifications imply. Instead, she sees it as flowing from the original tension built into the European nation-state model—the tension between state and nation, law and "the will of the people."

It was the entrenchment of the views that "only nationals could be citizens" and that the state is but an instrument of the "nation" that rendered the nation-state's response to the interwar refugee crisis more or less predictable. The hegemony of these views had the practical effect of transforming human rights into national rights: they became the exclusive legal possession of an ethnic majority people organized into a nation-state. In such a world, expulsion from a political community, coupled with denial of opportunity to become a rights-bearing member of the country of refuge, is tantamount to expulsion from what Arendt calls the "human artifice"—her shorthand for the institutional, cultural, and legal structures that demarcate civilized life. And this, Arendt stresses, is equivalent to being expelled from humanity altogether.

****

Was the identification of the "Rights of Man" with the "Rights of Peoples" underlying this state of affairs fortuitous, the result of mistaken interpretation or local prejudice? Arendt thinks not. After describing the vulnerabilities of minority peoples and the stateless, she embarks on a theoretical discussion of "the perplexities of the Rights of Man." Her intent is to draw out the historical and conceptual logic by which the "inalienable Rights of Man," originally formulated to apply to individual human beings, came to be identified with the Rights of Peoples. This identification was fraught with implications for ethnic minorities and stateless refugees alike. It contributed mightily to the decline of the nation-state and paved the way for replacement of the rule of law with a hierarchy of rights and privileges based upon ethnic identity.

According to Arendt,

> the Declaration of the Rights of Man at the end of the eighteenth century was a turning point in history. It meant nothing more nor less than that from then on Man, and not God's command or the customs of history, should be the source of Law.[64]

Viewed from this angle, the Declaration had two main consequences. First, it not only abolished the complex hierarchy of feudal society; it also made the constitutional and the political order, rather than social estates or the Church, the protector and guarantor of rights.

The second consequence was broader and more epochal. Considered as historical event, the Declaration of the inalienable Rights of Man signaled Man's "coming of age." This meant that the rights, freedom, and dignity of human beings were independent of any reliance upon an encompassing theological or metaphysical order. Whereas previously the rightness of all positive law was seen to have its ground in a "higher" Divine or Natural Law, it was now seen to be derived from the inalienable rights that Man, qua Man, inherently possessed. Moreover, no special laws were seen as necessary to protect these inalienable rights, since they in fact were the true ground of all (legitimate) law.

Man—and not God, Nature, or custom—now appeared as "the only sovereign in matters of law."[65] The possession of inalienable rights made Man an autonomous or "self-legislating" being (Kant). It seemed obvious that beings who carried the ground of all right and justice within themselves should not be coercively ruled by others. Hence, "it seemed only natural that the 'inalienable' rights of man would find their guarantee and become an inalienable part of *the right of the people to sovereign self-government*."[66] At the moment that Man appeared as the "only sovereign in matters of law," the People were proclaimed as the only sovereign in matters of government. Arendt underlines the supremely ironic result: "Man had hardly appeared as a completely emancipated...being who carried his dignity within himself...when he disappeared again into a member of a people."

This was less the result of any slipperiness built into the concept of autonomy than it was a problem built into the idea of inalienable human rights as such. "From the beginning," Arendt writes, "the paradox involved in the declaration of inalienable human rights was that it reckoned with an 'abstract' human being who seemed to exist nowhere, for even savages lived in some kind of social order."[67] Add to this the empirical fact that "natural" or "primitive" men rarely, if ever, enjoyed their "inalienable rights" and it became possible for Europeans to conclude that

> if a tribal or other 'backward' community did not enjoy human rights, it was obviously because as a whole it had not yet reached that stage of civilization, the stage of popular and national sovereignty, but was oppressed by foreign or native despots.[68]

The question of human rights thus came to be inextricably linked to the question of *national emancipation*. The full implications of this identification came to light only after WWI, when revolution, civil war, and mass denationalizations in Russia, Spain, and elsewhere created an enormous refugee crisis. An ever-growing population of stateless people appeared, one whose "elementary rights were as little safeguarded by the ordinary functioning of a nation-state in the middle of Europe as they would have been in the heart of Africa." Lacking the legal protections previously provided by their home countries, the stateless discovered that there was no institutional authority in their places of refuge willing to guarantee their "inalienable" rights.

It was not surprising, then, that stateless peoples became as convinced as the minority peoples that "loss of national rights was identical with loss of human rights, that the former inevitably entailed the latter."[69] Previously, legal protection of foreign nationals had been guaranteed by reciprocal treaties between nations: the French would guarantee a German national rightful treatment under law and the Germans would do the same for a French national. However, with the advent of revolutionary governments and subsequent destruction of the comity of European nation-states after WWI, this mechanism broke down completely. Once large numbers of people who were no longer citizens of any sovereign state appeared on the scene, the "inalienable" Rights of Man proved unenforceable. This was the case even in countries whose constitutions were explicitly based upon them, such as France.

Ironically, part of the blame for this can be traced back to the political thought of the nineteenth century, which took what Hegel had called the "great mental dawn" of the French Revolution for granted. Given the post-revolutionary rise of republics and constitutional monarchies, most thinkers believed the Rights of Man to be firmly established as part of the European cultural inheritance, one that required no further theoretical reflection:

> The reason why the concept of human rights was treated as a sort of stepchild by nineteenth century political thought...seems obvious: civil rights—that is, the varying rights of citizens in different countries—were supposed to embody and spell out in the form of tangible laws the eternal Rights of Man, which by themselves were supposed to be independent of citizenship and nationality. All human beings were citizens of some kind of political community; if the laws of their country did not live up to the demands of the Rights of Man, they were expected to change them, by legislation...or through revolutionary action.[70]

The decades following the end of WWI revealed the tragic naïveté of these nineteenth-century assumptions. For it was in this period that the gulf between the all-too-familiar phenomenon of politically oppressed groups (who had lost one or several rights) and the unprecedented situation of the stateless appeared. The latter, deprived of any government protection whatsoever, have lost not *some* but *all* their rights:

> The calamity of the rightless is not that they are deprived of life, liberty, and the pursuit of happiness, or of equality before the law and freedom of opinion...but that they no longer belong to any community whatsoever. Their plight is not that they are not equal before the law, but that no law exists for them; not that they are oppressed but that nobody wants even to oppress them. Only in the last stage of a rather lengthy process is their right to live threatened; only if they remain perfectly 'superfluous', if nobody can be found to 'claim' them, may their lives be in

danger. Even the Nazis started their extermination of the Jews by depriving them of all legal status (the status of second-class citizenship)...The point is that a condition of complete rightlessness was created before the right to live was challenged.[71]

Deprived of their place in the world, denied government protection, and persecuted not for anything they may have done, said, or thought but rather because of *who they were*, the stateless live in a condition of absolute vulnerability. Despite the significant growth of international law and organization in the period after WWII, the plight of sixty-five million-plus refugees in the world today reveals just how far we are from effectively dealing with the problem Arendt identified. Assuming that everyone is a citizen somewhere, that everyone has *some* home they can return to, we remain captive to nineteenth-century assumptions that prevent us from seeing a harsh global reality for what it actually is.

It is at this point that Arendt introduces her celebrated notion of "a right to have rights." "We become aware," she writes,

> of the existence of a right to have rights (and this means to live in a framework where one is judged by one's actions and opinions) and a right to belong to some kind of organized community, only when millions of people emerged who had lost and could not regain these rights because of the new global political situation.[72]

In a world where there are no longer any spaces that have not been incorporated into *some* political entity, the stateless are condemned to live a fugitive existence in the shadows of whatever nation-state they succeed in escaping to. The citizens and governments of those nation-states are more likely than not to view them as little more than parasites or "useless mouths."

Seen from this angle, it could be legitimately said that the stateless were (and still are) demonstrably worse off than the slaves of antiquity. Within ancient society, the slave was certainly not free. However, as Arendt points out, he nevertheless had a "distinctive character," a "place in society." The stateless person, on the other hand, possesses nothing beyond the "abstract nakedness of being human and nothing but human." The condition of the ancient Greek or Roman slave thus shows how it is possible for an individual to "lose all so-called Rights of Man without losing his essential quality as man, his human dignity."[73] It is "only the loss of a polity itself"—the loss sustained by the millions of stateless people between the wars—that "expels him from humanity."

This makes it sound as if the "right to have rights" is equivalent to the right to belong to *some* political entity capable of bestowing and protecting rights. That is, indeed, the preponderant sense of Arendt's notion. However, in the sentence citied above where she defines the "right to have rights," Arendt insists that, in addition to the right to "belong to some kind of organized community," the "right to have rights" entails the right to "live in a framework where one is judged by one's actions and opinions," and not by any ascribed identity (racial, ethnic, religious, etc.). In other words, the "right to have rights" means the right to be included in an, but not just *any*, organized political community. The recognition of a citizen's (or subject's) rights hinges, after all, on the presence of laws that spell out his civil and political rights, no matter how narrowly construed these may be. Thus, though it may undo the stateless person's expulsion from humanity, political membership *as such* is not enough.

What is the ground of such a "right to have rights"? Arendt's comments regarding the "cynical claims" of totalitarian regimes that inalienable rights do not exist, combined with her repeated invocation of human dignity, might lead one to assume that she believes the Rights of Man are, as the eighteenth-century thought they were, *natural* rights—something every human being possesses *a priori*, as it were. But, as the following passage reveals, this is not the case:

> When the Rights of Man were proclaimed for the first time, they were regarded as being independent of history and the privileges which history had accorded certain strata of society....Historical rights were replaced by natural rights, "nature" took the place of history, and it was tacitly assumed that nature was less alien than history to the essence of man....Today we perhaps better qualified to judge exactly what this human "nature" amounts to...Ever since a deeper knowledge of natural processes instilled serious doubts about the existence of natural laws at all, nature

has assumed a sinister aspect. How should one be able to deduce laws and rights from a universe which apparently knows neither the one or the other?[74]

This skepticism toward "natural rights" should not come as a total surprise. After all, Arendt not only aligned herself with the dismantlers of metaphysics and opposed the uncritical use of the category "human nature" (see Chapter 1). She also thought that the category of "nature" was itself highly misleading when used to describe political phenomena such as equality, freedom, and authority, all of which were made possible through the creation of an artificial, institutionally and legally articulated, public-political realm. Moreover, the category of nature was downright dangerous insofar as it led numerous British and European authors and statesmen to view the political world through the lens of evolutionary biology and "natural selection." This was a widespread tendency at the end of the nineteenth century, and it came to horrific culmination in what the historian Timothy Snyder has called Hitler's "ecological" view of the world as the site of an endless struggle for limited resources between different races.[75]

Is Arendt's rejection of "natural right" tantamount to an acceptance of history as the actual ground of "inalienable" rights? According to some, historical right is the only possible alternative to natural right.[76] Yet, Arendt thinks that "history and nature have become equally alien to us, namely in the sense that the essence of man can no longer be comprehended in terms of either category."[77] If the category of nature threatens to reduce the "essence of man" to something either metaphysically static or biologically determined, the category of history threatens to reduce it to either the sheer facticity of the past or to a progressive movement toward the realization of some future telos. In both cases, the sheer capacity to begin—a capacity which Arendt sees as central to the "essence of man"—is viewed as illusory or epiphenomenal.

Of course, all talk of "human nature" or the "essence of man" risks devolving into biological reductionism or theological (or rationalist) dogma. Yet, Arendt deploys both terms in OT, and in a way that is neither ironic nor overtly skeptical. The important thing to note in the present context is that she spurns nature and history equally as the ostensible grounds for "inalienable" rights. What, then, is left? For many, to say that human rights are "ground-less" in either the metaphysical or theological sense is equivalent to declaring them fictions—useful fictions, perhaps, but fictions nevertheless. Indeed, Arendt herself raises this issue in terms that defenders of the traditional distinction between positive right and law (on the one hand) and natural right and law (on the other) would no doubt find congenial:

> A conception of law which identifies what is right with the notion of what is good for—an individual, or the family, or the people, or the largest number—becomes inevitable once the absolute and transcendent measurements of religion or the law of nature have lost their authority. And this predicament is by no means solved if the unit to which "good for" applies is as large as mankind itself. For it is quite conceivable...that one fine day a highly organized and mechanized humanity will conclude democratically...that for humanity as a whole it would be better to liquidate certain parts thereof. Here, in the problem of factual reality, we are confronted with one of the oldest perplexities of political philosophy, which could remain undetected only so long as a stable Christian theology provided the framework for all political and philosophical problems, but which long ago caused Plato to say: "Not man, but a god, must be the measure of all things."[78]

For many social and political thinkers, the relativizing of all justice and right inherent in the "good for" formulation Arendt alludes to above is more than ample reason to revert to traditional Catholic Natural Law teaching. Yet, despite her long-standing interest in Christian theology (she wrote her doctoral dissertation on "St. Augustine's Concept of Love"), Arendt is no theologian. Nor does she think that the Enlightenment, liberalism, or something called "modernity" is to blame for this relativizing: she is actively hostile to any nostalgia for the *ancien régime*. What avenue, then, remains if we wish to avoid conceding that Burke's arguments against the Rights of Man were basically correct, and that all "the rights we enjoy spring 'from within the nations,' so that neither natural law, nor divine command, nor any concept of mankind…are needed as a source of law"?[79]

The only alternative Arendt offers is one that is neither certain nor, many would say, likely. Following her assertion that "history and nature have become equally alien to us," she notes that "humanity"— which for the eighteenth century was a kind of "regulative idea" or ideal—has "today become for us an inescapable fact."[80] We live in a globalized world, one which is interconnected in ways previous ages could scarcely conceive. In this situation, Arendt states, "humanity" has "in effect assumed the role formerly ascribed to nature or history." Given this context, the right to have rights—the right of every individual to belong to humanity and to have their elementary rights protected by some legally organized political entity—"should be guaranteed by humanity itself"—that is, by a humanity that has come of age and become a concrete reality.[81]

That this is not a relapse into the edifying clichés of the Enlightenment is made clear by Arendt's conclusion that "it is by no means certain whether this is possible." As long as international law takes the form of reciprocal agreements and treaties between sovereign states, a sphere "above the nations" (a sphere in which humanity, and not just sovereign states, could legislate and enforce agreements) is impossible. At the same time, any sort of "world government" would, as Kant rightly concluded, be an insufferable tyranny. From Arendt's perspective, the only hope seems to reside in the strengthening of international law and the creation of multi-state federal bodies.

Thus, while there have been many positive developments since the time Arendt wrote—for example, the creation of the European Union and the International Criminal Court in the Hague, as well as the growth of global civil society exemplified by organizations like Amnesty International and Doctors Without Borders—the basic situation remains much the same. Indeed, the contemporary revanchist insistence on national sovereignty, the closing of national borders to refugees escaping war and domestic chaos, and the mounting persecution of ethnic and religious minorities around the world underscore the fact that—while "humanity" may now indeed be a concrete reality, thanks to globalization—it is by no means the case that we have "come of age." Nor are we in a position to *guarantee* much of anything to the persecuted of the world, let alone the "right to have rights."

Arendt's analyses of the European pathologies of racism, tribal nationalism, and anti-Semitism provide much illumination in this regard. One can hardly emerge from reading the first two thirds of OT with naïve confidence that humanity is on track to guaranteeing basic human rights for all, or that a more cosmopolitan world is just around the corner. This is especially so given the stubborn persistence of these three pathologies. Our current situation might lead us to ask whether Arendt, in addition to providing historical genealogies of these pathologies, has anything to say about their underlying source. What is the root of the resentment and hatred that appears to animate all three?

As her review of Denis de Rougemont's book *The Devil's Share* makes abundantly clear, Arendt rejects any explanation that falls back upon the supposed fact of human sinfulness. Nor does she think, as did the eighteenth century, that the source of our woes is to be found in the persistence of prejudice, and that prejudice will be eliminated by the spread of education, enlightenment, and a wider recognition of the "self-evident truth" that "all men are created equal." The interwar refugee crisis unmasked this Enlightenment piety, proving beyond all doubt that "the world found nothing sacred in the abstract nakedness of being human."[82]

Equality, Arendt emphatically asserts, is not something *given* by nature. It is, rather, something *made* by men, the result of a collective decision to create a political community based upon law and justice—that is, upon the equality of citizens. Humanity will be able to guarantee the "right to have rights" only when the nation-states of the world agree that any state that abuses its sovereignty by stripping entire populations of their civil and political rights has committed an attack on the human status itself.

To repeat, this status is *not* something given by an anthropomorphic god, nor is it a consequence of our possession of reason or any other mental faculty. It is, rather, a function of the human capacity to *begin*, to create an artificial world distinct from nature in which legal and civic equality become possible. For it is only within such a public-political world that the idea of human dignity and the "right to have rights" can be recognized as fundamental to civilized life in the modern age.

These points are summed up by Arendt when she states "our political life rests on the assumption that we can produce equality through organization, because man can act in and change and build a common world, together with his equals and only with his equals."[83]

VI The destruction of the European class system and the rise of totalitarian movements

Thus far, I have traced Arendt's genealogy of some of the practices and attitudes that helped make totalitarianism possible in "civilized" Europe. These elements—imperialist expansionism, racism, the decline of the nation-state and the rule of law, and the creation of bureaucratic rule by decree for subject populations—were all well-established in Europe and European colonies prior to WWI. Yet, even if we grant Arendt the importance of these elements in the constellation that helped make totalitarianism possible, something important is clearly missing. How is it that totalitarian movements were able to come to power in the first place? What made the most poisonous ideological mixtures of these pathologies and practices attractive to millions of ordinary people in Central and Eastern Europe? What could possibly account for their popularity in the interwar period and beyond?

Arendt's answer to this question avoids falling into two recognizable traps. On the one hand, there are historians and political scientists who have emphasized the coup-like nature of the Nazi and Soviet ascensions to power, emphasizing the relative smallness of the party faithful in comparison to the population at large. On the other, there are those who have claimed that the Nazis and Bolsheviks came to power because their programs resonated with a deeply anti-Semitic German people and with a downtrodden and oppressed Russian populace eager to overturn a corrupt feudal-bourgeois order.

While both sides of the debate contain a kernel of truth, they are clearly inadequate as explanations. The first tendency is apologetic insofar as it argues that the movements and regimes in question were never propelled by broad popular support. To the question "what made totalitarian movements and regimes popular among ordinary people?" it answers that they were never that popular among the majority of Germans or Russians: guilt resides mainly with the leadership and with a minority of party fanatics. The second tendency goes too far in the other direction, presenting entire populations as animated by either murderous prejudice or chiliastic dreams of a purified society, one purged of all "corrupting" elements.[84]

In contrast to both these tendencies, Arendt emphasizes a fact we should never forget: totalitarian movements were indeed *mass* movements. They drew the body of their followers not from hyper-politicized "mob" elements (the milieu that gave birth to Hitler and Stalin), but from broad swaths of a population that had been previously politically apathetic. "Totalitarian movements," she writes,

> are possible wherever there are masses who for one reason or another have acquired the appetite for political organization. Masses are not held together by a consciousness of common interest and they lack that specific class articulateness which is expressed in determined, limited and obtainable goals.

She continues:

> The term *masses* applies only where we deal with people who either because of sheer numbers, or indifference, or a combination of both, cannot be integrated into any organization based on common interest, into political parties or municipal governments or professional organizations…It was characteristic [of the Nazi and Communist movements] that they recruited their members from this mass of apparently indifferent people who all other parties had given up on as too apathetic or stupid for their attention. The result was that the majority of their membership consisted of people who never before had appeared on the political scene. This permitted the introduction of entirely new methods into political propaganda, and indifference to the arguments of political opponents; these movements not only placed themselves outside and against the party system…they found a membership that had never been reached by it.[85]

Who, then, were these "masses"? Where did they come from and how did they come to play such a central role in the rise of totalitarian movements?

Arendt's answers to these questions can be read as an extension of Tocqueville's argument that the replacement of the *ancien regime's* caste society by a democratic *condition sociale* invariably gives rise to individualism, dissociation, and atomization. No longer connected to social ranks above and below them by a network of obligations and privileges, democratic individuals increasingly turn inward to family, friends, and the pursuit of private interests. They become increasingly alienated from one another and from society at large.

In an analysis parallel to Tocqueville's account, Arendt argues that WWI, combined with the collapse of the Austro-Hungarian and Russian Empires, effectively destroyed whatever remained of the *ancien regime* in Europe. The dissolution of Europe's *political* caste-structure paved the way for the breakdown of Europe's post-1789 *class* structure as well. This breakdown was accelerated by the economic depression of the 1930s, the effects of which were socially devastating. "Inflation destroyed the whole class of small property owners beyond hope for recovery...Unemployment, when it came, reached fabulous proportions, was no longer restricted to the working class but seized with insignificant exceptions whole nations."[86] Not only did many millions lose the relative security of their class position. They also lost their place in the world—that is, they lost their connection to the opinions and interests that had defined their class position and status. They became part of an ever-growing mass of individuals no longer meaningfully integrated into society, a mass that was politically apathetic and understandably hostile to a parliamentary party system designed to represent specific class interests.

Tocqueville had argued that the bourgeois desire for material well-being over all else could—and sometimes did—translate into impatience with democratic civic responsibilities and the desire for a "strong man." The latter—Napoleon and Napoleon III are good examples—quash political liberty but nevertheless maintain the authority and order the bourgeoisie saw as critical to the smooth accumulation of profit. While Arendt shares Tocqueville's appraisal of the corrosive effect of bourgeois materialism on civic responsibility and care for the "public thing," she is keen to point out the difference between attitudes that promote the appearance of "democratic despots" and those that pave the way for *totalitarian* rule. Thus, even though the bourgeois society of the nineteenth century excluded large portions of the population from political participation, Arendt argues that the individuals comprising these groups were still able to keep their personalities intact and pursue their self-interest.[87]

The same cannot be said for the millions who lost their class position, thanks to war, civil war, revolution, and economic depression. Unlike their working class and *petit bourgeois* forebears, these people were not simply excluded from the public realm. They had lost their place in society as well. For them, all that was solid truly had melted into air. The result, in Arendt's view, was that they internalized a sense of their own expendability, a feeling exacerbated by a society that had "so insistently and exclusively centered on the individual's success or failure in ruthless competition."[88]

Battered by events and increasingly aware of their own social superfluity, these traumatized masses abandoned the relentless but futile pursuit of self-interest. In their collective fury at an established order that had failed to protect them (and whose powers they perceived as "not so much evil as …stupid and fraudulent"), they were more than ready to be swept up by the dynamism of anti-bourgeois and anti-establishment radical political movements. In fact, Arendt thinks it was precisely the promise of transcending the politics of self- and sectional interests that made totalitarian movements (movements that "thought in continents and felt in centuries") attractive to masses of atomized and bitter individuals. Selflessness, previously the expression of the highest personal idealism, now became a curiously mass phenomenon.[89] Drawn by the idealism of the movement (which contrasted so sharply with bourgeois hypocrisy), "expendable" mass men abandoned concern for their individual well-being and embraced the ethos of total loyalty and willing self-sacrifice trumpeted by the Nazis and the Bolsheviks.

Arendt here confronts the mystery of why millions of ordinary people enthusiastically followed political leaders, parties, and movements willing to sacrifice the lives and welfare of entire generations for the sake of "victory" in the class or race struggle. The role played by totalitarian propaganda and ideology is obviously key, but not in the way we usually think it is. From Arendt's standpoint, it is not as if an inert populace in either Russia or Germany simply allowed itself to be brain-washed by fiendishly effective ministries of propaganda, such as the one led by Joseph Goebbels. Rather, she

stresses the *longing for fiction* that characterized atomized masses traumatized by war, civil war, and economic depression. In a period
when virtually every aspect of life had become nakedly and unbeara-
bly contingent—where "common sense" no longer seemed to make
sense—the need for simplifying, all-explaining ideological world-
views was pronounced. As Arendt puts it:

> While it is true that the masses are obsessed by a desire to escape
> from reality because in their essential homelessness they can no
> longer bear its accidental, incomprehensible aspects, it is also
> true that their longing for fiction has some connection with
> those capacities of the human mind whose structured consist-
> ency is superior to mere occurrence. The masses' escape from
> reality is a verdict against the world in which they are forced to
> live and in which they cannot exist, since coincidence has be-
> come its supreme master and human beings need the constant
> transformation of chaotic and accidental conditions into a man-
> made pattern of relative consistency.[90]

The appeal of Nazism and Bolshevism, then, lay not just in the fact
that they offered simple explanatory principles (the supposedly
all-determining historical "realities" of race and class struggle) but
in their logicality and their capacity to insulate the mind from a del-
uge of unwelcome and seemingly random facts and events. In "Ideology and Terror," the lecture she transformed into the concluding
chapter of the second and subsequent editions of OT, Arendt notes
the "three specifically totalitarian elements" that are "peculiar to all
ideological thinking":

> First, in their claim to total explanation, ideologies had the
> tendency to explain not what is, but what becomes, what is
> born and passes away....The claim to total explanation prom-
> ises to explain all historical happenings, the total explanation
> of the past, the total knowledge of the present, and the reliable
> prediction of the future. Secondly, in this capacity ideological
> thinking becomes independent of all experience from which
> it cannot learn anything new even if it is a question of some-
> thing that has just come to pass. Hence ideological thinking

becomes emancipated from the reality that we perceive with our five senses and insists on a "truer" reality concealed behind all perceptible things...Thirdly, since ideologies have no power to transform reality, they achieve this emancipation of thought from experience through certain methods of demonstration. Ideological thinking orders facts into an absolutely logical procedure which starts from an axiomatically accepted premise, deducing everything else from it; that is, it proceeds with a consistency that exists nowhere in the realm of reality.[91]

Thus, before seizing power, totalitarian movements use propaganda and ideology to

conjure up a lying world of total consistency which is more adequate to the needs of the human mind than reality itself; in which, through sheer imagination, uprooted masses can feel at home and are spared the never-ending shocks which real life and real experiences deal to human beings and their expectations.[92]

Hitler and Stalin's predictive pronouncements—about the fate of the Jews should war break out in Europe, or the fate of various "dying" classes in the Soviet Union—were couched in the language of "prophetic scientificality." The elimination of Jews from Europe or the class of prosperous peasants (kulaks) from Russia were presented as unavoidable conclusions drawn from supposedly incontrovertible premises, premises established by the pseudo-sciences of race and history. Of course, such events were hardly inevitable. Nevertheless, Hitler and Stalin used terror and violence to bring about their predictions, thus "demonstrating" the infallibility of their reasoning.

Arendt singles out the idea of a Jewish "world conspiracy" as the "most efficient fiction of Nazi propaganda." In the post-WWI environment of the Weimar Republic, German Jews (1% of the national population) had lost whatever power they once wielded as bankers to the Prussian state (a role that extended from Frederick the Great through Bismarck). Yet, while they had lost their "economic usefulness," they were surprisingly prominent in the arts, sciences, the professions of law and medicine, and politics. This prominence, combined with the structural weakness of their position in society, made the Jews the perfect ideological foil for the Nazis. Framed as a foreign, supra-national "race" that had established itself parasitically within the body of the German *Volk*, the Jews ceased to be a minority vulnerable to sporadic outbursts of Christian prejudice and became, instead, the defining "other" for the German national community— the *Volksgemeinschaft*. Nazi propaganda, according to Arendt,

> was ingenious enough to transform antisemitism into a principle of self-definition and thus to eliminate it from the fluctuations of mere opinion...This gave the masses of atomized, undefinable, unstable and futile individuals a means of self-definition and identification which not only restored some of the self-respect they had formerly derived from their function in society, but also created a spurious stability which made them better candidates for organization.[93]

As privileged possessors of German blood and members of the "naturally superior" Aryan race, the "isolated individuals of an atomized society" gained not only a new self-importance to offset whatever loss of social standing they might have suffered. They were also organized and integrated into an "organic" community based on the "absolute equality of all Germans"—that is, upon an equality "not of rights, but of nature."[94]

It is perhaps not surprising that such a newly self-important people, still smarting from a defeat they felt was the result of a "stab in the back" by the liberal (and, in some instances, Jewish) leaders of the Weimar Republic, would find in the Tsarist forgery "The Protocols of the Elders of Zion" less an exposé of Jewish world domination than a kind of manual of instruction. "The delusion of an already existing Jewish world domination," Arendt writes, "formed the basis for the illusion of future German world domination."[95] The lesson of the Protocols was not only that world domination was a "practical possibility," but that the key to its achievement lay in "inspired or shrewd know-how" and the right kind of organization. The Protocols were read as an authentic document revealing the secrets of such organization and the deceptive stratagems the achievement of global hegemony required. When Himmler said "we owe the art of government to the Jews," he did so with the Protocols in mind, underlining their importance by claiming that Hitler had "learned them by heart."[96]

This brings us to two factors Arendt saw as crucial to the success of totalitarian movements. The first concerns the forms of organization employed by totalitarian movements and parties, which she viewed as utterly novel: "They are designed to translate the propaganda lies of the movement…into a functioning reality, to build up, even under non-totalitarian circumstances, a society whose members act and react according to the rules of a fictitious world."[97] Totalitarian movements deploy front organizations for a dual purpose. On the one hand, they make the party and the aims of the movement appear more conventional and rational to the outside world than they in fact are. On the other, front organizations surround party members with a "protective wall," separating them from the outside world while also providing a reassuring "bridge back to normalcy." Without such a bridge, party members in the pre-power stage might "feel too sharply the differences between their beliefs and those of normal people, between the lying fictitiousness of their own and the reality of the normal world."[98]

Party members are thus related to and separated from "fellow travelers." Similarly, members of elite formations (the SS, the Bolshevik cadres) are both related to and separated from ordinary party members. According to Arendt, the idea behind totalitarian forms of organization is the creation of a "graduated hierarchy of militancy in which each rank is the higher level's image of the non-totalitarian world."[99] The resulting onion-like structure—with the Leader at its center—insures that both party members and elite formations are insulated from the prosaic world of facts and the standards of normal society. Indeed, it is this "normal society"—with its interest group politics, parliamentary procedure, and declining but still operative respect for brute social, political, and historical facts—that totalitarian movements such as the Nazis and Bolsheviks desired to destroy once and for all.

The realization of totalitarian ideological goals—of a totally classless society or unified *Volksgemeinschaft*—thus hinges upon the lack of "normal social relationships" so characteristic of atomized mass populations, as well as upon a party structure that insures ideological fiction is viewed as the only constant in a flux-filled world. This is a world from which factuality has been eliminated, thanks to mass man's peculiar mixture of "gullibility and cynicism" and the artfully cultivated "inability to understand facts as facts" characteristic of the elite formations who have been schooled in the most radical version of the party ideology.

The elite formations see the ideological clichés of the movement and belief in the leader's infallibility as little more than useful tools for organizing the masses. From their point of view, neither the masses nor ordinary party members realize that, with the right type of organization and sufficient ruthlessness, *everything is possible*. There is no set of "facts on the ground" that cannot be destroyed so that the world might be re-made to accord with the ultimate aims of the movement. Thus, according to Arendt, the superiority of the elite formations consists

> in their ability immediately to dissolve every statement of fact into a declaration of purpose…the elite formations understand that the statement, all Jews are inferior, means, all Jews should be killed; they know that when they are told that only Moscow has a subway, the real meaning of the statement is that all subways should be destroyed.[100]

Above the clichés of the movement and contemptuous of "all facts and all realities," the elite formations were bound together by their "firm and sincere belief in human omnipotence."[101]

To be sure, the transformation of reality to accord with what Arendt calls the "ideological super-sense" of the movement had its precedents in totalitarian propaganda and in the political organization that followed seizure of power. Thus, in the case of National Socialism,

> the assumption of a Jewish world conspiracy was transformed by totalitarian propaganda from an objective, arguable matter into the chief element of the Nazi reality; the point was that the Nazis *acted* as though the world was dominated by the Jews and needed a counter-conspiracy to defend itself. Racism for them was no longer a debatable theory of dubious scientific value but was being realized every day in the functioning hierarchy of

political organization in whose framework it would have been
very 'unrealistic' to question it.[102]

Totalitarian fiction thus supplied not only a reassuringly simple and
consistent explanation for an overwhelmingly complex and chaotic
world. It also supplied aims and principles that could be concretely
instantiated in the laws and political organization of a single state.
While ordinary citizens of Stalin's Russia or Hitler's Germany may or
may not have thought in terms of world domination, the Bolsheviks'
success in creating a "classless" society and the Nazis' success in
creating a racially organized *Volksgemeinschaft* apparently demonstrated
that the fiction was, indeed, more real than the shapeless and agoniz-
ingly contingent reality that had proceeded it.

VII Anti-Semitism

This brings us to Arendt's analysis of anti-Semitism in Part I of OT.
For first-time readers of *Origins*, the book's commencement with a
lengthy historical analysis of the rise of modern anti-Semitism and
Western and Central European Jewry's relation to state and society
is a bit mystifying. While anti-Semitism was clearly at the center of
the Nazis' ideology and murderous practice, it is not clear what role,
if any, it played in contributing to the conditions that made Stalin's
Russia possible. As Margaret Canovan has observed, while OT contains much on the antecedents of Nazi racism and anti-Semitism,
it contains little on "the Marxist background to Stalin's murderous
version of the class struggle"—a deficit Arendt later attempted to
redress in the never-completed book on "totalitarian elements in
Marxism."[103]

Nevertheless, a case can be made that it was anti-Semitism that "set
the whole infernal machinery" of totalitarian politics in motion. As I
noted earlier, Arendt's project in OT is both historical and theoretical.
On the one hand, she wanted to isolate the primary elements—the
events, attitudes, and practices—that contributed to making totalitarianism possible in Europe. On the other, she wanted to construct
an ideal type of what she viewed as an "unprecedented" form of political regime. Anti-Semitism merits inclusion in the list of elements
that made totalitarianism in Europe possible because, like racism and

imperialism, it was not simply a German but a pan-European phenomenon in the late nineteenth and early twentieth century.[104] In
this period, anti-Semitism ceased to be the expression of merely of
social prejudice or Christian antipathy toward the "older brother." It
became a *political ideology* attached to specific movements, events, and
parties in France, Austria, and Germany and contributed in no small
part to the ideology of pan-Slavism that Stalin was to appropriate
and exploit.

The thread uniting these parties and movements across Europe
was that they all saw the Jews precisely as the "Protocols of the Elders
of Zion" had portrayed them: powerful out of all proportion to their
numbers and hell-bent on dominating European and world politics.
Arendt remarks, "if a patent forgery like the "Protocols of the Elders
of Zion" is believed by so many people that it can become the text
of a whole political movement, the task of the historian is no longer
to discover a forgery...[but to explain why] the forgery is being believed."[105] Only then can one understand the "catalytic" role played
by anti-Semitism in the rise of totalitarian movements and regimes.

But how to proceed? According to Arendt, one important rule to
keep in mind was suggested by Tocqueville in *The Old Regime and the
Revolution*. In that work, Tocqueville made the acute observation that,
in the decades prior to the revolution, the French people came to
hate the aristocracy far more than ever before, in large part because
the aristocrats' "rapid loss of real power was not accompanied by
any considerable decline in their fortunes."[106] Arendt thinks it can
be demonstrated that political and social anti-Semitism in Europe
waxed as the power and influence of European Jewry waned. "Anti-
semitism," she writes, "reached its climax when the Jews had similarly lost their public functions [as bankers to the state] and their
influence and were left with nothing but their wealth."[107] Backing
up this thesis demands that Arendt, in addition to tracing the emergence of modern European anti-Semitism, provide an analysis of the
Jews' evolving relationship to the state and to society in Western and
Central Europe in the period between 1740 and 1914.

This task is inhibited by two widespread, essentially unhistorical,
"explanations" of why the Jews came to occupy what Arendt calls
the "storm center" of twentieth-century European politics. The first
is the idea that the Jews were picked out and blamed for the political,

economic, and social evils of the late nineteenth and early twentieth centuries precisely because their relative powerlessness made them prime candidates to be cast as scapegoats. The second is the "opposite doctrine" of an "eternal antisemitism" which sees hatred of the Jews as an indelible feature of world history for more than 2,000 years.

In addition to being unhistorical, Arendt objects to these two "explanations" for the following reasons. The trouble with the "scapegoat theory" is that it makes the choice of the Jews more or less arbitrary: any relatively powerless group could have easily served the same purpose. However, "an ideology which has to persuade and mobilize people cannot choose its victims arbitrarily."[108] The trouble with the "eternal antisemitism" idea is that it makes the focused analysis of any specific outburst of anti-Semitic hatred, no matter how horrific or unprecedented it might be, superfluous. If anti-Semitic hatred is a constant of history, then something like the Holocaust was inevitable—shocking, but hardly confounding or inexplicable. Moreover, the idea of "eternal antisemitism" serves to absolve the perpetrators of much of their personal responsibility for horror. They appear to be determined by historical forces operating over their heads and beyond their control.

This last point highlights another reason why Arendt is keen not just to set aside but to debunk these two "explanations." Each, in its own way, diminishes the importance and specificity of human action, judgment, and responsibility. The scapegoat theory is essentially functionalist in character: *someone* had to be blamed for Germany's defeat, the Great Depression, high unemployment, etc., so it might as well be the Jews. The masses (and, later, the perpetrators) merely react to events and strike out blindly at a powerless and innocent victim. Similarly, "eternal antisemitism" not only semi-absolves the perpetrators; it also implies that the Jews lack any agency whatsoever when it comes to defining their identity or determining their place within society.

This alerts us to a dual theme in Arendt's subsequent writing, namely her emphasis on contingency of history (in opposition to all doctrines of historical necessity or inevitability) and her equally strong emphasis upon moral agency and responsibility in politics. There are few among us who wish to mitigate, let alone absolve, the perpetrators of responsibility, no matter what the chain of command might have been. But many of us think that any reference to the victim's agency is the first step on a slippery slope to blaming the victim.

Of course, Arendt hardly wants to do that. OT was written out of rage at the perpetrators and the trends in European politics that brought them to power. Equally, it was written out of anguish for the millions who were killed or transformed into rightless refugees. While she harbors few illusions about the prospects of organized political resistance under established totalitarian regimes, she adamantly *does* think that the exercise of greater political responsibility—by the bourgeoisie, political elites, and socialist parties of the left—could have avoided the cataclysm of the twentieth century.

Had the bourgeoisie cared about politics and the public realm a fraction as much as they cared about profits and expansion; had national statesmen more staunchly resisted the economic and political forces undermining the nation-state; and had socialist and workers' parties cared about international politics and the gradual destruction of the nation-state system one-tenth as much as they cared about capitalist exploitation at home, then things might have been much different. One lesson of OT is that, in politics, no one is completely innocent—that is, without some degree of *political* responsibility. Of course, that does not mean that everyone is somehow "guilty." For Arendt, only the perpetrators of deeds—from the highest-ranking formulators of murderous policy down to the lowliest foot soldier or concentration camp guard—are *guilty*. But, prior to the triumph of totalitarianism or dictatorship, we all bear some responsibility for what happens in the public sphere. It's with these considerations in mind that one should read passages like the following:

> It is quite remarkable that the only two doctrines which at least attempt to explain the political significance of the antisemitic movement deny all specific Jewish responsibility and refuse to discuss matters in specific historical terms. In this inherent negation of the significance of human behavior, they bear a terrible resemblance to those modern practices and forms of government which by means of arbitrary terror, liquidate the very possibility of human activity.[109]

The phrase "Jewish responsibility" here *does not* refer to any purported Jewish responsibility for inciting anti-Semitism through the abuse of either power or position—a notion Arendt finds absurd and, as noted earlier, one she explicitly repudiates. Rather, it refers to the Jews' political behavior and social function after their nineteenth-century emancipation in Western and Central Europe. "An ideology which has to persuade and mobilize people cannot choose its victims arbitrarily." This means that leaders of proto-totalitarian movements seeking to destroy the "narrowness" of the nation-state had to choose victims who were marginal and relatively powerless, but whose history and function in European society made them plausible candidates to fill the role of a secret "power behind the throne" manipulating the course of events and the destinies of European peoples.

This is the rationale behind Arendt's contention that modern anti-semitism must be seen in the more general framework of the development of the nation-state, and at the same time its source must be found in certain aspects of Jewish history and specifically Jewish functions during the last centuries.[110]

> If in the final stage of disintegration, antisemitic slogans proved the most effective means of inspiring and organizing great masses of people for imperialist expansion and destruction of the old forms of government, then the previous history of the relationship between the Jews and the state must contain elementary clues to the growing hostility between certain groups of society and the Jews...If, furthermore, the steady growth of the modern mob—that is, of the *déclassés* of all classes—produced leaders who, undisturbed by the question of whether the Jews were sufficiently important to be made the focus of a political ideology, repeatedly saw them as the "key to history" and the central cause of all evils, then the previous relationship between Jews and society must contain the elementary indications of the hostile relationship between the mob and the Jews.[111]

Arendt's survey of the "history of the relationship between the Jews and the state" in modern Europe is wide-ranging. Schematically, she breaks it down into four main developments. First, the seventeenth and eighteenth centuries saw the development of nation-states in Western and Central Europe under the "tutelage" of absolute monarchs. Wealthy individual Jews were elevated to the status of court Jews who financed state affairs and handled financial transactions for their princes. This elevation of a few wealthy individual Jews had virtually no impact on either the majority of subjects (who continued to live within a mostly feudal order) or upon the Jewish people. Second, after the French Revolution, modern nation-states emerged in the form of republics or constitutional monarchies. The increased scale of their business transactions required "considerably larger amounts of capital and credit than the court Jews had ever been asked to place at the prince's disposal."[112] To meet this demand, Jewish financiers were compelled to draw increasingly upon the combined wealth of Central and Western European Jewry.

The third development concerns the rise of imperialism and the negative impact it had on the "intimate relationship between national governments and the Jews." Previously indifferent to politics and unwilling to tie up their capital in the state-sector, national bourgeoisies realized further expansion of their enterprises could be carried out only with the aid and intervention of the state. The "political emancipation of the bourgeoisie" not only deprived wealthy Jews of their exclusive position vis à vis the state. As we have seen, it also "undermined the very foundations of the nation-state and introduced into the European comity of nations the competitive spirit of business concerns."[113]

The final stage came about in the decades preceding the first World War, which saw wealthier Jews largely bereft of their previous function, status, and (limited) power. Never fully integrated into the class society that emerged after the fall of the *ancien régime*, they found themselves dangerously isolated. At the same time, the state—having surrendered its autonomy and ostensibly "universal" representative status to the financial interests of the bourgeoisie—came under attack from a range of increasingly hostile social and ethnic groups, many of which gravitated toward tribal nationalism and proto-totalitarian political movements.

Thus, the state—the legal-political institution that had emancipated the Jews in Western and Central Europe at the beginning of the century, granted them equal civil rights, and guaranteed that the wealthier among them fulfilled an important socio-political function—was under enormous pressure at the beginning of the new century, having lost it legitimacy in the eyes of many if not all of its citizen-subjects. Having allied themselves with governmental authority for many decades, Central and Western European Jews remained blind to the hollowing out of state authority by powerful economic interests and intensifying social discontent. Indeed, many of them perceived the decades immediately preceding WWI as (in Stefan Zweig's words) a "golden age of security" even though it was during this period that anti-Semitic political parties made their presence felt in France, Austria, and Germany. The Dreyfus Affair that wracked French social and political life from 1894 to 1904 constituted a veritable dress rehearsal for much that was to follow. Anti-Semitic rioting all over France was initiated by quasi-militarized groups and the mob's cries of "Death to the Jews!" echoed even in the salons of polite society.

According to Arendt, it was the peculiar position of Jews in Central and Western Europe—allied to the state, but never really integrated into class society—that made them oblivious to the new constellation in which they found themselves toward the end of the nineteenth century:

> Just as the Jews ignored completely the growing tension between state and society they were also the last to be aware that circumstances had forced them into the center of the conflict. They therefore never knew how to evaluate antisemitism, or rather recognize the moment when social discrimination changed into a political argument. For more than a hundred years, antisemitism had slowly and gradually made its way into almost all social strata in almost all European countries until it emerged suddenly as the one issue upon which an almost unified opinion could be achieved. The law according to which this process developed was simple: each class of society which came into conflict with the state as such became antisemitic because the only social group which seemed to represent the state was the Jews.[114]

Arendt argues that the rise of anti-Semitic political parties in France, Germany, and Austria in the early 1900s was preceded by a series of financial scandals, including the Panama Affair in France (in which a large number of French parliamentary representatives took bribes to keep quiet about how financially compromised De Lesseps' Panama Company had become) and the *Grundungsschwindel* or "Founders' Swindle" in Germany and Austria (in which an oversupply of investment capital following the Franco-Prussian War led to a speculation bubble, the crash of the Vienna stock market, and two decades of economic stagnation). Millions of shop and small property owners (the *petit bourgeois*) were ruined in each.

These millions quickly found themselves part of an ever-growing mass of *déclassé* individuals, which Arendt christens "the mob," the better to distinguish them from both a politically organized *people* and a socially coherent *class*. Their collective rage and resentment were directed at the state (the Third Republic in France was totally compromised) and at small-to-middling Jewish bankers who had extended loans during the investment fever that preceded each scandal. The historic connection between larger Jewish financial houses (such as the Rothschilds) and governments made it easy for unscrupulous agitators to argue that the Jews were responsible for the corruption of the state and the financial ruination of an entire social class, even though neither claim had any basis in fact.

The focusing of this rage was facilitated not just by the Jews' historic links to the state, but by their marginal yet clearly identifiable position *vis à vis* society. Arendt argues that "social discrimination, and not political antisemitism, discovered the phantom of 'the Jew.'"[115] The advent of Jewish emancipation in the early nineteenth century marked the end of such free social spaces as the Berlin salon of Rahel Varnhagen. In the salons of Rahel and other Berlin Jewesses, intellectuals, aristocrats, artists, and Jews had mixed without prejudice in a society outside the bounds of "official" society. However, once civil-political discrimination against the Jews ended, social discrimination began to kick in with a vengeance, first among formerly friendly aristocrats. Jewish notables, relying on their special relationship to the state, were content to leave Gentile society to itself and preserve their leadership positions within relatively autonomous Jewish communities.

The rapid disappearance of such "unofficial" social spaces left few avenues open to educated Jews who wanted to escape the narrow confines of their communities, forcing them into the position of the intellectual or literary "pariah" (who stood outside both the Jewish community and "official" society), the business-oriented "parvenu" (who established an independent social status through success in economic or professional pursuits), or the conformist (who slavishly mimicked the behavior and opinions of the majority). Each of these avenues had its pitfalls, as "Jews felt simultaneously the pariah's regret at not having become a parvenu and the parvenu's bad conscience at having betrayed his people and exchanged equal rights for personal privileges."[116]

The result was that "the majority of assimilated Jews…lived in a twilight of favor and misfortune and knew with certainty only that both success and failure were inextricably connected with the fact that they were Jews." For assimilated Jews, the so-called "Jewish question" lost all political significance and became an essentially psychological one, the inner burden carried by an individual who was constantly aware of his otherness no matter what the degree of his professional or personal success.[117] This situation changed in the last decades of the nineteenth century, as "polite society" in France, Austria, and Germany felt (largely out of boredom) an increasing attraction to the exotic "other": the criminal, the homosexual, the Jew. Delighting in "vice" and the "wicked," polite society found "exceptional" educated Jews adept at performing their "Jewishness" fascinating—a phenomenon Arendt finds amply documented in Proust's *Remembrance of Things Past*. With the initial explosion of the Dreyfus Affair, the appeal of such "exception" Jews became irresistible, since polite society—newly tolerant of criminality—was now convinced that, just as all homosexuals were "criminals" (and therefore appealing additions to the guest list) so all Jews were "traitors." The "vice" of Jewishness exerted an appeal every bit as strong as the "vice" of homosexuality. Unbeknownst to the Jews, this was, in fact, an extremely dangerous development. As Arendt notes, "Jews had been able to escape from Judaism into conversion; from Jewishness there was no escape. A crime, moreover, is met with punishment; a vice can only be exterminated."[118]

This threatening possibility loomed over France once the Dreyfus Affair had run its course, and it emerged once again as the "social glory" of German and Austrian Jews in the 1920s began to fade. This

short-lived glory in the eyes of high society was predicated upon
the "exciting" idea that the Jews were somehow secretly responsible
for WWI—a conviction shared by the "mob" of *déclassés*, who also
viewed the Jews as criminals, albeit without the enthralled fascination of their high society peers. In France, Germany, and Austria,
social philosemitism "always ends up by adding to political antisemitism that mysterious fanaticism without which antisemitism could
hardly have become the best slogan for organization."[119]

Once Judaism was transformed into "Jewishness" (a transformation effected, in part, by the psychologizing habits of assimilated Jewry) and once "Jewishness" was identified with vice by
high society and criminality by the mob, the path was opened to
a "passion-driven hunt of the 'Jew in general,' the 'Jew everywhere
and nowhere'"—something very different from earlier forms of
"merely" political anti-Semitism. The latter, Arendt notes, might
have produced anti-Jewish legislation and even mass expulsion, but
hardly "wholesale extermination."[120] It took the politicization of a
distinctively *social* antipathy toward Jews and "Jewishness"—an antipathy felt by *petit bourgeois* shop keepers and small property owners
who felt they had been ruined by Jewish bankers (first in the financial scandals of the late nineteenth century, then in the Great Depression) as well as by high society types who now found themselves
viscerally repelled by what they had previously found dangerously
appealing. Made vulnerable by their identification with a state apparatus that seemingly lacked all legitimacy, by their marginal position within class society, and by their own historical lack of political
experience and organization, European Jewry was ill-equipped to
either understand or effectively resist the forces behind their "fateful
journey to the storm center of events" of the twentieth century.

This analysis clarifies what Arendt meant by Jewish responsibility in
the fifty or so years prior to the catastrophe. Arendt *in no way* suggests
that the Jews were somehow "responsible" for their own destruction.
Nor does she suggest that they were "responsible" for the vicious ste-
reotypes created and promulgated by anti-Semites. Rather, she holds
the *leading elements* of central and western European Jewry responsible
for three things: first, for their undeviating faith in the effectivity of
the protection provided by state authority; second, for underwriting
the relative autonomy (and separateness) of Jewish communities, the

better to preserve their own positions of authority within them; and third, for adopting an individual strategy of parvenu-like assimilation to a class society that had no place for them as a group. A very different response—that of political organization and participation—arose only with the appearance of the Zionist movement. This was a movement predicated on the assumption, ironically shared by the anti-Semites, that the Jews never had and never would have a real social or political "home" in western or central Europe.

VIII Total domination and the destruction of human freedom

The penultimate chapter of OT, "Totalitarianism in Power," consists of three long sections: one on "the so-called totalitarian state," another on the role of the secret police, and a final section entitled "Total Domination." The final section contains an analysis of how totalitarian terror—spread by means of the search for ideologically defined "objective enemies" by the secret police (on one hand) and by enormous systems of work, concentration, and extermination camps (on the other)—all but achieves its goal of "changing human nature." It is in the camps that the totalitarians carry out what Arendt calls their "ghastly experiments" in *total* domination. By creating a veritable hell on earth in the camps, one in which a variety of techniques were deployed in order to "prolong the process of dying" for months at a time, the totalitarians were able to transform their victims from individual human beings capable of unpredictable action to interchangeable "bundles of reflexes." Total domination isolates and "stabilizes" individuals, literally dehumanizing them in order to eliminate the "problem" posed by human unpredictability, which the totalitarians viewed as the primary impediment to the acceleration of the "laws of movement" ostensibly laid down by either History or Nature.

   Before turning to her analysis of total domination, however, a word or two should be said about Arendt's description of the "so-called totalitarian state." As I previously mentioned, Arendt thinks the standard view of totalitarian regimes—one which sees them as monstrously inflated and monolithic "total" states—is quite misleading. The outstanding characteristic of totalitarian regimes is the same as that of totalitarian movements: a *dynamism* manifest in ever-increasing radicalization and the destruction of durable legal and institutional structures. While statesmen and politicians expected the Nazis and Bolsheviks to pursue predictable national interests once they had successfully seized power and liquidated their political enemies, the exact opposite took place. The seizure of power did not begin the process of transforming totalitarian movements into "normal," interest-pursuing nation-state governments. Rather, it began a rule by terror, one in which successive groups of innocent human beings were marked as "objective enemies" of the regime, destined to be liquidated as the evolutionary laws of History or Nature dictated. The actual political views of individuals (let alone the performance of acts of resistance or real crimes) did not matter to such ideologically guided determinations. The result was that *everyone* in a totalitarian regime soon realized that tomorrow he or she may be fated to become either victim or executioner. As Stalin's show trials amply demonstrated, party membership or loyalty to the regime was hardly a guarantee of survival.

Beyond the application of terror to an ever-expanding list of "objective enemies," Arendt thinks the totalitarian state was characterized by a marked shapelessness. Rather than a clear structure of authority, one finds a fantastic duplication of offices and a constantly shifting center of power (the Nazis excelled at this). The ministry or office that appeared to, and in some instances did, wield power one day became practically irrelevant the next. Aside from the Leader, the only stable point of power was the secret police. As Arendt remarks, in totalitarian regimes, real power "begins in secrecy." Far from resembling a monolithic state with a clearly defined bureaucratic hierarchy, totalitarian regimes combined the dynamism and radicalism of the movement with the mysterious opaqueness of secret societies. The body politic of the country is rendered "shock-proof" because of its shapelessness, while the characteristically totalitarian belief that *everything is possible* by means of the power of organization insures that the regime's behavior will never be guided by "merely" utilitarian interests.

Rule by terror is the path to total domination, and total domination is the path to the unhindered working out of the "laws" of Nature or History. From the point of view of the totalitarians, the problem is how to "fabricate something that does not exist, namely, a kind of human species resembling other animal species whose only 'freedom' would consist in 'preserving the species.'" Total domination "strives to organize the infinite plurality and differentiation of human beings as if all of humanity were just one individual," a materially homogenous and plastic entity that could be shaped and re-shaped in accordance with the dictates of the reigning ideological fiction (the hierarchy of the races; the classless utopian society). Totalitarian domination attempts to achieve this goal

> through ideological indoctrination of the elite formations and through absolute terror in the camps; and the atrocities for which the elite formations are ruthlessly used become…the practical application of the ideological indoctrination…while the appalling spectacle of the camps themselves is supposed to furnish the 'theoretical' verification of the ideology.[121]

Far from being a truism, Arendt's description of the camps as the "central institution" of totalitarian regimes was ahead of its time. By 1951, many people had seen the films the allies had made as they liberated camps like Bergen-Belsen, but the hellish Bruegel-like scenes of hundreds of emaciated corpses being bull-dozed into mass graves provoked incredulity as well as incomprehension. It took decades for the Holocaust to take its place in the popular imagination as a manifestation of radical evil, and longer for the Gulag to be appreciated as the clear horror it was. Even when the awful facts were finally grasped, there was a decided preference on the part of many not to "dwell on horrors." This was the case even in Israel, where—prior to the trial of Adolf Eichmann in Jerusalem in 1961—the destruction of European Jewry by the Nazis was seen by many native-born Israelis as almost an embarrassment, a sign of the weakness and apparent passivity of the victims.[122]

All the more reason to be surprised by Arendt's own "dwelling on horrors" in the penultimate chapter of OT. In one of the most striking passages of OT, she writes:

> The camps are meant not only to exterminate people and degrade human beings, but also to serve the ghastly experiment

of eliminating, under scientifically controlled conditions, spontaneity itself as an expression of human behavior and of transforming the human personality into a mere thing, into something that even animals are not; Pavlov's dog, which as we know, was trained to eat not when it was hungry, but when a bell rang, was a perverted animal. Under normal circumstances this can never be accomplished, because spontaneity can never be entirely eliminated insofar as it is connected not only with human freedom, but with life itself, in the sense of simply being alive. It is only in the concentrations camps that such an experiment is at all possible, and there they are not only "*la société la plus totalitaire encore réalisée*" (David Rousset) but the guiding social ideal of total domination in general.[123]

Readers who find this description of the nature and significance of the camps far-fetched might want to consult not just Rousset's *Les jours de notre mort* but also Primo Levi's *Survival in Auschwitz*. Levi's descriptions of the *Muselmänner* (Auschwitz slang for the "walking dead") bear an uncanny resemblance to the "living corpses" and the "ghastly marionettes with human faces" Arendt writes about. Levi, an Auschwitz survivor himself, does not venture any philosophical generalizations about the "bestial, desperate terror" which he and his fellow Jews experienced there: his primary purpose was to bear witness. Only "the fearful imagination of those who have been aroused by such reports but have not actually been smitten in their own flesh," Arendt thinks, can "afford to keep thinking about [these] horrors" and their human and historical significance.[124]

To speak of "murder" in the case of the camps like Auschwitz is, of course, hopelessly inadequate. "What meaning has the concept of murder," Arendt asks, "when we are confronted with the mass production of corpses?"[125] Yet, even Arendt is forced to use it:

The real horror of the concentration and extermination camps lies in the fact that the inmates, even if they happen to keep alive, are more effectively cut off from the world of the living than if they had died, because terror enforces oblivion. Here murder is as impersonal as the squashing of a gnat. Someone may die as the result of systematic torture or starvation, or

because the camp is overcrowded and superfluous human material must be liquidated...it is indeed as if there were a possibility
to give permanence to the process of dying itself and to enforce
a condition in which both death and life are obstructed equally
effectively.[126]

Whether confined to concentration, labor, or death camps, the "human masses sealed off in them are treated as if they no longer existed, as if what happened to them were no longer of any interest
to anybody."[127] It is this isolation and enforced oblivion that leads
Arendt to suggest a discomforting parallel to the Hades, Purgatory,
and Hell of Western imagination. The "skillfully manufactured unreality" of these carceral zones provokes "enormous cruelties" of
the sort previously perpetrated by European adventurers upon the
peoples of the "Dark Continent" during the imperialist era. Within
the "unreality" of these zones, extermination "looks like a perfectly
normal measure."[128]

Arendt goes on to make the even more discomforting suggestion
that the totalitarians' ability to create such a Purgatory and Hell—to
manufacture "right here on earth" what "for thousands of years the
human imagination had banished to a realm beyond human
competence"—exerted a strange fascination to "modern masses"
who themselves had lost faith in any Last Judgment. "Unable as yet to
live without fear and hope, these masses are attracted by every effort
which seems to promise a man-made fabrication of the Paradise
they had longed for and of the Hell they had feared."[129] The thought
of eternal punishment had been made bearable for previous ages
by the expectation of a Last Judgment and the possibility of divine
grace. Stripped of this faith, the human power attested to by the
camps could not but appear as awesome as it was arbitrary. No man
ever deserved such punishment—a punishment which can, "with
equal justice and injustice, be inflicted on anyone" in the perfected
terror state.[130]

However, the senselessness of the camps, as well as their anti-util-
ity, is only apparent. In reality, "they are more essential to the preservation of the regime's power than any of the other institutions." How
so? Arendt argues that without the concentration camps—without
"the undefined fear they inspire and the very well-defined training

they offer in total domination"—it is impossible for a totalitarian regime to inspire its "nuclear troops" [the SS or Bolshevik cadres] with
sufficient fanaticism or to "maintain a whole people in complete
apathy."[131] In addition to fulfilling these central functions, the camps
were also the "laboratories" in which "ghastly experiments in total
domination" could be carried out. It was in the camps that human
beings were reduced to "bundles of reflexes" and deprived of their
distinctively human capacity for spontaneous action.

A skeptical reader might object that this second description, rhetorically powerful as it is, corresponds to no actual historical reality
(the hideous "experiments" of Josef Mengele and others notwithstanding). Whatever purposes the camps may have filled, the destruction of human spontaneity and the reduction of human individuals
to specimens of the animal species mankind were not among them.
The skeptic will feel that Arendt has overreached, allowing herself to
be carried away by her theoretical imagination.

Arendt has an answer to such skepticism, and—while it may not
quiet all doubts—it certainly gives one pause:

> If we take totalitarian aspirations seriously and refuse to be mis-
> led by the common-sense assertion that they are utopian and
> unrealizable, it develops that the society of the dying established
> in the camps is the only form of society in which it is possible
> to dominate men entirely. Those who aspire to total domination
> must liquidate all spontaneity, such as the mere existence of in-
> dividuality will always engender, and track it down to its most
> private forms, regardless of how unpolitical and harmless these
> may seem. Pavlov's dog, the human specimen reduced to the
> most elementary reactions...is the model 'citizen' of a totalitar-
> ian state, and such a citizen can be produced only imperfectly
> outside the camps.[132]

Any attempt to begin to comprehend the incomprehensible—
Auschwitz-Birkenau, the Soviet Gulag—must begin, then, by taking
the aspirations expressed in Nazi and Bolshevik ideology seriously.
Here, we need to remember that the totalitarians did not "have" ideologies in the way other political movements or parties did. The totalitarians thought that their ideologies articulated not interests or goods

but the fundamental and underlying nature of reality as manifest in all-powerful "laws of movement." By means of the logic of a single idea—the race struggle dictated by Nature, the class struggle dictated by History—the past could be explained, the present made transparent, and the future predicted with certainty. In other words, from the totalitarian point of view, it wasn't just the unparalleled power of totalitarian political organization that guaranteed success. It was the grounding of that dynamic organization in the movement of Nature or History itself. Hence, the "ridiculous supersense" of totalitarian ideology—the world-rule of the Aryan race, the classless utopia of Communism—could, with sufficient tenacity and ruthlessness, be made concrete. Empirical reality could be rendered consistent with ideological fiction through the enslavement of "inferior" races and the physical liquidation of "dying" classes. As Arendt writes:

> It is chiefly for the sake of this supersense, for the sake of complete consistency, that it is necessary for totalitarianism to destroy every trace of what we commonly call human dignity. For respect for human dignity implies the recognition of my fellow-men or our fellow-nations as subjects, as builders of a world or co-builders of a common world. No ideology which aims at the explanation of all historical events of the past and at mapping out the course of all events of the future can bear the unpredictability which springs from the fact that men are creative, that they can bring forward something new that nobody ever foresaw.[133]

This is why Arendt thinks that what is at stake in the success of totalitarian regime is less the transformation of human *society* than of human *nature*. The concentration camps demonstrate that "human beings can be transformed into specimens of the human animal." More to the point, they demonstrate that "man's 'nature' is only 'human' insofar as it opens up to man the possibility of becoming something highly unnatural, that is, a man."[134] Divested of their juridical rights, denied the space of decision required for the exercise of their moral agency, and deprived of all outward traces of individuality (the shaved heads, the uniforms, the tattooed numbers), the victims of the concentration camp system emerge as perverse iterations of Rousseau's natural man, bare life that takes the form of "bundles of reflexes."

Here, one must bear in mind what Arendt calls the "necessary limitations of an experiment which requires global control in order to achieve conclusive results."[135] This fact, combined with the defeat of Nazism and the eventual fall of communism, may lead one to think that, however well-grounded Arendt's fears may have been, totalitarian regimes have been safely (and permanently) consigned to the past. The contemporary resurgence of authoritarianism, racism, nationalism, and anti-Semitism demonstrates just how premature such a judgment would be. Moreover, there is a larger issue. World-wide population growth, the increasing scarcity of basic natural resources such as water, and the accelerating loss of jobs due to the robotization have conspired to render hundreds of millions economically superfluous and—from a strictly utilitarian point of view—expendable. Arendt thought that "totalitarian solutions" to such problems as overpopulation and economic superfluousness could "well survive the fall of totalitarian regimes in the form of a strong temptation that will come up whenever it seems impossible to alleviate political, social, or economic misery in a manner worthy of man."[136] In recent decades, the problems have only grown more dire, and the temptation to resort to methods of mass expulsion, incarceration, and liquidation only stronger.

IX Ideology and terror: totalitarianism as an unprecedented regime form

In the second edition of OT Arendt replaced her original Conclusion with a long essay entitled "Ideology and Terror: A Novel Form of Government." This chapter distills Arendt's thoughts on the nature of totalitarianism and can be said to mark the book's turn to political theory proper (even though virtually all of material that preceded it is of relevance to the theory of politics).

Arendt frames her discussion by noting that

> if it is true that the elements of totalitarianism can be found by retracing the history and analyzing the political implications of what we usually call the crisis of our century, then the conclusion is unavoidable that this crisis is no mere threat from the outside.[137]

The pan-European character of the elements that helped give rise to totalitarianism—racism, imperialism, tribal nationalism, the decline of the nation-state—suggest that the totalitarian threat will remain long after the defeat of Nazism and the death of Stalin. The question then is whether the totalitarian form of government was a "makeshift arrangement," one that borrowed its methods and techniques from the well-known "arsenal of tyranny" and that owed its existence to an "accidental failure of traditional political forces"? Or whether, on the contrary, totalitarian government can be said to have a *nature* or *essence*, one comparable to yet clearly distinct from the basic regime types known since Plato and Aristotle?[138] The standard answer is to say that the forms of government created by Hitler and Stalin had some novel features, but that they were clearly examples of tyranny, which is perhaps the oldest form of political regime.

Tyranny has long been understood as the archetypal form of lawless government, one in which arbitrary power is wielded in accordance with the ruler's interests and against those of his subjects. The classic catalog of regime types—with monarchy, aristocracy, and democracy on one side, and the "perversions" of tyranny, oligarchy, and ochlocracy on the other—was articulated in terms of the basic distinction between *lawful* (legitimate) and *lawless* (illegitimate) power. The problem, Arendt maintains, is that the totalitarian form of government actually explodes "the very alternative on which all definitions of the essence of government have been based in political philosophy."[139] While contemptuous of the strictures of positive law and juridical fairness, totalitarian government turns out to be far from lawless:

It is the monstrous, yet seemingly unanswerable claim of totalitarian rule that, far from being "lawless," it goes to the sources of authority from which positive laws received their ultimate legitimation, that far from being arbitrary it is more obedient to these suprahuman forces than any government ever was before, and that far from wielding power in the interest of one man, it is quite prepared to sacrifice everybody's vital immediate interests to the execution of what it assumes to be the law of History or the law of Nature. Its defiance of positive law claims to be a higher form of legitimacy which, *since it is inspired by the sources*

themselves, can do away with petty legality. Totalitarian lawfulness pretends to have found a way to establish the rule of justice
on earth—something which the legality of positive law admittedly could never attain.[140]

Totalitarian "lawfulness," with its pretense to establish the *direct*
rule of justice on earth, thus doesn't bother to translate its "higher
law"—the law of Nature or History—into legal standards for individual human actors. Rather, it "applies the law *directly to mankind*,
without bothering with the behavior of men." The correct application of the laws of Nature or History to men as they are is expected
to produce a purified and plastic mankind as its result. In essence,
totalitarian policy "claims to transform the human species into an
active unfailing carrier of a law to which human beings otherwise
would only passively and reluctantly be subjected."[141]

Arendt's claim that totalitarian "lawfulness" represents something
radically new in Western political history may seem dubious. Hav-
en't a variety of chiliastic religious sects sought to apply their interpretation of God's law directly to man, no matter what the cost? And
didn't the Jacobins, acting in the name of truths vouchsafed them
by Reason, suspend the protections of positive law and resort to a
purifying Terror? Don't all appeals to a transcendent authority, given
by reason or revelation, contain the implicit threat of a *direct* and violent application of some higher law to the "raw material" of human
individuals? As noted in Chapter 1, Arendt herself would go on to
make such a claim in the critique of the Western tradition of political philosophy she mounts in *The Human Condition*. Like many liberals,
she feared all efforts to make an "absolute" (God, First Principles,
Platonic "ideas," etc.) the generative source of political power and
legitimate authority.

In "Ideology and Terror" she points out, however, that while
both Nature and God have been recurrently posited as transcendent
sources of authority by the Western tradition, the structure of legitimation and type of justice they implied were quite different from
totalitarian "lawfulness." Traditionally speaking, Nature or God were
"thought of as permanent and eternal," whereas positive laws were
seen as changing and changeable "according to circumstances." Nevertheless, positive law was viewed as possessing a *relative* permanence

compared to the ever-changing actions of individuals. Though relative, the permanence of positive law was viewed as deriving from the "eternal presence" of its ultimate source of authority (Nature, the Divinity).[142] Thanks to this grounding in a "permanent and eternal" source of authority, positive laws, though mutable, could fulfill their essential purpose: providing a stable context for the unpredictable actions of individuals.

The contrast with totalitarian "lawfulness" is striking. The laws appealed to by totalitarian ideology were not objective, stable, and permanent (as, for example, Divine Law or Jefferson's "self-evident truths" were clearly intended to be). Rather, they were *laws of movement*, expressive of an underlying reality which can be grasped only as a process of *development*. Arendt sees Marx and Darwin as the progenitors of a "tremendous intellectual change," one which "consisted in the refusal to view or accept anything 'as it is' and in the consistent interpretation of everything as being only a stage of some further development." Since the ideologies of Bolshevism and Nazism are rooted, respectively, in vulgarizations of the Marxian idea of social evolution and the Darwinian idea of natural evolution, it is not surprising to see them changing the meaning of "law" accordingly. Whereas law previously connoted "a framework of stability within which human actions and motions can take place," it now became "an expression of the motion itself."[143]

Bearing this change in mind, it becomes clear that totalitarian "lawfulness" means nothing other than the mimetic coordination of social and political policies with what the totalitarians perceived to be the demands flowing from creative-destructive motion of Nature (or History) itself. According to the Nazis, natural evolution demanded the elimination of "everything harmful and unfit to live" in order to realize a predestined and purified hierarchy of the races. According to the Bolsheviks, historical evolution demanded the liquidation of "dying" classes for the achievement of the classless society. In both cases, totalitarian "lawfulness"—the tracking of the creative-destructive motion of Nature or History—turns out to be synonymous with the application of terror. If, as the tradition teaches, *lawfulness* in the usual sense is the essence of non-tyrannical government and *lawlessness* is the essence of tyranny, then, Arendt suggests, *terror* should be seen as the essence of totalitarian domination.

Considered as the "execution" of pregiven and unalterable law of movement, terror systematically eliminates individuals for the sake of the species, "sacrifices the 'parts' for the sake of the 'whole.'"[144]

In totalitarian regimes, then, terror replaces positive law as the mediator between an absolute (trans-human) reality and the world of men. Yet, "mediator" is, in many respects, the wrong word in this context, since totalitarian terror attempts to channel the law of motion that is its absolute directly into human affairs. Whereas positive law articulates a bounded, durable, and relatively stable political realm, one that opens channels of communication between plural and spatially separated individuals, terror "substitutes for the boundaries and channels of communication between men a band of iron which holds them so tightly together that it is as though their plurality had disappeared into One Man of gigantic dimensions."[145]

This elimination of human plurality and the space required for communication between individuals highlights the anti-political character of totalitarian regimes. Politics, as Arendt will stress in all her subsequent work, is based on human plurality and presupposes a legally articulated space that enables communication between diverse individuals. Where the "hedges" of law have been destroyed, as they undoubtedly are by tyranny, the "living space of freedom" between men is replaced by what is, in effect, a desert, a "wilderness of fear and suspicion."[146]

Yet, as Arendt points out, even a desert is a space. Tyrannical terror may radically constrain freedom of movement and communication, yet it still leaves some room for "fear-guided movements and suspicion-ridden actions." On the other hand, total terror—the kind deployed by the Nazis and Bolsheviks—"presses men against each other," destroying the space between them by its "iron band" and thus eliminating the possibility of even fear-guided movements and actions. The ideologically articulated "law of movement" driving totalitarian terror generates an ever-expanding list of "objective" enemies. Regardless of the care an individual may exercise in monitoring his own words and actions, the party or Leader may well decide that the "laws of movement" now require the liquidation of all people in his category. Two examples suffice in this regard. Beyond the elimination of Communists, Socialists, Jews, Gypsies, homosexuals, the physically and mentally handicapped, and millions of "inferior"

Slavs, Hitler planned (post-war) to eliminate Germans with family histories of heart disease and had legislation drafted for this purpose. Likewise Stalin—having purged thousands in the party and military, destroyed the classes of "rich" peasants and the bourgeoisie, decimated the artists, intellectuals, and doctors, and imprisoned millions of "counter-revolutionary elements" in the Gulag—planned, in his final years, the liquidation of Soviet Jewry.

Total terror is thus no "makeshift" collection of brutal methods designed to achieve "strategically rational" ends (such as the Machiavellian ones of seizing and maintaining political power). There is no "economy of violence" here. The categories proliferate and the killing, torture, and imprisonment increase with time. Total terror "makes sense" only when viewed through the lens of ideological fiction. Then and only then can we grasp the fact that it is "supposed to provide the forces of nature or history with an incomparable instrument to accelerate their movement."[147] From the perspective of totalitarians intent on accelerating the process by which Nature or History re-shapes the human species, the problem is that—even though the desired outcome is "inevitable"—the process can be slowed down considerably by the resistance born of the very unpredictability of the "human material" from which the "animal species mankind" is to be fabricated. For Arendt, this unpredictability is a sign of the distinctively human capacity for spontaneous (free) action. Terror, "as the obedient servant of natural or historical movement," therefore has to eliminate not only specific freedoms such as those of speech, association, movement, etc. It must also eliminate "the very source of freedom which is given with the fact of the birth of man and resides in his capacity to make a new beginning."[148] Hence the "ghastly experiments" in total domination in the camps and the consistent application of terror everywhere else.

Here, we encounter the characteristically Arendtian theme of human *natality*, a theme made explicit in the closing lines of *The Origins of Totalitarianism*. "Beginning," she writes, "is the supreme capacity of man; politically, it is identical with man's freedom." She cites a phase from Augustine's *City of God: Initium ut esst homo creates est*—"that a beginning be made man was created"—before offering a gloss that, initially at least, looks more like an expression of faith than the result of historical or philosophical analysis: "This beginning is guaranteed by each new birth; it is indeed every man."[149] Coming, as it does, after a prolonged argument to the effect that it is indeed possible to "change human nature" and turn human beings into the equivalent of "bundles of reflexes," this may strike some as misplaced. Is it the result, perhaps, of a desire to provide a bit of hope, if not exactly a "happy ending," after so many pages on imperialism, racism, anti-Semitism, and the horrors of the concentration and extermination camps? To answer that question, we must turn to Arendt's most ambitious and philosophically original work, *The Human Condition*.

Summary

Despite the impression given by its title, *The Origins of Totalitarianism* is not a book devoted to uncovering the *causes* of totalitarianism. Arendt thought the advent of totalitarian domination in Europe was an unprecedented *event*, and that it was highly misleading to think that it had been "caused" by one or several factors (for example, nationalism, secularism, economic depression, etc.). Rather, in the book, she identified the *elements* she thought had come together to create a constellation in which this "novel form of government" became *possible* (but by no means inevitable). Encompassing a variety of events, practices, and attitudes, these elements included European imperialism from 1880 to 1914 (and the "political emancipation of the bourgeoisie" that unleashed it); European racism in theory and practice; the growth of anti-Semitism not as a prejudice but as a political ideology; Central European tribal nationalism born of the collapse of the Russian and Austro-Hungarian empires; the interwar refugee crisis created by revolution and civil war in Russia, Spain, and elsewhere; the decline of the nation-state in the face of such pressures; the invention of bureaucratic rule by decree as a device to rule subaltern populations; and an ever-increasing reliance on "government by the police" to deal first with refugees, then with entire national populations.

It should be stressed that this list of elements covers the events and developments from 1880 through WWII and is trans-European in scope. Totalitarianism as a phenomenon was not, in Arendt's view, rooted in particular national cultures or political traditions. Rather, it became possible because these disparate events, attitudes, and practices came together in post-WWI Europe in an unpredictable yet extraordinarily calamitous way.

In addition to describing the elements that contributed to making totalitarianism possible, OT also provides a survey of the central institutions of totalitarian regimes and the characteristic features of totalitarian domination. Taking aim at the common misconception that totalitarian regimes were monolithic "total" states, Arendt emphasizes their dynamism and ever-increasing radicalism. She also emphasizes the gap between factual reality and what she calls "totalitarian fictions" inscribed in the respective ideologies of National Socialism and Soviet Bolshevism. Both Nazism and Stalinism viewed the world as governed by "laws of movement," natural or historical "laws" made manifest in what the totalitarians saw as the fundamental realities of race or class struggle. According to totalitarian ideology, these "laws of movement" are playing out in history. They cannot be stopped, but they *can* be accelerated. Regimes can make the fiction real by liquidating "dying classes" and "inferior" races ahead of schedule.

"Total domination" becomes possible through the application of total terror, which operates on a qualitatively different level from the terror employed by the dictators and tyrants of the past. Terror is not a means for totalitarian regimes but their very essence. This is what distinguishes this "novel form of government" from all others, and it is the fact that makes all comparisons to the tyrannies and dictatorships of the past misleading. Above all, Arendt wants us to appreciate the radical novelty—the totally unprecedented character—of regimes whose central institutions were concentration and extermination camps. The primary totalitarian ambition was to transform mankind into a passive medium through which the "laws" of Nature or History could race to their supposedly predestined conclusion. For the Nazis, this was the victory of the Aryan "master race" in an all-encompassing "struggle of the races." For the Bolsheviks, it was the victory of the "universal" class—the proletariat—in a class struggle that has defined all history hitherto.

Notes

1 See Martin Jay, "The Political Existentialism of Hannah Arendt" in Jay, *Permanent Exiles* (New York: Columbia University Press, 1985) pp. 237–256.

2 Arendt, *Origins of Totalitarianism*, p. 440.

3 Arendt, "A Reply to Eric Voegelin" in Arendt, EU, p. 405; "Understanding in Politics" in Arendt, EU, p. 309.
4 Hannah Arendt/Karl Jaspers Correspondence 1926–1969, edited by Lotte Kohler and Hans Saner (New York: Harcourt Brace Jovanovich, 1992), p. 166.
5 Arendt, OT, p. 457.
6 Kateb, Hannah Arendt, p. 54.
7 Kateb, Hannah Arendt.
8 Arendt, EU, p. 403.
9 Arendt, "Outline: The Elements of Shame: Antisemitism-Imperialism-Racism" (1946), cited by Canovan, Hannah Arendt: A Reinterpretation, p. 28.
10 Arendt, EU, p. 316.
11 Arendt, OT, p. 125.
12 Arendt, OT, p. 125.
13 The structural character of such crises is one of the primary themes of Marx's Capital.
14 Arendt, OT, p. 126.
15 Arendt, OT, pp. 136–137.
16 Arendt, OT, p. 136.
17 Arendt, OT, p. 126.
18 Arendt, OT, p. 138.
19 Arendt, OT, p, 138.
20 See Marx's critique in "On the Jewish Question."
21 Arendt, OT, 215.
22 Arendt, OT, p. 158.
23 Arendt, OT, pp. 171–173.
24 Arendt, OT, p. 170.
25 Arendt, OT, pp. 176, 178.
26 Arendt, OT, p. 180.
27 Arendt, OT, pp. 180, 182.
28 Arendt, OT, p. 183.
29 Arendt, OT, p. 184.
30 Arendt, OT, p. 185.
31 Arendt, OT, p. 206.
32 Arendt, OT, p. 185.
33 Arendt, OT, p. 185.
34 Arendt, OT, pp. 192–193.
35 Arendt, OT, p. 300.
36 Arendt, OT, p. 236.
37 Arendt, OT, p. 211.
38 Arendt, OT, p. 211.
39 Arendt, OT, p. 214.
40 Arendt, OT, p. 212.
41 Arendt, OT, pp. 197–198.
42 Arendt, OT, p. 186.
43 Arendt, OT, p. 207.
44 Arendt, OT, pp. 223–224.
45 Arendt, OT, p. 222.
46 Arendt, OT, p. 230 (my emphasis).

47 Arendt, OT, p. 230 (my emphasis).
48 Arendt, OT, pp. 230–231.
49 Arendt, OT, p. 232.
50 Arendt, OT, p. 231.
51 Arendt, OT, p. 232.
52 Arendt, OT, p. 232.
53 Arendt, OT, p. 234.
54 Arendt, OT, p. 234.
55 Arendt. OT, p. 235.
56 Arendt, OT, p. 236.
57 Arendt, OT, p. 265.
58 Arendt, OT, p. 267.
59 Arendt, OT, p. 270.
60 Arendt, OT, p. 275.
61 Arendt, OT, p. 290.
62 Arendt, OT, p. 269.
63 Arendt, OT, p. 295.
64 Arendt, OT, p. 290.
65 Arendt, OT, p. 291.
66 Arendt, OT, p. 291.
67 Arendt, OT, p. 291.
68 Arendt, OT, p. 291.
69 Arendt, OT, p. 292.
70 Arendt, OT, p. 293.
71 Arendt, OT, pp. 294–295.
72 Arendt, OT, p. 296.
73 Arendt, OT, p. 297.
74 Arendt, OT, p. 298.
75 Timothy Snyder, Black Earth: The Holocaust as History and Warning (New York: Tim Duggan Books, 2015), pp. 1–14.
76 See Leo Strauss, Natural Right and History (Chicago: University of Chicago Press, 1965).
77 Arendt, OT, p. 298.
78 Arendt, OT, p. 299.
79 Arendt, OT, p. 299.
80 Arendt, OT, p. 298.
81 Arendt, OT, p. 298.
82 Arendt, OT, p. 300.
83 Arendt, OT, p. 301.
84 For the latter, see Karl Mannheim's influential Ideology and Utopia (New York: Harcourt, 1936).
85 Arendt, OT, pp. 311–312.
86 Arendt, OT, p. 267.
87 Arendt, OT, p. 313.
88 Arendt, OT, p. 312.
89 Arendt, OT, p. 315.
90 Arendt, OT, p. 352.

91 Arendt, OT, p. 470.
92 Arendt, OT, p. 353.
93 Arendt, OT, p. 356.
94 Arendt, OT, p. 360.
95 Arendt, OT, p. 360.
96 Arendt, OT, p. 360.
97 Arendt, OT, p. 364.
98 Arendt, OT, p. 366.
99 Arendt, OT, p. 367.
100 Arendt, OT, p. 385.
101 Arendt, OT, p. 387.
102 Arendt, OT, p. 362.
103 Arendt, THC, p. xxiii.
104 Arendt, OT, p. 94.
105 Arendt, OT, pp. 6–7.
106 Arendt, OT, p. 4.
107 Arendt, OT, p. 4.
108 Arendt, OT, p. 7.
109 Arendt, OT, p. 8.
110 Arendt, OT, p. 9.
111 Arendt, OT, pp. 9–10.
112 Arendt, OT, p. 14.
113 Arendt, OT, p. 15.
114 Arendt, OT, p. 25.
115 Arendt, OT, p. 61.
116 Arendt, OT, p. 66.
117 Arendt, OT, p. 67.
118 Arendt, OT, p. 87.
119 Arendt, OT, p. 87.
120 Arendt, OT, p. 87.
121 Arendt, OT, p. 438.
122 See Tom Segev, *The Seventh Million* (New York: Henry Holt and Company, 1991), pp. 345–366.
123 Arendt, OT, p. 438.
124 Arendt, OT, p. 441.
125 Arendt, OT, p. 441.
126 Arendt, OT, p. 443.
127 Arendt, OT, p. 445.
128 Arendt, OT, p. 445.
129 Arendt, OT, p. 446.
130 Arendt, OT, p. 447.
131 Arendt, OT, p. 456.
132 Arendt, OT, pp. 455–456.
133 Arendt, OT, p. 458.
134 Arendt, OT, p. 455.

135 Arendt, OT, p. 459.
136 Arendt, OT, p. 459.
137 Arendt, OT, p. 460.
138 Arendt, OT, pp. 460–461.
139 Arendt, OT, p. 461.
140 Arendt, OT, pp. 461–462 (my emphasis).
141 Arendt, OT, p. 462.
142 Arendt, OT, p. 463.
143 Arendt, OT, p. 464
144 Arendt, OT, p. 465.
145 Arendt, OT, p. 465.
146 Arendt, OT, p. 466.
147 Arendt, OT, p. 466.
148 Arendt, OT, p. 466.
149 Arendt, OT, p. 479.

Further reading

M. Canovan, *Hannah Arendt: A Reinterpretation of her Political Thought* (Cambridge: Cambridge University Press, 1992). [A full-scale study that gives priority to *Origins of Totalitarianism.*]

R. H. King and D. Stone, *Hannah Arendt and the Uses of History: Imperialism, Nation, Race, and Genocide* (New York: Berghahn Books, 2007).

S. J. Whitfield, *Into the Dark: Hannah Arendt and Totalitarianism* (Philadelphia: Temple University Press, 1980).

Three

Marx, labor, and the "rise of the social"

I Continuities and discontinuities

Many admirers of Arendt's *The Origins of Totalitarianism* are struck by the apparent discontinuity between it and *The Human Condition*. There seems to be an enormous gap between the very historical and concrete study of the "origins" of totalitarianism and the more philosophical approach Arendt takes in THC. Speaking broadly, it appears that Arendt had abandoned political science and political history for philosophical anthropology. Yet, despite the appearance of radical discontinuity there is a deep, albeit partly submerged, thematic continuity.

To be sure, the subject has changed. Arendt is no longer addressing anything like the question of what elements in modern European history contributed to making totalitarianism possible. Her concern in THC is with what medieval and early modern philosophy and theology referred to as the *vita activa*: the active life. From its earliest articulation in the Greek distinction between the *bios politikos* and the *bios theoretikos*, this notion had been contrasted with the *vita contemplative* or contemplative life. This was the life of the philosopher or monk who withdrew from the activities and concerns of daily life, the better to devote himself to a life of study, prayer, and contemplation of eternal things such as the order of the cosmos or the "harmony of the spheres."

The primary exponents of the contemplative life (Plato, Aristotle, Aquinas, Boethius, *et al.*) viewed it as clearly superior to the active life. The latter concerned itself with fulfilling the requirements and

demands of this world (for food, shelter, craft- and artworks, and political organization) while the former had its eye turned to a higher
realm of true Being or Divine perfection. Arendt's project in THC is
to examine the three activities traditionally viewed as constituting
the *vita activa*—labor, work, and action—but to do so in a manner
stripped of the distorting prejudices projected by an "otherworldly"
contemplative tradition.

It is in the course of this examination that Arendt extends and
deepens themes first encountered in OT. Most obviously, THC is centrally concerned with the basic phenomenon of human *plurality*—the
fact that men, not Man, "live on earth and inhabit the world." This
theme was first announced in her analysis of total domination and
the totalitarian ambition to destroy or uproot human plurality, the
better to create "one Man of gigantic dimensions." In THC the idea
of human plurality is unpacked in all its phenomenological richness, the better to provide insight into what Arendt believes to be
both the origin and (in a loose sense) goal of politics. Authentic
politics—which, for Arendt, means the activities of debate, deliberation, and decision concerning matters of public or common concern
performed by diverse yet equal citizens—presumes human plurality
not only as its *sine qua non* (that without which) but also as its *conditio
per quam* (causal basis). Plurality is both the essential condition for,
and the ultimate cause of, politics in any legitimate sense of the
word. The Arendtian emphasis on plurality means that politics is an
activity that must be distinguished in the strongest possible terms
from domination or rule (on the one hand) and bureaucratic administration (on the other).

Arendt's concern with the human capacity for spontaneous
beginning—a capacity viewed, in OT, as distinctively human but
increasingly endangered by new forms of terror, domination, and
determinism—also takes center stage in THC, most notably in the
chapter on action. In THC Arendt situates and makes concrete what
in OT seemed little more than a semi-pious wish inspired by a single phrase from Augustine ("because he is a beginning, man can
begin"). In her consideration of the fundamental characteristics of
political action, Arendt singles out its *initiatory* dimension. Real political action involves beginning and carrying through something with
one's peers. Such "acting in concert" is undertaken in full awareness

of the fact that there is no guarantee that the goal of the action will be achieved. What matters is the *initiation* and the *performance* of the action itself, regardless of whether it is successful.

Arendt thinks every Athenian citizen was aware of the initiatory and intersubjective dimensions of political action. We, on the other hand, have become accustomed to understanding political action as the strategic deployment of power or coercive means by elite political actors. As a result, we have lost sight of action's intersubjective, initiatory, and performative dimensions. Arendt thinks that the causes of this forgetting have far deeper roots in the Western tradition of political thought than most have previously imagined.

THC also deepens Arendt's thinking about the trends in modern life that encourage the subjection of politics and political life to natural or nature-like processes. First encountered in her description of the imperialist bourgeoise's success in getting statesmen to think in terms of expansion for expansion's sake; extended by her analysis of the bogus "naturalization" of European politics performed by race-thinking and "survival of the fittest" social Darwinism; and culminating in the totalitarian attempt to channel the "laws of movement" of Nature or History into the social and political realms, this theme resonates throughout THC. We find it in Arendt's description of the "rise of the social" and the concomitant channeling of what she calls the "life process" into the public realm, as well as in her description of modern man as an *animal laborans* chained to endlessly repetitive (and increasingly automatic) cycles of production and consumption.

Finally, THC is animated by Arendt's fearful sense that we have embraced accelerating economic, social, and technological changes without ever pausing to "think what we are doing"—to ourselves, the human artifice that houses us, and the earth upon which that artifice is built. She sees the dynamism of the modern age as undermining the durability of many of the structures that preserve culture and public life. This undermining effect is distinct from, yet oddly reminiscent of, the totalitarian destruction of the stable legal and institutional structures of the state. Increasingly, Arendt maintains, we live in a condition of economic, political, and technological flux. The Heraclitean character of this flux—a kind of "permanent revolution" without the revolution—means that the human-built world can no longer be what she thinks it once was and should be: a "home for mortal men."

Even with these continuities in mind, it is an overstatement to say that THC "organically developed" out of Arendt's work on OT.[1] The Arendt of THC is no longer the Arendt of OT. Not only has the subject and content changed. The form and even the style are different. Whereas in OT we encounter a work of sprawling historical and sociological ambition composed of similarly sprawling sentences, in THC Arendt adopts a more classic and (at times) almost aphoristic style. She articulates her many distinctions—between the public and the private, the social and the political, and between labor, work, and action—with an assurance and authority that is almost Olympian in character. There is little doubt in the reader's mind that this totally original work has been thought through from beginning to end, with every piece considered and put in exactly the right place. Her idiom is philosophical and universal (as befits a book titled The Human Condition), yet her descriptions of the activities of labor, work, and action are surprisingly concrete. They draw upon an enormous wealth of sources—from Greece, Rome, and the Bible through the works of such early moderns as Adam Smith and John Locke; from late moderns like Karl Marx and Friedrich Nietzsche to such near contemporaries as Gunnar Myrdal and Werner Heisenberg. Historical events—the Reformation, the discovery of the New World, the invention of the telescope, and the launching of the Russian satellite Sputnik in 1957—play a central role, yet are deployed sparingly, with Arendt giving them a largely symbolic or emblematic significance.

Arendt's attempt to "think what we are doing" by way of a "reconsideration of the human condition from the vantage point of our newest experiences and our most recent fears" takes the form of a phenomenology of the three activities that constitute the *vita activa*: labor, work, and action. This "systematic" part, comprising the central chapters of THC, is joined to a historical narrative about the philosophic and scientific origins of the modern age (in the last chapter of the book), as well a historical analysis of the changing place of labor, work, and action within Western culture's hierarchy of human activities.[2]

To briefly summarize: Arendt thinks that, while the ancient Greeks held that action—words and deeds in the public realm—possessed the highest dignity and greatest meaning, the early modern age elevated work, fabrication, and the criterion of utility to a dominant position. The modern age proper, ushered in by the Industrial Revolution, revealed the unsuspected productivity of human labor-power, previously limited by lack of technology and industrial-scale methods. If Hobbes, Locke, Smith, and utilitarian thinkers like Jeremy Bentham are the prophets of the first half of the modern age, Karl Marx clearly stands, in Arendt's view, as the prophet of its second half—a world in which labor, labor-power, and productivity rule supreme. Throughout, Arendt is concerned to trace the fall of action and the "shining brightness" of the public realm from the highest rank in the vita activa to the lowest. One need only compare Pericles' praise of the bios politikos in Thucydides to the disenchantment of many with politics and politicians today to see the surface plausibility of Arendt's argument.

As I noted in Chapter 1, the activity of politics has rarely been held in lower esteem than in our own time. Arendt wants to understand the changes in attitude—the broad evolution of mentalités—as well as the scientific and economic developments that produced this devaluation of both politics and the public realm itself. If she cannot hope to singlehandedly restore dignity to political action and public life, she can at least remind us of the meaning and dignity they once possessed. She hopes this exercise will lead us to reflect upon why we are currently so alienated from the public world and the activities that take place within it.

One large question remains: how did Arendt go from wanting to fill a gap in the analysis of OT (by means of a book project on the "proto-totalitarian elements in Marx's thought") to the altogether different and more inclusive project of THC? The outlines of an answer can be found in the manuscript of her Gaus Lectures. These were given at Princeton in 1953 under the title of "Karl Marx and the Western Tradition of Political Thought."

II Coming to terms with Marx and the tradition

Arendt's Gaus Lectures can be considered a sort of rough draft of THC. Hardly the one-sided indictment of Marxian thought her project title promised, "Karl Marx and the Great Tradition" is an examination of

Marx's relationship to Western political thought and philosophy. More precisely, the lectures are an examination of the perplexities generated by Marx's reliance upon traditional categories as he grappled with the historical developments—the industrial revolution, the emancipation of the working class, and the French and American Revolutions—that made his age unlike any other.

According to Arendt, Marx's great influence is due to the fact that he was "the only thinker of the nineteenth century to take its central event, the emancipation of the working class, seriously in philosophic terms."[3] After Marx, labor as a human activity "no longer belonged to the strictly private realm of life: it became a public political fact of the first order." And, while it may be doubted that Marx himself was ever "genuinely interested in politics," his "glorification of labor" could not fail "to introduce a complete reversal of all traditional political values" while simultaneously generating its own perplexities, paradoxes, and contradictions.[4]

What is the nature of this "reversal"? And how does it generate these paradoxes and "self-contradictions"?

Traditionally speaking, labor has always been associated with the needs of the body and biological reproduction. The Bible sees the "curse" of labor as punishment for Adam and Eve's disobedience to God, while the ancient Greeks saw it as an activity suitable only for slaves and women. In democratic Athens, male heads of households were largely freed from the daily grind of labor, and this gave them the leisure to participate in the city-state's robust political life. Women, slaves, and children, on the other hand, were confined to the privacy of the household, where they devoted themselves to the necessary (and endlessly repetitive) labor required for material subsistence and the reproduction of life.

It was because of the connection of laboring activity to "the strictly biological needs of our bodies" that it was deemed by the Greeks "to belong to the lower, almost animal-like functions of human life, and as such considered a strictly private matter."[5] Political life began where the private realm of the household ended. It took place in a sphere—the public realm—that by definition transcended the individual's daily "metabolism with nature" (to use Marx's phrase). The institution of slavery was thus seen as a necessary precondition for *politeuein*—that is, for those free activities of debate and persuasion that comprised the core of political life for the citizen. While Greek political life was *based* upon rule over slaves, Arendt emphasizes the fact that it was hardly comprised by the activities of ruling and being ruled. Contra Aristotle, rulership is not the heart of politics. Considered as an activity, it was seen, rather, as a "pre-political condition of *politeuein*, of being political."[6]

Politics thus began with liberation from the daily routine of labor, an activity that was itself viewed as bereft of any dignity or meaning. In the ancient Greek (Athenian) conception, politics consisted largely in the forms of speech (including debate, deliberation, persuasion, and judgment) that took place *between* equal citizens as they attended to public business in the *agora*, the assembly, the executive council, and the large juries known as dikasteries. With the decline of polis life in the fourth century BCE, these forms of speech (and the activities that went with them) lost much of their luster. Increasingly, philosophers such as Plato and Aristotle came to view the activity of philosophizing (*philosophein*) as the paradigmatic free activity. They correspondingly downgraded politics and *politeuein* to the status of instrumental activities required to procure the order and stability needed for pursuit of the contemplative life.

At this point, the distinction between *rulers* and *ruled* invaded the political realm directly, with Plato and (less dramatically) Aristotle framing the burdensome yet necessary activity of rulership as both the core of political life and the most important precondition for the safe pursuit of the philosophical life. The original experience of a political life based upon, but in no way consisting in, rulership was forever lost. It is no accident that Aristotle's typology of regime forms (kingship, aristocracy, polity) and their respective "perversions" (tyranny, oligarchy, democracy) is a catalog of *forms of rule*. Nor is it an accident that the conviction that politics and rulership are identical went virtually unchallenged for the next 2,000 years.

The first to truly challenge this conviction was Karl Marx. He reversed the tradition not only by insisting that *praxis* ranked higher than philosophy and contemplation. He also reversed it by insisting that labor—previously considered the lowest of all human activities—was in fact the highest and most distinctively human activity. If the first reversal challenged the 2,000-year-old hegemony of the philosophical-theological ideal of the *vita contemplativa*, the second reversal (the elevation of labor) challenged both the philosopher's ideal *and* the pre-philosophic political tradition of the polis as well.

However, unlike his challenge to the *bios theoretikos*, Marx's challenge to the *bios politikos* was in many respects unwitting. I say "unwitting" because Marx remained very much an heir to the Western philosophical tradition even as he rebelled against it. This made him susceptible not only to the Platonic-Aristotelian devaluation of political action and *politeuein*; it also led him accept their dubious identification of politics with *rule*. Arendt believes that it is on the basis of this identification of politics with rule—and the effacement of the original experience of political life it implied—that both Marx's "glorification of labor" and his untraditional (but not very political) idea of a universal freedom became possible.[7]

"Universal" freedom—the freedom of man not as citizen, household head, or philosopher, but *qua* man—implied not just the abolition of rulership in the political sphere, but in the social and economic sphere as well. Philosophically speaking, the basic idea behind universal freedom—namely, that no man can be free if he rules over others; that both master and slave (or capitalist and proletarian) are necessarily unfree—is given its most classic expression Hegel's dialectic of lordship (*Herrschaft*) and bondage (*Knechtschaft*) in the *Phenomenology of Spirit*. But that dialectic, as well as Marx's appropriation of it, had its *political* roots in the French and American revolutions and its *social* roots in the Industrial Revolution and the advent of "free" labor in the service of capital.

The political revolutions had been fought in the name of universal *political* (or civic) equality. Among their achievements they could count the emancipation of the working classes, at least insofar as these revolutions eliminated serfdom and provided basic civil and political rights to all. The Industrial Revolution, on the other hand, radically transformed social and economic relations in order to accommodate the unprecedented dynamism of early capitalism. It revealed the unsuspected, seemingly unlimited productivity that resided in the lap of human labor-power. The speed and thoroughness of this transformation, coupled with the surprising realization that the age-old "curse" was the driving force behind it all, led both Hegel and Marx to the idea that man forms or creates himself through labor.

In Arendt's telling, the social and economic transformation wrought by the Industrial Revolution, coupled with the violent transformation of the political world by the French and American revolutions, were the basic experiences that led Marx to advance his three fundamental theses: "first, *Labor is the Creator of Man*; second, *Violence is the midwife of History* (...); and third...*Nobody can be free who enslaves* others."[8]

As Arendt points out, "each of these propositions expresses in quintessential form one of the decisive events with which our own era began." The Industrial Revolution had transformed the relentless, repetitive, and subsistence-oriented "curse" of labor into a Faustian world- and humanity-shaping power. In the French and American revolutions, violence was no longer the haphazard slaughter and conquest of previous ages, but the vehicle for the emergence of a new body politic. The *philosophes* had perceived the idea of a just society, and it appeared that this idea "needed nothing but the helping hand of violence to be realized." Finally, the most important consequence of the French and American revolutions—the positing of the utterly un-traditional idea of a *universal* equality in place of the older notion of an *equality of peers*—gave rise to the idea of a "society in which nobody should be a master and nobody a servant." It gave rise, in other words, to a novel idea of freedom, one *not* predicated upon some form of rulership (as freedom always had been in the tradition) but defined rather in terms of a newly assumed incompatibility between liberty and rulership of any kind.

Arendt argues that "the basic self-contradiction in which Marx's whole work...is caught" arises from his "glorification" of labor and violence (on the one hand) and what she calls his "obsession" with this new form of universal freedom (on the other). From the standpoint of the tradition, the results could hardly be more unorthodox:

> For when Marx stated that labor is the most important activity of man, he was saying in terms of the tradition that not freedom but necessity [in the form of laboring activity] is what makes man human. And he followed this line of thought throughout his philosophy of history, according to which the development of mankind is ruled by, and the meaning of history contained in, the law of historical movement, the political motor of which is class struggle and whose natural irresistible driving force is

the development of man's laboring capacity. When under the influence of the French Revolution he added to this that violence is the midwife of History, *he denied in terms of the tradition the very substantial content of freedom contained in the human capacity of speech.* From this it follows...that history...shows its true, undistorted face only in wars and revolutions; and that political activity, if it is not direct, violent action, must be understood as either the preparation of violence or the consequence of past violence.[9]

While Arendt pursues the political, social, and cultural effects of the glorification of labor at length in *The Human Condition*, in the Gaus Lectures she focuses on Marx's assumption that *violence* (or the preparation for it) is the heart of political action and as such revelatory of the true content of history: class struggle.

Marx's conviction concerning violence was, according to Arendt, "not less heretical in terms of the tradition than his conviction concerning labor [as the vehicle of man's self-creation]." From Greek philosophy through Christian theology, the tradition had always assumed that speech was far more revelatory of truth and meaning than any form of action (let alone the "mute" one of violence) ever could be. In contrast, Marx views most speech, including legal and political norms and structures, as ideology, that is, as pretexts or rationalizations for violent or coercive acts (such as expropriation and exploitation). Marx's "basic distrust of speech" and the theory of ideology that follows from it express what Arendt thinks is the peculiarly modern conviction—established by Copernicus, Galileo, and Descartes—that being and appearance have parted company. One must, as a result, somehow "get behind" appearances. In Marx's case, this translated into the imperative of getting behind the economic, legal, political, and ethical discourses of bourgeois society in order to grasp the truth of the historical process.

However, while Marx's glorification of labor, his devaluation of speech, and his conviction that violence is the "midwife of history" are all untraditional, they occur within a categorial framework which is, Arendt thinks, entirely traditional. Ultimately, they are grounded in the original Greek contrast between necessary activities (such as labor) and free ones (such as politics for the citizen and philosophizing for the philosopher).

The proof of this assertion may be found in the "basic self-contradiction" that haunts Marx's thought. This contradiction expresses itself in such fundamentally Marxian ideas as the notion that violence is needed to abolish violence; that the goal of history is to end history; and that labor "is the only productive activity of man but that the development of man's productive forces will eventually lead to the abolition of labor."[10] Arendt believes that this self-contradiction is most strikingly expressed in the few passages in The German Ideology where Marx outlines his ideal future society. While acknowledging that these sentences (about "hunting in the morning, fishing in the afternoon, rearing cattle in the evening, and criticizing after dinner") are frequently dismissed as utopian, Arendt argues that they in fact "constitute the center of Marx's work and express most clearly its original impulses." Indeed, "if utopia means that this society has no topos, no geographical and historical place on earth, it is certainly not utopian: its geographical topos is Athens and its place in history is the fifth century before Christ."[11]

This is a penetrating insight, one that at first seems far-fetched but which, given a moment's thought, seems undeniable and even obvious. In Marx's future society,

> the state has withered away, there is no longer any distinction between rulers and ruled and rulership no longer exists. This corresponds to life in the ancient Greek city-state, which, although it was based on rulership over slaves as its pre-political condition, had excluded rulership from the intercourse of its free citizens.[12]

The abolition of the fixity of the modern capitalist division of labor together with the ultimate abolition of labor itself (insofar as it is experienced as a "curse") are the two defining characteristics of Marx's future socialist society and of the epochal move from what Marx calls the "realm of necessity" to the "realm of freedom."

Arendt's point is that Marx's "realm of freedom" is all but indistinguishable from the "almost complete leisure society" created by Athenian democracy in the fifth century. It is indeed a polis without slaves. However, Marx's version is a society from which the political activities that filled the leisure time of the male Athenian citizens—the activities of debate and deliberation, taking part in the assembly, judging in the juries, etc.—have vanished. Where there are no social classes, not only is there no need for a *state* (to enforce class rule), there is also no need for *politics*. In Marx's "free association of producers," the common good is no longer a subject of debate or disagreement. Individuals devote themselves to a broad range of freely chosen activities as they pursue their individual and social self-actualization. All that is left of politics is the rump of essential administrative functions that can, in Lenin's famous phrase, "be performed by any cook."

Marx's ideal society, then, is a "polis without slaves" but also a polis without *politics*. The very activities the Greeks viewed as constituting the "realm of freedom" were ostensibly transcended in socialist society. In the meantime, political action itself was identified with the revolutionary violence that would bring about the ultimate transition from the capitalist "realm of necessity" to the socialist "realm of freedom." The crucial point for Arendt is that Marx's devaluation of the political activities of debate, deliberation, and persuasion is by no means peculiar to him, let alone ascribable to a vehement, not to say blasphemous, desire to somehow "undo" the tradition. Rather, Arendt thinks Marx was simply following in Plato and (to a lesser degree) Aristotle's footsteps. After all, it was they who effected the first, deepest, and most influential devaluation of politics and *politeuein*, albeit in the name of philosophy and the contemplative life.

Marx's lack of awareness of what Arendt calls the "intimate relation between speech and freedom" has its roots in the Platonic devaluation of opinion and persuasion (on the one hand), and in the deep forgetfulness of polis experience manifest in Aquinas' rendering of the Aristotelian statement that "man is, by nature, a *political* animal" (*zōōn politikon*) as "man is, by nature, a *social* animal" (*animal socialis*). This, Arendt notes, "is a banality for which one would not have needed Aristotle." With this translation—which was to become authoritative for the tradition and, indeed, for Marx himself—

> the word politikon no longer meant a unique, outstanding way of life, of being-together, in which the truly human capacities of man, as distinguished from his more animal characteristics, could show and prove themselves. It had come to signify an all-embracing quality that men share with many animal species.[13]

This forgetting of the political experience of the polis—of the free-dom, dignity, and intrinsic worth of *politeuein*—was also facilitated by Plato's negative view of persuasive speech (*peithein*), which was the very medium of Greek political life. The limits of persuasion—so starkly demonstrated by the trial and condemnation of his teacher Socrates—led Plato to equate *peithein* not with freedom, but with "ar-bitrary compulsion through words." And it led him, in his political philosophy, to "substitute for this arbitrary compulsion the *coercion of truth*."[14] Since, in Plato's view, "truth was essentially speechless and could be perceived only in the solitude of contemplation," Platonic man "was already not a 'speaking' but a rational animal, that is, a being whose chief concern and enlightenment lay in himself, in his own reason and *not* in the faculty of speech."[15] The Platonic con-ceptions of truth and reason testified to the moment when "when men of thought and men of action went their separate ways"; the moment when the Periclean harmony of speech and deeds gave way to what Nietzsche would call the "fateful distinction" between *theory* and *practice*. Plato's definition of man as a rational rather than political animal opened an "abyss" between thought and action that Arendt thinks has "never since been closed."[16]

One result of this separation of *knowing* and *doing* is what Arendt later refers to as "Plato's tyranny of truth," in which those who know command those who execute or put into practice the truths revealed to reason. Another result—a distinctively modern one—is that

> all thinking activity that is not simply the calculation of means to obtain an intended or willed end...came to play the role of an 'afterthought'....Action, on the other hand, *became meaningless, the realm of the accidental and haphazard upon which no great deeds any longer shed their immortal light.*[17]

In order to escape the "melancholy haphazardness" (Kant) and the "incoherence and immorality" (John Adams) of the course of hu-man events, one had to posit some greater than human force work-ing "behind the backs" of men.

This is what Kant, Hegel, and Marx did, albeit each in their own way. Behind human discord, Kant saw a "ruse of nature" working to develop our talents and capacities, while Hegel saw Spirit (*Geist*) developing itself and coming to self-transparency in the course of a historical process that otherwise appeared to be little more than a "slaughter-bench." And, although Arendt does not draw this particular conclusion in her Gaus Lectures, Marx can be seen as heir to both the Platonic distinction between knowing and doing (*theoria* and *praxis*) *and* the Kantian-Hegelian conviction that words and deeds are ultimately meaningless unless they can be placed within a grand historical process with a clear purpose or direction.

Such a historical process can be framed as the unfolding of human capacities and consequent moral progress (Kant), the universal "coming to consciousness" of human freedom (Hegel), or the realization of the "realm of freedom" in the form of a classless society (Marx). In all three thinkers, freedom is not something tangibly expressed by acting and speaking men but is rather the result of a long historical march driven by Nature, *Geist*, or the evolution of forces and relations of production. *History*, in other words, is seen by the moderns as the route by which the "problem" of human freedom is solved. Arendt thinks that Aristotle, writing during the decline of the Greek polis, was "the last for whom freedom is not yet 'problematic' but inherent in the faculty of speech." He still knew what had been self-evident to those who shared or remembered political life in the Greek city-state: that men, "so long as they talk to each other and act together in the modus of speech, are free."[18]

What Arendt calls "the basic inconsistency of Marx's teaching," then, arises less from the untraditional nature of his fundamental theses (labor is the creator of man; violence is the midwife of history; nobody can be free who rules over others) than it does from his transposition of the Greek idea of freedom from a context presuming a pre-political rule over others to one that viewed *any* form of rulership as illegitimate. Marx retains the Greek criterion of no-rule among equals as constitutive of freedom while glossing over what the Greeks—and, indeed, the tradition at large—had assumed to be the deep and fundamental incompatibility between *freedom* and the *equality of all*:

> Universal equality cannot exist with freedom as the pre-political condition of political life and with the absolute rule over laborers; it is the latter that makes it possible for free citizens to

escape the coercive necessities of biological life, at least to the extent that such necessities demand of man's specific activities. Marx's own formulation that freedom is incompatible with rule over others only enhances this difficulty. If it were true, a Greek might have answered him by saying that then freedom was impossible: all men would be slaves of necessity—the necessity to eat and to live, to preserve and regenerate life. Not only are slaves not human, but no man is fully human under these conditions.[19]

This transformation of the Greek ideal of civic freedom into an ideal of universal (human) freedom based on a similarly universal notion of equality was itself enabled, Arendt claims, by a redefinition of the concept of man that occurred in late antiquity and that was intimately linked to the decline of the polis. "Only when the philosophers had definitely (and not only theoretically, as with Plato) broken with the polis," Arendt writes, and only "when political homelessness had become the status of a great many people in the world," did they conceive of man "in an entirely unpolitical way, that is, independent from the way in which he lived together with his equals."[20] This new "universal" concept of man was ultimately to provide the basis for the universal concept of equality that came to the fore in early modern age. The basic idea is that a traditional category—in this case, equality—is detached from its original political context and given an increasingly un-situated or "universal" form. As Arendt notes,

> never before our own time has equality meant in terms of political reality that literally everyone is everyone else's equal.... Originally equals were only those who belonged to the same group, and to extend this term to all men would have been to render it meaningless.[21]

At this point, it is easy to imagine the reader objecting "original context be damned! Universal human equality is the only morally defensible form of equality." Arendt would certainly agree with this statement. She had no desire to restore the hierarchy of the *ancien régime*, let alone the morally repugnant institution of slavery. What she would like us to see, however, is the way freedom loses its content and equality its shape or structure when they are so thoroughly detached from legal and institutional articulation. Thus, in the ancient world, the decline of polis life led to a loss of interest in "worldly" forms of civic freedom and an increasing fixation on the amorphous and intangible "inner freedom" preached by the Stoics and early Christians. The modern redefinition of equality—as universal and inherent in individuals *qua* human beings—points to a similar loss of interest in (or forgetting of) the positive or constitutive dimension of political structures and activities. With this loss of interest, "legitimate" political power comes to be viewed as a way to preserve natural or "pre-civil" rights and liberties (Locke), or as an ideologically disguised tool of class rule.

Marx took the latter view of so-called "legitimate" political power, especially with respect to the *faux* egalitarianism manifest in its bourgeois (liberal or republican) forms. His ideal society is expressive of the wish for what one might call a "post-political" world based upon a non-political (social) form of human equality and solidarity.[22] The extent to which Marx was "obsessed" by the idea of a universal equality that transcended not just all limited political forms but politics per se can be seen, according to Arendt, from "his concept of the future as a classless and nationless society, that is, a society in which universal equality will have razed all political boundaries between men." Echoing a theme from her analysis and critique of the European nation-state form in OT, Arendt claims that what Marx fundamentally failed to see was that "like all frontiers these boundaries [between relatively permanent and distinct political associations] give protection together with limitation, and not only separate but also bind men together."[23]

When it came to the achievement of universal equality, Marx was famously skeptical about the efficacy of civil and political rights.[24] As for the basis of human equality, he certainly did not believe that it was a transcendental endowment universally granted by a divine Creator (as Locke and Jefferson maintained). "Marx's greatness," Arendt writes,

and the reason for his enormous influence on modern political thought and movements, was that he discovered the positive

character of this [universal] equality in the nature of man himself, that is, in his conception of man as labor force.[25]

Arguing that it was not *reason* but rather our laboring capacity that
was distinctively human, Marx disposed of the Platonically inspired
definition of man as the *animal rationale*, putting in its place a conception of man as a self-creating or self-forming *animal laborans*. In so
doing, he grounded human equality in a faculty or power that all
human beings can be said to possess *qua* human beings and to possess in equal measure (as opposed to reason, a faculty philosophers
have historically viewed as unevenly distributed along class, race,
and gender lines). The point in the present context is that, for Marx,
both equality and freedom are grounded in a capacity possessed by
man *qua* laboring subject. They are utterly stripped of the tangible
and worldly—intersubjective and public—quality which had distinguished them in the Greek world.

****

Marx's suspicion of the political realm, combined with his "glorification" of labor, led him to characterize his ideal post-political
society as a "free association of producers" in which necessary administrative functions could be performed by "any cook." Conceptually speaking, the Marxian idea of praxis—as encompassing man's
"metabolism with nature," his potential for "all-sided" or unalienated production, and his revolutionary-practical activity—manages
to conflate the constituent components of the *vita activa* into one
all-purpose category. The most important point, underlined by the
analysis given in THC, is that Marx's praxis—whether considered
as labor, as production, or as political violence—has virtually no
connection to what the Greeks understood by *praxis*. They reserved
that category for words and deeds in the public realm, which they
pointedly distinguished from labor and fabrication as well as from
violence.

The sublimation of *praxis* in the Greek sense by Marx's overly inclusive concept of praxis lies at the root of the Marxian substitution of *administration* for *politics*. This substitution—originally intended
by Marx as a way of transposing the Greek criterion of freedom as

"no rule" from a sphere defined by an "equality of peers" to one characterized by truly *universal* equality—has been fraught with consequences for the Marxist tradition. It can be said to be responsible, in whole or in part, for the state-centric and supremely high-handed bureaucratic rule we typically associate with self-styled "Marxist" regimes. As Arendt observes in her Gaus Lectures, "administration was supposed to be no rule, but it can actually be only rule by nobody, that is, bureaucracy, a form of government without responsibility." She extends this thought in THC by noting that "the rule by nobody is not necessarily no-rule; it may indeed, under certain circumstances, even turn out to be one of its cruelest and most tyrannical versions."[26]

On the other hand, Marx's "dignification of labor" and his undifferentiated concept of praxis point to what Arendt considers to be an undeniable and fundamental fact about our age:

> The one decisive difference of our own world from all previous ages, the dignification of labor, has already acquired the doubtful status of a commonplace, and this in little more than a century. Marx's prophecies may have been wrong in almost all respects...But in this one respect—in his conviction that the future belongs to man as a laboring animal, to those, that is, who have nothing but their laboring capacity, whom he called the proletariat—he was so right that we, even today, are hardly aware of it...We live in a society in which men consider their activities primarily as laboring activities, in the sense that their end is "the preservation of individual life," and themselves primarily as owners of labor power. It is in this sense that those who manifestly do not labor, who do not earn their living through labor, are considered parasites.[27]

Two things need to be noted about this passage. First, Arendt is *not* saying Marx was right when he predicted that capitalism would wind up producing nothing but impoverished members of the working class (a prediction based on his "immiseration of the workers" thesis in *Capital*). Rather, she is saying that Marx clearly saw the outline of a "laboring society" on the horizon and that *that* is indeed the type of society we now live in. Second, to the objection that the professional athlete, the classical musician, or the professor are not "laborers" or "jobholders," Arendt would undoubtedly reply "oh, yes they are!"

Prior to the Industrial Revolution and its enormous expansion of the division of labor, social identity was determined primarily in terms of the "estate" (aristocracy, clergy, bourgeoisie, or peasantry) an individual belonged to. We, however, live a world in which an individual's primary identity is seen as a function of the type of labor—i.e. the type of job—he or she performs. In a laboring society, we *are* what we *do*: lawyer, professor, sheet metal worker, fireman, forest ranger, etc. Insofar as we are all "jobholders," we are all laborers—that is, individuals who sell their labor-power for roughly fixed rates and fixed periods of time. This is what Arendt means when she states that "we live in a society in which men consider their activities primarily as laboring activities." Her point (and Marx's) is not only that this is something *new*, but that it is *laboring* activity—and not membership in an "estate," civic body, or anything else—that now defines our horizon of value.

Seen from a Greek perspective—and, indeed, from Marx's perspective as well—the advent of a laboring society means that the "realm of necessity" has expanded far beyond the household, to the point where it englobes almost everything. Marx dreamed of a society in which accelerated technological innovation and the rapid expansion of *forces* of production would take place within a revolutionized set of *relations* of production. Under such conditions, the working class could conceivably be emancipated from having to earn their daily bread by occupying a fixed place in the division of labor. But for *that* to happen—for a society to come into being in which everyone (and not just the independently wealthy) could "hunt in the morning, fish in the afternoon, tend cattle in the evening, and criticize after dinner"—it is not enough that private ownership of industry and productive capacity gives way to some form of socialized ownership. The latter, after all, hardly does away with the coercive force of the division of labor. Rather, as Marx himself was well aware, the realm of necessity would somehow have to dialectically transform itself into the realm of freedom.

Here we encounter what Arendt deems to be "the only strictly utopian element in his [Marx's] thought." Still cleaving to the traditional idea—derived from the Greeks—that "the realm of freedom begins where laboring ends," Marx is left with the unhappy choice between subjecting *all* to the necessity of labor (something the Greeks would equate with the elimination of freedom as such) or emancipating man from labor altogether. In the Gaus Lectures, Arendt claims that the latter option is "something that in all probability is just as impossible as the early hope of the philosophers to free man's soul from his body."[28] This is one conclusion she will substantially revise, if not altogether abandon, in her critique of Marx in THC.

III The public realm and the "rise of the social"

The criticism of Marx that Arendt mounts in the Gaus Lectures leads her (and us) back to the origins of the Western tradition of political and philosophical thought. Despite his Cold War status as the intellectual forebear of one form totalitarian domination, Marx does indeed serve as a "bridge" to a tradition rendered fragmentary and remote by the horrific events of the mid-twentieth century.

Arendt underlines the connection between the beginning of the Western tradition (in Plato and Aristotle) and its end (in Marx) in the final section of her Gaus Lectures. Stressing how, for both Plato and Aristotle, the philosophical life was the only truly *free* one, she concludes by effectively setting the stage for the far-reaching critique of the Western tradition's contemplative prejudices she will undertake in THC:

> Our tradition of political philosophy, unhappily and fatefully, and from its very beginning, has deprived public affairs, that is, those activities concerning the common public realm that come into being wherever men live together, of all dignity of their own. In Aristotelian terms, *politics is a means to an end; it has no end in and by itself.* More than that, the proper end of politics [from the point of view of Plato and Aristotle] is in a way its opposite, namely, nonparticipation in political affairs, *schole*, the condition of philosophy, or rather the condition of a life devoted to it. In other words, *no other activity* appears as anti-philosophical, as hostile to philosophy, as political activity in general and action in particular...[29]

As Arendt will argue at length in THC, the anti-political prejudice of philosophical critics such as Plato and Aristotle comes to color the entire Western tradition. Marx may well have set himself against the contemplative tradition (and its greatest modern representative, Hegel), but his thought gives remarkably strong expression to the Platonic-Aristotelian devaluation of the public realm and such distinctively political activities as debate, deliberation, and the exchange of opinion. These activities, along with the "state of being" they manifest (the freedom of the *bios politikos*), are discarded as "mere" opinion, ideology, or obfuscation. Politics is stripped of intrinsic dignity and worth (it is no "good in itself") and converted into what is, at best, a means to "some allegedly higher [non-political] end": making the world safe for philosophy (Plato), cultivating moral virtue (Aristotle), or emancipating the working class and creating a "post-political" future (Marx).

The critique of the tradition is, however, only one dimension of the highly original and densely argued text that is The Human Condition. After a "Prologue" in which she states her primary aim—to "think what we are doing"—Arendt provides a relatively short chapter on what she means by "the human condition" before turning (in Chapter 2) to a longer discussion of the age-old distinction between the public and private realms. Here, she argues that these two spheres, once clearly separated realms of experience, have increasingly merged in the modern age. What Arendt calls the "rise of the social" creates a world that lacks either a genuine public or private realm. Our world is one in which the economic imperatives of the household sphere have migrated and effectively taken over the public-political realm. Instead of citizen deliberation concerning matters of public concern and the question of how we should live together, we get governmental administration, planning, and regulation of the socio-economic sphere.

Before proceeding, a word should be said about Arendt's somewhat unorthodox use of terms. We are all familiar with the distinction between public and private, especially as it applies to our own lives. And we often use "social" in order to describe a certain type of event (a "social engagement") or thing (a "social problem"). However, to see Arendt endowing something called "the social" with the power of eroding or effacing the distinction between public and private—not to mention the capacity to "devour" the spheres of experience these terms once designated—is more than a bit mystifying.[30] What can she possibly mean? The political theorist Hanna Pitkin was only half-joking when she titled her book on Arendt's concept of "the social" *The Attack of the Blob*. In THC, the term indeed seems to have taken on a life of its own.[31]

Making sense of "the rise of the social" demands, first, that we attend to Arendt's delineation of the public and private realms. In presenting a historically based account of these two realms, Arendt is not adumbrating a *theory* of the public or private sphere so much as providing a quasi-phenomenological *description* of what she takes to be their defining or essential characteristics. It is precisely because Arendt thinks that the distinction between these two realms has been blurred by "the rise of the social" that she turns to the ancient Greeks, the better to present the original distinction in its starkest possible form. The resulting contrast is somewhat stylized but illuminating nonetheless.

Picking up on themes developed in the Gaus Lectures, Arendt returns to the Greek contrast between a public realm (the sphere of the polis) in which citizens debated matters of common concern, and a private realm (the sphere of the household or oikos) where husbands, wives, slaves, and children attended to the pressing requirements of biological and material reproduction. "The distinctive trait of the household," she tells us, "was that in it men lived together because they were driven by their wants and needs…Natural community in the household was…born of necessity, and necessity ruled over all activities performed in it."[32] The realm of the polis was the realm of freedom and *politeuein*, and it was assumed "as a matter of course" that "mastering the necessities of life in the household was the condition for freedom of the polis."[33] For the Greeks, "mastering the necessities of life" in the household sphere entailed the male head of household exercising rule or mastery over all those within it, employing coercion and violence when necessary. Thus, the household sphere was rigidly hierarchical, "the center of the strictest inequality."[34]

The polis, on the other hand, knew only free and equal citizens: "To be free meant both not to be subject to the necessity of life or to the command of another *and* not to be in command oneself. It meant neither to rule nor be ruled."[35] An obvious but important implication of this Greek understanding is that the male head of household—its "ruler"—had to leave it and enter the public realm if he was to know the reality of either freedom or equality. Making a point she will return to in *On Revolution*, Arendt observes that for the Greeks *equality* and *freedom* were virtually identical. They were both distinguishing features of the condition of "no rule" that defined the public realm. As she did in her Gaus Lectures, Arendt emphasizes the fact that not only did the Greeks *not* see any contradiction between public (political) equality and private (household) inequality; they also assumed the latter to be the absolute, indeed ineliminable, precondition of the former. The Greek citizen experienced daily the starkness of this contrast between the public and private realms. He simply had to step out of his house and encounter his fellow citizens on their way to the agora or assembly in order to appreciate it. Though it sounds odd to us—conditioned as we are to think of freedom as the freedom *from* politics—the Greek citizen knew that "freedom is located exclusively in the political realm."[36]

At this point in her analysis, Arendt has defined the freedom found in the public realm in strictly negative terms: *not* being subject to the necessity that rules the household, *not* being subject to the command of another, *not* being in command oneself. But what, according to Arendt, is the *positive* nature of the freedom the Greeks experienced when they crossed the boundary separating the private realm from the public? In answering this question, we encounter several of the key elements of Arendt's mature political theory. First, freedom is something *public*—that is, worldly and tangible. Second, human *plurality* is the basis not only of political action but of the reality of the public realm itself. And third, the robust political equality and freedom enjoyed by the Greeks and other authentically political actors has a distinctively *agonistic* or competitive character.

The idea of "public freedom" is not unknown to modern Western political thought and practice. Indeed, Arendt makes it the centerpiece (along with public spirit and public happiness) of her analysis of the modern revolutionary tradition initiated by the French and American revolutions. Yet, as Arendt points out in her essay "What is Freedom?," the Western tradition of philosophy and theology has focused almost entirely on the problem of free will—that is, on the nature and experience of the willing *self*.[37] The interior struggle of a will divided against itself—a struggle "discovered" and focused upon intently by St. Paul and Augustine—sets the stage for centuries of philosophical speculation of whether "free will" is fact or fiction. In her political theory, Arendt sets the so-called "problem of freedom" firmly aside, but only after blaming our philosophical and theological tradition for identifying freedom with the will in the first place. This identification is the origin of a recurring pattern in Western political thought, one in which freedom is equated with the sovereignty or autonomy of a single (individual or collective) will.

If, like Arendt, we set the "problem" of freedom aside, what is left? For Arendt, there is little question: what is left are the words and deeds that occur on a public stage in the political realm. The *fact* that, through their deliberations, citizens can initiate new and unpredictable things (such as the Athenian expedition to Sicily in 415 BCE, or the creation of a new form of government by the delegates to the constitutional convention in Philadelphia in 1787) is sufficient testimony, Arendt thinks, to the existence of a tangible or worldly form of freedom. Such freedom occurs not *within* individual persons but *between* them, when they speak and act together in an established public realm (such as the Athenian assembly) or engage in a deliberative process that brings forth a new one (as in the American constitutional convention).

Even at this stage, we can detect an important shift in emphasis as Arendt moves from her description of freedom as a "state of being" enjoyed by Greek household heads (in the Gaus Lectures) to the specifically *public* form of freedom described in THC. While the underlying contrast of freedom versus necessity remains the same, the *public* from of freedom explored in THC is not so much a "freedom from" certain activities as it is a "freedom for" a set of specifically political (or civic) activities. "Tangible" freedom, in other words, is manifest in words spoken and the deeds performed by citizens who assemble for the sake of the polis. Thus, while the leisure or "state of being" afforded by liberation from daily chores can be enjoyed by household heads as individuals, *public* freedom is manifest only in the *political* activities of diverse yet equal citizens debating and deciding matters of common concern.

This brings us to the central role human plurality plays in the constitution of the public realm (the "space of freedom") and in Arendt's mature political thought more generally.

The theme of human plurality had, of course, been introduced in the "Ideology and Terror" chapter of OT. In that book, however, plurality was deployed largely as a contrasting pole to the "one Man of gigantic dimensions" Arendt thought the totalitarians were bent on creating. In THC, the importance of plurality as a (if not the) central concept in Arendt's political thinking is announced at the start of the very first chapter ("*Vita Activa* and the Human Condition"). Here, she tells us that action, "the only activity that goes on directly between men," corresponds to "the human condition of plurality, to the fact that men, not Man, live on earth and inhabit the world" and that this plurality is "specifically *the* condition—not only the *conditio sine qua non*, but the *conditio per quam*—of all political life."[38] If there was no plurality—if, for example, human beings were all the same, namely human, without at the same time being unique individuals—there would be few differences between individual perspectives on common matters, and hence no real need for politics. However, the absence of plurality would mean not just the end of diverse perspectives on a shared public world, but the disappearance of worldly objective reality as such. Arendt writes:

> The reality of the public realm relies on the simultaneous presence of innumerable perspectives and aspects in which the common world presents itself and for which no common measurement or denominator can ever be devised. For though the common world is the common meeting ground of all, those who are present have different locations in it, and the location of one can no more coincide with the location of another than the location of two objects. Being seen and heard by others derive their significance from the fact that everybody sees and hears from a different perspective. This is the meaning of public life, compared to which even the richest and most satisfying family life can offer only the prolongation or multiplication of one's own position with its attending aspects and perspective.... Only where things can be seen by many in a variety of aspects without changing their identity, so that those who are gathered

around them know they see sameness in utter diversity, can worldly reality truly and reliably appear.[39]

This passage has elicited much commentary. Arendt stresses the way the common world acquires depth and public reality (its "three dimensionality," so to speak) *only* through the perspectival contributions made possible by unconstrained human plurality in a particular time and place. Whether we are talking about the public realm of ancient Athens or that of post-revolutionary America, the reality of each depends upon the active expression of diverse opinions emanating from a wide range of perspectives on the same "object" or thing. The last qualification is crucial. As Arendt observes, "If the sameness of the object can no longer be discerned, no common nature of men, least of all the unnatural conformism of a mass society, can prevent the destruction of the common world."[40]

This can happen where privatization and isolation (whether the result of tyranny or less tangible cultural forces) have imposed or fostered a widespread withdrawal from politics and the public world. But the "destruction of the common world" can happen in other ways as well. It can happen when public opinion is divided up along ideological lines and "siloed" in media echo chambers where one encounters only like-minded commentators and fellow citizens. And it can happen when "alternative facts" are so widely disseminated that the sameness underlying the public-perspectival constitution of political things dissolves in a haze of lies and disinformation. Finally, it can happen when "perspectives" are reified and made expressive of group identity rather than individual viewpoints or opinion.

This latter possibility has come to the fore with the recent rise of identity politics across the political spectrum. It has become increasingly common to assume that it is nearly impossible for an individual from one group to understand or fully appreciate the perspective of an individual from another. Moreover, it is often claimed that the most pressing task facing marginalized or oppressed groups is less the exchange of opinions than the cultivation of a strong sense of agency among its members. Contemporary political theory has seen a variety of attempts to square the latter imperative with the idea/ideal of a public sphere. Nancy Fraser's idea of "subaltern counter-publics" (e.g. the feminist public sphere, the black public sphere, the gay and lesbian public sphere) has been one of the more suggestive and influential. What such counter-publics provide is the political education and experience necessary for more effective participation by these groups in what might be called the "official" or civic public sphere.[41]

While hardly blind to the need for better civic integration of racial, ethnic, and religious minorities, Arendt would not have viewed the contemporary fragmentation of the public along lines of group identity as a sign of political health. The analysis of the decline of the nation-state in OT makes that perfectly clear. Nor would she have viewed the category of "citizen" as an underhanded way of disguising power differentials between groups divided by class, race, or gender.[42] Her insistence upon the need to maintain the integrity of the public realm and the category of citizenship is a theme that runs throughout her work.

Left-leaning critics frequently complain that Arendt's insistence on this score is the residue of either an outmoded eighteenth-century republicanism or of the "polis-envy" typical of much post-Kantian German philosophy. However, these same critics often find themselves attracted to the third feature of Arendt's "positive" concept of political freedom, namely, the *agonistic* quality of the public realm in which such freedom finds adequate expression.

"Agonistic" derives from the Greek word *agonistes* (contestant) and refers to the intensely competitive nature of Greek life, at least as it was interpreted by Jacob Burckhardt, Friedrich Nietzsche, and Werner Jaeger. These writers viewed the ancient Greeks as turning virtually everything into some form of competition, whether it be athletics, war, drama, or poetry. Even philosophy, in the form of Socratic dialogue, retained more than a trace of this agonistic spirit (although in an earlier essay Arendt credits Socrates with attempting to tame an agonism that threatened to spiral out of control).[43]

Politics too was an intensely competitive activity for the Greeks, and not merely in the sense that elites such as Pericles competed in the assembly to persuade their fellow citizens of the superior wisdom of their recommended policies. A competitive spirit animated the political activity of ordinary citizens as well. As individuals, they took pride in their participation and in their knowledge of politics and public affairs, a fact eloquently testified to by Pericles' Funeral

Oration. Arendt is only slightly exaggerating when she observes that "the public realm itself, the polis, was permeated by a fiercely agonal spirit where everybody had constantly to distinguish himself from all others, to show through unique deeds or achievements that he was the best of all (*aien aristeuein*)."[44]

An agonistic public sphere of the sort described by Arendt appeals to radical democratic theorists otherwise put off by her perceived "elitism." For these theorists, agonistic freedom means the freedom to actively and publicly *contest* regnant policies, practices, and concepts insofar as these support the power differentials built into the status quo. In THC, Arendt does not gloss the Greeks' agonism in quite this way. However, there can be little doubt that her overall conception of the public realm is more spontaneous, energetic, and rebellious than that espoused by many *deliberative* democrats. The latter, often following Jürgen Habermas' analysis in *The Structural Transformation of the Public Sphere*, focus on the giving of arguments and the "right to justification" possessed by ordinary citizens confronting high-handed governmental or corporate powers. Deliberative democrats view "agonism" as too distant from the rationalist heritage of the Enlightenment and, at the same time, as too close to the "politics is struggle" motif that runs through the political writings of Max Weber and Carl Schmitt. The suspicion they feel toward an "Arendtian-agonistic" conception of the public sphere more than matches the enthusiasm expressed by their "radical democratic" counterparts.

If we stick to her political theory rather than to the uses to which it has been recently put, the truth is that Arendt offers a middle way between the Scylla of an unconstrained agonism and the Charybdis of a process-oriented deliberative politics. In other words, her "agonistic public sphere" is as much about debate and deliberation as it is about spontaneity and resistance. The fact that these two dimensions are often seen as mutually exclusive tells us more about the contemporary political climate than it does about the intentions underlying her turn to a Greek-inspired conception of the public realm.

What are these intentions? Why does Arendt feel compelled to turn to a "model" of the public sphere so removed from contemporary conditions and understandings? Answering these questions takes us back to the issue of what she means by "the rise of the social" and why she thinks it is of such paramount importance.

Mapping the Greek distinction between the public and private realms provides Arendt with a screen on which she can project the modern "rise of the social" in its sharpest outline. This is important if only because a phenomenon as broad, deep, and temporally extended as the "rise of the social" is hard to see unless we have a clear contrasting background. The difficulty is exacerbated by the fact that we currently assume that managing socio-economic affairs is and always has been the primary concern of the political sphere—its *raison d'être*, so to speak. This assumption, Arendt thinks, is deeply rooted—historically and intellectually—in the modern age:

> That politics is nothing but a function of society, that action, speech, and thought are primarily superstructures upon social interest, is not a discovery of Karl Marx but on the contrary is among the axiomatic assumptions Marx accepted uncritically from the political economists of the modern age. This functionalization makes it impossible to perceive any serious gulf between the two realms; and this is not a matter of a theory or an ideology, since with the rise of society, that is, the rise of the "household" (*oikia*) or of economic activities to the public realm, housekeeping and all matters pertaining formerly to the private sphere of the family have become a "collective" concern. In the modern world, the two realms constantly flow into each other like waves in the never-resting stream of the life process itself.[45]

As the inheritors of a "functionalizing" approach to politics—one that views the state as a juridical-administrative superstructure whose job it is to protect a pre-existing (and far more extensive) sphere of production and exchange—we take it for granted that the proper role of government is to regulate the economy in accordance with the interests of society at large. "Society" here denotes a distinctively modern form of human association, one in which "the fact of mutual dependence for the sake of life and nothing else assumes public significance and where the activities connected with sheer survival are permitted to appear in public."[46] This is a form of association created by the rise of market society, the Industrial Revolution, and the emergence of capitalism.

Together, these developments separated workers from the tools or means of production (on the one hand) while revolutionizing, concentrating, and interconnecting vastly expanded forces of production (on the other). Labor and the productive process moved quite literally out of the private household and took up residence in what Arendt, following the Swedish economist Gunnar Myrdal, calls the "national household." If in OT Arendt had argued that the migration of economic concepts to the political realm laid the groundwork for imperialism and the decline of the nation-state, in THC she argues that a more basic and profound instrumentalization of politics flowed from the work of the classical political economists. Authors like Adam Smith, David Ricardo, and James Mill reified disparate and often conflicting economic interests into the conceptual fiction of an underlying *social* interest. They thereby endowed the new and often harsh economic order with misleadingly benign, socially beneficial powers (courtesy of the "hidden hand" of the market). By doing so, they unintentionally paved the way for socialist critics like Marx to claim that *society*—and not the nation-state, a particular class, or a group of individual entrepreneurs—was the real agent behind economic growth and should, by right, be the *direct* recipient of the benefits this growth produced.

The important point here is that both advocates and critics of a *laissez-faire* capitalist economy took it for granted that the entity they were dealing with was not the political association per se, but "society" defined in terms of its economic power, interests, and relationships. In other words, the political association became an *economic polity*—a "national household." Henceforth, it would view its population less as citizens than as potential laborers who needed training and education if they were to become productive "members of society" and contributors to the nation's overall economic strength. The "rise of the social" thus refers to the economic absorption of the political in the modern age, a process that has been a central theme in the work of such contemporary theorists as Habermas and Michel Foucault. There are clear links between Arendt's analysis of the "rise of the social" (with its "irresistible tendency to grow, to devour the older realms of the public and the private") and Habermas' idea of the colonization of the "lifeworld" by the "system," as well as between her analysis and Foucault's influential concepts of biopower and governmentality.[47]

Unsurprisingly, what concerns Arendt most about this absorption of the political by the economic is the way it denatures the public realm and undercuts the human plurality that sustains it. What the Greeks viewed as a space for the "sharing of words and deeds" by equal yet diverse citizens becomes the site of administration and bureaucracy (the "rule by nobody").[48] In a world in which "the life process itself" has been "channeled into the public realm" what is required is not the spontaneous *action* and judgment of agonistic citizens, but rather the predictable ("normalized") *behavior* of laborers.[49] The enormous expansion of productive forces—and with it, the sphere of laboring activity itself—thus unleashes an "unnatural growth of the natural" and a corresponding growth of the sort of conformist behavior Arendt thinks typical of mass societies. The reduction of the vast majority to "specimens" of the *animal laborans* means that, at the moment it becomes economically and technologically possible to guarantee the survival of the species "on a world-wide scale," humanity itself may well be "threatened with extinction."[50]

Is Arendt saying that "human nature" is once again under attack, but this time by capitalist modernity rather than totalitarianism? On the face of it, this certainly appears to be the case. After all, didn't she conclude OT by observing that the very threats raised by totalitarianism may well reappear under non-totalitarian circumstances?

The last thing Arendt wants to do is to suggest (*à la* Herbert Marcuse's *One-Dimensional Man* or Horkheimer and Adorno's *Dialectic of Enlightenment*) that we are victims of a "soft" totalitarianism in the form of consumer capitalism. For Arendt, there is absolutely no analogy between the concentration camp and the shopping mall. That said, the channeling of the necessities of the life process into the public sphere obviously encourages the growth of a technocratic or bureaucratic approach to governance. And this in turn severely limits the spaces and opportunities for meaningful political participation by ordinary citizens. To the objection that our recent politics have become *too* "populist" and/or agonistic in temper, one need only observe that neither the mass rally nor internet trolling are examples of public debate, deliberation, persuasion, or judgment.

Before answering the question of whether THC offers a modified version of Arendt's "human nature is under attack" claim from OT, we must first note her rejection of the category of "human nature" in the former work. "Nothing entitles us," she writes,

> to assume that man has a nature or essence in the same sense as other things…If we have a nature or essence, then surely only a god could know and define it, and the first prerequisite would be that he be able to speak about a 'who' as though it were a 'what.'[51]

Rather than basing herself on some dubious thesis about human *nature*, Arendt begins her investigation with an enumeration of "the basic conditions under which life on earth has been given to man."[52] These are "life itself, natality and mortality, worldliness, plurality, and the earth."[53] Of course, "the human condition comprehends more than the conditions under which life has been given to man." As Arendt observes, "whatever touches or enters into a sustained relationship with human life immediately assumes the character of a condition of human existence."[54] This introduces a degree—or perhaps more than a degree—of cultural and historical variability into the idea of "the human condition," a locution that might otherwise appear to designate something as static and immutably given as "human nature."

Here, a glance at Heidegger's *Being and Time* is perhaps helpful. In opposition to the Cartesian model of a contemplative consciousness set over against a world composed of material but perhaps unknowable objects, Heidegger argued (in Division I of *Being and Time*) that we are always already *in* the world. In Heidegger's usage, "world" means the totality of referential or practical contexts (e.g. a workshop) within which individual entities (e.g. a hammer) appear—first as "equipment" we employ without reflection, and only later (if at all) as "objects" standing over against a subject who has adopted a self-consciously "theoretical" or detached attitude. Human existence—*Dasein*—thus has the fundamental character of an always already *involved* "being-in-the-world." However, as Division II of *Being and Time* makes clear, the "world" that *Dasein* inhabits changes as culture and civilization itself changes. *We* are conditioned by our world no less than the Greeks or Aztecs were conditioned by theirs, even though the respective "worlds" in question are dramatically different. What both Heidegger *and* Arendt wish to emphasize is the conditioned—that is, finite, worldly, and involved—character of human existence as such.[55]

This is the background against which we should read Arendt's descriptions (in the "Prologue" to *THC*) of the three activities constitutive of the *vita activa*. Labor, work, and action are to be understood as "those general human capacities which grow out of the human condition and are permanent, that is, which cannot be irretrievably lost so long as the human condition itself is not changed."[56] This leaves the door open to the possibility that either the "basic" or more supplemental conditioning elements of the human condition could change so radically that one or even all of these "general human capacities" desert us. If that were to happen, Arendt argues, humanity as we know it would indeed become "extinct."

That this thought is not quite as outlandish as it might first appear is made clearer by if we turn to two hypothetical, but by no means implausible, instances of such a profound change in our existential circumstances. With regard to the possibility that a radical change in one of the "basic conditions" under which "life on earth has been given to man" might produce a correspondingly radical change in us, one need only consider the environmental degradation that has occurred over the last 200 years, thanks to the Industrial Revolution and its globalized aftermath. If current trends continue, more than a few experts have predicted that the earth (which Arendt refers to as "the very quintessence of the human condition") will become uninhabitable in the not-too-distant future.[57]

Should these predictions come true—that is, should human beings ultimately be forced to leave the earth and inhabit another planet—a technologically produced and controlled environment would take the place of earthly nature (on the one hand) and the artificial yet durable "world" created by civilization and political association (on the other). Our descendants would still be members of the human *species*, but they would no longer be the worldly and earth-bound mortals known by the Greeks and virtually every other human civilization down to our own. "Humanity" may not totally disappear under these circumstances, but it would certainly have to be radically reconceived. So too would the conditioned activities that once comprised the *vita activa* on earth.

With regard to the second possibility, in which a radical change in one or more of the "supplemental" conditioning elements that define the human condition occurs, Arendt herself provides us with an example. It is quite possible, she thinks, that automation and technology will soon succeed in liberating society from what for millennia seemed the inescapable "curse" of labor. Were that to happen, she observes, we would find ourselves "confronted with a society of laborers without labor, that is, *without the only activity left to them.* Surely nothing could be worse."[58]

Arendt here is not going for dystopian shock-effect. Rather, she is underlining what happens when our distinctively human capacities are deprived, over time, of the worldly locations or spaces required for their full or even partial exercise. Invaded by economic matters or "household" concerns, the public realm invariably shrinks as government becomes increasingly bureaucratic in character. The kind of civic abilities that once flourished in more open, local, and accessible public spaces—among them the capacities for deliberation, persuasion, and "acting in concert"—atrophy. Similarly, as society assimilates its jobholder-laborers to ever-accelerating cycles of production and consumption, the capacity to create and sustain the kind of durable artifacts and institutions that define public culture also withers.

Having "devoured" the relatively autonomous spheres of (political) action and (culture-defining) work, the "unnatural growth of the natural" unleashed by the "rise of the social" creates a population familiar only with the activity of labor. The point of Arendt's warning is that we are on verge of rendering *that* activity obsolete as well, creating a world where most if not all of the necessary tasks required for material reproduction are carried out by machines.[59] In such a world—one in which the survival of the species is increasingly guaranteed "on a world-wide scale" while our general human capacities for action, work, and even labor atrophy—the existence of humanity is indeed threatened, if for no other reason than that our distinctively human capacities wither once the spaces required for their exercise disappear.

****

I want to conclude this section by briefly considering another aspect of Arendt's "rise of the social" thesis, namely, her insistence that *social* problems are not *political* problems and that, overall, they are best left to the experts. This assertion appears baffling on two counts. First, what are social problems if not *political* problems? Second, why on earth would Arendt want to assert that the types of public spaces required for citizen participation are rapidly disappearing as bureaucratic rule extends its domain, *and then* hand over to the bureaucrats many of the very issues that are at the heart of political debate and contestation today?

More than any of the other distinctions she is famous for drawing (between public and private, power and force, political action and violence, etc.), Arendt's distinction between the *social* and the *political* has made her readers balk. If "the social" is the enemy of the public and the political, where does that leave citizens of contemporary liberal or social democracies? Aside from foreign affairs, virtually all our political problems appear to be social ones. Education, health care, affordable housing, gender and race relations: it's hard to conjure such issues away, let alone claim that they are somehow *not* political, especially given the passions they raise. Whether encountering this distinction for the first or the hundredth time, it's safe to say most readers of Arendt have or will have reactions similar to that expressed by the philosopher Richard Bernstein in 1972. Addressing Arendt directly at a Toronto conference held in her honor, Bernstein vehemently took exception: "You know darn well that—at least, for us, now—one can't consistently make that distinction!"[60] The content of much of our politics is irreducibly social in character. To insist otherwise, as Arendt apparently does, runs the risk of erecting a concept of the political that is detached from reality and overly formalist in character.

Arendt's response to Bernstein and others voicing this criticism is illuminating but frustrating. She suggests that problems like housing have a "double face." The *social* face—the need for adequate housing—is the side of the issue she thinks there is already agreement upon: "There shouldn't be any debate about the question that everybody should have decent housing."[61] If this is the case, then the only question facing us is a technical one: What are the best, most efficient and cost-effective, *means* for getting adequate housing to those in need of it? Like all questions focused strictly on means, Arendt thinks this one is best left to the experts. On the other hand, whether such housing ought to be racially integrated (whether by law or some other form of mandate) is a question about *ends*, that is, about justice and the type of political community we want to create and maintain. Here, Arendt thinks, there will invariably be differing legitimate opinions about what course of action best serves justice and the common good. Where ends as well as means are involved, there we have a *political* (as opposed to purely technical) question, one that needs to be addressed by *citizens* and not simply by the experts.

Broadly speaking, this is a coherent position to take. It acknowledges that there is a connection, not an abyss, between the social and political sides of things. And it acknowledges that there is a role for administration and government that goes well beyond that of the "night watchman state" envisioned by such early liberal political theorists as John Locke. However, for a contemporary American reader, Arendt's parsing of the social/political distinction will appear too optimistic by half. The things Arendt evidently assumes any decent society will want to provide (adequate housing, education, health care, etc.) through appropriate administrative mechanisms are precisely the things Americans disagree about. There is at present no consensus that would enable us to spin off (as Arendt apparently assumes we can) the management and delivery of basic social goods while retaining our citizenly prerogatives with regard to more authentically political questions.

Here, we broach issues that come to the fore with Arendt's treatment of "the Social Question" in *On Revolution*, which I will discuss in Chapter 5. For now, I want to turn to the core of THC—the phenomenological descriptions of the three activities that comprise the *vita activa*. I begin with labor in this chapter and will treat work and action in the next.

IV Labor and necessity

At the beginning of her chapter on labor, Arendt notes that it will offer criticism of Marx, albeit criticism which eschews the reduction of the "great man's" thought to totalitarian or proto-totalitarian elements.

Readers expecting a full-scale critique of Marx will, however, be somewhat disappointed. It is not that Arendt fails to engage Marx's thought at a deep level (she does). Rather, it is because in the "Labor" chapter, Arendt treats Marx's "glorification of labor" as emblematic of a deeply rooted cultural-historical shift of attitude, rather than as the essential core of Marxian socialism. Labor, the component of the *vita activa* that the Greeks viewed as closest to animal life and worthy only of slaves, is elevated to a position of unquestioned preeminence—not just by Marx, but by the classical political economists he criticized (Smith, Ricardo, Mill). Arendt, in other words, positions Marx against the backdrop of an era dazzled by the sudden and unexpected exponential increase in the productive capacity of human labor.

Of course, much of the credit for this increase can be traced back to the Industrial Revolution and the introduction of mechanized means of production. But, as Marx points out in the famous opening pages of the *Communist Manifesto*, the chief contribution of machine production, when combined with the removal of feudal restrictions on trade and investment, was to awaken the dormant powers that previously existed in the "lap of labor."[62] Once the bounds imposed by the lack of industrial technology and a "free market" in labor were overcome, human labor-power could reveal what it was really capable of: virtually unlimited commodity production as well as the creation of the global system of trade and manufacture such vastly increased productive capacity required. Laboring activity, for millennia focused on subsistence, now revealed an astonishing fertility. Not only was labor now viewed as the source of all value (Arendt traces the "labor theory of value" back to Locke's *Second Treatise*); it was also seen as capable of providing society at large with an ever-expanding surplus. For both the early advocates of free-market capitalism and for Marx, it was this expanding surplus that made it possible, in principle, to leave the "realm of necessity" imposed by the daily struggle for subsistence behind once and for all and enter into a "realm of freedom." The availability of cheap and plentiful commodities—equitably distributed by either efficient markets or rational economic planning—would consign the "curse" of subsistence-driven labor to the dustbin of history. Of course, man's "metabolism with nature" (Marx) would still require labor, but it would be labor freed from its age-old thralldom to nature.

Or would it? The Marxian image of humanity as a kind of demiurge, a collective subject that tames, transforms, and "humanizes" nature through its ever-expanding laboring activity, is in fact misleading—at least from Arendt's perspective. The burden of the "Labor" chapter in THC is to argue that the Marxist (and capitalist) glorification of labor and productivity does not so much "humanize" nature as assimilate humanity to it. The more society centers on the expansion and acceleration of cycles of production and consumption, the more the economic system takes on a life and rhythm of its own. Increasingly it functions in a manner akin to the "automatic" natural processes (such as respiration and circulation) by means of which the individual organism and species sustain themselves. In other words, the more the "life process" of society comes to dominate our lives and our public world, the more we find ourselves assimilated to natural or pseudo-natural processes. The result is that, rather than entering a "realm of freedom" virtually freed from labor, humanity finds itself reduced to the *animal laborans*—the laboring animal.

This capsule summary reveals the way THC amplifies and transforms ideas first encountered in OT. There, the reader will recall, Arendt highlighted the bogus naturalism animating European imperialism, racism, and tribal nationalism. By substituting economic categories for political ones, the European bourgeoisie succeeded in making "expansion for expansion's sake" and the competition for empire a "natural" imperative of the (hitherto territorially bounded) nation-state. Either you expand, gaining more land, population, and resources in the process, or you remain within your fixed boundaries and stagnate, wither, and die. Similarly, the substitution of racial categories for political ones turned the domination of native populations into a nature-imposed evolutionary duty (the "white man's burden"), while the rejection of civic-political ties in favor of more "natural" identities based on soul, blood, or inheritance (Burke) signaled a root-and-branch repudiation of the entire "artificial" world of politically bounded and institutionally articulated nation-states.

The "Labor" chapter in THC extends these thought trains to the glorification of "productive" labor in the modern age. This glorification—anticipated by Locke and Smith, consummated by the work of Marx—underwrites the subsumption of the political by the social that Arendt sees as characteristic of the modern age. The realm of necessity grows as the "life process" of society is channeled into the space previously reserved for the sharing of words and deeds by diverse civic equals. Human plurality is uprooted—not by terror in the name of deterministic ideologies, but rather by an ever-expanding economic system that depends upon predictable behavior and widespread conformity for its smooth ("automatic") functioning. It is hardly surprising that, in the course of the modern age, the political realm comes to be viewed either as an entrenched obstacle on the way to the creation of a "free association of producers" (Marx), or as a parasitic source of unwarranted interference in the otherwise "naturally" self-regulating behavior of markets (Smith).

For the past two centuries, the priority of man's "metabolism with nature" over all other activities has been presumed, as has the priority of the economic over the political. From Arendt's point of view, the importance of Marx's theory lies in the fact that it offers the most profound analysis of how and why labor—once viewed as the lowest and most despised of all human activities—comes to occupy the hegemonic position it does in the modern age. But Marx's theory is also important, she thinks, because it reveals the fundamental contradiction built into the idea that a "realm of freedom" could, in fact, be created on the basis labor's ever-increasing productivity. I should point out that, in generalized form, this is an idea that underlies both socialist and capitalist ideology. Arendt is therefore hardly indulging in hyperbole when she dubs Marx's thought "the theory of the modern age."

****

Viewed from the standpoint of the history of Western civilization, the cultural hegemony of labor over both action and work is a relatively recent, one might even say novel, phenomenon. In her chapter on labor, Arendt highlights this novelty as well as the radical departure that labor's glorification represents, at least from the standpoint of the traditional hierarchy of human activities. Contrary to what some of her critics have claimed, Arendt's point is not to argue that the Greek ranking of human activities (which placed action at the apex, with work and labor far below) got it right, and that we should somehow effect a "transvalutation of values" that would bring us more in line with our classical heritage. The rhetoric of her chapter on "Action" notwithstanding, Arendt was profoundly aware that there was no going back to what Hegel had called the "beautiful freedom" of the Greeks.

From Arendt's point of view, "thinking what we are doing" means recognizing the newness and relative strangeness of our hierarchy of activities, as well as the values, attitudes, and unthought presuppositions upon which it rests. In order to accomplish this, the self-proclaimed project of THC, Arendt must do more than criticize Marx (or Smith or Locke, for that matter). She must also provide us with a description of the essential characteristics of labor, work, and action, showing how the specific differences between these activities have been eroded or covered over—first by the contemplative tradition represented by Plato, Aristotle, and Christian thought; second by the rise of capitalism and the valuing of labor's productivity above all else.

It is for this reason that the central chapters of THC—chapters that focus on "those general human capacities which grow out of the human condition and are permanent, that is, which cannot be irretrievably lost so long as the human condition itself has not changed"—combine a historical-critical narrative with more straightforward phenomenological descriptions of the activities themselves. The situation is further complicated by the fact that Arendt habitually turns to historical figures (Marx, Locke, Plato, and Pericles, among others) and texts (Greek poetry and drama, the Old and New Testaments, etc.) in order to flesh out the descriptive and historical dimensions of labor, work, and action. In general, she is most concerned to get us to see the *differences* between activities which *modern* thought and practice (to say nothing of the contemplative tradition) have conflated.

This effort can sometimes leave the impression that Arendt reifies the activities of labor, work, and action into distinct "natural kinds," stipulating both an essence and an appropriate social location for each while denying the legitimate possibility of overlap in practice. It is indeed the case that, for Arendt, the attitudes and activities characteristic of *homo faber* are distinct from those of the *animal laborans*, just as the attitudes and activities of a public-spirited political actor are distinct from those of either the fabricator-craftsman or the "laboring animal." However, that does not mean these distinct activities, or the agents who carry them out, occupy hermetically sealed chambers. Such ironclad separation may have been dominant in the slave economies of the ancient world, but it is hardly so in the modern age.

Thus, in section 30 of THC ("The Labor Movement") and at greater length in *On Revolution* Arendt emphasized the fact that, despite the anti-political (non-public and often isolating) aspects of laboring activity, the European working classes have been at the forefront of some of the most important political actions of the nineteenth and twentieth centuries. While the intense bodily effort of their labor may have effectively isolated them for lengthy periods of time, their liberation from serfdom during and after the French Revolution allowed them to appear, for the first time, on the European public stage. Here, they played a central political role in the modernization and revolutionary re-constitution of society. Contrary to the elitist assumptions of Plato and Aristotle, in Arendt's view being a laborer or a craftsman does not render one *a priori* incapable of public spirit or authentically political action. She *does* think that the *mentalities* of the *animal laborans* and *homo faber*—mentalities she views as characteristic of the late modern and early modern periods, respectively—have anti-political implications when extended to the public domain. However, this extension is the result of broad intellectual and cultural shifts of the sort she traces in THC. These, however, are initiated by philosophers, scientists, political economists, and social theorists—*not* workers.

Bearing these qualifications in mind, the bulk of Arendt's theoretical energy in THC is devoted to disentangling the nature and modes of *political* action from metaphors, concepts, and analogies philosophers and theorists have taken from the realms of labor and work and projected onto the public realm (Plato's "craftsman" analogy in the *Republic* being perhaps the most famous and enduring).[63] Only after this task has been accomplished can we see just how radically philosophical and theological prejudice, in tandem with the "rise of the social," have denatured both the public sphere and political action.

The first step in this disentangling process is recovering the distinction between the activities of *labor* and *work*. This distinction is by no means self-evident and, as Arendt herself admits, will probably strike many readers as unusual. Nevertheless, Arendt thinks the reality of a distinction between "the work of our hands" and the "labor of our bodies" is both experientially and linguistically indisputable. All the Western languages, ancient and modern, have different words for labor and work (*labore* and *fabricari*, *travailler* and *ouvrer*, *arbeiten* and *werken*, etc.). Moreover, the results of these activities—the goods consumed in the course of daily life (food, fuel, etc.) that are "produced" by labor and the durable use objects and artifacts (tables, artworks, buildings, etc.) fabricated by work—are clearly different in nature.[64]

Why, then, are the activities of labor and work so often conflated, both by thinkers within the Western tradition and in our daily experience? And what implications, if any, does this conflation have for the nature and prospects of political action and the public realm in the modern age?

With respect to the tradition, it is, as Arendt notes, unsurprising that the ancient Greeks ignored the distinction between the activities of work and labor. The operative distinction for them was whether an activity was carried out in the relative "darkness" of the private realm (the household) or in the "bright light" of the public space (the assembly or agora). Was the activity in question undertaken primarily for private reasons (subsistence, money-making, the pursuit of a trade), or was it engaged in out of care and concern for public affairs? From this standpoint, even the great sculptors and artisans of classical Greece were viewed as *banausoi*—men whose chief interest was the pursuit of their craft and *not* the public matters discussed in the marketplace and the assembly. Like those who labored and whose chief interest lay in subsistence, "banausic" craftsmen were viewed as less than ideal candidates for citizenship (Aristotle recommending against their inclusion).

While the ancient neglect of the difference between work and labor is understandable, it is more than a bit perplexing that the modern age "should not have brought forth a single theory in which *animal laborans* and *homo faber*, 'the labor of our body and the work of our hands,' are clearly distinguished."[65] This perplexity is rooted in the fact that the modern age reversed not just the traditional rank of the *vita activa* and *vita contemplativa*, but also the traditional hierarchy within the *vita activa* itself, glorifying labor and elevating the *animal laborans* "to the position traditionally held by the *animal rationale*."[66] The ground of this revaluation was, of course, the exponential growth in the productivity of labor that came with the onset of the industrial revolution. This unprecedented increase struck both Smith and Marx, leading them to draw a fundamental distinction between "productive" and "unproductive" labor—a distinction Arendt sees as making the characteristically modern identification of labor and work possible.

How does this happen? "It is indeed the mark of all laboring," Arendt writes,

> that it leaves nothing behind, that the result of its effort is almost as quickly consumed as the effort is spent. And yet this effort... is born of a great urgency and motivated by a more powerful drive than anything else, because life itself depends upon it.

However, the distinction between productive and unproductive labor effectively assimilates the durable use objects produced by work to the urgently needed (and invariably short-lived) consumer goods produced by labor. In the modern age, the fleeting "products" of labor are created at an ever-accelerating rate, to the point where they come to be identified with productivity as such. Overwhelmed by the "unprecedented productivity of Western mankind," Marx and the thinkers that followed him had

> an almost irresistible tendency to look upon all labor as work and to speak of the *animal laborans* in terms more fitting for *homo faber*, hoping all the time that only one more step was needed to eliminate labor and necessity altogether.[67]

We tend to take the resulting "equation" of labor with work for granted. This equation makes sense if we—like Marx and the classical political economists he criticized—view "society" as the quasi-organic subject of economic reproduction and growth. As Arendt observes:

> The social viewpoint is identical...with an interpretation that takes nothing into account but the life process of mankind, and within its frame of reference all things become objects of

consumption. Within a completely 'socialized mankind,' whose sole purpose would be the entertaining of the life process—and this is the unfortunately quite unutopian ideal that guides Marx's theories—the distinction between labor and work would have completely disappeared: all work would have become labor because all things would be understood, not in their worldly, objective quality, but as results of living labor power and functions of the life process.[68]

Let us say that Arendt is right about this. What would be so terribly wrong with reducing all work to labor and viewing the use objects produced by work in much the same light as we view the consumer goods produced by labor? The short answer is that it would dissolve the durable or "thing character" of the world by converting the human artifice that stands *between* man and nature into a collection of material inputs which, like other consumer goods, are consumed by the "life process" of society. (The so-called "urban renewal" of the 1960s and 1970s, during which well-established neighborhoods were replaced by interstate highways and soon-to-decay public housing units, demonstrates what happens when this attitude guides alterations to the built environment.) When this happens, there is nothing left to prevent the repetitive rhythms of production and consumption from determining the life of the individual as well as society. Arendt thinks this danger only increases with the automation of the production process:

> The danger of future automation is less the much deplored mechanization and artificialization of natural life than that, its artificiality notwithstanding, all human productivity would be sucked into an enormously intensified life process and would follow automatically, without pain or effort, its ever-recurrent natural cycle. The rhythm of machines would magnify and intensify the natural rhythm of life enormously, but it would not change, only make more deadly, life's chief character with respect to the world, which is to wear down durability.[69]

The human capacity for spontaneous action would be absorbed by these pseudo-natural rhythms, while the public sphere would be shaped in accordance with the economic imperatives of the business cycle or the centrally planned economy. The "life process of society" comes to exercise a tyranny next to which Marx's "fetishism of commodities" looks almost benign.

The allusion to the "fetishism of commodities"—the process by which, according to Marx, "the definite social relation between men" under capitalism assumes "the fantastic form of a relation between things" in the marketplace—highlights an aspect of Arendt's analysis of the distinction between labor and work that readers schooled in Marxist thought will likely find bizarre. This is her insistence on the *positive* role played by reification in endowing not just the products of work, but the "products" of thought and action as well, with a tangible and lasting reality.

> Human life, insofar as it is world-building, is engaged in a constant process of reification, and the degree of worldliness of produced things, which all together form the human artifice, depends upon their greater or lesser permanence in the world itself.[70]

The human artifice is created not just by craftsmen and builders, but by artists, poets, and historians as well—that is, by all who objectify ("reify") and memorialize the words, thoughts, and deeds of others. Taken together, these two types of reification provide humanity with a *home* within which it becomes possible to live a recognizably *human* life. Without this "reified" world, Arendt argues, birth and death would lose their specifically human significance:

> The birth and death of human beings are not simple natural occurrences but are related to a world into which single individuals, unique, unexchangeable, and unrepeatable entities, appear and from which they depart. Birth and death presuppose a world which is not in constant movement, but whose durability and relative permanence makes appearance and disappearance possible, which existed before any one individual appeared into it and will survive his eventual departure. Without a world into which men are born and from which they die, there would be nothing but changeless eternal recurrence, the deathless everlastingness of the human as of all other animal species.[71]

Arendt's reflections on the intensification of the "life process" of society, combined with her conviction that "without a world between
men and nature, there is eternal movement, but no objectivity," underline her fear that life in the modern age is becoming ever more
"naturalized," divested of both its capacity for free action and its
distinctive humanity. The preponderant sense of the "Labor" chapter
is that Marx's "system of labor" contributes to this naturalization,
not just through his glorification of this activity but also through
his overall conception of the labor process as the human species'
"metabolism with nature." Arendt seizes on this locution, the better
to convict Marx of holding a naturalistic, quasi-positivistic view of
the "human animal" in constant interchange with its natural environment through labor:

> When Marx defined labor as 'man's metabolism with nature,'
> in whose process 'nature's material (is) adapted by a change of
> form to the wants of man,' so that 'labor has incorporated itself
> with its subject,' he indicated clearly that he as 'speaking phys-
> iologically' and that labor and consumption are but two stages
> of the ever-recurring cycle of biological life. This cycle needs
> to be sustained through consumption, and the activity which
> provides the means of consumption is laboring. Whatever la-
> bor produces is meant to be fed into the human life process al-
> most immediately, and this consumption, regenerating the life
> process, produces—or rather reproduces—new 'labor power,'
> needed for the further sustenance of the body.[72]

Defenders of Marx would point out that he was less a positivistic
"naturalist" than he was quasi-romantic humanist, one who railed
against the "Manchester system" and the way it turned the individual worker's distinctively human activity—labor—into a prolonged
exercise in alienation and self-denial. Borrowing Hegel's idea of a
self-defining subject (while rejecting his focus on the cultural or
"spiritual" [geistlich] side of things), Marx saw the laborious "metabolism with nature" as the route by which humanity had created
("formed") itself. On the one hand, the development of an increasingly specialized division of labor enabled the species to fully develop
and unfold its talents, knowledge, and capacities. On the other, this

same division of labor forced the vast majority to spend their lives in mind-numbing, effectively animalizing labor. Individual workers were thus alienated from their "species-activity" (self-formative labor), as well as from nature (reduced to simple raw material), their fellow men (who are either competitors on the labor market or exploiters of labor-power), and—finally—their own social being or "species-essence" (*Gattungswesen*). The products of labor loom over them as so many alien powers, condemning them to a lifetime of endless toil and drudgery rather than serving as the means by which they might develop their full range of talents and positively relate themselves to their fellow men.

Marx saw such alienation as a *historical* and not existential phenomenon, one that left open the possibility of *unalienated* labor in the future. "Objectification" need not take the alienating form of the production of commodities for profit and exchange. As Marx wrote in his "Notes on James Mill's *Elements of Political Economy*" (1843):

> Let us suppose that we had produced as human beings. In that event each of us would have *doubly affirmed* himself and his neighbor in his production. (1) In my *production* I would have objectified the *specific character* of my *individuality* and for that reason I would both have enjoyed the *expression* of my own individual life during my activity and also, in contemplating the object I would experience an individual pleasure, I would experience my personality as an *objective, sensuously perceptible* power *beyond all shadow of doubt.* (2) In your use or enjoyment of my product I would have the *immediate* satisfaction and knowledge that in my labor I had gratified a *human* need, i.e., that I had objectified *human nature* and hence had procured an object corresponding to the needs of another *human being.* (3) I would have acted for you as the *mediator* between you and the species, thus I would be acknowledged by you as the complement of your own being, as an essential part of yourself. I would thus know myself to be confirmed both in your thought and your love. (4) In the individual expression of my own life I would have brought about the immediate expression of your life, and so in my individual activity I would have directly *confirmed* and *realized* my authentic nature, my *human, communal* nature.[73]

It is odd that Arendt does not cite this passage, since it points so clearly to the underlying tension running through the entirety of Marx's thought. On the one hand, Marx was aware that man's "metabolism with nature," required for reproduction of both individual and species, was an endless cycle of production and consumption and (in that sense) the least worldly of human activities. It produced not durable products but rather life itself. On the other, not only did Marx think of labor as a process of "objectification" (*Vergegenständlichung*) and as the "supreme world-building capacity of man"; he also thought of it as the privileged vehicle for human interaction, the forming of moral relationships, and the self-actualization of the individual.[74] The freedom of the "free association of producers" prophesied in this passage as well as The German Ideology therefore hinges, crucially, on humanity making a technologically aided leap from the "realm of necessity" (in which the form of labor is determined by the imperatives of subsistence and commodity production) to the "realm of freedom." As Marx wrote in a famous passage from Vol. 3 of *Capital*:

> In fact, the realm of freedom actually begins only where labor which is determined by necessity and mundane considerations ceases; thus in the very nature of things it lies beyond the sphere of actual material production...Freedom in this field can only consist in socialized man, the associated producers, rationally regulating their interchange with Nature; and achieving this with the least expenditure of energy and under conditions most favorable to, and worthy of, their human nature. But it nonetheless still remains a realm of necessity. Beyond it begins that development of human energy which is an end in itself, the true realm of freedom, which, however, can blossom forth only with the realm of necessity as its basis.[75]

Here, we encounter what Arendt describes as the "flagrant contradiction" at the center of Marx's thought. This is his vision of a society of emancipated laborers who are, ultimately, to be emancipated from their "distinctively human activity"—labor—as well. "Only when labor is abolished can the 'realm of freedom' [finally] supplant the 'realm of necessity.'"[76] In true Hegelian fashion, labor's increasing productivity and inherent fertility would enable it to overcome and transcend itself:

> The true meaning of labor's newly discovered productivity [in the modern age] becomes manifest only in Marx's work, where it rests on the equation of productivity with fertility, so that the famous development of mankind's 'productive forces' into a society of an abundance of 'good things' actually obeys no other law and is subject to no other necessity that the aboriginal command, 'Be ye fruitful and multiply,' in which it is as though the voice of nature herself speaks to us…Marx's consistent naturalism discovered 'labor power' as the specifically human mode of the life force which is as capable of creating a 'surplus' as nature herself. Since he was almost exclusively interested in this life process itself…the question of a separate existence of worldly things, whose durability will survive and withstand the devouring processes of life, does not occur to him at all.[77]

Arendt's underlying claim is that Marx's "realm of freedom," made possible through the industrial-technological unleashing of the fertility inherent in human labor-power, is actually not a society of *producers* at all. It is, rather, a society of *consumers* who—once liberated from the drudgery of manual labor and an inflexible division of labor—have the leisure time to pursue a wide range of activities (hunting in the morning, fishing in the afternoon, etc.).[78] The "polis without slaves" is realized, but only ironically. Not only has its *rasion d'être* (the provision of a public stage for the "sharing of words and deeds" by citizens) been removed, so has all concern with the *institutionalization of freedom.* The latter, of course, is a—if not the—central concern of political theory and the primary question addressed by virtually all constitutional theory.

"Transcending" the political sphere altogether, Marx's theory thus leaves us, according to Arendt, with a vision of happiness centered on vastly expanded leisure time and potentially unlimited opportunities for consumption. Arendt is notably dismissive of what she calls the hope that "inspired Marx and the best men of the various workers' movements," namely, the hope that free time and the liberation of the working class from the drudgery of labor would result in the pursuit of other, "higher" activities:

> A hundred years after Marx we know the fallacy of this reasoning; the spare time of the *animal laborans* is never spent in anything but consumption, and the more time left to him, the greedier and more craving his appetites.[79]

Anyone who thinks Arendt's criticism of Marx is on point but, after the collapse of the Soviet bloc, moot, has clearly missed her meaning. Marx's theory is the "theory of the modern age" and not simply because he exemplifies the modern conflation of labor with work, or because he traces labor's value-creating power back to a nature-like fertility in human labor-power itself. Rather, Marx's theory deserves this title because he, more than any of his contemporaries, so clearly limned the horizon of the "laboring society" created by the Industrial Revolution and the emancipation of the working class, articulating (albeit uncritically) both its naturalistic/naturalizing presuppositions and the idea of happiness animating it.

It is important to emphasize here that *both* capitalism and socialism produce societies organized around the priority of the "life process," the productivity of labor, and the mentality characteristic of the *animal laborans*. They both strive toward the same goal: abundance and a "realm of freedom" defined almost entirely in terms of leisure and consumption.[80] The "specter" of a consumer's society is not the antithesis of Marx's vision but, in many respects, the only plausible outcome of his—and our—desire to dignify labor while nevertheless seeking to escape from it. If, as Marx thought (and many think today), automation will soon provide an escape from the "curse" of labor altogether, then we might well witness the creation of what Arendt calls a "true consumers' society." This is a society in which "painless consumption," once the privileged preserve of a parasitic elite, could become the primary activity of the majority. As Arendt writes:

> The specter of a true consumers' society is more alarming as an ideal of present-day society than as an already existing reality. The ideal is not new; it was clearly indicated in the unquestioned

assumption of classical political economy that the ultimate goal of the *vita activa* is growing wealth, abundance, and the "happiness of the greatest number.' And what else, finally, is this ideal of modern society but the age-old dream of the poor and destitute, which can have a charm of its own so long as it is a dream, but turns into a fool's paradise as soon as it is realized…

[Already] the universal demand for happiness and the widespread unhappiness in our society (…) are among the most persuasive signs that we have begun to live in a labor society which lacks enough laboring to keep it contented.[81]

The recent rise of artificial intelligence and the unnerving approach of what some have called a "world without work" reveals Arendt's prescience in this regard.

Summary

The Human Condition is Arendt's most theoretically ambitious and philosophically deep work. It had its origins in a study of Karl Marx's thought that Arendt had proposed as a follow-up to OT. She never published the Marx book, and much of its material found its way into THC. The gap between Arendt's approach in OT (leaning heavily on history and political science) and the one she utilized in THC (most often viewed as a contribution to philosophical anthropology) is large. Larger still, apparently, is the gap between her analysis of radical political evil in OT and her celebration of political action and the *bios politikos* in THC. Yet, this second gap is only seeming. In fact, OT presented totalitarian domination as a form of anti-politics, one predicated on the suppression not just of political opposition, but human plurality and diversity. THC followed this analysis up with a more philosophical (phenomenological) exploration of the nature of the public realm, the constitutive role of human plurality in all authentically political relationships, and the gradual effacement of the political by what Arendt calls "the rise of the social" in the modern age.

Arendt's Gaus Lectures on "Karl Marx and the Great Tradition" are the linchpin for understanding how what was originally intended as a study of the "proto-totalitarian elements" in Marx's thought evolved into a study of Marx's relationship to the "great tradition" of

Western political philosophy that began with Plato and Aristotle. In the lectures, Arendt stresses the fact that Marx, standing on the other side of the abyss created by the event of totalitarian domination in Europe, was far more a creature of that tradition than its destroyer (as some have claimed). She zeros in on what she calls Marx's "glorification of labor" as the key to understanding his project of creating a "polis without slaves," but also without the political activities of debate, deliberation, and decision that constituted political life for the ancient Greeks.

The lectures thus set the stage for THC, providing as they do a sketch of what authentically political relationships looked like (with the *polis* as model), an analysis of Plato and Aristotle's criticisms of the democratic politics of no-rule (*isonomia*), and—finally—Marx's abortive attempt to fuse *human* (rather than political) equality with freedom in a classless utopia from which the need for *action* had been expunged, rendered superfluous by the final overcoming of class conflict. It remained for THC to parse more explicitly what Arendt meant by "the public realm," how it was threatened by the advent of early capitalism (the "rise of the social"), and how Marx's "glorification of labor" effectively inverted the traditional hierarchy of the *vita activa*, placing what had been deemed the lowest form of human activity—the labor required for the material and biological reproduction of the species—at the top, while radically devaluing *action*, the sharing of words and deeds in the public realm.

Notes

1   See Margaret Canovan, *Hannah Arendt: A Reinterpretation of Her Political Thought* (Cambridge: Cambridge University Press, 1992), p. 7.
2   Arendt, THC, p. 5.
3   Hannah Arendt, *Thinking Without a Bannister: Essays in Understanding, 1953–1975*, edited by Jerome Kohn (New York: Schocken Books, 2008), p. 12. Hereafter cited as TWB.
4   Arendt, TWB, p. 13.
5   Arendt, TWB, p. 14.
6   Arendt, TWB, p. 14.
7   Arendt, TWB, p. 15.
8   Arendt, TWB, p. 16.
9   Arendt, TWB, p. 18.
10 Arendt, TWB, p. 18.
11 Arendt, TWB, p. 20.

12 Arendt, *TWB*, p. 20.
13 Arendt, *TWB*, p. 23.
14 Arendt, *TWB*, p. 24 (my emphasis).
15 Arendt, *TWB*, p. 24 (my emphasis).
16 Arendt, *TWB*, p. 25.
17 Arendt, *TWB*, p. 25.
18 Arendt, *TWB*, p. 26.
19 Arendt, *TWB*, pp. 29–30.
20 Arendt, *TWB*, p. 27
21 Arendt, *TWB*, pp. 26–27.
22 See Carl Schmitt, *The Concept of the Political*, translated by George Schwab (Chicago: University of Chicago Press, 1996).
23 Arendt, *TWB*, p. 28.
24 See Karl Marx, "On the Jewish Question" in Marx, *Writing of the Young Marx on Philosophy and Society*, edited and translated by Lloyd D. Easton and Kurt H. Guddat (Indianapolis: Hackett Publishing Company), pp. 216–248.
25 Arendt, *TWB*, p. 28.
26 Arendt, *THC*, p. 40.
27 Arendt, *TWB*, pp. 36–37.
28 Arendt, *TWB*, p. 38.
29 Arendt, *TWB*, p. 39.
30 Arendt, *THC*, p. 45.
31 Hanna Pitkin, *The Attack of the Blob: Hannah Arendt's Concept of the Social* (Chicago: University of Chicago Press, 1998).
32 Arendt, *THC*, p. 30.
33 Arendt, *THC*, p. 31.
34 Arendt, *THC*, p. 32.
35 Arendt, *THC*, p. 32.
36 Arendt, *THC*, p. 31.
37 Arendt, "What Is Freedom?" in *BPF*, pp. 142–144.
38 Arendt, *THC*, p. 7.
39 Arendt, *THC*, p. 57.
40 Arendt, *THC*, p. 58.
41 Nancy Fraser, "Rethinking the Public Sphere" in *Habermas and the Public Sphere*, edited by Craig C. Calhoun (Cambridge: MIT Press, 1992), pp. 109–142.
42 The locus classicus is Marx's "On the Jewish Question." For a contemporary restatement of this perspective, see Iris Marion Young's *Justice and the Politics of Difference* (Princeton: Princeton University Press, 2011).
43 Hannah Arendt, "Socrates," in Arendt, *The Promise of Politics*, edited by Jerome Kohn (New York: Schocken Books, 2004), pp. 16–17.
44 Arendt, *THC*, p. 41.
45 Arendt, *THC*, p. 33.
46 Arendt, *THC*, p. 46.
47 Arendt, *THC*, p. 45.
48 Arendt, *THC*, p. 40.
49 Arendt, *THC*, p. 40.
50 Arendt, *THC*, p. 46.

51 Arendt, THC, p. 10.
52 Arendt, THC, p. 7.
53 Arendt, THC, p. 11.
54 Arendt, THC, p. 9.
55 See the discussion in my *Arendt and Heidegger: The Fate of the Political* (Princeton: Princeton University Press, 1996), chapter 4.
56 Arendt, THC, p. 6.
57 See David Wallace-Wells, *The Uninhabitable Earth: Life After Global Warming* (New York: Crown Publishing Group, 2019).
58 Arendt, THC, p. 5.
59 Mill, *On Liberty*, p. 122.
60 Hannah Arendt, "On Hannah Arendt" in *Hannah Arendt: The Recovery of the Public World*, edited by Melvyn Hill (New York: St. Martin's Press, 1979), p. 316.
61 Arendt, "On Hannah Arendt" in Hill, ed., p. 318.
62 Karl Marx and Friedrich Engels, *The Communist Manifesto* (New York: Verso, 1998), p. 41.
63 Plato, *The Republic*, 501a.
64 Arendt, THC, p. 80.
65 Arendt, THC, p. 85.
66 Arendt, THC, p. 85.
67 Arendt, THC, p. 87.
68 Arendt, THC, p. 89.
69 Arendt, THC, 132.
70 Arendt, THC, p. 96.
71 Arendt, THC, pp. 96–97.
72 Arendt, THC, pp. 98–99.
73 Karl Marx, *Excerpts from James Mill's* "Elements of Political Economy" in Karl Marx, *Early Writings* (London: Penguin, 1992), pp. 277–278.
74 Arendt, THC, pp. 98–99, 101.
75 Karl Marx, *Capital*, v. 3, in *The Marx-Engels Reader*, edited by Robert C. Tucker (New York: W. W. Norton and Company, 1978), p. 441.
76 Arendt, THC, p. 104
77 Arendt, THC, pp. 106 and 108.
78 Marx, "The German Ideology" in *Writings of the Young Marx on Philosophy and Society*, pp. 424–425.
79 Arendt, THC, p. 133.
80 Khrushchev's famous "we will bury you" speech referred not to nuclear annihilation, but greater economic productivity.
81 Arendt, THC, pp. 133–134.

Further reading

G. Kateb, *Hannah Arendt: Politics, Conscience, Evil* (Totowa: Rowman & Allanheld, 1984).
H. F. Pitkin, *The Attack of the Blob: Hannah Arendt's Concept of the Social* (Chicago: University of Chicago Press, 1998).

Four

Work, action, and the modern age

I Work and the human artifice

Arendt's chapter on "Work" in THC is something of an intermezzo between her chapters on labor and action. Nevertheless, the chapter plays an essential role—not just because it sheds more light on her distinction between labor and fabrication *qua* activities, but also because it clarifies what she means when she refers to the *worldlessness* of the "laboring animal," which she contrasts with the *worldliness* of man the fabricator or "builder" and man the political actor. Perhaps most importantly, it sketches Arendt's understanding of how the "human artifice" provides a stable framework for, and essential backdrop to, the meaning-creative power of words and deeds.

We have already seen some of the basic contrasts Arendt makes between the activities of labor and work. Whereas labor is governed by natural necessity, which compels it to churn out *consumer goods* in never-ending cycles of production and consumption, work creates *use objects*—durable things that, taken together, form the artificial world that stands between us and nature. In contrast to the ideals of the *animal laborans* (leisure, rest, and painless consumption), the ideals of *homo faber*—the "fabricator of the world"—are durability, permanence, and stability.[1]

Of course, sustained use can wear even the most seemingly "permanent" of human artifacts down, ultimately requiring their replacement. As with all things human, "permanence" is a relative term. The essential point is that a given historical-cultural "world" of things lasts for generations, whereas consumer goods are destined to quickly disappear in the "life process." It is this trans-generational lastingness that enables the constituent items of the human artifice to stand apart from nature *and* from the specific individuals who produced them. This independence, in turn, is what makes it possible for the man-made world to provide a "home for mortal men." As Arendt writes,

> the things of the world have the function of stabilizing human life, and their objectivity lies in the fact that…men, their ever-changing nature notwithstanding, can retrieve their sameness, that is, their identity, by being related to the same chair and the same table.[2]

Without this world composed of relatively permanent things, we would find ourselves exposed to the "sublime indifference" of nature directly, subject to an "overwhelming elementary force" that would compel us to "swing relentlessly in the circle of [our] own biological movement."[3]

Even with the protection afforded by the relatively permanent world of things created by *homo faber*, man as *animal laborans* is caught in the "cyclical movement of the body's life process" and so subject to necessity.[4] And though he may enlist tamed animals in the endless process of nourishing human life, he remains forever the "servant of nature." Nothing could be less true of the attitude and activity characteristic of *homo faber*, who regards nature as little more than the supplier of the raw material required for his various projects. Indeed, the material needed to make or build something "is already a product of human hands which have removed it from its natural location." Such removal is invariably *violent*: we must kill the life process of a tree if we require wood, and we must violently interrupt "one of nature's slower processes" in order for iron, stone, or marble to be "torn out of the womb of the earth." The element of violence and violation is thus "present in all fabrication," and *homo faber*, the "creator of the human artifice," has always been "a destroyer of nature."[5] Far from being the servant of nature, *homo faber* regards himself as its lord and master.

This points to another decisive difference between the activities of labor and work or fabrication. Whereas labor—the maintenance of the life process—is endless and cyclical in nature, the activity of fabrication always has a definite beginning and an equally definite end. The end is the creation of a specific product: a table, a chair, a building. The beginning is a preconception or "model" of the object or entity to be produced. Guiding the actual step-by-step process of fabrication, the model may be either physical (a blueprint) or merely mental (an idea) in character. It is important to note that the model pre-exists the actual work process and is, so to speak, "outside" the fabricator. "Alone with his image of the future product," homo faber is, according to Arendt, "free to produce, and again facing alone the work of his hands, he is free to destroy."[6] Homo faber chooses his model, material, and tools; he decides when to start his work and when the product he desired to create is finished. The animal laborans knows no such freedom.

From the standpoint of homo faber, the production process is nothing more than the means by which to accomplish the predesignated end: the creation of a concrete product that adequately corresponds to or embodies its ideal model. This is not to say that the model disappears at the end of the production process. On the contrary.

> It is of great importance to the role fabrication came to play within the hierarchy of the vita activa that the image or model whose shape guides the fabrication process not only precedes it but does not disappear with the finished product, which it survives intact.[7]

It is this fact, Arendt believes, that provided the backdrop for Plato's theory of ideas, as well as his reinterpretation of political action as a form of making or fabrication. In Arendt's view, this reinterpretation became—for reasons I discuss in the next section—virtually canonical for the Western tradition of political theory and philosophy.

The crucial point in the present context is that the categories of means and ends "entirely determine" the process of making as such. "The fabricated thing is an end product in the twofold sense that the production process comes to an end in it (...) and that it [the process] is only a means to produce this end."[8] The same cannot be said of labor. The "end" of labor comes only with its exhaustion, and the "products" it creates are immediately fed back into the laborer's life process. Such consumables are less "means" by which a specific and limited end is procured than the cyclically necessary inputs required to sustain the reproduction of labor and labor-power. Within the life process itself

> it is idle to ask questions that presuppose the category of means and end, such as whether men live and consume in order to have strength to labor or whether they labor in order to have the means of consumption.

The cyclical and repetitive rhythm of the labor process blurs the distinction between means and end, to the point where it becomes impossible for the *animal laborans* to clearly distinguish between the two:

> If we consider this loss of the faculty to distinguish clearly between means and ends in terms of human behavior, we can say that the free disposition and use of tools for a specific end product is replaced by the rhythmic unification of the laboring body with its implement, the movement of laboring itself acting as the unifying force...What dominates the labor process and all work processes which are performed in the mode of laboring is neither man's purposeful effort nor the product he may desire, *but the motion of the process itself and the rhythm it imposes upon the laborers....* The point is that nothing can be mechanized more easily and less artificially than the rhythm of the labor process, which in turn corresponds to the equally automatic repetitive rhythm of the life process and its metabolism with nature.[9]

Mechanization accelerates and intensifies the rhythm of the life process, to the point where industrial automation begins to mirror what Arendt describes as the "automatism" of natural processes. The latter are self-moving, in no way dependent upon any agent or agency to start them going or to direct them to their ostensible end (they have none). The "things of nature" (e.g. a tree) are inseparable from the developmental sequences that bring them into being, and these are constantly repeating themselves in a cyclical, never-ending motion. When it comes to natural processes, then, the categories of *homo faber* and his world—purpose, instrumentality, means and ends, etc.—simply do not apply. The point here is that the automation of the human life process similarly effaces the (previously clear) distinction between the production process and the product itself:

> As matters stand today, it has become as senseless to describe this [automatized] world of machines in terms of means and ends as it has always been senseless to ask nature if she produced the seed to produce a tree or the tree to produce the seed.[10]

At this point, Arendt makes a startling claim, challenging the grounding assumption of both Marx's analysis of commodity fetishism and Max Weber's parallel analysis of the bureaucratization of the world.[11] For both Marx and Weber, the late modern age is characterized by the fact that instruments created by man to increase his power and agency (such as machine technology and the "human machine" of bureaucracy) come to take on a life of their own, subjecting their ostensible "masters" to the imperatives of capitalist accumulation and bureaucratic rationality. For Marx, a key goal of the overthrow of capitalism was the restoration of man to his rightful place as master of, rather than slave to, the machine economy. For Weber, the hypertrophy of bureaucracy meant that state take-over of the economy had to be avoided at all costs, lest citizens of industrialized nations be reduced to the status of "the *fellahs* of ancient Egypt."[12]

For Arendt, this reversal of ends and means is less troubling than the mechanization of the life process, which effaces the very distinction between them. From her perspective,

> the question…is not so much whether we are the masters or the slaves of our machines, but whether machines still serve the world and its things, or if, on the contrary, they and the automatic motion of their processes have begun to rule and even destroy world and things.[13]

As my summary indicates, she thought that the "rise of the social" and automation clearly promoted the latter possibility, reducing all that is worldly, durable, and relatively permanent to the level of consumer goods to be fed into the life process. Writing in 1958, when the promise of industrial development and technological advance seemed almost unlimited (and entirely benign), she sounded a cautionary note. She does not offer a blanket denunciation of the "evils of technology," but rather a philosophical account of its existential ramifications in the late modern world:

> For a society of laborers, the world of machines has become a substitute for the real world, even though this pseudo world cannot fulfill the most important task of the human artifice, which is to offer mortals a dwelling place more permanent and stable than themselves….the natural processes on which it [the world of machines] feeds increasingly relate to the biological process itself, so that the apparatuses we once handled freely begin to look as though they were "shells belonging to the human body as the shell belongs to the body of a turtle." Seen from the vantage point of this development, technology in fact no longer appears "as the product of a conscious human effort to enlarge material power, but rather like a biological development of mankind in which the innate structures of the human organism are transplanted in an ever-increasing measure into the environment of man."[14]

In recent times, the evolutionary view of the relation between humanity and technology referred to in the passage above has been shorn of its more ominous overtones and become an article of faith among technophiles. We are repeatedly told that technology, in the form of artificial intelligence and genetic engineering, is in the process of speeding up the evolution of the human species. A brave new world of human-machine hybrids, equipped with longer lifespans and enhanced intelligence, awaits. Whether one regards this prospect with hope or horror, the possibility of "permanent revolution" in the field of biotechnology clearly bodes ill for the future durability of the human artifice.

****

Such possibilities, however, lie in the future. In the last sections of her chapter on work, Arendt focuses neither on the present nor the future, but on the historical high-water mark of the instrumental-utilitarian worldview associated with *homo faber*. In order to create durable artifacts—in order to create the human artifice—*homo faber* must first create and use tools. It is from his use of tools that "the most fundamental experience of instrumentality arises." This experience determines all work and fabrication, so that within the "world of work," it is "indeed true that the end justifies the means." The end does more than that: it creates and organizes the means themselves. Thus,

> the end justifies the violence done to nature to win the material, as the wood justifies killing the tree and the table justifies destroying the wood. Because of the end product, tools are designed and implements invented...During the work process, everything is judged in terms of suitability and usefulness for the desired end, and nothing else.[15]

Confined to the sphere of fabrication, the hegemony of the standards of suitability and usefulness are not a problem. This hegemony is to be expected, arising as it does out of the concrete experience of fabrication and the use of tools. A potential problem arises, however, when the craftsman's focus on utility *within* the production process becomes the standard for judging things outside or beyond it. A curious property then begins to reveal itself:

> The trouble with the utility standard inherent in the very activity of fabrication is that the relationship between means and end on which it relies is very much like a chain whose every end can serve again as a means in some other context. In other words, in a strictly utilitarian world, all ends are bound to be of short duration and to be transformed into means for some further end.[16]

Why does this pose a problem? Essentially, Arendt argues, because

> the ideal of usefulness permeating a society of craftsmen—like the ideal of comfort in a society of laborers or the ideal of acquisition ruling commercial societies—is actually no longer a matter of utility but of meaning. It is 'for the sake of' usefulness in general that *homo faber* judges and does everything in terms of 'in order to.'[17]

Arendt's thesis in the second half of the "Work" chapter is that—
thanks to the dramatic growth of production and trade in the late
eighteenth and early nineteenth centuries—*homo faber's* characteristic
attitude toward the world and the things was universalized, transformed not just into a philosophy (utilitarianism) but also a hegemonic worldview. One standard, one criterion—utility—rose above
and displaced all others.

The dominance of utilitarianism *qua* worldview meant that every
particular and limited end would now be evaluated with an eye toward its relative utility for the achievement of some larger (yet to be
defined) end, which end itself would be similarly evaluated. In this
way, "utility established as meaning generates meaninglessness." The
infinite regress suggested by any fully consistent utilitarianism can
be checked only when we designate someone or something an "end
in itself." It was this regress that Lessing thematized when he asked
"and what is the use of use?" and that Kant sought to put a halt to
when he insisted that Man was an "end in himself" and therefore
should never be treated as a "mere means."

Arendt is at pains to point out that the problem is not instrumentality per se, nor the means/end category. Within the domain of the
fabrication experience, an instrumentalizing attitude and the consistent deployment of the means/end category are both inescapable
and perfectly legitimate. What *is* a problem is "the generalization of
the fabrication experience in which usefulness and utility are established as the ultimate standards for life and the world of men."
An anthropocentric utilitarianism in which Man is "the measure of
all things" cannot but degrade the world and the things in it to the
status of mere means:

> The instrumentalization of the whole world and the earth,
> this limitless devaluation of everything given, this process of
> growing meaninglessness where every end is transformed into
> a means and which can be stopped only by making man him-
> self the lord and master of all things, does not directly arise out
> of the fabrication process; for from the viewpoint of fabrication
> the finished product is as much an end in itself, an independ-
> ent durable entity with an existence of its own, as man is an
> end in himself in Kant's political philosophy. Only in so far as

fabrication chiefly fabricates use objects does the finished product again become a means, and only in so far as the life process takes hold of things and uses them for its purposes does the productive and limited instrumentality of fabrication change into the limitless instrumentalization of everything that exists.[18]

The last sentence of this passage is crucial if we wish to understand the reasoning behind Arendt's analysis. The "instrumentalization of the whole world and earth"—the treatment of the human artifice and the planet earth itself as mere means—comes about when an emergent utilitarianism intersects with the "rise of the social" and the channeling of society's life process into the public sphere. This occurs at a moment in European history—the latter half of the eighteenth century—when population growth, new methods in agriculture and industry, and an increasing identification of economic with political power led to economic expansion and the acceleration of man's "metabolism with nature."

At the start of this process, the mentality of *homo faber* is ascendant and the public realm largely takes the form of the "exchange market." Individual producers leave the isolation of their respective workshops to appear in public, display their wares, and receive the esteem owed to expert practitioners of their craft. It is in the public exchange market of the early modern age that *homo faber* enters into relationships with others, specifically through the buying and selling of products. Unlike the *animal laborans*, then, *homo faber* is "fully capable of having a public realm of his own, even though it may not be a political realm, properly speaking."[19] With the mechanization of production in the Industrial Revolution, however, individual craftsmen are replaced by ever-larger teams of laborers, each performing narrower and narrower tasks requiring little or no expertise, for hours on end. Absorbed by physical effort and the needs of his body, the "worldless and herd-like" *animal laborans* is, according to Arendt, "incapable of building or inhabiting a public, worldly realm."[20] It is for this reason that Arendt somewhat jarringly refers to the exchange market of the early modern age as the "last public realm"—i.e. the last place where independent producers/citizens came together in public as a regular part of their daily lives. With the advent of factory labor, there was neither the need nor the time for producers to appear in public. The temporary isolation of the workshop gave way to the permanent isolation of the *animal laborans* trapped in the cycle of production and consumption.

II Action, meaning, and tangible freedom

Arendt's chapter on action has long been considered the heart of THC. In the 1960s, it inspired participants in the civil rights and antiwar movements. Since then, it has proved an enormously fertile ground for scholars, students, and—last but by no means least— critics of her thought. It is easy to see why. The "Action" chapter presents what many critics have termed Arendt's "Greek" theory of political action, a theory that apparently privileges the heroic, agonistic, and "dramaturgical" aspects of political action over its ethical, solidaristic, and deliberative dimensions.

While this characterization is a distortion, it is (as we shall see) not entirely without basis. Arendt's description of the public realm as a "space of appearances" indicates the presence of a certain theatrical element in her overall conception of political action. The primary reason for this is that she sees authentic political action as, first and foremost, the expression of a tangible or *public* freedom. Such political action is manifest in the words and deeds of diverse equals who, motivated by some matter of common concern, take leave of the private sphere and enter the "bright light of the public." Here they "act in concert" in order to initiate some change in the realm of human affairs. Whether they are *successful* in effecting this change is, to a certain extent, beside the point. The important thing is that these individuals break with the routines of everyday life and bravely display their capacity for spontaneous initiation and joint action. In other words, it is the *performance* of political *actors* on a public *stage* that is the most tangible expression of our distinctively human freedom. It is hardly by chance that Arendt invokes the "virtuosity" of memorable political actors, or that she reminds us of the "close relationship" between politics and the performing arts.[21]

If we view political action from this angle—from the standpoint of its *performance*—we see that it has an inherent (and not merely instrumental) meaning or value. This may seem counterintuitive, especially given our ingrained habit of thinking about political action almost entirely in terms of means and ends. It becomes decidedly less counterintuitive, however, when we stop to consider how often the defeated cause in a protest, rebellion, or revolution is the one that elicits our respect and admiration. It is precisely because the individuals involved in such episodes are willing to defy the odds and take action, sacrificing their private interests for the sake of the "public thing," that their words and deeds become worthy of re-membrance and memorialization. Thus, in *On Revolution*, Arendt cites the Paris Commune, the Russian Revolution of 1905, the revolutions in Germany in 1918–1919, and the Hungarian uprising against the Russians in 1956 as examples of "defeated causes" that heroically express the human capacity for spontaneous action against the odds.

In each of these instances, the political actors in question were ordinary people—workers, soldiers, citizens—who fought for their freedom and for the creation of a new (republican) form of gov-ernment. However, the paradigmatic political actors in THC are markedly different: they are the action and politics-hungry citizens praised by Pericles in his famous Funeral Oration. These citizens—the male heads of Athenian households—come together in order to debate, deliberate, and decide upon all important public action, legislation, and judgment. They view their equality as essentially po-litical in character and regard care for the polis and its "space of free-dom" as their highest calling. In the words of Pericles, "we do not say a man who takes no interest in politics is a man who minds his own business; we say rather that he has no business here at all."[22] Yet, compared to the heroic rebels of *On Revolution*, Pericles' Athenians are far less likely to elicit our admiration. After all, the leisure necessary for the pursuit of their political calling depended upon the coerced labor of slaves, women, and children in the household sphere.

As her Gaus lectures indicate, Arendt was hardly blind to the dom-ination that made the "beautiful freedom" of the Greeks possible. Indeed, as we have seen, she highlighted it. Nevertheless, she would defend her idealization of the Athenians in THC by reminding her readers that the Greeks invented not only *politics* but also *democracy*. The study of their political attitudes and practices enables us to see how the distinctive characteristics of *authentic* politics—civic equality; the expression of plurality; the activities of popular debate, deliberation, and decision—are also those of any democracy worthy of the name.

A central leitmotif of the "Action" chapter is how philosophers like Plato and Aristotle were not just critics of democracy but of politics, at least as it was understood by the Greeks. For the Greeks, politics demanded the presence of civic equality (a citizen body rather than a ruler and his subjects) and a commitment to the medium of persuasive speech (as opposed to appeals to the authority of God or Nature).

However predisposed we might be to accept Arendt's view that democracy and "the political" dovetail, most of us would probably agree with Benjamin Constant's judgment that modern representative democracy, predicated upon the defense of individual rights and liberties, is superior to a direct democracy of the Greek type.[23] And, from a moral point of view at least, there seems to be little contest between the two. It took a long time, but modern representative democracy did abolish slavery and, in the name of individual rights and liberties, ultimately gave women the same political and civil rights as men while doing away with such typically Greek practices as civic banishment. Yet, while the moral superiority of modern representative democracy is patent, politically speaking things are much less clear. It is this fact that Arendt wants to highlight in her chapter on "Action" and in THC overall.

In this section, I begin by discussing what Arendt considers to be the key phenomenological characteristics of political action. The emphasis here is on action's public, initiatory, and revelatory or disclosive dimensions. Unlike labor (which she viewed as endlessly repetitive and determined by nature) and unlike work (which she saw as governed by instrumentality), action has, according to Arendt, an overlooked but indisputable meaning-creative capacity. Not only do the individual actor's words and deeds reveal his or her unique (public) identity; they simultaneously contribute to the creation of what Arendt describes as a "subjective" web of meaningful relationships and enacted stories. It is this web that overlays and endows with meaning the "objective" world of things comprising the human artifice.

I turn next to consider the "frailty" Arendt sees as built into political action and the realm of human affairs generally. This frailty is manifest in action's "inherent unpredictability" as well as in what Arendt refers to as the "futility, boundlessness, and uncertainty of outcome" that accompanies all action. Action is *unpredictable* because it grows out of the human capacity to spontaneously interrupt the largely automatic behaviors that characterize daily life. It is *boundless* because the ripple effects of any action in a given constellation are potentially unlimited. It is *uncertain of outcome* and often *futile* because—as *political* action—it occurs in a public context that is defined by, and unthinkable apart from, the presence of other actors. The boundlessness and unpredictability of *their* actions create a broad range of unforeseeable consequences, making the attainment of the political actor's original goal uncertain and even unlikely. Since political action "rarely, if ever, achieves its goal," it is difficult to escape its apparent futility.[24]

Arendt saw the Greek polis as creating a context that limited and compensated for the inherent frailty of action. By providing an institutionally articulated space for political action and for the remembrance of words and deeds, the polis supplied a partial remedy for the lack of control and the "futility" experienced by all who act in a plurality-defined context. Elite critics of Athenian democracy such as Plato and Aristotle saw matters in a quite different light. In their view, the democratic polis exacerbated the problem of action's futility, largely because it accommodated human plurality when it should have curtailed it. Hence, their attempt to convince their fellow citizens to think politics in terms of a set of metaphors imported from the field of fabrication. In the fabrication process, the craftsman—the possessor of specialized skills and expert knowledge—remains in control from beginning to end, a veritable "sovereign." The price of such control in the political realm was, of course, the re-introduction of the ruler/ ruled distinction and the coercive treatment of the citizen body by a philosophic or aristocratic ruling elite ostensibly "expert" in the domains of virtue and politics.

Arendt argues that Plato and Aristotle, through the sheer force of philosophic conceptualization, managed to make their "substitution of making for acting" canonical for the Western tradition of political thought. As we will see below, the result was the *effacement* of the essential phenomenal characteristics of political action; the *bracketing* of its most important constitutive condition (human plurality); and the *destruction* of its most tangible and essential creation (the non-sovereign civic freedom of the public realm). In short, Arendt sees the Platonic-Aristotelian substitution of making for acting—a substitution driven by the desire for sovereignty and control—as responsible for the anti-political and anti-democratic bias of much if not all of Western political theory.[25]

****

At the beginning of her chapter on "Action," Arendt writes that "human plurality, the basic condition of both action and speech, has the twofold character of equality and distinction":

> If men were not equal, they could neither understand each other and those who came before them nor plan for the future and foresee the needs of those who will come after them. If men were not distinct, each human being distinguished from any other who is, was, or will ever be, they would need neither speech nor action to make themselves understood. Signs and sounds to communicate immediate, identical needs and wants would be enough.[26]

At first glance, this passage seems to be claiming that human plurality, "the condition of both action and speech," is a kind of natural fact from which one can derive the normatively robust notions of "equality" and "distinction." Yet it is a grave error to read Arendt in this fashion. She is not arguing that, simply due to the fact of human plurality, we can rest assured that "all men are created equal" and that we are all "by nature" unique individuals. As individual instances of the human species, each of us possesses a "distinctness," to be sure, but this is a quality shared "with everything that is."[27] The specifically *human* form of distinctness (what Arendt calls "unique distinctness") exists only insofar as it is expressed in speech and action—i.e. only insofar as there is a *public world* in which matters that transcend "immediate, identical needs and wants" (for food, water, shelter, sex, etc.) can be discussed and acted upon. Individual members of the human species possess the *potential* for unique distinctness, but there is no God or nature-given guarantee that this potential will be actualized or expressed.

Arendt's very next paragraph makes this perfectly clear. It cannot help but be shocking to those of us who have been brought up in a culture that regards *natural* equality as the ground of rights and political equality, and which also insists upon the inherent "uniqueness" of the individual no matter how conformist in belief or behavior that individual might actually be:

> Speech and action reveal this unique [human] distinctness. Through them, men distinguish themselves instead of being merely distinct; they are the modes in which human beings appear to each other, not indeed as physical objects, but *qua* men. This appearance, as distinguished from mere bodily existence, rests on initiative, but it is an initiative from which no human can refrain and still be human. This is true of no other activity within the *vita activa*. Men can very well live without laboring, they can force others to labor for them, and they can very well decide merely to enjoy the things of the world without themselves adding a single useful object to it; the life of an exploiter or slaveholder may be unjust, but they are certainly human. *A life without speech and without action*, on the other hand…is literally dead to the world; *it has ceased to be a human life because it is no longer lived among men.*[28]

As "laboring animal" man is absorbed by the bodily effort required to fulfill his immediate needs. This bodily absorption renders him effectively worldless, one member of the "animal species mankind" amongst others. As *homo faber*, he is isolated from his fellow men, at least as long as he is fully engaged in the fabrication process. It is only through action and speech that he appears before an audience of peers, attains a "unique distinctness" or identity, and becomes fully human. Through action and speech, we transcend the demands of the body and the isolation of work and come to "insert ourselves into a human world."

Unlike labor, this insertion is "not forced upon us by necessity." And, unlike work, it is not "prompted by utility."[29] It rests on the *initiative* of the individual who, for one reason or another, is prompted to risk action, to begin or say something unpredictable and unexpected. As we have seen, it is this capacity to spontaneously begin that Arendt thinks distinguishes human beings from animals (who are determined by need, instinct, and environment). Arendt dubs this human capacity for spontaneous initiation "natality," arguing that it is through initiatory action or speech that the individual brings about his or her "second birth." We should therefore view such action and speech not so much as the beginning of something, but "of somebody, who is a beginner himself."[30]

In making this assertion, Arendt once again invokes Augustine's phrase ("that there be a beginning, man was created, before whom there was nobody"). She cites this phrase, however, not as an authoritative metaphysical-theological claim with which she finds herself in accord. Rather, for her, it is an emblem or motto of what she, following Heidegger, viewed as a crucial component of human being. Arendt uses "natality" to designate a feature of our temporal (existential) constitution rather than to make a claim about a "faculty" that human beings have been transcendentally endowed with by God or nature. The contingency and "startling unexpectedness" that characterize action *in the world* and *with others* disappear the moment we misconceive natality as the inner core of a "true" or non-phenomenal self, an essence that somehow precedes and determines existence. Natality is *not* rooted in the "autonomous" individual will; nor can the "abyss of freedom" it opens be bridged through the imposition of a bogus teleological "necessity" upon the realm of human affairs. Insofar as natality designates the human capacity for spontaneous or radical beginning, it stands for something that is, from a metaphysical point of view at least, *groundless*.

"If action as beginning corresponds to the fact of birth," Arendt writes,

> if it is the actualization of the human condition of natality, then speech corresponds to the fact of distinctness and is the actualization of the human condition of plurality, that is, of living as a distinct and unique being among equals.[31]

This remark prefaces two characteristically Arendtian claims. The first is the *closeness* if not inseparability of speech from action. "Speechless action would no longer be action," she tells us, adding that "no other human performance requires speech as to the

same extent as action."[32] The second and more controversial claim is
that our "unique identity"—*who* we are—is disclosed by our words
and deeds, and *not* by our individual idiosyncrasies, psychological
depths, personal beliefs, or good intentions:

> In acting and speaking, men show who they are, reveal actively
> their unique personal identities and thus make their appear-
> ance in the human world...The disclosure of "who" in contra-
> distinction to "what" somebody is—his qualities, gifts, talents,
> and shortcomings, which he may hide or display—is implicit
> in everything somebody says and does. It can be hidden only
> in complete silence and perfect passivity, but its disclosure can
> never by achieved as a willful purpose, as though one possessed
> and could dispose of this "who" in the same manner as he has
> and can dispose of his qualities. On the contrary, it is more than
> likely that the "who," which appears so clearly and unmistaka-
> bly to others, remains hidden from the person himself, like the
> *daimōn* in Greek religion which accompanies each man through-
> out his life, always looking over his shoulder from behind and
> thus visible only to those he encounters.[33]

This passage makes two things clear. First, while the disclosure of
"who" an individual is "is implicit in everything [that he] says and
does," the individual in question is never the producer of his identity or the "author" of his story. This may seem questionable in an
age of image-making and variations on modernist self-fashioning *à
la* Proust and Nietzsche, but outside the confines of advertising and
the narcissism of "styling," it is undoubtedly true. Second, the disclosive dimension of action and speech becomes apparent "where
people are *with* others and neither for or against them—that is, in
sheer human togetherness."[34] For action's agent-disclosing capacity
to achieve "full appearance," it needs "the shining brightness we
once called glory," which is "possible only in the public realm."[35]
   Arendt's analysis of the agent-disclosive capacity of political
action—combined with her description of the *polis* as a "space where
freedom as virtuosity can appear" and her seemingly rigid distinction between public and private—has led some to conclude that she
favors a heroic politics, one devoted largely to competitive displays

of Machiavellian *virtu* (skill or ability) by elite political actors such as Pericles or Alcibiades.[36] This conclusion is wide of the mark, but the "Action" chapter provides some evidence to support it. Achilles is invoked as a paradigmatic example of the rare hero whose short life "delivers into the narrator's hands the full significance of his deed."[37] Pericles' Funeral Oration is similarly invoked as an example of a political actor (rather than a poet or historian) providing his fellow citizens with their own monument, a lasting testament to the immortal fame their heroic deeds and achievements have already won for them.[38]

These two examples make it seem as if the point of Arendt's agonistic politics is the expression of individual or collective energy in the pursuit of glory. If this were the case, she could plausibly be charged with being a reactionary celebrant of toxic masculinity, such as we find in the Homeric heroes' competitive displays of masterly violence or in the predatory behavior of imperial Athens itself. But, of course, it is not. The story of Achilles is cited not as a normative example of political action (Achilles' status as ruler and killing machine nullify that possibility), but rather to underline the virtual impossibility of any actor remaining in control of the meaning of his life story. Like Achilles, he would have to die a quick death following his one "glorious deed" to even approximate such control. Similarly, Pericles' Funeral Oration is cited not as a normative example of political speech (the bumper sticker version of which would be "We are the greatest!"), but rather as an indicator of the importance the Greeks attached to the *polis* as a vehicle for organized remembrance.

One reason for such repeated misreadings is that Arendt's critics fixate on action's agent-disclosive capacity at the expense of what she sees as its broader meaning-creative capacity. Action not only discloses the "who" of the agent, but also illuminates the "what" of the public world in its various aspects. Experientially, the two cannot be separated:

> Action and speech go on between men…and they retain their agent-revealing capacity even if their content is exclusively "objective," concerned with the matters of the world of things in which men move, which physically lies between them and out of which arise their specific, objective, worldly interests. These

interests constitute, in the word's most literal significance, something which *inter-est*, which lies between people and can therefore relate and bind them together. Most action and speech is concerned with this in-between, which varies with each group of people, so that most words and deeds are *about* some worldly objective reality in addition to being a disclosure of the acting and speaking agent.[39]

That which is public—the "in-between" of the human artifice—relates and separates not just by providing a stage for, or backdrop to, agent-disclosive action. Rather, it "relates and separates" by providing precisely the objects, institutions, and matters of common concern that elicit the actor's speech and his interlocutors' (or audience's) attention in the first place. Narcissistic self-display detached from worldly concerns may typify celebrity culture and the politics that has recently grown up around it, but it has little if any connection to the agent-revealing speech about the common world that Arendt describes in this passage.

Here I should point out that selfless, committed actions by ordinary people on behalf of some worldly or common interest are just as agent-disclosive or "revelatory" as the more classical (male and heroic) examples Arendt is wont to cite. The primary difference has to do with *whose* story gets told and whose *public self* is monumentalized by means of "organized remembrance."[40] It should be emphasized that Arendt herself engages in the rescuing and remembrance of ordinary people's stories when she highlights the "defeated causes" of the Paris Commune, the 1905 Russian Revolution, the workers- and soldiers-councils of the 1918–1919 German revolution, and the 1956 Hungarian revolt in *On Revolution*. In these pages, she can truly be said to be the "Homer of the losers."

Arendt describes the relation between the self- and world-disclosive dimensions of action by means of the metaphor of the (subjective) "web of human relations" that overlays the "in-between" of the common (objective) world:

> Since this disclosure of the subject is an integral part of all, even the most "objective" intercourse, the physical, worldly in-between along with its interests is overlaid and, as it were,

overgrown with an altogether, different in-between which consists of deeds and words and owes its origin exclusively to men's
acting and speaking directly to one another. This second, subjective in-between is not tangible, since there are no tangible
objects into which it could solidify; the process of acting and
speaking can leave behind no such results and end products. But
for all its intangibility, this in-between is no less real than the
world of things we visibly have in common. We call this reality
the "web" of human relationships, indicating by the metaphor
its somewhat intangible quality.[41]

Whenever an agent acts, he acts into an "already existing web" of
human relationships. This web, a function of the human condition
of plurality, is characterized by "innumerable conflicting wills and
intentions." Action's intrusion into such a pre-existing web invariably creates unforeseen consequences, consequences that deflect the
actor from achievement of his original goal. Indeed, such unforeseen consequences may well (and often do) bring about a state of
affairs directly opposite that intended by the actor. Thus, because
action always occurs in the medium supplied by the "web of human
relationships," the actor is "never merely a 'doer,' but also and at the
same time a sufferer."[42] While frustrating all attempts to "produce" a
state of affairs analogous to the way a craftsman produces his product, this web nevertheless constitutes a medium "in which action
alone is real." As a result, Arendt claims, it "'produces' stories with
or without intention as naturally as fabrication produces tangible
things."[43]

   These stories are real (as opposed to fictional) accounts of the
consequences, intended and unintended, "produced" by the actor's
action. Considered by themselves, apart from any subsequent reification in a poem, document, or artwork, they "tell us more about
their subjects, the 'hero' in the center of each story, than any product of human hands ever tells us about the master who produced
it."[44] We can know *who* somebody is only "by knowing the story
of which he is himself the hero—his biography, in other words."[45]
Broadly speaking, this is an epistemological claim about the possibility of knowing another person's concrete identity. We can only
know *who* somebody is (or was) if something approximating their

whole story—a truthful if not entirely full account of their "words and deeds"—becomes available to us. It might be objected that truthful, let alone full, accounts of *any* actor's words and deeds are hard to come by. However, this objection misses Arendt's fundamental point, which is that identity takes shape through—is constituted by—narrative and is, as a result, inseparable from "story-telling."[46] Once again, the all-important qualification here is that the stories told are truthful (fact-based) ones, and not fictions of a novelistic or propagandistic sort. The latter types of stories are fabrications in the literal sense of the word, whereas the former (the "true" sort) can be said to have been produced by the agent's words and actions themselves.

There is an interesting connection here between Arendt's account of the self- and world-disclosive character of *action* and the early Heidegger's account of *Dasein's* "authentic disclosedness" in *Being and Time*.[47] In Arendt's account, the "world" produced by *homo faber* is an artificial one composed of use objects and instrumental relationships. This is a world in which instrumentality (in the form of the "in order to") threatens to overwhelm the "for the sake of" if *homo faber's* utilitarian mentality becomes hegemonic. In *Being and Time*, Heidegger presents the "world" of *Dasein's* being-in-the-world as a totality of referential contexts which are themselves composed of "in order to" relationships. The famous example of the workshop in *Being and Time* underlines the fact that any given referential context is not composed by a heap of unrelated things, but rather of interrelated *equipment* that is "ready-to-hand" for a variety of possible projects *Dasein* might undertake.

The point for Heidegger is twofold. Not only is our primary relationship to the world a practical (as opposed to contemplative) one. We are also *absorbed* by the equipmental relations that compose these referential contexts, contexts that—taken as a totality—constitute our "world." Viewed from the perspective of everyday existential involvement, everything in the world—planes, houses, schools, newspapers, public institutions—has the fundamental character of equipment for living. As long as these things function smoothly, we don't give them much thought. As a result, our "being-in-the-world" takes on a certain automatic or, as Heidegger would say, "inauthentic" quality. It is only when we are brought up short by the thought of our *own* death, our "ownmost possibility for being," that we are able to break away from such absorption in the everyday. We then become free for the disclosure (and practical projection) of deeper, more "authentic" possibilities for living. According to Heidegger, these possibilities are implicit in, yet dimmed down by, the world as we encounter it on an everyday basis. The illumination of greater than quotidian possibilities and a fuller thematization of the "for the sake of" thus hinge upon a confrontation with our own mortality.

Arendt retains the Heideggerian emphasis on the disclosure of meaning as a defining feature of human *being*. For Arendt, however, it is our *natality*—our capacity for initiatory action with others—and not our *mortality* that is revelatory of a dimension of (non-instrumental and worldly) meaning implicit in the "web of human relationships." The "shining brightness of the public realm" attests to initiatory action's capacity to illuminate the world and transcend everyday utilitarian concerns. It is this possibility that eludes *homo faber* (absorbed as he is by instrumentality) as well as the *animal laborans* (who is absorbed by bodily needs and the endless effort to meet them).

Arendt's strong emphasis upon the initiatory dimension of action traces back to her conviction that totalitarianism had (for a time) uprooted plurality, reducing human beings to the level of "perverted animals" capable of reactive behavior but not free ("spontaneous") action. Yet, if Arendt's focus on *beginning* as the *sine qua non* of action is understandable in light of OT, her focus on action's disclosive or revelatory capacity is less so. Many who might agree with her statement that "freedom is the *raison d'être* of politics" may well find themselves dubious about her linkage of *worldly meaning* and *individual identity* to politics, political action, and the public realm. The Greeks may have thought in these terms, but why should we?

The answer to this question is tied to German philosophy's response to modernization and secularization in the nineteenth and twentieth centuries. For some—for example, Hegel and Marx—the destruction of the *ancien regime* by the French Revolution and the industrialization that followed pointed to a future in which man could fashion *rational* political and economic arrangements and so come (finally) to feel at home in the world. For others—e.g. Nietzsche and Heidegger—modernization and secularization contributed mightily to the "death of God" and the feeling of meaninglessness generated by incredulity toward the idea of an otherworldly ("transcendent") source of meaning. The other side of the Promethean liberation promised by Hegel and Marx was nihilism and the suspicion that Western culture was uniquely and profoundly self-undermining. As Nietzsche put it in The Will to Power, "the highest values devaluate themselves."[48]

Politically speaking, Arendt's debt to the republican heritage of the French Revolution (so evident in OT) places her closer to the "modernist" Hegel and Marx than to the vehemently anti-modernist (and politically retrograde) Nietzsche and Heidegger. However, she was convinced that Nietzsche and Heidegger had identified, if not the "inner logic" of the West's self-undermining, at least a nihilistic *cultural dynamic*. Modernity's relentless "instrumentalization of everything that exists" deprived this world of meaning at the very moment the "death of God" put paid to the idea of an otherworldly source. Alienation from the world increased as Western man retreated further and further into the self.

Like Nietzsche and Heidegger, Arendt thought this cultural dynamic had deep historical roots, going back at least as far as Plato. She did not, however, view the artist's capacity to create beautiful illusions (Nietzsche) or the poet's capacity to disclose new worlds (Heidegger) as adequate responses to either the original Platonic-Christian devaluation of the world or its modern, activist and instrumentalizing, counterpart. Indeed, she saw Nietzsche and Heidegger's respective responses as themselves symptomatic of something that had characterized Western philosophy and political theory from the very beginning: the oblivion of *praxis*.

From the beginning—since Plato—the Western tradition has sought to escape the "futility, boundlessness, and uncertainty of outcome" that attends all action in the public world. Arendt sees the tradition as animated by the need to find a "substitute for action [*praxis*]," one that provides an escape from "the haphazardness and moral irresponsibility inherent in a plurality of agents." The theoretical "solutions" to the problem posed by action's "frailty" are all oddly similar. "Generally speaking, they always amount to seeking shelter from action's calamities in an activity where one man, isolated from all others, remains master of his doings from beginning to end."[49] That activity is, of course, fabrication, and the attempt to replace *acting* with *making* is what links Plato's craftsman analogy in the *Republic* and *Statesman* to Nietzsche's "artist's metaphysics" and Heidegger's view of the state as the "setting-into-work of truth."[50]

Between Plato and these two great anti-Platonists we find virtually endless variations on what Arendt calls the "traditional substitution of making for acting." Machiavelli and Rousseau both invoke the Platonic figure of the great legislator who works the raw material of "the people" into balanced or beautiful form, even though neither of them relies upon anything like Plato's "eternal" models of justice and harmonious proportion. Similarly, Hobbes' *Leviathan* is a set of instructions for how to construct a durable and unified state, one in which the sovereign power monopolizes the public realm and plurality is effectively neutered. As we have seen, Marx's work model of action, combined with his "glorification of labor," radically undercuts both plurality and exchange of opinion in the name of unalienated production and the realization of our "species essence."

Even Aristotle, whose basic distinction between *praxis* and *poiēsis* seems to place him in the pro-action, pro-plurality camp, is seen by Arendt as succumbing to the Platonic temptation of recoding *acting* as a form of *making* (his positing of naturally given *ends* toward which virtuous action and the "formation of character" should strive is a case in point).[51] Finally (albeit unmentioned by Arendt in *THC*), there are the formative projects of the Bolsheviks and the Nazis, each of which depends upon the trope of the people as material awaiting the shaping hand of the Party. Suffice it to say the list is long and could be expanded indefinitely.[52]

The "frailty" of action is no mirage born of a tradition animated by vehemently anti-democratic prejudice. Arendt attests again and again to the phenomenological *reality* of action's unpredictability, boundlessness, and uncertainty of outcome. Her point is that these are constitutive aspects of political action as such—i.e. of action as it occurs in the context of human plurality. The "traditional substitution of making for acting" is guided by an *anti-political* idea of freedom: the self-contained freedom of the artist-fabricator who stands apart and above his human raw material. In the modern age, such freedom is increasingly identified with the will of the monarch or "the people" conceived as an autonomous, self-shaping collective subject. As Arendt notes in her essay "What is Freedom?":

> Within the conceptual framework of traditional philosophy, it is indeed very difficult to understand how freedom and non-sovereignty can exist together or, to put it another way, how freedom could have been given to men under the condition of non-sovereignty. Actually it is as unrealistic to deny freedom because of the fact of human non-sovereignty as it is dangerous to believe that one can be free—as an individual or as a group—only if he is sovereign. The famous sovereignty of political bodies has always been an illusion which, moreover, can be maintained only by the instruments of violence, that is, with essentially nonpolitical means. Under human conditions, which are determined by the fact that not man but men live on the earth, freedom and sovereignty are so little identical that they cannot even exist simultaneously...If men wish to be free, it is precisely sovereignty they must renounce.[53]

The apparent paradox of "non-sovereign freedom" dissolves once we acknowledge that a citizen body is composed of diverse equals who have different perspectives—and hence different opinions—on issues of common concern. Debate, deliberation, and persuasion are less the tools of "democratic will formation" than they are the stuff of the ongoing activity of politics, an activity that takes place in a public realm whose very existence depends on the preservation of human plurality and a diversity of perspectives.[54] The "will of the people" may be a necessary constitutive fiction of modern democracies, but to view it as denoting the will of an actually existing subject (one similar to Rousseau's moi commun) is to fall back into the fantasies of collective sovereignty that, as Arendt observed in OT, drove the majoritarian ethnic tyrannies of the nineteenth and twentieth centuries and that continue to exert such a dangerous attraction today.

But are there no political ways of containing the unforeseen, boundless, and potentially destabilizing effects of action, short of curtailing diversity, equality, and plurality? Arendt thinks there are, and that we can find inspiration in the "solution" practiced by the Greeks and in the two faculties—promising and forgiving—that enable political communities to bind themselves to the future while coping with the misfortunes, mistakes, and evils of the past.

The *polis* was the solution to the problem of action's "frailty" for the pre-philosophic Greeks. The founding of the *polis* was rooted not in the desire for subsistence or security—other pre-*polis* forms of village and political organization could supply those. What prompted the Greeks to organize themselves into city-states composed of equal citizens was, in Arendt's view, the desire to provide a durable institutional space for the thing that made living together worthwhile in the first place: the sharing of words and deeds. This conviction about where the true value of living together lay went back to the Homeric Greeks, who episodically left their (separate and isolated) households in order to combine in such enterprises as the Trojan War. These instances of joint effort yielded the "great words and deeds" subsequently memorialized by the poet.

From the standpoint of the citizenry of the *polis, that* experience remained in the distant past. Yet it still retained much of its normative force (Homer had long been, and continued to be, the "teacher of all Hellas," Plato's desire to either censor or banish the poets notwithstanding). The point of life was to say or do something worthy of remembrance by the community; to show oneself to be, if not *the* best, then among the best. Thus, the *polis* served a dual function:

> First, it was intended to enable men to do permanently, albeit under certain restrictions, what otherwise had been possible only as an extraordinary and infrequent enterprise for which they had to leave their household. The polis was supposed to multiply the occasions to win 'immortal fame,' that is, to multiply the chances for everybody to distinguish himself, to show in deed or word who he was in his unique distinctness...[second, it] was to offer a remedy for the futility of action and speech; for the chances that a deed deserving fame would not be forgotten, that it would actually become "immortal," were not very good.[55]

Arendt's gloss on the intention behind the foundation of the *polis* may strike us as idealistic and far-fetched, as least until we remember that this was indeed a supremely agonistic (competitive) culture, and that Athens experienced an "incredible development of gift and genius" once it rid itself of its tyrants. Moreover, she is hardly alone in her emphasis on how the city-state provided the ordinary citizen with an identity and meaning that, thanks to collective remembrance, transcended the short span of mortal life. As Hegel observed with respect to the ancient Roman example, *death* "must have become truly terrible" for the individual once he ceased to be a republican citizen and, forever banished from the public realm, became a private, "atomized" subject of imperial power.[56]

Perhaps unsurprisingly, it is at this point that Arendt cites Pericles' Funeral Oration, virtually verbatim as it appears in Thucydides. The *polis*

> gives a guaranty that those who forced every sea and land to become the scene of their daring will not remain without witness and will need neither Homer nor anyone else who knows how to turn words to praise them.[57]

I previously mentioned the importance of "organized remembrance" as a vehicle for the creation and preservation of meaning in a world otherwise determined by the repetitiveness of labor and the instrumentality of work. One would be hard-pressed to deny that "organized remembrance" is indeed the medium through which a polity narratively constitutes its identity and that of its citizens. However, at this point in her description of the "Greek solution," Arendt makes a rather extraordinary claim:

> According to this self-interpretation, the political realm rises directly out of acting together, the "sharing of words and deeds." Thus action not only has the most intimate relationship to the public part of the world common to us all, but is the one activity which constitutes it. It is as though the wall of the polis and the boundaries of law were drawn around an already existing public space which, however, without such stabilizing protection could not endure, could not survive the moment of action and speech itself.[58]

The *polis*, then, exists to memorialize the "words and deeds" of its citizens. However, it first appears as a kind of add-on to the "public part of the world" these words and deeds have already created through their sheer performance. Arendt qualifies this latter claim with an "as though." Regardless, it is passages like these that have given readers of THC the impression that action has an indisputable priority over law and institutions in Arendt's thought. This impression is strengthened when she observes that Plato and Aristotle "elevated lawmaking and city-building to the highest rank in political life" (because in them men "act like craftsmen") and then proceeds to insist that "this is no longer or rather, not yet action (*praxis*) properly speaking, but making (*poiēsis*)."[59] As man's most "disclosive" activity, then, political action not only possesses an *existential* priority for Arendt; it also (apparently) possesses an *ontological* and *temporal* priority as well.

This impression, though strong, is nevertheless mistaken and points to the hazards of reading THC as a full or complete statement of "Hannah Arendt's political philosophy." As we saw in Chapter 2, Arendt's encounter with totalitarianism led her to stress the fundamental importance of precisely those man-made institutional and legal structures that totalitarian regimes either ignored or destroyed outright. And, as we shall see in Chapter 5, in *On Revolution*, she argues that it is the American *constitution* that is the most significant and lasting *political* contribution of the "age of revolution." Action, then, in order to appear and be remembered, demands a public "space of appearances"—a public realm—and this realm demands legal-institutional articulation if it is to survive the fleeting moment of action. The Athenians, of course, had their laws and institutions, and—even though Arendt does not focus on them in THC—it was these laws and institutions that provided the democracy with its basic structure and which made its "space of freedom" possible.

But even such a legally and institutionally articulated "space of freedom" requires something more than the words, deeds, and their memorialization to keep it going. It requires *power*.

Like her discussion of the relation of freedom to non-sovereignty, Arendt's treatment of power in THC challenges our preconceptions. For most of us, political power is a coercive force: it is the ability to "impose one's will," to act with the expectation of obedience from those one commands. The is how Max Weber defined power, and it is precisely this type of "sovereign" power that the liberal tradition has attempted to limit through a variety of constitutional mechanisms and restraints. These restraints, however, do little to change its fundamental nature.[60] Regardless of the type of regime one lives under, political power is what Weber said it was: "power backed up by violence."[61] The only question is the extent to which that power is (or is not) limited.

In stark contrast to Weber's definition, Arendt defines power as "the human ability not just to act, but to act in concert." Power "is never the property of an individual; it belongs to a group and remains in existence only so long as the group keeps together."[62] At first, this definition may seem to merely collectivize what remains a fundamentally coercive power. This impression vanishes the moment we remember that, for Arendt, the essential mode of political action is persuasive speech. To act means to initiate something by (first) persuading one's peers, through argument and debate, to pursue a particular policy or initiative, and (second) carrying through on this initiative by acting in concert with them.[63]

On this understanding, the actor who initiates is never a ruler or authority (he is not one who simply commands) and his co-actors are never his hierarchical inferiors. The distinction between those who know and command (on the one hand) and those who merely do or execute (on the other) is, according to Arendt, a Platonic one, arrived at by way of his analogy between the statesman and the craftsman. It codifies the idea that moral-political knowledge is a species of "expert knowledge," one that is possessed only by the philosophically wise or the divinely appointed. Regardless of form, this distinction obviously takes aim at the heart of democracy. It brackets the medium of persuasive speech (peithò) in the name of "Truth," simultaneously undercutting the plurality of opinion (doxa) that makes politics as a way of being-together possible. Not for nothing does Arendt refer to "Plato's tyranny of truth."[64] This a tyranny that has been pursued by a wide range of philosophical, ideological, and religious movements, all bent—as indeed Plato was—on effecting radical moral reform from above in the name of some Absolute (the will of God, the "end" of History, the order of Nature).

In contrast to the coercive force deployed by such absolutist regimes to either destroy or monopolize public space, power—understood as the ability of plural individuals to "act in concert"—is, in fact, the "lifeblood" of the public realm. It lies in the actuality of a robust public-political life, the sheer fact of ongoing debate, deliberation, and acting together by citizens in the public sphere. Such a participatory political life can take a variety of forms, from the Athenian assembly to the New England town hall meetings described by Tocqueville, or (more recently) the mass demonstrations in Poland and East Germany that helped bring down the ruling Communist regimes in both countries. To this list could be added the civil rights and antiwar movements in America during the sixties and the anti-nuclear movement of the seventies and eighties. The movement for gay and lesbian rights, hardly foreseen by Arendt, would also fit this paradigm, at least if we view it less as a struggle for recognition and more as a struggle for equal civil and political *rights* (hard as it is to separate these two dimensions). The point is less what kind of action earns the Arendtian honorific of "political" than the *fact* of energetic "acting together" for the sake of creating, preserving, or augmenting a public realm open to all.

For Arendt, what stimulates and generates power (in the form of citizens' acting together) is, at bottom, care for the public world and the desire for public freedom. This care is as manifest in the seemingly mundane tasks Tocqueville called "local administration" (such as jury service and town hall meetings) as it is in those extraordinary moments where ordinary citizens attempt to reclaim or reconstitute a public realm monopolized by a ruling party, colonial power, or dominating racial, ethnic, or religious group. Wherever "power" in the Weberian sense remains firmly in the hands of a party, bureaucracy, or set of private interests, there power in the Arendtian sense is lacking. Tyranny can, of course, destroy power by means of violence and terror (the Tiananmen Square massacre in 1989 is a good example), or prevent its development in the first place. However, violence and terror can never substitute for power, nor can they create anything more than a sham public sphere consisting solely of staged spectacles and carefully managed rituals and symbols.

The existential significance of initiatory action, disclosive speech, institutionally grounded remembrance, and plurality-based political power is summed up by Arendt's gloss on the "melancholy wisdom" of *Ecclesiastes*: "Vanity of vanities; all is vanity....there is no new thing under the sun,...there is no remembrance of former things; neither shall there be any remembrance of things that are to come with those that shall come after." This sentiment, Arendt argues, is not the fruit of a specifically religious experience, but arises "wherever and whenever trust in the world as a fit place for human appearance, for action and speech, is gone":

> Without action to bring into the play of the world the new beginning of which each man is capable by virtue of being born, 'there is no new thing under the sun'; without speech to materialize and memorialize, however tentatively, the 'new things' that appear and shine forth, 'there is no remembrance'; without the enduring permanence of a human artifact, there cannot be 'any remembrance of things that are to come with those that shall come after.' And without power, the space of appearance brought forth through action and speech in public will fade away as rapidly as the living deed and word.[65]

The *alienation from the world* manifest, not only in *Ecclesiastes* but also in early Christianity, is profound, and for entirely understandable historical reasons: neither the ancient Hebrews nor the early Christians could lay claim to a public-political world of their own. What remained to them was messianic hope in the coming of a Redeemer who would either end their exile and restore their kingdom *or* dispense a Final Judgment on the things of this world and bring about a kingdom of His own: Divine rule on earth.

The Bible, of course, means different things to different faith traditions, sects, and individuals. It would be absurd to reduce it to an expression of simply *one* message or affect. Nevertheless, it is undeniable that the Bible *does* express, in both its Hebrew and Christian versions, a degree of alienation from the world that the average citizen of ancient Athens or the Roman Republic would have found incomprehensible. Seen through a Biblical lens, *amor mundi*—love of the world—is not something to be cultivated and expressed through interaction with one's fellow citizens in the public realm. It is, rather, something one should strive to overcome. Augustine's relentless unmasking of all pagan public-political virtues in the *City of God* tells us all we need to know on this score.

The final chapter of THC, "The *Vita Activa* and the Modern Age," shifts the discussion away from the contrast between the "pagan" pursuit of *worldly immortality* and the Christian pursuit of *eternal salvation* to the consideration of *modern* world alienation. Arendt thinks this alienation is pervasive, to the point of being a characteristic if not defining feature of modernity itself.

III The modern age: world alienation and life as the highest good

If the specter of Auschwitz looms over much of OT, the threats of ecological disaster and nuclear annihilation loom over the final chapter of THC. In Arendt's view, capitalism and modern revolutions in science have set off processes that are truly "boundless," creating logics of unlimited capital accumulation (on one hand) and equally unlimited technological development (on the other). These processes have created a political world in which nuclear war and the annihilation of all organic life on earth is far from unthinkable, and an economic world in which consumerism and ecologically unsustainable wastefulness rule supreme.

From Arendt's point of view, then, mankind is heedlessly hurtling toward the destruction of the earth (the "very quintessence of the human condition"), either through the depredations of a capitalist "waste economy" or through the seemingly inevitability of a full-scale nuclear exchange. "Thinking what we are doing" has thus never been more imperative. At a less apocalyptic level, Arendt thinks that modernity's very dynamism all but guarantees the disappearance of the stability and durability of the "human artifice." The "world" constituted by relatively stable political, cultural, and domestic institutions falls victim to the constantly revolutionizing forces of capitalist accumulation and technological development. As Marx wrote in the *Communist Manifesto*, "all that is solid melts into air."[66] This is one Marxian insight that Arendt totally agrees with.

****

Arendt begins her discussion of the modern age by telling us that three events "stand at its threshold" and "determine its character." These are: the discovery of America and "the ensuing exploration of the whole earth"; the Reformation, whose expropriation of ecclesiastical property led to the "primitive accumulation" that kick-started capitalism and what Arendt calls "the accumulation of social wealth"; and, finally, the invention of the telescope and "the development of a new science that considered the nature of the earth from the standpoint of the universe."[67] The first two may be seen as the events precipitating the development of modern earth and world alienation, respectively. However—and somewhat surprisingly, given the importance she attaches to the world alienation generated by capitalism and its ever-intensifying focus on the "life process of society"—Arendt observes that

> compared with the earth alienation underlying the whole de-
> velopment of natural science in the modern age, the withdrawal
> from terrestrial proximity contained in the discovery of the
> globe as a whole and the world alienation produced in the two-
> fold process of expropriation and wealth accumulation are of
> minor significance.[68]

How do the discovery of America, on the one hand, and the Reformation, on the other, help precipitate the development of earth alienation (an entirely new phenomenon) and modern world alienation (an entirely different form of "withdrawal from the world" from that practiced by religious and philosophical ascetics of the pre-modern era)?

Arendt's answer is that the discovery of America and the globe as a whole had the effect of simultaneously enlarging the known world while effectively shrinking the earth, both practically and imaginatively. Well before the invention of steam ships and air travel, the "surveying capacity of the human mind" made it possible for man to "disentangle" himself from his proximate earthly concerns and create the mental distance requisite for the objectification of the entire globe. "Before we knew how to circle the earth," Arendt remarks, "we brought the globe into our living rooms to be touched by our hands and swirled before our eyes."[69] Indeed, the invention of the airplane, which gives us the ability to leave the surface of the earth at any moment, is "like a symbol for the general phenomenon that any decrease of terrestrial distance can be won only at the price of putting a decisive distance between man and earth," that is, "of alienating man from his immediate earthly surroundings."[70]

The objectification of the globe by our "surveying capacity" is the beginning of an "earth alienation" that is consummated in space travel and in the hope that "mankind will not remain bound to the earth forever."[71]

The genesis of modern world alienation from the Reformation has a twofold aspect. First, there was the expropriation of Church property in England and Germany in the sixteenth century, a process that was followed by numerous enclosure acts in Britain in the eighteenth and nineteenth centuries. Expropriation of Church property also accompanied the French Revolution, although in this case, the right of peasants to their own holdings was legally affirmed. Arendt discusses none of these cases in detail but instead points to a generalized expropriation of Church and peasantry in the course of the Reformation. In the case of the peasantry, this meant the destruction of private property as it had been understood since antiquity (namely, as a "privately owned share of a common world") and the loss of their very place in the world. "Expropriation," Arendt writes, "the deprivation of certain groups of their place in the world and their naked exposure to the exigencies of life, created both the original accumulation of wealth and the possibility of transforming this wealth into capital through labor." The result was that the new laboring class "stood not only directly under the compelling urgency of life's necessity but was at the same time alienated from all cares and worries which did not immediately follow from the life process itself."[72]

To this forcible "alienation from the world" imposed on the peasant class via the expropriation of their property, Arendt adds the "innerworldly asceticism" described by Max Weber in *The Protestant Ethic and the Spirit of Capitalism*. Weber had argued that the most important spiritual precondition of capitalism lay in the relentless work ethic practiced by the Calvinist strand of early Protestantism. According to the Calvinist doctrine of predestination, there was nothing one could do in terms of "good works" to change the fate of one's soul, since this fate had already been decided by an omniscient God at the Creation. Nevertheless, the Calvinists believed that devotion to (and success in) one's calling might well be a sign of God's grace and membership in the small group of a "saintly" elect who—unlike the vast majority of sinful mortals—were not damned for all eternity.

The existential anxiety created by the doctrine of predestination thus gave birth to a work ethic which demanded that the enjoyment of the fruits of one's labors be perpetually deferred, and that profits be continuously reinvested as capital. The result was an ethos that was *ascetic* without being otherworldly (like the monk's); an ethos that generated intense and uninterrupted activity *in the world* but which lacked any trace of *amor mundi* (love of the world). As Arendt puts it:

> The greatness of Max Weber's discovery about the origins of capitalism lay precisely in his demonstration that an enormous, strictly mundane activity is possible without any care for or enjoyment of the world whatever, an activity whose deepest motivation, on the contrary, is worry and care about the self. *World alienation, and not self-alienation as Marx thought, has been the hallmark of the modern age.*[73]

Thus, while *earth* alienation proceeds (in part) from the human surveying capacity's newfound ability to objectify the entire globe, world alienation proceeds from expropriation and from a new (and intensely disciplined) focus upon the process of capital accumulation as such. Accumulation for the sake of accumulation led the Calvinist to view the world as little more than a supplier of "valueless" raw material to be consumed by production and given value by labor.

The resulting worldview was neatly summed up by Locke when he proclaimed that God gave the world to "the industrious and the rational," imposing upon the rational European Christian the duty to labor and create value out of what had hitherto lain "waste."[74] What Locke could not foresee was the way the process of (social) wealth accumulation in the form of investment capital would eventually take over everything, undermining the stability of the world by instituting a "constant process of change" in the form of ever-accelerating cycles of production and consumption. According to Arendt, while the "life process of society" remains "bound to the principle of world alienation from which it sprang," in its mature form this process can continue "only provided that no worldly durability and stability is permitted to interfere, only as long as all worldly things, all end products of the production process, are fed back into it at ever-increasing speed."[75] The process of wealth accumulation as we currently know it is possible "only if the world and the very world-liness of man are sacrificed." In fully developed capitalism, the world alienation manifest in the Protestant ethic gives way to the *worldlessness* of the *animal laborans*.

Important as the "withdrawal from terrestrial proximity" and world alienation are, they pale in significance compared to spe-cific form of earth alienation generated by the development of modern science. Arendt explains how Galileo's confirmation of the Copernican hypothesis (by means of the newly invented telescope) led astronomers to abandon the geocentric standpoint upheld by the Church and Aristotelian science. They proceeded to adopt a universal or "cosmic" standpoint, one in which the earth was no longer the center of God's Creation and a presumably closed cosmos, but rather just one more object in a potentially infinite universe. This was the "Archimedean point" long dreamed of by Western science, an ideal extra-terrestrial standpoint which remained a mere dream so long as scientists continued to ground their astronomical theories and observations on earthly sense experience.

With Galileo's discovery, the millennia-old sense-based certainty that the sun revolved around the earth was revealed to be a complete illusion. Once this illusion was shattered, the geocentric cosmos of divinely ordered ends or "perfections" (a hierarchical cosmos in which man occupied a privileged place) gave way to a decentered view, one in which the formulation of natural laws eschewed all reference to final causes. Liberated from medieval (Aristotelian) tel-eology, science no longer sought to explain the "why" of the cosmos but focused instead on the "how" of astronomical and earthly events; that is, it focused on the invisible physical and chemical processes that produced these events. Nature and the cosmos were no longer "texts" to be deciphered, but rather mechanisms to be explained in terms of efficient causation. This task was facilitated greatly by the *mathesis universalis* of Newton and the new physics. The shattering of geocentric illusion, made possible by the *event* of the telescope's invention, thus paved the way for the scientific revolution and the massive expansion of human knowledge and technological power that it fostered.

But while the scientific men of the "learned societies" may have exulted in the prospects opened by the new mathematical physics, the response of the philosophers was quite different. Starting with Descartes, it was the philosophers and not the scientists who "registered with unequalled precision the enormous shock of the event."[76] For what Galileo's destruction of the geocentric illusion demonstrated was that—contrary to what Arendt calls "the common creed of pagan and Hebrew antiquity, [and] of Christian and secular philosophy"—*truth did not reveal itself.*[77] Nor were our five senses or human reason created specifically by God or Nature to receive it. The conclusion was inescapable. If neither truth nor reality were *given* through our senses or the "eyes of the mind," then "there is nothing left to be taken on faith; *everything must be doubted.*"[78] It is only through the rigorous bracketing of the "world of appearances" that we can "hold out [any] hope for true knowledge."[79]

Arendt rehearses the radical or "universal" nature of Cartesian doubt, as well as the "ingenuity" of his *Dieu trompeur* thesis, at some length. *Pace* Heidegger, her point is not to give priority to philosophers over men of science when it comes to grounding an age.[80] Rather,

> the point, in our context, is that both despair and triumph are inherent in the same event. If we wish to put this into historical perspective, it is as if Galileo's discovery proved in demonstrable fact that both the worst fear and the most presumptuous hope of human speculation, the ancient fear that our senses, our very organ for the reception of reality, might betray us, and the Archimedean wish for a point outside the earth from which to unhinge the world, could only come true together, as though the wish would be granted only provided we lost reality and the fear consummated only if compensated by the acquisition of supramundane powers.[81]

On the one hand, the invention of the telescope and discovery of the Archimedean point make the formulation of the genuinely universal laws of astrophysics possible. On the other, these events demonstrated the necessity of taking nothing on faith; of not grounding our knowledge on the authority of Aristotle, divine revelation, or the testimony of our senses. The only things we could *really* know were the "clear and distinct ideas" of mathematics and logic, together with whatever conclusions we could generate through the methodologically rigorous procedures of hypothesis, experiment, and verification. The vistas of human knowledge thus seemed to expand indefinitely at the very moment humanity was compelled to abandon the idea of a self-disclosing reality.

The philosophers quickly realized the existential-epistemological implications of this situation. Henceforth, the only knowledge we could be certain of would be that produced in terms of vocabularies, theories, and methods we ourselves have created. For even "though one cannot know truth as something given and disclosed," man can nevertheless "know what he makes himself."[82] If the universal doubt arising from the shock of Galileo's discovery were to be assuaged, it seemed there was no alternative to moving the Archimedean point into man himself.[83] Arendt sees Descartes' *cogito ergo sum* argument as commencing the "subjectivism" of modern philosophy. Modern philosophy's proliferation of a "great variety of introspections" (from English phenomenalism and sensualism to German Idealism and pragmatism) makes sense when we view these various retreats to the self as a response to the loss of the world of appearances induced by Galileo's shattering of the geocentric illusion.[84]

While the philosophers were attempting to come to grips with the epistemological and existential implications of a world well lost, scientists were abandoning the traditional approach of "letting Nature guide its movements" and deploying a far more aggressive approach in order to "compel Nature to answer [their] questions."[85] The invisible forces behind observable phenomenon were forced to reveal their secrets to the experimental method. However, while the "world of the experiment" increased man's power of making and acting "far beyond what any previous age dared to imagine in dream or phantasy," it also had the effect of sealing him within "the prison of his own mind":

> The moment he [man] wants what all ages before him were capable of achieving, that is, to experience the reality of what he himself is not, he will find that nature and the universe 'escape him' and that a universe construed according to the behavior

of nature in the experiment and in accordance with the very principles which man can translate technically into a working reality lacks all possible representation.[86]

Yet, for the scientists at least, the realization that the experimental method revealed not the innermost secrets of the universe but only patterns imposed by the human mind lay in the somewhat distant future.[87] In the meantime, the experimental method, combined with the *reductio scientia ad mathematicam* and the invention of ever-more sophisticated measuring instruments, enabled scientists not just to recreate and manipulate natural processes in their laboratories, but (ultimately) to "import" cosmic processes that nowhere appear on earth into the human artifice itself. Nuclear fission is a good example of such an "imported" process, and we are all familiar with the results. The fruit of modern science's triumphant earth alienation is nuclear weapons: the real possibility of the destruction of not just all organic life but the earth itself.[88]

Compounding the danger, in Arendt's view, is the fact that, at the very moment we have learned how to import such processes, we have lost the "capacity for universal thought" and for deliberative self-direction—that is, for thinking and talking intelligently about what we are doing as we avail ourselves of such God-like powers. Arendt, it should be noted, is not "anti-science." However, she does think that scientific and technological innovation continually outstrips public discourse and the capacity of ordinary citizens and politicians alike to discuss them in a sober and informed way. The result is that the advances—in weapons technology, artificial intelligence, genetic engineering—continue to pile up as public discourse about them remains stuck at the level of either bad science fiction or theologically rooted prejudice.

Given her penchant for citing stories and examples from the Hebrew bible and the New Testament, some readers may feel that Arendt's criticism of the modern age is itself an expression of theologically rooted prejudice. I think reading her in this way is a mistake. However, it is hard to deny that Arendt's emphasis upon (a) the finitude of the human condition and (b) the need to preserve the stability and durability of the human artifice gives her work a culturally conservative cast. While lauding initiatory action in the

public-political realm, she seems almost to dread it when it occurs in the spheres of science and technology. Modernity's sheer
dynamism—equally manifest in capitalism's transformation of the
globe and in successive waves of scientific and technological innovation over the past 200 years—undercuts virtually everything she
holds dear. If we were confined to the evidence supplied by THC
alone, it would be hard to label her as even a "reluctant" modernist.[89]

The last sections of THC are devoted to telling the story, first, of
how the *vita activa* asserted its broad superiority over the *vita contemplativa* in the modern age; and, second, of how the modern "victory
of *homo faber*" and his instrumental-utilitarian outlook was quickly
undone by the elevation of life itself to the position of the highest
good or *summum bonum*.

Arendt sees the reversal of the hierarchical order between the *vita
contemplativa* and the *vita activa* as a necessary consequence of the shattering of the geocentric illusion and our previous trust in the world
of appearances and the evidence given by our senses:

> After being and appearance had parted company and truth was
> no longer supposed to appear, to reveal and disclose itself to the
> mental eye of a beholder, there arose a veritable necessity to hunt
> for truth behind deceptive appearances. Nothing indeed could be
> less trustworthy for acquiring knowledge and approaching truth
> than passive observation or mere contemplation. In order to be
> certain, one had to *make sure*, and in order to know one had to
> do. Certainty of knowledge could be reached only under a two-
> fold condition: first, that knowledge concerned only what one had
> done himself—so that the ideal of knowledge became mathemat-
> ical knowledge, where we deal only with the self-made entities of
> the mind—and second, that knowledge was of such a nature that
> it could only be tested by more doing.[90]

It is important to note that the reversal in question actually concerned
the relationship between *thinking* and *doing*, while contemplation
itself—as least in its original sense of "beholding the truth"—faded
from the scene. Thinking becomes the handmaiden of doing. At first,
the doing in question was the activity of experimental science; later
it came to encompass virtually all the productive and world-building

activities of *homo faber*. Contemplation itself "became altogether meaningless" in this new dispensation. Truth was no longer something given and eternal, but rather something actively *made* through hypothesis and experiment. As such, it was subject to revision and replacement as practical needs changed and methods of verification became ever more precise.

Thus, not only had the respective positions of the *vita contemplativa* and the *vita activa* reversed themselves: with the passage to modernity, the former ceased to have any genuine significance at all. The dissolution of "the concept of truth underlying our whole tradition" was, of course, a blow to the standing of philosophy, which proceeded to lose the privileged position in the hierarchy of human activities it had held since Plato and Aristotle. The collapse of the ideal inscribed in the *vita contemplativa* meant that philosophy could no longer pretend to be the pursuit of philosophical wisdom ("Truth"). It had to settle instead for logic, epistemology, and the various forms of introspection mentioned above.

Arendt thinks that an even more significant reversal (at least in terms of its worldly effects) occurred within the framework of the *vita activa* itself, when the attitudes and activities of *homo faber* rose to predominance during the seventeenth and eighteenth centuries. This hegemony was manifest not only in the approach of the new science, but also in the "modern discovery of history" by Vico and the new "science of politics" invented by Hobbes. In the physical sciences, one could know only what could be recreated in the laboratory by experimental means: natural processes construed as chains of efficient causation, the totality of which comprised what Kant, following Newton, called the "mechanism" of nature. But, according to Vico, the same basic reasoning meant that genuine knowledge was possible in the field of historical studies as well, for had not man "made" history? If we can only know what we ourselves have made, then historical study would seem to have an equal, if not greater, claim to legitimacy as a field of "scientific" inquiry.

Moreover, was not the polity itself something artificial, constructed by men out of laws and institutions as well as definitions of right and wrong? Hobbes argued that once the idealistic Aristotelian quest for the "natural" end or perfection of man and the political association was abandoned, it became possible to analytically resolve the polity into its constituent parts, much in the way one takes apart a watch to see how it works. The fundamental human passions—the efficient but invisible causes of the polity's life and movement— could be revealed, as Descartes taught, through a process of introspection. With the true causes of political order and disorder thus identified, the objectively necessary powers of the sovereign could be definitively cataloged. The polity itself could then be shored up or, if necessary, reconstructed on a firm logical and scientific (rather than merely speculative) basis.[91]

According to Arendt, it was the new science's focus on causal or developmental *processes* rather than the things themselves that enabled not just the natural scientist, but the historian and political philosopher as well, to claim that they had finally uncovered genuine, solidly grounded knowledge. She even goes so far as to assert that the real "break with contemplation" was consummated "not with the elevation of man the maker to the position formerly held by man the contemplator," but rather with "the introduction of the concept of process into making" by way of the experiment. "Compared with this," Arendt tells us, "the striking new arrangement of hierarchical order within the *vita activa*, where fabrication had come to occupy a rank formerly held by political action, is of minor importance."[92]

It is of "minor importance" because the hierarchical relationship between political action and fabrication within the *vita activa* had, in a sense, been reversed already by the "traditional substitution of making for acting" first performed by Plato. Within the framework established by this substitution, the experience of contemplation was transformed from an attitude of speechless wonder at the order of the cosmos to one of rational appreciation of the perfection of the models or ideal "forms" of things beheld by the eye of the mind. Contemplation as speechless wonder—*thaumazein*—gave way to contemplation as *theoria*. The latter is actually a reified version of an experience known by every craftsperson—namely, the mental "beholding of the model" that proceeds and guides the fabrication process as well as providing the craftsman with the standards necessary for evaluating his finished product.[93]

It is this "inner affinity" between contemplation and fabrication— between *theoria* and *poiēsis*—that kept these two activities in each other's orbit (so to speak) even after the modern age elevated "man the maker" into the position formerly held by "man the contemplator." Or, as Arendt puts it, if "the modern challenge to the priority of contemplation over every other kind of activity had done no more than turn upside down the established order between making and beholding, it still would have remained in the traditional frame- work." But, in fact, this framework was "forced wide open" when the understanding of fabrication shifted focus from the *product* and its guiding model to the *process* of fabrication itself—in other words, when it shifted from the question of "what a thing is" to the ques- tion of "how and through what means and processes it had come into being and could be reproduced."[94]

Arendt's argument here is abstract and hinges on what some might consider a fine (and perhaps not especially relevant) distinction. Yet, even though THC's overall reliance upon the "traditional framework" provided by the distinction between the *vita contemplativa* and *vita activa* occasionally obscures rather than facilitates her argument, Arendt's main point is clear. While these two ways of life (or *bioi*) may indeed have changed places in the hierarchy of human activities following the tri- umph of *homo faber's* utilitarian attitude, the *structure* of which they were both a part remained intact. Thus, well after it crossed the threshold of modernity, Western humanity could still understand itself—its activities and specific attributions of value—in terms of a categorial structure in- stituted long ago (a point Arendt emphasized *vis à vis* Marx in her Gaus lectures). At the foundation of this structure was the basic distinction between a mutable world of appearances, on one hand, and an im- mutable cosmos (or realm of "true Being"), on the other. The former provided the political actor with a context in which it was possible to win "immortal fame," while the latter provided the philosopher with an eternal order fit for contemplation.[95]

This entire conceptual edifice, Arendt argues, was "forced wide open" once the category of process (or "development") achieved intellectual and scientific hegemony in the latter half of the nine- teenth century. "The turning point in the intellectual history of the modern age," she writes,

> came when the image of organic life development—where the evolution of a lower being, for instance the ape, can cause the appearance of a higher being, for instance man—appeared in

the place of the image of the watchmaker who must be superior
to all watches whose cause he is.[96]

The replacement of the mechanistic worldview of *homo faber* with
an evolutionary or developmental one meant not only that the
pre-modern distinction between this world and the philosopher's
world of "true Being" could no longer be sustained.[97] It also meant
that the fundamental distinction between *subject* and *object*—basic to
virtually all post-Cartesian philosophy—could itself no longer remain intact:

> The split between subject and object, inherent in human con-
> sciousness and irremediable in the Cartesian opposition of man
> as a *res cogitans* to a surrounding world of *res extensae*, disappears
> altogether in the case of a living organism, whose very sur-
> vival depends upon the incorporation, the consumption, of
> outside matter. Naturalism, the nineteenth century version of
> materialism, seemed to find in life the way to solve the prob-
> lems of Cartesian philosophy and at the same time to bridge the
> ever-widening chasm between philosophy and science.[98]

In the resulting "process reality," not only was there nothing left
to contemplate; the distinction between action and fabrication was
itself blurred to the point of all but disappearing in an ever-flowing
stream of History or Life itself. The instrumental worldview of *homo*
faber, having gained victory over both action and contemplation in
the earlier part of the modern age, went down to defeat as the newly
hegemonic category of process rendered the distinction between
means and ends, the "in order to" and the "for the sake of," ever
more tenuous.

But however much metaphors of process, development, and evolution may have displaced those of efficient causality, instrumentality, and utility, we are still left with the mystery as to why, with the
modern rise of the *vita activa*, it was *labor* that came "to be elevated
to the highest rank of man's capacities." Nor does this displacement
provide an adequate explanation as to how, given what Arendt calls
the "diversity of the human condition and its various capacities,"
life itself came to enjoy the status of the "highest good" in the latter

half of the nineteenth century, to the point of overruling "all other considerations."[99]

Even though the argument of THC provides a certain amount of foreshadowing, Arendt's answer to these questions is still a bit surprising:

> The reason why life asserted itself as the ultimate point of reference in the modern age and has remained the highest good of modern society is that the modern reversal [of the *vita activa* and the *vita contemplativa*] operated within the fabric of a Christian society whose fundamental belief in the sacredness of life has survived...[both] secularization and the general decline of the Christian faith....The modern reversal followed and left unchallenged the most important reversal with which the Christian faith had broken into the ancient world...For the Christian "glad tidings" of the immortality of individual life had reversed the ancient relationship between man and the world and promoted the most mortal thing, human life, to the position of immortality.[100]

The Christian reversal of the classical relationship between man and the world was "disastrous" for the esteem in which political activity had once been held. Thanks to the Christian reversal, it now sank "to the level of an activity subject to necessity, destined to remedy the consequences of human sinfulness on one hand and to cater to the legitimate wants and interests of earthly life on the other." The aspiration to worldly immortality—previously the "greatest inspiration" and motivation for political action—now came to be seen as little more than vainglory.[101] The immortality of individual life was substituted for the "potential immortality" of the body politic. Life on earth, which necessarily ends in death, was only "the first and most miserable stage" of the individual's *eternal* life.[102]

All of this is, of course, a long way from the naturalism permeating the second half of the nineteenth century and the biologism that dominated the early part of the twentieth. Arendt's fundamental point, however, is that the modern age "continued to operate under the assumption that life, and not the world, is the highest good of man."[103]

At this stage, the various threads of THC begin to come together. The fact that "world alienation, and not self-alienation as Marx thought, is the hallmark of the modern age" is not due simply to the "innerworldly asceticism" born of the Protestant ethic and the spirit of capitalism; nor is it primarily the result of the distrust of the "world of appearances" born of Galileo's discovery and Descartes' radical doubt. Even in combination, the overall effect of these phenomena might well have remained limited were it not for the long-established cultural background of Christianity's rejection of this world and longing for eternal life. Once we take that background into account, the fact that even the most articulate modern critics of the tradition assumed the "priority of life over everything else," the world and earth included, becomes far more comprehensible. Indeed, it assumed the status of a "self-evident truth" for virtually all of them, from Thomas Jefferson to Friedrich Nietzsche.[104]

It is important here to be clear about the fact that Arendt is not indicting Christianity *tout court* in the manner of Machiavelli or Gibbon. Nor is she claiming that the Christian roots of Western culture made modernity's deep world and earth alienation somehow inevitable. Deploying an admittedly implausible counterfactual, she observes that our culture could have had a quite different trajectory had the discovery of the Archimedean point taken place 1,700 years earlier, when "not life but the world was still the highest good for man."[105] More to the point, she underlines the fact that what matters today is not the *immortality* of life but the assumption that *life itself* is the highest good. While this assumption is "clearly Christian in origin," that "constitutes no more than an important attending circumstance for the Christian faith."[106] Throughout THC, Arendt remains firm in her conviction that human history is constituted by *events*, not by the unfolding of the "inner logic" of ideas or the capitalist mode of production.

It is for this reason that she can plausibly claim that "before Galileo, all paths still seemed to be open." "The only thing we can be sure of," she writes, "is that the coincidence of the reversal of doing and contemplating with the earlier reversal of life and world became the point of departure for the whole modern development."[107] That is to say: when, in the early modern age, the *vita activa* was liberated from its dependence upon the opposing, but nevertheless constitutive, pole of the *vita contemplativa* (a liberation effected by the innerworldly asceticism of Weber's Calvinists, on one hand, and the rise of the new experimental science, on the other), the sole reference point that remained was not the world, but life itself. The freeing of the active life from any ground in either "true Being" or the world of appearances (liberation from the latter being the dual legacy of Christianity and Cartesian doubt) is what ultimately made it possible for the *process* of man's "metabolism with nature" to take center stage, intellectually and culturally as well as practically. Once this happened, *homo faber's* defeat at the hands of the "worldless" *animal laborans* in virtually all spheres of life—economic and sociological as well as cultural and intellectual—became a *fait accompli*.

IV   Conclusion

It is difficult to sum up a book as *sui generis* as *The Human Condition*. In it, Arendt provides accounts of: (a) the nature and origins of the public-political realm in the West; (b) the effect the rise of capitalism and market society had on this realm; (c) the phenomenological characteristics of labor, work, and action; (d) the roles modern capitalism, science, and technology have played in fostering alienation from the durable public world and from our planetary home; and (e) the deeply rooted cultural and intellectual reasons why life as such has become, over the course of the last two centuries, the highest good for Western (and perhaps even global) civilization. Considered as a stand-alone work, it seems almost to inhabit a different (decidedly more philosophical and abstract) intellectual universe than *The Origins of Totalitarianism*.

At the beginning of the previous chapter, I noted some broad thematic continuities between the two works, including their shared focus on the importance of human plurality; their common concern with the human capacity for "spontaneous" action; and their quite similar worries about the assimilation of political and social life to nature or nature-like processes. I want to conclude this chapter by underlining, once again, a few of the themes that connect THC and OT. I do this not to suggest, as some have, that the main points of Arendt's later work can all be found (*in utero*, as it were) in OT. It is crucial to see just how significantly Arendt develops, revises, and expands these themes in her later work. The progression is hardly linear, and Arendt provides precious few explicit links back to her earlier conclusions. Hence the need to briefly revisit them.

The first and most obvious link connecting OT and THC is the characteristically Arendtian concern with *beginning*—with the human capacity for unpredictable or spontaneous action. In OT, this capacity (which Arendt views as the root of any freedom worthy of the name) is presented as having been targeted for obliteration by totalitarian regimes. They did this not out of any simple lust for domination (Augustine's *libido dominandi*), but rather out of the desire to remove obstacles to the accelerated motion of the "laws" of History (Bolshevism) or Nature (Nazism). Arendt's concluding gesture toward an existential ground for our initiatory capacity ("that a beginning be made man was created, said Augustine. This beginning is guaranteed by each new birth; it is indeed every man") expands, in THC, into a theory of political action in which *natality*—the human capacity to interrupt all "automatic" or seemingly inevitable chains of events—plays the key role.

Arendt argued in OT that human spontaneity can, under certain extreme conditions, be destroyed. In THC, she argues that the transformation of the public-political realm into a "national household" threatens, if not to destroy our most distinctively human capacity, then at least to marginalize it as *behavior* replaces *action*. Contrary to our expectations, THC offers no guarantees, no set of "ontological foundations," that assure us that human spontaneity cannot be severely curtailed or even blotted out. There is only the hope, the possibility, that Arendt sees inscribed in the birth of every individual.

A second continuity emerges when we consider Arendt's contention that the ever-accelerating cycles of production and consumption born of capitalist accumulation combine with increasingly frequent scientific and technological revolutions to create a "process reality"—a Heraclitean flux in which the solidity and durability of the world all but dissolves. This thesis obviously echoes her descriptions of the totalitarian destruction of all stable legal and institutional structures in order to accelerate the motion of the "laws" of History or Nature. The totalitarians wanted to uproot (or at least neutralize) everything that stood in the way of these "irresistible" laws of movement and thereby create a kind of "process reality" of their own. Of course, Arendt would never be so irresponsible as to suggest that modern capitalism or science is "totalitarian" in her specific sense of the word. What she fears is the Faustian dynamism she sees as driving all three phenomena.

A third broad continuity surfaces when we compare Arendt's treatment (in OT) of a bourgeois class intent on turning the polity into a tool or servant of economic interests with her thesis about the "rise of the social" in THC. The animating fear, in both instances, is of the permanent colonization of the public realm by forces intent on facilitating the unlimited accumulation of wealth, without any regard for the preservation of institutional integrity and durability. In THC, however, this fear is not generated by the actions or sensibility of a particular social class, but by society itself—that is, by the emergence of the modern socio-economic realm, a realm which absorbs what had previously been the discrete realms of public and private. The "rise of the social" produces a fundamental change in the nature of the reality we inhabit, a change whose cultural roots go much deeper than the rise of the middle class and triumph of self-interest over civic responsibilities.

Finally, both works suggest that civilized life, as well as the preservation of rights and freedom, depend on the ability of the political association to provide what Arendt calls a "home for mortal man." In OT, this idea emerges in its most poignant and literal form, guiding Arendt's analysis of the interwar refugee crisis, statelessness, and the central contradictions afflicting the nation-state as a political form. In THC, the idea of "having a place in the world" returns, but in far more general and even metaphorical form. It takes on a decidedly existential resonance, a resonance perhaps not inappropriate in a work entitled The Human Condition but one which points us to a problematic philosophical assumption not found in OT.

While severely critical of German Idealism and its "rainbow bridge of concepts," Arendt—at least in THC—apparently shares with Hegel, Schelling, and some of the romantics the view that "being at home in the world" is, or should be, our genuine human vocation. Arendt, of course, differs from her German idealist predecessors, as well as from Marx, in that she believes our condition of existential "homelessness" is a function of world, rather than self, alienation. Nevertheless, the underlying assumption of all three positions—Idealist, Marxian, and Arendtian—is that alienation, *qua* alienation, is self-evidently bad. Coming from a political thinker who valued independent judgment, critical distance, and the ability to think for oneself almost as much as she valued the *bios politikos*, this is more than a bit perplexing. A more plausible response to the experience of modernity would be to say that we must come to feel "at home" in not-being-at-home. Of course, *radical* alienation from the world is as dangerous as Arendt said it was: it destroys the possibility of any practically effective care for the world. However, *moderate* alienation from one's own community and culture is and has been the essential precondition of all genuinely critical thought since Socrates.

Summary

Arendt's chapters on work and action are among the most important in THC. The chapter on work focuses on what Arendt calls "man's world-building capacity"—that is, upon the human ability to create an artificial world (composed of buildings, institutions, machines) that stands *between* man and nature. The products of work, unlike those of labor, are not ephemeral. They are not consumer goods that provide the materials necessary for the reproduction of labor-power. In contrast to the "products" of labor, the products of work possess a durability that lasts over many generations. The positive role of work in providing a "home for moral man" is potentially undercut, however, by the extension of the characteristic attitudes and categories of *homo faber* to all things, the public realm included. The pervasive role of the means/end category in all spheres and the dominance of a utilitarian attitude toward the world are markers of the early modern triumph of *homo faber*. Yet, this triumph is relatively fleeting, as technology and machine production combine to assimilate the activity of work to the natural (or pseudo-natural) rhythms of the labor process.

Action, the sharing of words and deeds in the public realm, pre-supposes the existence of an artificial world created by work. It also presupposes human plurality, the "fact that men, not Man, live on earth and inhabit the world." Political action appears primarily in the mode of persuasive speech. Politics, as opposed to domination or coercion, can be described as the art of reaching decisions through public discussions conducted by diverse and equal citizens. It consists of the oratory, debate, deliberation, and judgment that such citizens share about matters of common (public) concern. Action is characterized by its initiatory character: to act is to begin. Action is also characterized by contingency and lack of control: the unexpected is to be expected in the political realm. Moreover, beginning something in a sphere characterized by the presence of other acting beings means that action rarely, if ever, achieves its intended goal. The seeming "haphazardness" of political action—its irreducible "frailty" or lack of sovereign control—led Plato and Aristotle to reinterpret action (*praxis*) as a form of making (*poiēsis*). This "substitution of making for acting" proves foundational for the Western tradition of political philosophy. It expresses the anti-democratic and anti-political prejudices not just of Plato and Aristotle, but of many other canonical political philosophers as well.

Notes

1 Arendt, THC, p. 126.
2 Arendt, THC, p. 137.
3 Arendt, THC, p. 137.
4 Arendt, THC, p. 143.
5 Arendt, THC, p. 139.
6 Arendt, THC, p. 144.
7 Arendt, THC, p. 141.
8 Arendt, THC, p. 143.
9 Arendt, THC, p. 146 (my emphasis).
10 Arendt, THC, p. 152.
11 For the parallel, see Karl Löwith, *Max Weber and Karl Marx* (New York: Routledge, 1993).
12 Max Weber, *Economy and Society*, Vol. II, edited by Gunther Roth and Claus Wittich (Berkeley: University of California Press, 1978), p. 1402.
13 Arendt, THC, p. 151.
14 Arendt, THC, p. 153. The quotes are from Heisenberg.
15 Arendt, THC, p. 153
16 Arendt, THC, p. 153.
17 Arendt, THC, p. 154.
18 Arendt, THC, p. 157.
19 Arendt, THC, p. 160.
20 Arendt, THC, p. 160.
21 Arendt, BPF, pp. 151–153.

22 Thucydides, *History of the Peloponnesian War*, trans.by Rex Warner (New York: Penguin Books, 1972), p. 147.
23 Benjamin Constant, "The Liberty of the Ancients Compared to That of the Moderns" in *Political Writings*, edited by Biancamaria Fontana (New York: Cambridge University Press, 1988), pp. 310–318.
24 Max Weber makes this point strongly in "Politics as a Vocation." See Weber, *FMW*, p. 117.
25 This may seem too blanket an assessment for some. However, the fact remains that, for the greater part of two and a half millennia, "democracy" was viewed as among the worst possible political regimes.
26 Arendt, THC, pp. 175–176.
27 Arendt, THC, p. 176.
28 Arendt, THC, p. 176.
29 Arendt, THC, pp. 176–177.
30 Arendt, THC, p. 177.
31 Arendt, THC, p. 178.
32 Arendt, THC, pp. 178–179.
33 Arendt, THC, p. 179.
34 Arendt, THC, p. 180.
35 Arendt, THC, p .180.
36 See Hanna Pitkin, "Justice: On Relating Public and Private" in *Hannah Arendt: Critical Essays*, edited by Lewis P. Hinchman and Sandra K. Hinchman (Albany: SUNY Press, 1994), pp. 261–288.
37 Arendt, THC, p. 194.
38 Arendt, THC, p. 197.
39 Arendt, THC, p. 182.
40 The emergence of "women's history" and history "from below" is, among other things, precisely the attempt to tell stories that haven't—until relatively recently—been told, and to make them part of our "organized remembrance."
41 Arendt, THC, pp. 182–183.
42 Arendt, THC, p. 190.
43 Arendt, THC, p. 184.
44 Arendt, THC, p. 184.
45 Arendt, THC, p. 186.
46 In recent years, the "narrative constitution of identity" has become something of a cliché in literary studies.
47 See D. Villa, *Arendt and Heidegger: The Fate of the Political* (Princeton: Princeton University Press, 1995).
48 Friedrich Nietzsche, *The Will to Power*, translated by Walter Kaufmann and R.J. Hollingdale (New York: Vintage Books, 1968). p. 9.
49 Arendt, THC, p. 220.
50 See Martin Heidegger, "The Origin of the Work of Art" in Heidegger, *Poetry, Language, Thought*, edited by Albert Hofstader (New York: Harper and Row, 1971), pp. 15–86.
51 Arendt, THC, p. 196.
52 As Arendt observes in a footnote, "Recent political history is full of examples indicating that the term "human material" is no harmless metaphor." See THC, p. 188.

53 Arendt, BPF, p. 163.
54 Arendt, THC, p. 57.
55 Arendt, THC, p. 197.
56 G.W.F. Hegel, "The Positivity of the Christian Religion" in Hegel, *Early Theological Writings*, translated by T. M. Knox (Philadelphia: University of Pennsylvania Press, 1975), p. 157.
57 Arendt, THC, p. 198.
58 Arendt, THC, p. 198.
59 Arendt, THC, p. 195.
60 Weber, *Economy and Society*, p. 53.
61 Weber, "Politics as a Vocation" in FMW, p. 119.
62 Hannah Arendt, *On Violence* (New York: Harcourt Brace & Company, 1970), p. 44.
63 Arendt, THC, p. 189.
64 Arendt, *The Promise of Politics*, p. 12.
65 Arendt, THC, p. 204.
66 Marx and Engels, *The Communist Manifesto*, p. 38.
67 Arendt, THC, p. 248.
68 Arendt, THC, p. 264.
69 Arendt, THC, p. 250.
70 Arendt, THC, p. 251.
71 Arendt, THC, p. 1, quoting the funeral obelisk of "one of Russia's great scientists."
72 Arendt, THC, pp. 254–255.
73 Arendt, THC, p. 254.
74 John Locke, *Two Treatises of Government*, edited by Peter Laslett (New York: Cambridge University Press, 1988), p. 291.
75 Arendt, THC, p. 255.
76 Arendt, THC, p. 273.
77 Arendt, THC, p. 276.
78 Arendt, THC, p. 274.
79 Arendt, THC, p. 274.
80 See Heidegger, "The Age of the World Picture" in Martin Heidegger, *The Question Concerning Technology and other Essays*, translated by William Lovitt (New York: Harper and Row, 1977).
81 Arendt, THC, p. 262.
82 Arendt, THC, p. 282.
83 Arendt, THC, p. 284.
84 Arendt, THC, p. 272.
85 Immanuel Kant, *The Critique of Pure Reason*, translated by Norman Kemp Smith (New York: St. Martin's Press, 2007), Bxiv.
86 Arendt, THC, p. 288.
87 Arendt, THC, p. 261, quotes Eddington and Heisenberg to this effect.
88 Kateb, *Hannah Arendt: Politics, Conscience, Evil*, p. 160.
89 Cf. Seyla Benhabib, *The Reluctant Modernism of Hannah Arendt* (Thousand Oaks: Sage Publications, 1996).
90 Arendt, THC, p. 290.
91 Arendt, THC, pp. 298–299.

92 Arendt, THC, p. 301.
93 Arendt, THC, p. 302.
94 Arendt, THC, p. 304.
95 Arendt, THC, pp. 18–20.
96 Arendt, THC, p. 312.
97 Cf. Nietzsche, "How the True World Becomes a Fable" in Nietzsche, *Twilight of the Idols/The Anti-Christ*, translated by R. J. Hollingdale (New York: Penguin Books, 1968), pp. 40–41.
98 Arendt, THC, pp. 312–313.
99 Arendt, THC, p. 313.
100 Arendt, THC, p. 314.
101 Arendt, THC, p. 314.
102 Arendt, THC, p. 316.
103 Arendt, THC, p. 318.
104 Arendt, THC, p. 319.
105 Arendt, THC, p. 319.
106 Arendt, THC, p. 319.
107 Arendt, THC, p. 320.

Further reading

S. Benhabib, *The Reluctant Modernism of Hannah Arendt* (Thousand Oaks: Sage Publications, 1996).
D. Villa, *Arendt and Heidegger: The Fate of the Political* (Princeton: Princeton University Press, 1995). [Focuses on Arendt's theory of political action and her critique of the tradition, as well as her debt to Heidegger.]

Five
Revolution, constitution, authority

I Violence and the meaning of revolution

Albrecht Wellmer has written that *On Revolution* represents Arendt's "settling of accounts" with the Marxist revolutionary and liberal constitutionalist traditions.[1] This is an accurate yet ultimately insufficient characterization. Viewed in terms of her *oeuvre*, *On Revolution* stands as Arendt's fullest and most explicit account of what authentic political action looks like in the modern age. Basing herself on a probing contrast of the political experience of the French and American revolutions, Arendt focuses on three main points. First, she emphasizes that revolutions are "the only political events which confront us directly and inevitably with the problem of beginning"—with whether and how plural political actors can interrupt the course of history and create, through spontaneous joint action, a new form of government and a new "space for freedom." The answer to the question of whether such a radical beginning is possible is by no means obvious, particularly given influential interpretations of revolutionary events which emphasize either unsuspected historical continuities (such as Tocqueville's *The Ancien Regime and the Revolution*) or the dialectical unfolding and development of latent possibilities (such as we find in Hegel and Marx).

Second, Arendt argues that the "revolutionary spirit"—the confidence displayed by the French and American revolutionaries that the flow of time can indeed be interrupted—was itself something new and characteristically *modern*. Unlike the "Glorious Revolution" of 1688 in England, the revolutions of the eighteenth century were hardly "revolutions back" to established patterns of institutional behavior and political practice. The modern concept of revolution, Arendt tells us, was "inextricably bound up with the notion that the course of history suddenly begins anew, that an entirely new story, a story never known of told before, is about to unfold."[2] While the *novelty* of what they were undertaking was clear to the revolutionaries from the start, the *plot* of the "new story" they had begun became manifest "to actors and spectators alike" only in the course of revolutionary events. Self-government and civic equality had all but disappeared from the Western world in the 1,300 years stretching from the fall of Rome through the feudal period and the *ancien regime*. It was against this European backdrop of rulership and subjection that the "plot" of the revolutionary story appeared. It was, in Arendt's words, "unmistakably the emergence of freedom."[3]

The question is what type of freedom did the revolutions aim at? At the time of *On Revolution's* publication (1963), Arendt's answer was more than a little controversial since it went against the grain of received wisdom. For generations, the American Revolution had been interpreted largely along Lockean lines. It was seen as a revolution whose primary aim was constitutional (limited) government and the preservation of property and civil liberties (or "lives, liberties, and estates," in Locke's famous phrase). This interpretation received its canonical expression in Louis Hartz's influential *The Liberal Tradition in America* (1955). *On Revolution* broke sharply and dramatically with this view, arguing that the American and French revolutions were—at least in their early phases—equally committed to the ideal of republican citizenship and the creation and preservation of *political* (and not just civil) liberty. Active self-government under law was the point of the revolutionary republican *constitutio libertatis*—the constitution of liberty.

It is in underscoring this third point that Arendt both departs from and enriches the analysis of political action found in *The Human Condition*. The most notable departure is found in *On Revolution's* emphasis upon the fundamental importance of authoritative *written* constitutions in the creation and preservation of "new spaces of freedom." From Arendt's perspective, the legal and institutional articulation of such spaces provided—or should have provided—the opportunity for every citizen to become a "participator in the government of

affairs" (Jefferson) should he or she choose. Arendt's constitutionalism is thus markedly different from more familiar liberal variants, if
only because its *raison d'être* is a decidedly "positive" (political) form
of freedom instead of the usual "negative" liberty (or freedom from
interference) we typically associate with constitutional limited government. While Arendt makes no explicit reference to Isaiah Berlin's
famous distinction (not surprising, given his well-documented hostility toward her), her development of the contrast between *political*
and *civil* liberties in OR is extensive enough to call it to mind. However, unlike many of her civic republican predecessors (Machiavelli
and Rousseau, for example) she is at no point neglectful or dismissive of civil liberties. She sees the protection of basic individual
liberties as a feature of any *civilized* form of government, whether
monarchical, democratic, or republican in form.

This is an important point, if only because liberals since Benjamin
Constant have been leery of the republican emphasis on political
participation over individual rights and liberties. Constant's famous
lecture "The Liberty of the Ancients Compared to that of the Moderns" (1819) made the case that the tragic mistake of the French
revolutionaries was to try to resurrect the "collective sovereignty"
prized by the ancient republics of Rome and Athens in the modern
world, with predictably dire results. Such freedom has no place in
modern constitutional regimes, Constant argued, where liberty is primarily understood as the right of the individual to choose his or
her own profession, place of residence, faith, partner, etc. without
interference from the state.

A superficial reading of OR might lead one to conclude that Arendt
has committed the same sin as the revolutionaries Constant so devastatingly criticized. Yet such a conclusion is off base for several reasons. First, there is Arendt's critique of the perennial identification
of freedom with *sovereignty*, whether of a collective or national sort.
Second (and relatedly), there is her extensive criticism of Rousseau
and Robespierre's reliance upon the idea of a singular and ideally
unanimous "will of the people" as the source of both legality and
power. Third, there is her strongly maintained distinction between
opinions (which constitute the medium of politics and which she sees
as formed and expressed by individuals) and *interests* (which are intrinsic to a variety of social groups who desire to see their particular

interests advanced by elected representatives). Fourth, and drawing upon her analysis in OT, there is her distinction between a politically organized *people*—one that participates in a public realm that contains institutionalized spaces for the sharing of opinions and debate, deliberation, and decision—and unorganized *masses* who are susceptible to various shifting public moods and to ideological manipulation. While each of these criticisms and distinctions are open to contestation, they nevertheless reveal just how misguided any *direct* application of Constant's critique to Arendt's brand of republicanism is, despite her own undeniably strong criticism of representative government.

OR enriches the conception of political action found in THC by shifting the focus away from agonistic or heroic political actors to the consideration of the self-organizing political capacities of ordinary citizens (the elite status of the French and American "men of the revolutions" notwithstanding). In the last chapter, "The Revolutionary Tradition and its Lost Treasure," Arendt draws our attention to a largely overlooked political phenomenon, one that accompanied virtually all the key revolutionary moments in Europe following 1848. This is the regular emergence of the council system. That system, which in all cases was spontaneously organized by ordinary citizens, appeared in Paris during the Prussian siege of 1870 and the creation of the Paris Commune in 1870–1871. It appeared again in Russia during the wave of spontaneous strikes in 1905, giving birth to grassroots political leadership in the form of workers' councils (or *soviets*), a form of leadership that reappeared during the February Revolution of 1917. During the revolutionary period of 1918–1919 in Berlin, workers' and soldiers' councils created a *Rätesystem* that they hoped would become the cornerstone of the new form of government following the demise of the *Kaiserreich*, while during the same period, a short-lived *Räterepublik* actually came into existence in Bavaria. Finally, and most thrillingly for Arendt, the council system re-emerged in the Hungarian Revolution of 1956.[4]

From the standpoint of "professional revolutionaries" (such as the Bolsheviks) and hard-headed "realists" such as Max Weber, the councils were political ephemera destined for quick demise in the face of counter-revolutionary violence or the establishment of one-party revolutionary dictatorships. From Arendt's perspective, however, they were hugely significant since they pointed to nothing less than a "new type of republican government." This would be a federal republic in which political power would no longer be monopolized by a centralized state bureaucracy or by whatever political party happened to be victorious on the parliamentary "battlefield of elections" (Weber). It would be a republic in which *authority* was generated from the bottom up rather than the top down; in which *power* was created by citizens "acting in concert" rather than through a state monopoly on the legitimate means of violence; and in which ordinary citizens were assured access to "spaces of freedom" at the local level. The latter would indeed enable them—and not just professional politicians or administrators—to become "participators in the government of affairs" should they so choose.

****

Given Arendt's penchant for making distinctions, it is perhaps not surprising that she begins *On Revolution* by telling us what a revolution is *not*. Considered as a *political* phenomenon, revolution cannot be equated simply with the attempted violent overthrow of an established government. If it were, then *coups d'état* and slave revolts would have to be considered revolutions, which they obviously are not. For Arendt, "revolution" refers to a specifically *modern* type of political phenomenon: the act of a people's liberation from domination that leads to the *constitutional foundation of a new body politic and a new form of government*. *Violent* struggle, even war, may be a necessary precondition to the beginning of the "new story" thus commenced, but it does not determine, let alone embody, the sum and substance of the revolution itself.

Arendt is aware that this assertion is counterintuitive, especially given the apparent inseparability of war and revolution in the twentieth century. However, her two chosen models—the American and French revolutions—provide her with a certain degree of back-up. What makes these two revolutions paradigmatic in her view is not the violent overthrow of an oppressor, but the fact that the men who carried them forward saw their primary task as *the foundation of a new body politic* by means of a new constitution. Despite all their differences, it is this common thread linking the French and American

revolutions that enables Arendt to state that "under modern conditions" the act of foundation "is identical with the framing of a
constitution." Thus it is that "the calling of constitutional assemblies
has become the hallmark of revolution ever since the Declaration of
Independence initiated the writing of constitutions for each of the
American states..."[5]

Even granting Arendt this key point, the skeptic will want to object that war and violence were central elements of both revolutions.
The American colonies fought an eight-year war in order to liberate themselves from their English "motherland," while the French
Revolution produced wars of both defense and aggression against
powerful and inveterately hostile European monarchies. However,
contrary to the skeptic's impression, Arendt has no desire to deny
the interrelatedness of war and revolution. Rather, what she wants
to avoid is the habitual *reduction* of revolution to war or violent social
struggle. Such reduction has the effect of converting what is a quintessentially *political* phenomenon into an un- or even anti-political
one. That this is no mere terminological quibble is borne out by the
fateful Marxist-Leninist equation of revolution with the violent seizure of state power by a vanguard party. It is similarly borne out by
the ideology of a people's collective self-formation through violence
propounded by such anti-colonialist theorists as Frantz Fanon.[6]
Hence, Arendt's staunchly held conviction that "only where change
occurs in the sense of a new beginning, where violence is used to
constitute an altogether different form of government, to bring about the formation of a new body politic...can we speak of revolution."[7]

In attempting to "save the phenomenon" of political revolution
from conflation with either war or violence, Arendt revives the
quandary we first encountered in the conception of political action
presented in THC. In that work, she drew a strict distinction between
the debate, deliberation, judgment, and decision-taking characteristic of meaningful political action and speech (on the one hand)
and the sheerly instrumental character of speechless violence (on
the other).

That politics is talkative while violence is mute is a recurrent theme
in Arendt. It is this very muteness that precludes violence from having any intrinsic meaning, reducing it to the status of a mere means
or technique. Where violence rules "everything and everybody must

fall silent." It is this silence that leads Arendt to call violence "a marginal phenomenon in the political realm."[8] As previously noted, for Arendt, this realm is a space of meaningful appearances. It is for this reason that political phenomena "in contradistinction to physical matters" stand in need of speech and articulation. They need "something which transcends mere physical visibility as well as sheer audibility, in order to be manifest at all."[9] While the political theorist or thinker may have a good deal to say about *justifications* for war or revolutionary violence, the phenomenon of violence itself—an instrumentality of last resort deployed by nation against nation, or class against class—is largely a matter of strategy and tactics. As such, it is a matter for military men and other "technicians" of violence.

In OR Arendt recalibrates the distinction between action and violence in terms of a distinction between *revolution and the foundation of freedom* (on the one hand) and *liberation from domination* (on the other). The *struggle for liberation*—whether from a colonizer, a ruling class, a one-party dictatorship, or an ethnic majority—is likely, though not necessarily, to be violent, while the *revolutionary foundation* of a new body politic demands speech, persuasion, compromise, and joint action. Liberation—e.g. the American war with Britain in the eighteenth century, or the nationalist struggles against imperialist domination in Africa, the Middle East, and Eastern Europe in the twentieth—"may be the condition of freedom but by no means leads automatically to it." Even the intention of liberating is, Arendt writes, "not identical with the desire for freedom."[10] Getting rid of the oppressor is one thing; constituting a new form of government where political freedom is a reality is another. The progression from the "negative" task of liberation to the "positive" one of constitution is by no means guaranteed. Historically speaking, it has been the exception rather than the rule, something the examples of the French and American revolutions bear out in their own distinct ways.

The equation of revolution with violence may very well be the primary obstacle to grasping its significance as a *political* phenomenon. However, the meaning, specificity, and (most importantly) the *modernity* of revolution are threatened by other habits of mind as well. Foremost amongst these is the tendency to view revolution not as a peculiarly *modern* political phenomenon, but rather as an event that recurs throughout the West's political history. It is common, for example, to refer to the civil war in Corcyra (427 BCE) recounted in Thucydides' History as a "revolution," and to do the same with respect to the two oligarchic coups in Athens (in 411 and 404 BCE). In similar fashion, the Nazi seizure of power in 1933 was described by Hitler himself as part of the "National Socialist revolution" and has been seen by historians such as George Mosse as part of a broader "fascist revolution" that occurred across Europe during the interwar period.[11]

In each of these instances, the word "revolution" designates a change in government effected by the seizure of power. However, this equation of revolution with the seizing of power or similar instances of dramatic political change is hugely misleading. The ancients were, of course, well-acquainted with political change (as the histories of Thucydides, Livy, Tacitus, and Polybius all attest). They, however, viewed the rise and fall of states against the backdrop of a cyclical concept of time, one in which patterns of growth, corruption, and decline in the political realm mirrored those in the natural. Thus, no matter how great a "motion" in the realm of human affairs might be (and the Peloponnesian War was certainly a "great" motion, the greatest ever experienced by the Greeks, according to Thucydides), the arc it traced had appeared before and would doubtless appear again. As a result, what Arendt calls the "pathos of novelty"—the overwhelming sense on the part of leading actors of the French and American revolutions of the utterly unprecedented character of their endeavor—was entirely absent from antiquity. For the ancients, there could be nothing like a revolutionary interruption—a radical break or a genuinely new beginning—in history because history in the modern (progressive and linear) sense simply did not exist for them.[12] The greatest political changes invariably fell back into a cyclical motion whose different stages were preordained and recurred eternally.

But couldn't one argue (and this is a second obstacle to grasping the specifically modern character of revolution) that Christianity's introduction of a rectilinear time concept made the idea of such an interruption in history—of an absolute beginning—available to all? On one level, this is obviously the case. The birth of Jesus constituted just such a break, a "new beginning" cosmically separating one epoch from another as if by an abyss. This fact has enabled some

conservative commentators to suggest that the revolutionary tradition and its "pathos of novelty" are actually little more than secularized versions of the Christian view of history, albeit encumbered
with eschatological expectations directed at the here and now rather
than at the end of time. And it has enabled religiously oriented commentators of a more liberal bent to suggest that revolutions are not
so much modern as they are "essentially Christian" in character. This
thesis is usually backed up by the suggestion that Christian teachings
are "revolutionary in and of themselves."[13]

Arendt rejects both arguments. In the case of the first, she rightly
points out that the "Christian concept of history, as formulated by
Augustine, could conceive of a new beginning only in terms of a
transmundane event breaking into and interrupting the normal
course of secular history."[14] This event—the coming of Jesus—was
indeed singular: it happened once and would not happen again until the end of time. Meanwhile, as Augustine's repeated emphasis
on man's fallen nature and the illusory character of Roman/pagan
notions of virtue and glory makes all too clear, the course of human
affairs in the secular realm remained bound to the old cycles determining the rise and fall of empires. The idea that a new beginning in
"the city of man" might give rise to a durable public realm with its
own potential "immortality" would have struck Augustine as both
illusory and blasphemous: "It is the world that will pass away; man
will live forever."[15] As for the idea that Christian teachings are themselves revolutionary in essence and therefore lie at the root of most
modern revolutions, Arendt is notably curt:

> The fact is that no revolution was ever made in the name of
> Christianity prior to the modern age, so that the best one can
> say in favor of this theory is it needed modernity to liberate the
> revolutionary germs of the Christian faith, which obviously is
> begging the question.[16]

We are now in a position to understand why Arendt feels justified in
categorically stating that

> the modern concept of revolution, inextricably bound up with
> the notion that the course of history suddenly begins anew, that

an entirely new story, a story never known or told before, is
about to unfold, was unknown prior to the two great revolutions at the end of the eighteenth century.[17]

Yet it would be wrong to frame the *original* motivations of the so-
called "Founding Fathers" in America or the members of the Constituent Assembly in France in terms of a characteristically modern
embrace of novelty as such. One strong *leitmotif* of On Revolution is how
what started out as a movement for restoration of the "rights of free-
born Englishmen" in America and those of regional *parlements* and
other "intermediary powers" in France turned into a *revolution* in the
modern sense only when protests against specific abuses perpetrated
by George III and Louis XVI transformed themselves, in the press of
events, into a rejection of monarchical government as such. (We find
just such a progression encapsulated in the argument and rhetoric of
the Declaration of Independence.) "The point of the matter," Arendt
writes,

> is that the enormous pathos of the new era, which we find in
> almost identical terms and in endless variations uttered by the
> actors of the American as of the French Revolution, came to the
> fore *only after they had come much against their will to a point of no return*.[18]

This observation is significant for several reasons. First, it reminds us
of what Arendt called the "boundlessness" of action in THC, and her
associated claim that the political actors are not *fabricators* who start
with a plan and then execute it (the "traditional substitution of making for acting" notwithstanding). Second, it underscores just how
radical and unprecedented the revolutionary endeavor was for the
eighteenth-century "men of revolution." Despite their great achievements and shared sense of the "pathos of novelty," the thought of
an *absolute* political beginning remained troubling even for them. The
puzzle of how to invest something *radically new*—a new body politic
and a new form of government—with anything like binding authority weighed heavily on their minds. It even inclined some of
them (for example, Thomas Paine) to continue to cast their endeavor
in conservative terms, as the retrieval of previously well-established
liberties.[19]

Third, the sheer contingency of their interruptions of the normal course of history made the men of both revolutions anxious to detect some current of necessity underlying the epoch-making events they had brought about. It seemed that greater than human forces needed to be summoned in order to account for a historical break of such magnitude. Providence, historical necessity, and (in France at least) the irresistible movement of the *torrent révolutionnaire* were among the forces political actors and observers alike invoked in order to account for what had previously been unimaginable.

Here we encounter one of the strongest thematic links between OR and Arendt's earlier works. In OT Arendt argued that totalitarian ideologies elevated the "laws of movement" of Nature and History to the status of all-determining forces. In THC, she extended that analysis to the "rise of the social"—that is, to the idea that the modern hegemony of society's "life process" was rendering human existence ever more predictable, establishing the reign of conditioned economic *behavior* over the spontaneous *action* of the political realm. In comparison to the two earlier books OR seems markedly more optimistic in outlook, focusing as it does on the human capacity for joint action and radically new beginnings.[20] But while OR presents both the French and American revolutions as quintessential examples of spontaneous (unpredictable) political action, it also tells the story of how both revolutions managed to lose their way, coming under the sway of deterministic forces and theories and ultimately betraying the "revolutionary spirit" that had animated them in the first place.

In the case of the French Revolution, the "plot thread" of the revolutionary story—the emergence of freedom—is lost in the course of the revolution itself. Concern with the constitution of a new form of government gives way to what Arendt sees as the Jacobin desire to solve the "social question" (the grinding poverty endured by millions in France) by means of revolutionary violence. In the case of the American Revolution—a revolution that *succeeded* in creating a new "space for freedom" through the constitutional foundation of a new form of government—this loss occurs far more gradually, as waves of poor European immigrants come to America in the late nineteenth and early twentieth centuries seeking not republican liberty but rather a land of "milk and honey." Political freedom gives way to the forces of necessity as hunger and poverty (on the one hand) and the desire for material comfort and unlimited consumption (on the other) deprive both revolutions of their original *raison d'être*. For Arendt, the lamentable result is a European revolutionary tradition in which *authentic* revolutions are equated with *social* revolutions, and an American revolutionary tradition that denies its own radicalism through the identification of freedom with civil liberties and the free market.

It is here that the insight of Wellmer's observation comes into sharpest focus. For in addition to calling our attention to the political stakes of revolution—the creation and preservation of a space for positive political freedom (or, in Lincoln's famous phrase, government "of the people, by the people, and for the people")—*OR* does indeed represent Arendt's "settling of accounts" with both the Marxist and liberal revolutionary traditions. In her view, rather than "preserving and augmenting" new spaces of positive political freedom, both traditions have a hand in destroying them. This is an exceptionally severe verdict, especially *vis à vis* the liberal revolutionary tradition descending from Locke. One task of the present chapter is to probe the reasons she arrived at it.

II Historical necessity, the "social question," and the politics of authenticity

Throughout Arendt's work, there is an unusually intense focus on the metaphors through which men make sense of, and often distort, political phenomena and experience. In the case of her analysis of totalitarianism, the structuring metaphors of both Bolshevik and Nazi ideology are biological (organic and developmental) in nature. Ultimately, they are grounded in a vulgarization of Darwin's ideas, one in which the "survival of the fittest" gives way to a struggle of classes or races with a predetermined, historically or naturally necessary, outcome. In THC, Arendt's focus shifts away from the ideologies of the twentieth century to the foundational metaphors of the Western tradition of political philosophy itself. Here, the "traditional substitution of making for acting" takes the leading role in effectively obliterating the plurality, unpredictability, and boundlessness that characterize genuine forms of political action.

In OR, this focus on metaphors which shape and distort our perception of political phenomena becomes, if anything, more intense. Arendt's overarching goal, however, remains the same. She wants to draw our attention to the way actors and theorists in the Western tradition have persistently denied or obscured the unpredictable and non-sovereign nature of political action, preferring to portray it instead as something that is both *determined* (by natural, economic, or historical factors) and *instrumental* in character. Given this concern with how metaphors shape our perceptions, we should not be surprised when Arendt commences the main part of OR by tracing the genealogy of the word "revolution" back to Copernicus' *De revolutionibus orbium coelestium*. In that work, "revolution" designated "the regular, lawfully revolving motion of the stars, which, since it was known to be beyond the influence of men and hence irresistible, was…characterized neither by newness nor by violence."[21] It was this astronomical sense of the word that provided the metaphorical grounding for the idea of political revolution as a "swinging back" into a preordained order—precisely the idea of revolution that guided the "Glorious Revolution" of 1688 in England.

It was later (and more authentically modern) revolutionaries who were to introduce the elements of novelty and violence into the meaning of the word "revolution." These elements were "conspicuous by their absence" from the original astronomical sense of the word. However, one key element of the original metaphor *was* retained by the later "men of revolution." This was the emphasis on the sheer *irresistibility* of the motion in question. Arendt claims that "we know…the exact date when the word 'revolution' was used for the first time with an exclusive emphasis on irresistibility and without any connotation of a backward revolving movement." The date in question was July 14, 1789, the day the people stormed the Bastille in Paris. It was on that day that Louis XVI, hearing of the event, exclaimed "*C'est une revolt!*," only to be corrected by his informant, the Duc de La Rochefoucauld-Liancourt, who replied "*Non, Sire, c'est une revolution.*"[22]

Arendt cites this anecdote because she thinks it clearly shows how the old astronomical metaphor, "which carries its meaning down from the skies to the earth," shifts its emphasis from the idea of a lawful and regular movement to that of an irresistible one, "beyond human power to arrest it."[23] In Liancourt's phrase, the *irresistibility* of revolution is now coupled with a sense of its *irrevocability*. Unlike 1688, the storming of the Bastille signals a revolution in which there can and will be *no going back*. The question, then, is what was it that Liancourt saw in the storming of the Bastille that prompted him to use the word "revolution" is this new and distinctively modern sense?

Arendt answers this question with one of the more remarkable passages to be found in an *oeuvre* studded with remarkable passages:

> Behind [his] words, we still can see and hear the multitude on their march, how they burst into the streets of Paris, which then still was the capital not merely of France but of the entire civilized world—the upheaval of the populace of the great cities inextricably mixed with the uprising of the people for freedom, both together irresistible in the sheer force of their number... What from then on has been irrevocable, and what the agents and spectators of revolution immediately recognized as such, was that the public realm—reserved, as far as memory could reach, to those who *were* free, namely carefree of all the worries that are connected with life's necessity, with bodily needs—should offer its space and its light to this immense majority who are not free because they are driven by daily needs.[24]

The wall that had closed off the public realm to the poor (not only for the entire history of France, but the West itself) was now irrevocably breached. With this breach and subsequent revolutionary popular action, "an entirely new imagery begins to cluster around the old metaphor" and "an entirely new vocabulary is introduced into political language."[25] It is the streaming of the Parisian poor into the "bright light of the public" that led the revolutionary orator Camille Desmoulins to speak of the *torrent révolutionnaire*, the German radical Georg Forster to write about "the majestic lava stream of the revolution which spares nobody and which nobody can arrest," and Robespierre himself to invoke images of *la tempete révolutionnaire*—a "mighty storm wind" which asserts "the grandeur of man against the pettiness of the great."[26]

The metaphors of torrent, lava stream, and storm wind were all used to denote an irresistible historical process. Coined by the actors themselves, these metaphors expressed their shared incredulity that mere mortals could have been the authors of such world-shaking events, events that could hardly have been imagined, let alone planned, prior to their occurrence. They had all been royalists in 1789, yet in a few short years they not only executed a particular king but came to denounce kingship as "an eternal crime."[27] They had formulated a constitution dedicated to the principle of radical decentralization, yet—again in a few short years—they possessed a centralized revolutionary government, one that was not only at war with the established monarchies of Europe, but increasingly victorious against them.

These and other unimaginable events served to buttress the feeling that a force greater than man had intruded upon the course of history. Unable to control the course of events, the leaders of the French Revolution ceased to think of themselves as free agents consciously shaping a new republic.[28] The contrast with the leaders of the American Revolution is, in this regard, striking. The latter remained, from start to finish, animated by the sentiment that "man is the master of his own destiny, at least with respect to political government."[29] In France, however, the Revolution was increasingly viewed as having a life, being, and agency of its own. It overturned monarchy, created and destroyed constitutions, raised up popular heroes one day and guillotined them the next. This hypostatization of the Revolution was to become so widespread that in subsequent years it became almost second nature to interpret "every violent upheaval, be it revolutionary or counter-revolutionary, in terms of a continuation of the movement originally started in 1789."[30]

In the short run, of course, the Revolution was a failure. The first French republic lasted a mere twelve years, from 1792 to 1804. However, according to Arendt, the "well-known shock of disillusion" experienced by the revolutionary generation quickly transformed itself into a feeling of awe "at the power of history itself." For the *philosophes* of the Enlightenment, only monarchical despotism "seemed to stand between man and his freedom to act." In the aftermath of the French Revolution, however, "a much more powerful force had suddenly arisen which compelled men at will, and from which there was no release, neither rebellion nor escape."[31] This was the force of history and of historical necessity, a force given crowning philosophical expression (in Arendt's view) by Hegel.

The last generation or two of Hegel scholarship has tended to cast a skeptical light on the claim—made by Berlin and Popper as well as Arendt—that Hegel thought of necessity in historical, rather than conceptual or logical, terms. Yet, while the myth of "historical inevitability" and a dialectic that proceeds in mechanical thesis-antithesis-synthesis lockstep dies hard, it is important to give Arendt her moment. For there is no denying that Hegel, with his notions of a self-moving *Geist* and the "cunning of reason" (*List der Vernunft*), encouraged the idea that there was a *logic* to the unfolding of history and that the underlying purpose guiding the entire process was the realization of freedom. These notions, taken up by Marx and reinterpreted along positivist lines by Engels (who spoke of "laws of history" and who famously dubbed Marx the "Darwin of history"), played a key role in the formation of Bolshevik ideology, an ideology which, as we have seen, took the idea of historical necessity and "laws of motion" quite seriously.

Arendt's reading of Hegel is clearly anachronistic. Like Berlin, Popper, and even Adorno, she cannot help but read Hegel through the lens of the horrific political experience of the twentieth century. Yet, despite its anachronism, Arendt's reading is insightful, revealing as it does one source of what she calls "the magic spell of historical necessity." This spell first appeared amongst revolutionaries in the mid-nineteenth century and gained considerable strength with the October Revolution in Russia. In Arendt's view, it has burdened and distorted the understanding of revolution ever since.

For Arendt, the most far-reaching *theoretical* consequence of the French Revolution "was the birth of the modern concept of history in Hegel's philosophy."[32] In contradistinction to antiquity's cyclical concept of history (in which mortal men performed memorable deeds against the backdrop of the rise and decline of city-states and empires) and Christianity's rectilinear concept (punctuated and given whatever meaning it might possess by the strictly transmundane events of Christ's birth and the Last Judgment), Hegel's conception held that Truth and Meaning actually revealed themselves in the realm of history and politics, now seen as a developmental process. They revealed themselves, that is, "in precisely the domain of human experiences which the philosophers unanimously had ruled out as the source or birthplace of absolute standards."[33] Arendt thinks—and there is compelling evidence for this in Hegel's *Lectures on the Philosophy of History*—that "the model for this new revelation by means of a historical process was clearly the French Revolution."[34]

The extraordinary influence of German post-Kantian philosophy on European thought in the twentieth century is due, Arendt thinks, to the fact that, with Hegel, it "left the sphere of mere speculation and attempted to formulate a philosophy which would correspond to and comprehend conceptually the newest and most real experience of the time."[35] However, the this-worldly focus of German philosophy after Kant did not signal a revival of interest in the public realm and political action as such. Rather, these were of philosophical interest only insofar as they provided key markers in what Hegel called "progress in the consciousness of freedom." It was the *historical process itself* that gave actions and events their meaning, not vice versa. Thus, the French Revolution did not yield "a new political science for a new age," as Tocqueville had demanded. Rather, it yielded a *philosophy of history*, one in which "everything that had been political—acts, and words, and events—became *historical*."[36]

For Arendt, the fallacy of "this new and typically modern philosophy" consists "in describing and understanding the whole realm of human action, not in terms of the actor and the agent, but from the standpoint of the spectator who watches a spectacle."[37] In the process-narrative constructed by the "backward glance of history" (Hegel's "owl of Minerva"), political actions and events took on a seeming continuity and inevitability. This would not have posed a problem in the political world were it not for the fact that political actors themselves—awed by the power of history and under the influence of Hegelian or quasi-Hegelian modes of thought— increasingly took the standpoint of spectators to a process whose "inevitable" stages they thought they knew in advance, thanks to the original pattern of movement set out by the French Revolution.

It is hardly surprising, then, that revolutionaries in the nineteenth and twentieth centuries came to view themselves "not merely as successors of the men of the French Revolution," but as "agents of history and historical necessity." The "obvious and paradoxical result" of this tendency was that "instead of freedom, necessity became the chief category of political and revolutionary thought."[38] This paradox was not the result of the revolutionaries' uncritical belief in the truth of the Hegelian metanarrative about "progress in the consciousness of freedom." Rather, it was the result of the Hegelian characterization of the *motion* of history itself. This motion

> is at once dialectical and driven by necessity: out of the revolu-
> tion and counter-revolution, from the fourteenth of July to the
> eighteenth Brumaire and the restoration of the monarchy, was
> born of the dialectical movement and counter-movement of
> history which bears men on its irresistible flow like a powerful
> undercurrent, to which they must surrender the very moment
> they attempt to establish freedom on the earth.[39]

Hence, the "famous dialectics of freedom and necessity in which both eventually coincide," which Arendt calls "perhaps the most terrible and, humanly speaking, least bearable paradox in the whole body of modern thought."[40]

Is Arendt being unfair to Hegel here? Perhaps. As already mentioned, the primary sense of "necessity" in Hegel is conceptual rather than historical. However, since history according to Hegel unfolds in terms of "the concept," the history of the world takes the form of a rational (and in that sense a *necessary*) process. It is therefore not implausible to suggest that it is with Hegel that the internal link between freedom and necessity is established, with "abstract" conceptual necessity taking its "concrete" form in the shape of world history. Of course, it is a long way from the Hegelian dialectics of freedom and necessity to the ideological formulations we find in Lenin, let alone Stalin. The position of Marx in this process of vulgarization is, of course, equivocal, since his version of "dialectical materialism" never lost sight of historical contingency, irony, and the relative autonomy of the political and cultural spheres. It is only by alloying Hegel in his most "popular" form (the *Lectures on the Philosophy of World History*) with Marx at his most positivistic or "scientific" that Arendt is able to bridge the sizeable gap between Hegel and Marx (on the one hand) and Lenin and Stalin (on the other).

Hegel's substitution of historical motion for political action is not the only factor behind the elevation of necessity to its paradoxical, preeminent, and (from Arendt's point of view) disastrous place in revolutionary thought after 1848. The apparent irresistibility of the torrent *révolutionnaire* and the French Revolution had a material base: the naked bodily needs of millions of hungry workers and peasants. As Arendt puts it, "behind the appearance [of irresistibility] was a reality, and this reality was biological and not historical, though it appeared now perhaps for the first time in the full light of history."[41] The necessity of our biological needs and automatic bodily processes is, according to Arendt, "the most powerful necessity of which we are aware." *Historical* necessity would have remained a largely philosophical idea had it not been associated, almost from the beginning, with the *biological* necessity—the sheer bodily need—that suddenly burst into the public realm with the appearance of the poor during the French Revolution.

When this happened, Arendt argues, the astronomic imagery behind the pre-Hegelian idea of necessary, cyclical and regular historical motions

> lost its old connotations and acquired the biological imagery which underlies and pervades the organic and social theories of history, which all have in common that they see a multitude— the factual plurality of a nation or a people or a society—in the image of one supernatural body driven by one, superhuman, irresistible general will.[42]

This was *le peuple*, the undifferentiated macro-subject of Jacobin and virtually all subsequent revolutionary political rhetoric. Arendt's point is that this lack of differentiation—this obliteration of human plurality and diversity of opinion—was not simply metaphorical but had its roots in something undeniably real: the mass poverty of eighteenth-century France.

The millions in danger of starving in France did indeed speak with one voice, at least at the beginning. They wanted *bread*, not a new "space of freedom" for debate, deliberation, and the exchange of opinion. According to Arendt, it was under the "absolute dictate" of their bodily needs that "the multitude rushed to the assistance of the French Revolution, inspired it, drove it onward, and eventually sent it to its doom."[43] If this isn't clear enough, she goes on to state that when poor appeared on the political scene, "necessity appeared with them." The result was that "the power of the old regime became impotent and the new republic was still-born; freedom had to be surrendered to necessity, to the urgency of the life process itself."[44]

Arendt appears to be dangerously close here to "blaming the victim" when it comes to accounting for the ultimate failure of the French Revolution. This impression is given some credence by her treatment of the "Social Question"—"what we may better and more simply call the existence of poverty"—in OR. She wants to assert two rather uncomfortable theses. First, she maintains that the existence of mass poverty renders the constitution of political freedom virtually impossible; second, she maintains that such poverty cannot be alleviated by *violence*, by so-called "revolutionary" means. The upshot is that it was only in America, blessed by nature's bounty and liberated from Old World poverty, that a *political* revolution had a real chance of succeeding. In France, on the other hand, the explosive appearance of the *malheureux* onto the political scene made the transformation of the "Rights of Man" into the "rights of the Sans-Culottes" almost predictable. Moved by the plight of the poor, the Jacobin leaders soon came to view the rights to "dress, food, and the reproduction of their species" as far more pressing and important than the creation of a new form of government. In this regard, Arendt cites Robespierre: "*La République? La Monarchie? Je ne connais que la question sociale.*"

If one views the existence of widespread poverty as (still) the most pressing problem we face, the stance Arendt takes in the second chapter of OR seems both cold and elitist. She appears to be arguing that the poor are the greatest obstacle to the creation of enduring republican constitutions, and (more generally) that they are the biggest threat to the creation of "tangible" freedom anywhere in the world. Indeed, many have read her chapter on "The Social Question" as a frontal attack not just on misguided notion that *revolutionary violence* can solve the problem of poverty, but upon social democratic reforms and movements more generally.

A few observations are in order here. First, Arendt is not arguing that things would be better if the poor had somehow been kept out of the "bright light of the public" and forever consigned to the obscurity in which they had labored for millennia. Rather, she is arguing that the problem of poverty can be solved, if it can be solved at all, only through expert administration and technological advances. Her view that it can't be solved by revolutionary violence ("expropriating the expropriators") has, unfortunately, been borne out by the tragic fate of the Russian, Chinese, and numerous other social revolutions. The sad truth of the matter is that "no revolution has ever solved the 'social question' and liberated men from the predicament of want."[45]

Second, she is not suggesting, à la Marie Antoinette, that if they can't get bread the poor might consider eating cake, just as long they don't disturb the sanctity or integrity of the public realm. Arendt takes poverty seriously and takes pains to emphasize its "acute misery" and "dehumanizing force." Placing them under the dictate of their bodies—that is, of sheer biological necessity—poverty robs the poor of the opportunity of ever knowing real freedom.

Third and perhaps most importantly, Arendt doesn't blame the malheureux for the failure of the French Revolution. Rather, she places the blame squarely on Robespierre and his fellow Jacobins. It was they who allowed their compassion for the poor to distract them from the political project of establishing a new constitution and creating a new form of government. Robespierre himself was by no means unaware of the gravity of this detour from the task of foundation: "We shall perish because, in the history of mankind, we missed the moment to found freedom."[46]

The transformation of the Rights of Man into the rights of the Sans-Culottes was, according to Arendt, "the turning point not only of the French Revolution but of all revolutions that were to follow."[47] Yet it took more than fifty years before this transformation, this "abdication of freedom before the dictate of necessity," found its theorist in Karl Marx. "The greatest theorist the revolutions ever had," Marx was, however, "much more interested in history than in politics." He therefore neglected, "almost entirely," what Arendt calls "the original intention of the men of the revolutions," namely, the foundation of freedom in a political-constitutional order.[48] That Marx paid no attention to the problem posed by the institutionalization of freedom is clear from his early essay "On the Jewish Question" (1843), which curtly dismisses the very category of "political emancipation" (and with it the entire topos of the so-called "bourgeois" revolutions).

Marx thought the French Revolution failed to make the transition from an order predicated on domination to a "realm of freedom" because it was unable to provide a solution to the "social question." From this, he concluded that freedom and poverty were incompatible—a thesis more or less in agreement with Arendt's own view of the matter. However, unlike Arendt, he saw the cause of poverty as ultimately political in nature: poverty's roots lay in the exploitation of the labor power of the many by the few. It was for this reason that he concluded that the solution to the social question could lie only in an armed revolution. The overthrow of the dominating class and the abolition of private property would return socially created wealth to the community from which it had sprung. Poverty, if not entirely abolished, would be transformed into a marginal affair, one that no longer determined the fate of the majority.

Arendt's targeting of Marx's conviction that only a violent social revolution could effectively solve the "social question," enabling entrance into the "realm of freedom," echoes themes from her Gaus Lectures. There she focused on three of Marx's fundamental theses: first, that labor is the "creator of man"; second, that "violence is the midwife of history"; and third, that "nobody can be free who enslaves others." In OR, she probes the ground of the second thesis, arguing that

> Marx's transformation of the social question into a political force is contained in the term 'exploitation,' that is, in the notion that poverty is the result of exploitation through a 'ruling class' which is in possession of the means of violence.[49]

By "reducing property relations to the old relationship which violence, rather than necessity, established between men," Marx was able to summon up a spirit of rebelliousness "that can spring only from being violated, not from being under the sway of necessity."[50] Poverty becomes a political, rather than a natural, phenomenon, "the result of violence and violation rather than of scarcity."

Here, Arendt is questioning not whether the exploitation of labor *exists* but whether it, rather than scarcity or necessity, was the primary basis of the poverty that many millions in Europe endured prior to, and in the course of, the Industrial Revolution. She clearly thinks it was not, pointing out (as she had in the Gaus Lectures) that the model behind Marx's explanation of poverty is the ancient institution of slavery. That institution did indeed presuppose a "ruling class," one that directly employed means of violence in order to "force a subject class to bear life's toil and burden for it."[51] The modern age and the Industrial Revolution emancipated this subject class, liberating it from the institution of slavery and from its immediate masterly taskmasters. "Free" workers now appeared to be in a position where they could recover their ability to act and rebel against an exploitative system whose ultimate sanction lay in the bourgeois class control of the state and the army.

This was the possibility implicit in the application of Hegel's master/slave dialectic to the Industrial Age. To this possibility, Marx added what he and others had thought they had learned from the *torrent révolutionnaire* of the French Revolution: namely, that the "stronger taskmaster" of the workers' daily needs and wants would *compel* them to rise up and achieve *human* (and not merely political) emancipation. This, Arendt observes, is probably "the most potent reason why he [Marx] was so eager to believe with Hegel in a dialectical process in which freedom would rise directly out of necessity."[52] In later years, the revolutionary *élan* of a young Marx who had seen "man-made violence and oppression...where others had believed in some necessity inherent in the human condition" gave way to a mature Marx who saw instead "the iron laws of historical necessity lurking behind every violence, transgression, and violation."[53]

In other words, the last trace of revolutionary spontaneity—the workers' decision to revolt—now disappeared in the face of a "science of history," a science in which the *life process itself* was seen as the primary "actor." It was the "compelling urges of the life process" (made concrete by the immiseration of the proletariat) that would inevitably produce a social revolution. According to Arendt, the goal of this revolution in Marx's view was no longer the liberation of men from the oppression of their fellow men but rather the liberation of the life process of society "from the fetters of scarcity" imposed by the strictures of bourgeois private property. Not freedom but abundance "became...the aim of the revolution."[54]

How accurate an account of the nature and trajectory of Marx's revolutionary thought is this? The leading figures of the Western

Marxist tradition, from Lukács to Habermas, have all sought to elevate the humanist concerns of the young Marx over the more positivistic formulations found in his later thought. Yet, Arendt's interpretation of Marx in OR does not really hinge upon spotlighting his later ambition to be the founder of a "science of history" with supposedly law-like regularities. It hinges, rather, upon showing the way two types of necessity—the historical necessity suggested by Hegel's philosophy of history and the biological necessity that turned the Parisian poor into a *torrent révolutionnaire*—came to be synthesized in his thought.

The end result is not merely a theory of revolution that questions the "pathos of novelty," but one which actually denies the capacity of human beings to interrupt the course of history through joint action alone. Historical discontinuities, when they occur, are really the result of forces beyond human control. This is something the French revolutionaries increasingly felt as the momentum of the Revolution swept them up before sweeping them away, and it is something which Marx (with the arc of the French Revolution in mind) felt demanded a generalized theoretical account. His success in this regard, Arendt suggests, can be measured in terms of hegemonic position held by the French Revolution in the modern revolutionary tradition. This paradigmatic status comes at the expense of the American Revolution, a revolution which concerned "not the order of society, but the form of government" and was thus, in the eyes of many, not a "real" revolution at all.

****

In noting how Arendt doesn't blame the poor for the failure for the French Revolution, I mentioned that she thought the real cause was to be found in the way the leaders of the revolution allowed their feelings of compassion for the plight of the poor to overwhelm their commitment to the constitutional foundation of a new form of government. Since compassion for the poor has always been a relatively rare commodity, and since "to avert one's eyes from the misery and unhappiness of the mass of humankind was no more possible in eighteenth-century Paris…than it is today in some European, most Latin American, and nearly all Asian and African countries," this seems a curious fixing of blame.[55] It comes into better focus once we take account of her argument about the un- or anti-political nature of both compassion and pity.

Arendt's pages on compassion and pity in OR are among the most counterintuitive, and perhaps shocking, in all her work. Our immediate response to someone who argues that compassion is an anti-political passion, one potentially destructive of both politics and the public realm, is to suspect that person of heartlessness. Given her demonstrated empathy for the victims of imperialism and totalitarianism in OT, it is clear that Arendt was not heartless. What, then, led her to indict compassion and pity in OR?

Arendt's argument is complex, wending its way from Robespierre and the Jacobins back to Rousseau's cult of sentiment and forward to Melville and Dostoevsky's reflections (in Billy Budd and The Brothers Karamazov) on the unworldliness of goodness and the limits of human compassion. For our purposes, it is Arendt's elucidation of the Robespierre-Rousseau connection that is most illuminating. It weaves together the strands of revolutionary compassion, unity, virtue, and authenticity into a broader argument about the perils of privileging the "natural man" over the citizen and the sovereign will of the nation over positive laws and institutions.

This broad argument harks back to Arendt's exploration of the "perplexities of the rights of Man" in OT and is part of her overall attempt to alert us to the dangers of the persistent tendency to reduce politics to nature—i.e. to natural or natural-seeming forces and characteristics. As we have seen, any and all such attempts—from the imperialist appeal to race and biology, to the totalitarian invocation of the "laws" of Nature or History, to the channeling of society's "life process" into what was once a relatively autonomous public-political realm—have the effect of effacing human plurality while simultaneously destroying the integrity of the one sphere in which human freedom can become a tangible, phenomenal reality.

In Arendt's view, the emergence of compassion as the driving force in revolutionary politics was a function of the distance that separated the bourgeois and middle-class "men of the French Revolution" from the mass of their poor and suffering compatriots. The downfall of the monarch did little to heal the long-established rift between the government and the nation. The revolutionary governments "were neither of the people nor by the people, but at best for the people, and at worst a 'usurpation of sovereign power' by self-styled representatives."[56] The liberation from monarchical tyranny "spelled freedom only for the few and was hardly felt by the many who remained loaded down by their misery."[57] A second liberation—a liberation from poverty and the yoke of necessity— was apparently required if freedom was to become a reality for ordinary Frenchmen. The achievement of this second liberation de- manded a supreme effort of solidarization with the people on the part of their "self-styled representatives," a solidarization effected through *compassion*. It was the "capacity to suffer with the 'immense class of the poor'" accompanied by "a will to raise compassion to the rank of the supreme political passion" that Robespierre and the Jacobins thought essential.[58] For them, virtue "meant to have the welfare of the people in mind, to identify one's will with the will of the people—*il faut que volonté UNE.*"

This effort as solidarization, following on the heels of the Girondins' failure to produce a constitution establishing repub- lican government, marked a profound shift in the nature and self-understanding of the Revolution:

> The Revolution had come to its turning point when the Jacobins, under the leadership of Robespierre, seized power, not because they were more radical but because they did not share the Girondins' concern with forms of government, because they believed in the people rather than in the republic, and 'pinned their faith on the natural goodness of a class' rather than on institutions and constitutions: 'Under the new Constitution,' Robespierre insisted, 'laws should be promulgated "in the name of the French people" instead of the "French Republic."[59]

This shift in understanding may have been produced by the course of the Revolution itself, but the terms in which it was cast were clearly Rousseauist in origin. In the *Discourse on Inequality*, Rousseau had proclaimed *pitié* to be "the most human reaction to the suffering of others, and therefore the foundation of all authentic, 'natural' hu- man intercourse,"[60] thus paving the way for the Jacobins' elevation of compassion to the rank of "supreme political virtue." Moreover,

in *The Social Contract* Rousseau replaced the ancient Roman idea of the
"consent of the people" (predicated on the idea of plurality) with
the notion of a *general* (singular and virtually unanimous) will of the
people. This was the *volonté générale*, from which all legitimate power
and legislation supposedly sprang. The shift from a civic or institutionally mediated form of solidarity to a compassion-based one,
combined with the parallel shift from the old idea of consent to law
to the idea of a collective will that *expressed itself through* law, created
an entirely new political optic. In this new field of vision, "the enduring unity of the future political body was guaranteed not in the
worldly institutions which this people had in common, but [rather]
in the will of the people of themselves."[61]

   This analysis resonates with Arendt's earlier description of how
the "Rights of Man" came to be transformed into the "Rights of
Peoples" in OT. However, in OR Arendt is less concerned with the
fate of human rights than she is with the way that Rousseau and
Robespierre's grounding of law and power in the (sovereign) will of
the people creates instability (on the one hand) and effaces plurality (on the other). Indeed, "Rousseau took his metaphor of a general will seriously and literally enough to conceive of the nation as
a body driven by one will." But the "enduring unity of a people
inspired by one will," Arendt observes, "must not be mistaken for
stability." Like the will of an individual, the will of the people had
to be understood as capable of changing direction without losing its
identity. As supreme legislator, the general will could not be viewed
as conclusively bound by any law, no matter how "fundamental."
After all, Rousseau reasoned, "it would be absurd for the will to bind
itself for the future."[62]

   Arendt sees this doctrine as at the root of the "fateful instability
and faithlessness of revolutionary governments" that was to follow.
This instability was a price that Robespierre and his compatriots
were willing to pay, since for them Rousseau's theory provided an
"ingenious means to put a multitude in the place of a single person
[the sovereign]." The general will, as conceived by Rousseau, was
"nothing more or less than what bound the many into one."[63] The
theoretical question was *how* the general will—a popular will that
came from all and applied to all, one that authentically expressed
the common or public interest—was to be identified and separated

out from the welter of individual or partial interests present in the national community.

Rousseau dealt with this difficulty, in Arendt's view, by transposing the idea of a unifying external enemy of the nation into the breast of each and every citizen. When it comes to articulating the general will in domestic affairs, the enemy is not the foreign invader but the *particular interests* of the individual citizen. It is the latter that constantly threaten to warp his view of the common good and pervert his sense of the general interest. Thus, when it comes to determining whether a proposed law is or is not in accord with the general will, what matters is not any *public* process of debate and deliberation but rather the *introspective* process of self-examination. It is only by stimulating an inner conflict between my selfless or citizenly side (on the one hand) and my particular interests as an individual (on the other) that I achieve clarity concerning the proposed law's harmony with the general will.[64] In Rousseau, the virtuous exercise of the people's legislative power thus depends upon the presence of an *âme déchirée* in the breast of every citizen. The passion of the "soul torn in two" takes the place of the argumentative, opinion-based reason found in both public deliberation and in the inner dialogue of thought.

It is at this stage of her Rousseau interpretation that Arendt seemingly leaves the text of *The Social Contract* behind. It would be more accurate to say that she imposes the lens provided by *Émile* and *La nouvelle Heloise* upon it. Since "the two in one of the soul" is first and foremost a conflict and not a dialogue, "it engenders passion in the twofold sense of intense suffering and intense passionateness." It was to this "emphasis upon suffering" that Rousseau, in Arendt's estimation,

> owed the enormous, predominant influence over the minds of the men who were to make the Revolution and who found themselves confronted with the overwhelming sufferings of the poor to whom they had opened the doors of the public realm to its light for the first time.[65]

Selflessness was no longer framed primarily in terms of the citizenly ethos of the common good found in *The Social Contract*. Rather, in the minds of Robespierre and the revolutionaries, it came to be equated with the ability to lose oneself in the sufferings of others. For them, "the magic of compassion was that it opened the heart of the sufferer to the sufferings of others, whereby it established and confirmed the 'natural' bond between men which only the rich had lost." Where compassion—the "capacity for suffering with others"—ended, there, it was assumed, vice began.[66]

Though she doesn't put it in quite these terms, Arendt is arguing that Robespierre's Rousseauian conviction that "the heart is the source of political virtue" profoundly altered the meaning of *corruption* in the republican and revolutionary traditions. From Tacitus to Machiavelli and *The Social Contract*, corruption meant the hegemony of private or selfish interests over public-spiritedness and other tangible forms of patriotic selflessness (for example, the willingness to die in defense of one's country). However, in the spirit of the Rousseau's proto-Romanticism, Robespierre and the Jacobins redefined corruption. It now stood for the diffidence and artificiality of so-called "good" society, the lack of heartfelt compassion for the sufferings of the poor. The latter, untainted by the pretense and artificiality of their social superiors, were viewed as "naturally good."

This redefinition had two broad and far-reaching consequences. First, it made the traditionally republican concern with the establishment of durable worldly institutions appear suspect. What was once seen as the *raison d'être* of the Revolution was now viewed as the apparently heartless evasion of the most important thing: the immediate amelioration, by whatever means necessary, of the misery of the poor. Second, it led the revolutionaries to repeatedly call attention to the depth of their compassion and the genuineness of their commitment as individuals to *les malheureux*. Purity of heart, rather than tangible deeds and words, became the standard by which virtue was measured. The politics of authenticity was born.

The problem is that compassion "by its very nature" cannot be ignited by the sufferings of "a whole class or a people." Compassion "cannot reach out farther than what is suffered by one person and still remain what it is supposed to be, co-suffering."[67] Carried into the public realm by Robespierre and the Jacobins, the passion of compassion quickly becomes something else: pity. Pity, Arendt writes, "because it is not stricken in the flesh and keeps its sentimental distance, can succeed where compassion always will fail;

it can reach out to the multitude and…enter the marketplace."[68]
Unlike the *principle* of solidarity, which enables the fortunate or well-
off to establish a "community of interest" with the unfortunate or
oppressed in the name of the general idea of human dignity, the
sentiment of pity has, according to Arendt, "just as much vested interest in the existence of the unhappy as thirst for power has a vested
interest in the existence of the weak."[69] Since it is an emotion rather
than idea, it is also potentially boundless. The boundless suffering of
the masses is likely to elicit an equally boundless pity on the part of
those who would help them.

This, Arendt suggests, is what happened in the case of Robespierre
and the Jacobins. The Revolution witnessed the downfall of legal and
political authority along with the sudden appearance in the public
realm of the previously excluded poor. *Les malheureux* wanted bread,
not a new constitution or form of government. Their need was violent and, in Arendt's estimation, essentially pre-political in character. To Robespierre and the Jacobins, it "seemed that only violence
could be strong and swift enough to help them."[70] Thus it was that
Robespierre's "pity-inspired virtue" ran roughshod over law and
due process, ultimately giving birth to the Terror. "*Par pitié, par amour
pour l'humanité, soyez inhumains!*" became the credo of the French (and
later the Russian) Revolution.

I should note that Arendt does not question the genuineness of
either Robespierre's or Lenin's compassion for the poor. Her point
is not that their embrace of violence revealed them to be the wolves
in sheep's clothing they always were. Rather, she thinks that it was
the very boundlessness of their pity for the poor that made them
"so curiously insensitive to reality in general and to the reality of
persons in particular, whom they felt no compunction in sacrificing
to their 'principles,' or to the course of history, or to the cause of revolution as such."[71] Sad to say, this insensitivity to "reality in general
and the reality of persons in particular" has been the distinguishing
mark of many if not all of the social revolutions of the nineteenth
and twentieth centuries. And it is here that Arendt's overarching
contrast between the French and American revolutions comes into
sharpest focus, revealing the stakes of her oft-criticized—and seemingly somewhat arbitrary—distinction between the social and the
political:

The direction of the American Revolution remained committed to the foundation of freedom and the establishment of lasting institutions, and to those who acted in this direction nothing was permitted that would have been outside the range of civil law. The direction of the French Revolution was deflected *almost from the beginning* from this course of foundation through the immediacy of suffering; it was determined by the exigencies of liberation not from tyranny but from necessity, and it was actuated by the limitless immensity of both the people's misery and the pity this misery inspired. The lawlessness of the 'all is permitted' sprang here still from the sentiments of the heart whose very boundlessness helped in unleashing a stream of boundless violence.[72]

Arendt's analysis here contains elements of Hegel's critique (in the *Phenomenology of Spirit*) of the French Revolution and the Rousseau-inspired cult of the heart. This link is apparently confirmed when she turns her attention to another consequence of viewing the heart as the source of political virtue: the relentless search for hypocrisy and lack of true commitment among the revolutionaries themselves. If patriotism was indeed a thing of the heart, then the inner motivations of all the leading revolutionary actors had to be endlessly interrogated lest the "reign of virtue" turn into the "rule of hypocrisy." This "never-ending attempt to ferret out hypocrites" was a fight which could "only end in defeat," with the Revolution devouring its own children.[73] As Arendt observes, "it was the war upon hypocrisy that transformed Robespierre's dictatorship into the Reign of Terror."[74]

What leads Arendt to make this unwelcome link between compassion and terror? The answer is simple enough. By making pity and compassion the *sine qua non* of political virtue, Robespierre and the Jacobins placed the question of individual *authenticity* at the very center of the revolutionary project. If the heart was the standard, then it is not surprising that leading actors of the French Revolution felt compelled to rhetorically display the purity of their innermost motives in public. Only in this way could any of them demonstrate the authenticity of their virtue and patriotism. Of course, the moment any individual attempts to perform publicly what ostensibly lies hidden in the depths of his heart, he opens himself to self-doubt as well as the doubt of others. Is the pure revolutionary virtue he appeals to authentic, or is he just playacting? Is he a true patriot, or is patriotism merely a mask he wears in public, the better to fool himself and others? According to Arendt, the "demand that everybody display in public his innermost motivation" actually "demands the impossible" and threatens to transform all political actors into hypocrites.[75] A perpetual suspicion of motives and an ethos of unmasking enter the public realm, with predictably dire results.

Right-leaning historians have long viewed the French revolutionary terror as the egg from which the terror of the Russian and Chinese revolutions hatched. At first glance, it appears that Arendt is guilty of the same gross over-simplification. It is important to note, then, that she clearly distinguishes between Robespierre's "terror of virtue" and later forms of left-wing *totalitarian* terror. Robespierre's suspicion-driven terror was directed against "a hidden enemy and a hidden vice" within the ranks of the revolutionaries and political elites; it *was not* directed against arbitrarily selected groups of ordinary people whose only "crime" was their group identity. Or, as Arendt puts it, in the case of the French Revolutionary terror, "it was a question of stripping the mask off the disguised traitor, not of putting the mask of the traitor on arbitrarily selected people in order to create the required impersonators in the bloody masquerade of a dialectical movement."[76]

Of course, we all encounter hypocrites—people who say one thing and do another—on an almost daily basis. At one level, it is the most ordinary vice imaginable. Why, then, does hypocrisy—this "vice that covered up vices"—become such a "monster" in the course of the French Revolution? What turns such a common vice into a crime worthy of death?

The answer to this question leads Arendt to take up the relationship between being and appearance, "one of the oldest metaphysical problems in our tradition." We know, from reading THC, that she thinks the public realm is a "space of appearances" in which the political actor appears before his or her peers in speech and deed. From a *political* or public perspective, what can be seen and heard by all constitutes reality.[77] And we know from reading both THC and the essay "What is Freedom?" that she thinks of the political actor in semi-theatrical terms, as someone who appears on a public stage and who is judged according to the *virtu* or virtuosity that he or she displays. "Great words and deeds" are *performed*, and it is this dimension of public performance that marks them as *political* in the first place.[78] The public or performing self of, say, a Lincoln or a Pericles is distinct from their respective private selves. Their private lives and inner motivations are irrelevant to their respective greatness as political actors. What matters are the *principles* (e.g. equality, honor, greatness) which inspire and become tangibly manifest in their public words and deeds.

In contrast, the politics of authenticity that first emerges with Rousseau, Robespierre, and (later) Lamartine equates the inner or "natural" self with the *true* self. It places a premium upon the display of what is normally hidden: one's innermost motivations. Performance again is key, but it is a type of performance that implicitly denies its theatrical or "artificial" dimensions. Words, deeds, and principles here matter less than the public revelation of the ostensibly "authentic" self of the political actor.

Viewed from this perspective, the corruption of the *ancien regime* was manifest in the theatrical spectacle and stylized artificiality of court life at Versailles. This was, after all, a social world in which saying one thing (to curry favor and build social credit) and doing another (to advance interests or indulge appetites) was universal. For Rousseau and his admirers, the hypocrisy of court life revealed its rottenness, a rottenness even more glaring when juxtaposed to the simplicity and honesty (or "natural goodness") of ordinary poor people. Nature was good while society—built on artifice, rank, and status—was bad. For Rousseau's revolutionary followers, the Revolution offered nothing less than "the opportunity of tearing the mask off the face of French society, of exposing its rottenness." Once the corrupt façade had been destroyed, the "unspoiled, honest face of *le peuple*" could emerge in its place.[79] The revolutionary exposure of the *ancien regime's* corruption would, in due course, be but a prelude to the Revolution "tearing off the mask of its own children." This latter, potentially endless, unmasking of hypocrisy and lack of patriotism among the revolutionaries themselves was the true *raison d'être* of Robespierre's "terror of virtue."

Although we have become mostly inured to hypocrisy, "phoniness" is a perpetual complaint we lodge against politicians.

"Authenticity" thus remains one of the most precious of commodities on the contemporary political scene. In this respect we are heirs to Rousseau and Robespierre's anti-theatrical prejudice, a prejudice whose roots go all the way back to Plato. Yet the suspicion of "masks" and the vehement rejection of any distinction between a political actor's public and private selves not only facilitates the marketing of a bogus "authenticity." It also undermines the very legal and institutional structures that articulate, protect, and preserve our civil rights and liberties. The recent wave of resentment-fueled populism in both Europe and America reveals how belief in a leader's "authenticity" encourages indifference to, not to say contempt for, established legal and constitutional safeguards.

Arendt did not live to see the current crisis, but OR suggests she wouldn't have been completely surprised by it. In a discussion that echoes her description of the rightlessness of refugees in OT, she suggests that the Roman idea of a legal *persona* was intended to provide a public artificial self, one that would protect the otherwise naked and vulnerable bodily self of the individual citizen. "The distinction between a private person in Rome and a Roman citizen," she writes,

> was that the latter had a persona, a legal personality, as we would say...Without his persona, there would be an individual without rights and duties, perhaps a 'natural' man—that is, a human being or *homo* in the original sense of the word, *outside the range of law and the body politic of citizens.*[80]

The citizen's legal persona is thus a kind of protective mask, one that replaces the natural differences between individuals with a set of codified general protections that are the same for all.

Technically speaking, the "Declaration of the Rights of Man and the Citizen" promulgated by the National Constituent Assembly in 1789 *should* have provided something similar. Given their hatred of masks and their Rousseau-like privileging of the "natural," however, the men of the French Revolution ultimately had "no conception of the persona, and no respect for the legal personality which is given and guaranteed by the body politic." To the contrary: they believed that the Revolution had emancipated nature herself, as it were, liberated the natural man in all men, and given him the Rights of Man to which each was entitled, not by virtue of the body politic to which he belonged but by virtue of being born.[81]

By making the Rights of Man prior to and independent of any artificial or "merely positive" law, the Revolution severely undercut the protections provided by an individual's possession of a legal personality. While "artificial," legal personality had been historically understood as inviolate. With the advent of the Reign of Terror and the ferreting out of the insufficiently patriotic, Robespierre and the Jacobins managed to tear away not only the mask of social hypocrisy, but the "mask" of a protective legal persona as well. The result "was the exact opposite of true liberation and true equality."[82]

At this point in her argument, Arendt returns to a topic broached twelve years earlier in OT. "The perplexities of the Rights of Man," she writes, "are manifold, and Burke's famous argument against them is neither obsolete nor 'reactionary.'" In distinction from the colonial American bills of rights, upon which the Declaration of the Rights of Man was modeled, they were meant to spell out primary positive rights, inherent in man's nature, as distinguished from his political status, and as such *they tried indeed to reduce politics to nature.* The colonial bills of rights, on the contrary, were meant to institute permanent restraining controls upon all political power, and hence presupposed *the existence of a body politic and the functioning of political power.*[83]

The charge that the Rights of Man, as formulated by the French Revolution, amount to an attempt to "reduce politics to nature" is a surprising and—in light of her in indictment of similar attempts by totalitarian movements—an exceptionally serious one. Given the widespread influence of natural rights theories in the seventeenth and eighteenth centuries, Arendt's charge appears unpersuasive—at least on the face of it. However, if we bear in mind the primacy of the "natural" in Rousseau's writings and the force of the "social question" in the minds of Robespierre and the Jacobins, it appears less dubious:

The new body politic was supposed to rest upon man's natural rights, upon his rights insofar as he is nothing but a natural being, upon his right to 'food, dress, and the reproduction of the species,' that is, upon his rights to the necessities of life.[84]

This return to her argument about the "rights of the *Sans-Culottes*" is what enables Arendt to conclude that "of the men of the Revolution only those survived and rose to power who became [the masses'] spokesmen and surrendered the 'artificial,' man-made laws of a not yet constituted body politic to the 'natural' laws which the masses obeyed." These laws expressed "the forces of nature herself," the force of the body's "elemental necessity" most of all.[85]

Arendt's interpretation of the course of the French Revolution rests less on her linkage of natural rights with natural necessity than it does upon the assertion that the "social question"—the poverty of millions—loomed largest in the minds of Robespierre and the Jacobins. Recent historical studies such as Patrice Higonnet's *Goodness beyond Virtue* suggest reasons to be skeptical of that assertion.[86] Nevertheless, Arendt is clearly correct in her historical judgment that it was the French Revolution—a *social* as well as political revolution—and not the more purely political American Revolution that provided the paradigm for revolutionary action in the nineteenth and twentieth centuries. The romantic appeal of "expropriating the expropriators" notwithstanding, she is likewise correct when she states that "no revolution has ever solved the 'social question' and liberated men from the predicament of want." It is hard to dispute her conclusion that "nothing…could be more obsolete than the attempt to liberate mankind from poverty by [the] political means [of violent revolution], nothing could be more futile or more dangerous."[87]

III Republicanism, the "pursuit of happiness," and corruption

While she specifically states that "nothing could be less fair than to take the success of the American Revolution for granted and to sit in judgment over the failure of the men of the French Revolution," the casual reader of OR might well conclude that Arendt is doing precisely that.[88] Not only were the British colonies free of the massive poverty of the Old World; they were also articulated politically "from top to bottom." In the words of John Adams, the inhabitants of the colonies were "formed by law into corporations or bodies politic" and possessed "the right to assemble…in their town halls, there to deliberate upon the public affairs." Indeed, it was "in these assemblies of towns or districts that the sentiments of the people were formed in the first place."[89] This access to public spaces of debate and deliberation gave the colonists in America the experience of *public* happiness, the kind of happiness available only to those who participated in self-government and the joint management of public affairs.

This experience of public happiness was unknown to the European Enlightenment and the *hommes de lettres* of pre-revolutionary France. Their reading of ancient histories had cultivated a "taste and a passion" for the *idea* of public freedom, even though neither group had experienced its actuality themselves. As a result, the political education of the *hommes de lettres* who would lead the French Revolution was "theoretical in the extreme." They had "no experience to fall back upon, only ideas and principles untested by reality to guide and inspire them."[90] Nevertheless, like the *philosophes* who preceded them, they were convinced that freedom was no inner gift or capacity (as it had been for the Stoics and early Christianity), but rather something that "could only exist in public." Freedom was a "tangible worldly reality," one that emerged in a "man-made public space or market-place" where, through the words and deeds of citizens, it became "visible to all."[91]

The ideal of a public freedom, gleaned from the histories of Greece and Rome, gave the *hommes de lettres* a certain fellow feeling with the poor. Like the poor, they too labored in obscurity, subject to an enforced exile from the public-political realm—an exile they found increasingly intolerable. The passion for the *idea* of public freedom thus came to be confused with the "much more vehement"—and much more concrete—hatred of masters, of those responsible for the banishment of the poor and the men of letters from the "bright light of the public."[92] In Arendt's view, the fact that this "passionate hatred" failed to produce a successful revolution is not surprising. It was "incapable of even grasping, let alone realizing, the central idea of revolution, which is the foundation of freedom, that is, the foundation of a body politic which guarantees the space where freedom can appear."[93]

It is at this stage that we encounter OR's central theme of the con-stitution of liberty—the *constitutio libertatis*. For those enthralled by the performative idea of political action in THC, Arendt's focus on constitutions in OR is a bit unnerving: the legal and institutional ar-ticulation of the public-political realm now takes pride of place over the "agonistic" action of the ancients. Yet, while there is clear shift of emphasis as Arendt transitions from her Greek-inflected descrip-tion of political action to her analysis of modern revolution, there is no self-contradiction. The question has become how, under modern conditions, is it possible for initiatory political action to create a new public-political realm and start a new (republican) story. Arendt's answer to this question is clear and unequivocal:

> Under modern conditions, the act of foundation is identical with the framing of a constitution, and the calling of consti-tutional assemblies has quite rightly become the hallmark of revolution ever since the Declaration of Independence initiated the writing of constitutions for each of the American states, a process which prepared and culminated in the Constitution of the Union, the foundation of the United States.[94]

In the modern era, "revolution on the one hand, and constitution and foundation on the other, are like correlative conjunctions."[95] If we find this hard to comprehend, it is because of the paradigmatic status of the French Revolution in the revolutionary tradition (a sta-tus due, in no small part, to the brilliance of Marx's theorization). Yet, to the men of the eighteenth century, "it was still a matter of course that they needed a constitution to lay down the boundaries of the new political realm and to define the rules within it." Only through the constitutional creation of a new legally and institution-ally articulated political space would it be possible for the "passion for public freedom" and the "pursuit of public happiness" to "re-ceive free play for generations to come."[96] In Arendt's view, the "men of the American Revolution" had a firm grasp of this fact and, as a re-sult, were able to create a constitution with lasting of authority. This authority was grounded on an act of foundation comprised of two stages: first, the debates, deliberations, and composition performed by the delegates to the Constitutional Convention in Philadelphia;

second, the ratification process carried out by each of the original thirteen colonies.

The deputies of the Third Estate were, in Arendt's view, most likely following the American precedent when they swore the Tennis Court Oath to remain in session until they produced a new national constitution that would be "duly accepted by royal power." However, unlike their American counterparts, the constitution they produced was "neither accepted by the king nor commissioned and ratified by the nation." The result was that the Constitution of 1791 "remained a piece of paper," a document whose authority was shattered even before it went into effect. It was to be followed in "quick succession by one constitution after another" in an "avalanche of constitutions" that lasted well into the twentieth century.[97]

What accounts for the durable authority of the American Constitution and the failure of so many revolutionary and post-revolutionary constitutions in France to achieve a similar status? I will defer answering this question until the next section, which deals with the problem of authority. Suffice it to say here that the independent decision of the deputies of the Third Estate to form a National Assembly, combined with the "top down" character of the constitution they presented to the nation, fatally undermined the Constitution of 1791. This document was hardly the product of any dialogue between, let alone joint action by, the deputies and their constituents. It was, broadly speaking, the product of the many lawyers among the deputies of the Third Estate, and thus bore more resemblance to the "expert" constitutions drawn up by legal specialists in interwar Europe than to the American model. With the Jacobin victory over the Girondins in 1792, the "social question" moved front and center, rendering the legal niceties of constitutional debates all but superfluous in comparison with the immediate and dire needs of the poor. The "great tragedy" of the French Revolution—its failure to create a durable republic or "house where freedom can dwell"—stands out all the more sharply against the backdrop of the achievement of the American "founding fathers." Arendt, it is true, does not take the American success "for granted." Nevertheless, she certainly appears to use it as a standard for measuring the depth and seriousness of the French Revolution's failure.

Yet reading Arendt as the celebrant of American constitutional success and the diagnostician of French constitutional failure is not entirely accurate. No sooner than her post-mortem on the French constitution of 1791 is complete, she makes the following pronouncement:

> However, even in America where the foundation of a new body politic succeeded and where therefore, in a sense, the Revolution achieved its actual end, this second part of revolution, to assure the survival of the spirit out of which the act of foundation sprang, to realize the principle [of public happiness] which inspired it...was frustrated almost from the beginning.[98]

Why was this second part of the revolution—the preservation of the "revolutionary spirit"— frustrated? What factors contributed to making the American Constitution at best only *half* successful? Arendt focuses on what she sees as an ambiguity in the rhetoric of the Declaration of Independence in order to provide the outlines of an answer.

In "A Summary View of the Rights of British America, 1774" (a paper prepared for the Virginia Convention), Thomas Jefferson had written that when "our ancestors" left the "British dominions in Europe," they had exercised "a right which nature has given all men,...of establishing new societies, under such laws and regulations as to them shall seem most like to promote *public* happiness."[99] Arendt comments that if Jefferson was right and "it was in quest of 'public happiness'" that the "free inhabitants of the British dominions" emigrated to the New World, then the American colonies "must have been the breeding ground of revolutionaries from the beginning."[100] For *public happiness* demanded *public freedom*. Such freedom consisted in "the citizen's right of access to the public realm" conjoined to a "share in public power" and an overall ability to be what Jefferson called "a participator in the government of affairs."[101] According to Arendt, the fact that "happiness" denoted a share in public power

> indicated strongly that there existed in the country, prior to the revolution, such a thing as 'public happiness'...The people went to the town assemblies, as their representatives were later to go to the famous Conventions, neither exclusively because of duty

nor, and even less, to serve their own interests but most of all because they enjoyed the discussions, the deliberations, and the making of decisions.[102]

This, obviously, is a robustly republican interpretation of the phrase "public happiness," one that stands in apparently sharp contrast to the Declaration's insistence upon the "unalienable rights" of "life, liberty, and the pursuit of happiness." Generations of Americans have understood the latter phrase in a distinctively Lockean or "liberal" mode; namely, as the right to pursue one's *private* happiness in whatever non-public sphere (domestic, economic, religious, or cultural) one chose. This raises a question: did Jefferson change his mind between 1774 and 1776? Or did his famous "felicity of the pen" fail him when he elided the "pursuit of public happiness" to the "pursuit of happiness" simpliciter?

Arendt plumps for the second alternative, remarking that Jefferson was probably "not very sure in his own mind which kind of happiness he meant when he made its pursuit one of the inalienable rights of man."[103] The entrenched presumption that the pursuit of *private* welfare trumps *public* happiness in the American republic was, Arendt thinks, in no small part enabled by Jefferson's equivocation. Yet, she categorically states that the Declaration "still intends us to hear the term 'pursuit of happiness' in its twofold meaning: private welfare as well as the right to public happiness, the pursuit of well-being as well as being a 'participator in public affairs.'"[104]

Arendt is suggesting that Jefferson's Declaration and the Revolution itself should be interpreted in strongly *republican*, rather than more familiar liberal, terms. Readers encountering Arendt's thesis for the first time might see this as wishful thinking on the part of a latter-day republican, one who can't resist projecting her preferences back onto the historical and documentary record. However, a number of highly influential works of history from the late 1960s and early 1970s (including Bernard Bailyn's *Ideological Origins of the American Revolution*, Gordon Woods' *The Creation of the American Republic, 1776–1787*, and John Pocock's *The Machiavellian Moment: Florentine Political Thought and the Atlantic Republican Tradition*) have bolstered such a strongly republican interpretation of the Revolution, qualifying if not displacing the more familiar Lockean-liberal narrative.

I should note that Arendt's view is not (or not simply) that there was a virtuous, public-spirited republican founding followed by a swift and predictable decline into privatism and the pursuit of self-interest. Such a narrative would merely repeat the standard republican story (to be found in Tacitus, Machiavelli, and Rousseau) about how private interests corrupt and ultimately destroy the civic virtue upon which all free republics rely.

Arendt's story deviates from the classic republican narrative of corruption and decline in that she emphasizes a certain equivocation or lack of clarity in the minds of the Founders themselves. She makes a point of drawing our attention to the fact that the Founders—Jefferson included—were the heirs to two traditions that served to obscure the republican character of the Revolution's inspiration as well as its aspirations. The first was the English tradition of "lawful monarchical rule" that they had grown up with, a tradition which confined the happiness of the King's subjects to the realms of family and business. The second was a Christian theological tradition which valued the salvation of one's eternal soul above all else, a tradition that viewed the assumption of public responsibilities as a sad necessity in a world populated by sinners.

If the English tradition inclined the Founders to view civil *rights* and the sanctity of the private sphere as the foremost guarantees of an *individual* (rather than public) liberty, the Christian tradition inclined them to view participation in public affairs as a "burden," and even to go so far as to question whether *public* happiness existed at all. The weight of close to a thousand years of monarchical rule combined with Christian prejudices to elevate the "negative" conception of liberty (the freedom *from* politics) over the more positive one (the freedom *for* politics) inherited from the ancients. It is, as a result, not totally surprising that what Arendt calls the "second meaning" of the pursuit of happiness—the pursuit of *public* happiness—soon came to be forgotten. Nor is it surprising that, with the success of the Revolution and the solid establishment of the new republic, the emphasis shifted "from the contents of the Constitution, that is, the creation and partition of power...to the Bill of Rights, which contained the necessary constitutional restraints upon government."[105]

Like her argument about the generally republican character of the American Revolution, Arendt's assertion that the protection of civil liberties, property, and the pursuit of private happiness was not the sole (or even the most important) guiding principle of the American or French revolutions will strike some readers as dubious. To counter such skepticism she notes that "the guarantee of civil liberties and the pursuit of private happiness had long been regarded as essential in all non-tyrannical governments where the rulers governed within the limits of law." If nothing more was at stake than civil liberties and private happiness, then

> the revolutionary changes of government, the abolition of monarchy and the establishment of republics, must be regarded as accidents, provoked by no more than the wrongheadedness of the old regimes. Had this been the case, reforms and not revolution…should have been the answer.[106]

It was the evolution of the revolutions themselves, from movements aiming at the restoration of established rights to anti-monarchical struggles aiming at the creation of new bodies politic, that sharpened the distinction between public and private and that brought the conflict between their respective principles—between public freedom, public happiness, and public spirit (on the one hand) and civil rights, private happiness, and the pursuit of interest (on the other)—to the fore. Whatever lack of clarity there may have been dissolved in the course of events as the "enormous role" played by "the conflict between private interests and public affairs" became increasingly difficult to ignore. When liberation from monarchical oppression was finally achieved, revolutionaries on both sides of the Atlantic were confronted by a stark choice.

For the Americans, the question was

> whether the new government was to constitute a realm of its own for the 'public happiness' of its citizens, or whether it had been devised solely to serve and ensure their pursuit of private happiness more effectively than had the old regime.

For the French, it was a question of whether

> the end of revolutionary government lay in the establishment of a 'constitutional government' which would terminate the

reign of public freedom through a guarantee of civil liberties
and rights, or whether, for the sake of 'public freedom,' the Revolution should be declared in permanence.[107]

The overarching question, in both cases, was whether the *revolutionary
spirit* that presided over the founding of the new republics could, or
even should, be preserved.

Both Jefferson and Robespierre were convinced it should be,
yet differed markedly on the question of how this might best be
achieved. Robespierre opted for the creation of a revolutionary government, one that would extend the Revolution and delay a constitutional settlement, rooting out the corrupting influence of private
interests in the name of public liberty. Jefferson, on the other hand,
firmly supported the American Constitution. He worried, however,
that the system it put in place failed to provide access to public spaces
at the local or grass roots level, thus stripping ordinary citizens of
the opportunity to participate in public debate, deliberation, and
decision. Hence, his proposal to "divide the counties into wards"—
into "elementary republics" that would enable ordinary citizens to
"do what they had been able to do during the years of revolution,
namely, to act on their own and participate in public business as it
was being transacted from day to day."[108] This opportunity was not
available at the state or even the county level, which he regarded as
"far too large and unwieldy to permit immediate participation."[109]

Arendt thinks Jefferson's proposal was clearly the result of fore-
boding about how

> dangerous it might be to allow the people a share in public
> power without providing them at the same time with more
> public space than the ballot box and with more opportunity to
> make their voices heard than on election day.[110]

Without access to public spaces for debate, deliberation, and opinion
formation with their peers, citizens would increasingly come to view
the political process as a vehicle for the protection and advancement
of their private (individual or group) interests. The "mortal danger"
Jefferson feared was that this elevation of private interests over public goods would become ingrained, and that the citizen body would

become "corrupt" in the classical republican sense of the word. The danger of corruption—of citizens who habitually elevated the pursuit of their private interests over the attainment of public goods—appeared unavoidable in a constitutional system that gave "all power to the people in their private capacity" without establishing a space for them to act in "their capacity for being citizens."[111]

Arendt completely agrees with Jefferson's diagnosis of the problem. She also agrees, in principle, with his solution to it. However, she doesn't regard Jefferson's ward system as the best or even the most plausible corrective for the Constitution's deficiencies. A far better solution, in her eyes, would have been to incorporate the townships themselves into the Constitution's decentralized scheme for distinct powers at the federal, state, and county levels. After all (and as Jefferson was well aware), it was the public spirit of the New England townships, with their long-standing practice of regular town meetings and local administration of public affairs, that had provided the engines of the Revolution. Arendt here takes a page from Tocqueville's *Democracy in America*, which stressed the "democratic and republican" character of the townships and their vital importance in creating and maintaining a love of public liberty and the habit of civic participation among ordinary citizens.

Arendt deploys this Tocquevillian insight to come to a quite un-Tocquevillian conclusion. In her view, the fact that the Founders *failed* to include the townships in their constitutional scheme more or less guaranteed their decline—both as centers for local administration and as generators of civic participation. She finds Tocqueville's assurance that civil society and a robust associational life could prevent a descent into privatism and *individualisme* completely unconvincing. Whereas civic republicans from Machiavelli onward thought that the conflict between public goods and private interests reflected an irreducible tension between two spheres of life, Tocqueville taught that associational membership could reveal the "close tie" between public and private interests, a possibility he saw confirmed in the universal American endorsement of the idea of "self-interest rightly understood." Arendt does not reject the idea that civil society might provide a possible home for political action, but she *does* reject the idea that self-interest is, or ever could be, "enlightened" (as the doctrine of "self-interest, rightly understood" had taught).[112] In her view, civil society is unable to perform the successful mediation between public and private interests, as Tocqueville (and Hegel, to a degree) had argued. At best, it can provide a venue adjacent to the "official" public sphere, a venue in which citizens can join together to advocate for, or protest against, specific governmental policies or actions.

The rejection of the doctrine of "enlightened self-interest" has important consequences for Arendt's argument in OR. Not only does it sharpen, once again, the distinction between public and private; it also leads her to reiterate familiar civic republican and participatory ideas about the importance of the *vivere civile* and the need for direct democracy at the local level. Arendt's not entirely deserved reputation as the doyenne of participatory democracy can be traced to the presence of these themes in her work, as well as to the biting critique of *representative* democracy set out in OR. While there are certainly precedents for the critique of representative institutions in the republican tradition (for example, Rousseau's in the *Social Contract*), the degree of Arendt's hostility is still surprising, especially in light of her overall enthusiasm for the ingenious "system of power" found in the American Constitution.

In order to understand Arendt's hostility toward representative government—her inability to appreciate what George Kateb has termed the "moral distinctiveness of representative democracy"— we first need to be clear about her distinctions between plural *opinions* (on the one hand) and mass "public opinion" and *interests* (on the other).

As we've seen, Arendt thinks that human plurality is the *conditio sine qua non* of politics and authentically political relations. In the public realm, this plurality is expressed through the medium of opinion— *doxa*. She views all forms of Platonism, Christianity included, as attempts to replace the plurality-based politics of diverse opinions with an authoritarian politics of univocal Truth. The devaluation of *doxa* in the Western philosophical and theological tradition is, of course, dwarfed by the totalitarian terror-driven attempt to efface human plurality altogether. Arendt never failed to point out the difference between an authoritarian politics founded on a transcendental "Truth" and a totalitarian politics based on ideological fiction. However, the one thing these two projects *do* share is the desire to replace a public realm constituted by diverse perspectives with one grounded on an enforced unity and the elimination of difference.

The politics of plurality is fundamentally a politics of plural opinions expressed by diverse equals in a shared public space. Opinion is the stuff of any politics based on persuasion rather than coercion. A doxastic politics so conceived is threatened not only by an authoritarian politics of a supposedly unquestionable "Truth," but also by what we currently refer to as "public opinion." The latter, an increasingly potent force in modern mass societies, is the object of incessant polling and quantitative assessment. What such polling measures, however, are not the opinions formed, tested, and purified through public debate and deliberation, but rather the public's mood or sentiment at a particular moment in time.

In this regard, Arendt points out that the founders' preference for a republic over a democracy resulted from the fact that they understood democracy to be a form of government in which "*public opinion* was held to rule where *public spirit* ought to prevail." The sign of this perversion, they thought, was to be found in the "unanimity of the citizenry."[113] Arendt fundamentally agrees with the founders' on this point and drives her argument home by borrowing a phrase from James Madison. "Opinions," she writes,

> never belong to groups but exclusively to individuals, who 'exert their reason coolly and freely,' and no multitude, be it the multitude of a part or of the whole of society, will ever be capable of forming an opinion. Opinions will arise wherever men communicate freely with one another and have the right to make their views public.[114]

This assertion calls to mind Arendt's statements in THC that "the reality of the public realm relies on the simultaneous presence of innumerable perspectives and aspects" and that "being seen and being heard by others derive their significance from the fact that everybody sees and hears from a different position."[115] Such statements might create the impression that the diversity of opinion Arendt so prizes is solely a function of our "different locations" in the common world—our different "subject positions." But that, of course, is not what Arendt means. The contemporary notion of "subject positions" encourages us to think of opinions and points of view as largely a function of one's racial, class, or gender identity. Thus, just as we have come to equate *opinion* with public *sentiment*, so we have also come to equate *differences in perspective* with *differences in group identity*. In neither case is the opinion or perspective in question viewed as the product of an active engagement with the views, opinions, or perspectives of others. Such active engagement occurs, Arendt thinks, in the course of actual public debate and deliberation and by way of the process she describes as "representative thinking":

> Political thought is representative. I form an opinion by considering a given issue from different viewpoints, by making present to my mind the standpoints of those who are absent; that is, I represent them. This process of representation does not blindly adopt the actual views of those who stand somewhere else, and hence look upon the world from a different perspective; this is a question neither of empathy, as though I tried to be or to feel like somebody else, nor of counting noses and joining a majority, but of being and thinking in my own identity where actually I am not. The more people's standpoints I have present in my mind while I am pondering a given issue, and the better I can imagine how I would feel and think if I were in their place, the stronger will be my capacity for representative thinking and the more valid my final conclusion, my opinion.[116]

Individual opinion formation thus presupposes public debate (through which I become acquainted with the opinions and standpoints of others) and representative thinking (through which I develop my imaginative capacity for viewing a public matter from a variety of perspectives, while nevertheless retaining my own individual standpoint).

Opinion formation so construed is obviously quite different from reportage of how we *feel* about a particular politician or policy at a given point in time. It is similarly far removed from any inner conflict between the universal and particular aspects of our will, a conflict whose stimulation Rousseau recommended as the best way to elucidate the general will. Contrary to the tradition and to contemporary usage, opinion is not a feeling or impression located somewhere between total ignorance and genuine knowledge, but a *rational faculty* all are capable of developing by means of public argument and individual thought and imagination. What is at stake is not the attainment of "truth," the achievement of a "rational consensus," or the leveling and homogenization of viewpoints. Rather, what is at stake is a fuller articulation of each citizen's "opening to the [public] world" as well as the plurality that underlies both our common world and our political relations. Opinion, in short, is not something to be transcended, but rather something formed and expressed by individual citizens through debate, deliberation, and representative thinking.[117] As such, it is the lifeblood of the public realm.

If opinions belong to individuals, interests—on the other hand—are the property of groups. They are pre-political in nature, embodying the social and material goods constitutive of (or desired by) a particular social group. American politics has long been understood and framed in terms of "interest group politics" and Harold Lasswell's 1936 contention that politics is about "who gets what, when, and how" continues to guide (implicitly if not explicitly) much of contemporary American political science.

Of course, attention to the role of *material* interests in politics predates American political science. It even predates Marx. Aristotle, for example, was well aware of their importance. Our contemporary understanding of the relative legitimacy of interests in politics can be traced back to the luxury debate of the eighteenth century. This debate pitted proponents of republican civic virtue (like Ferguson and Rousseau) against liberal or proto-liberal advocates of commerce and an expanding division of labor (like Hume and Smith). For the former, particular interests clearly *subverted* the general will, undermining the *patria* and contributing to the dissolution of the common good. For the latter, the common good was not something to be viewed as separate and distinct from the myriad interests of market actors. Rather, they viewed the common good as nothing other than an aggregate of these very "selfish" interests.

The crucial point for Arendt is that interests, unlike opinions, can be *represented*. They are not formed through debate and deliberation in the public realm; rather, they exist fully formed in the socio-economic sphere. Outside the public-political realm proper, they attempt to steer policy and legislation in directions favorable to the group's goals and desires. Representative government is the ideal vehicle for interest group politics, and not merely because representatives are susceptible to lobbying and pressure tactics. The very theory of representative government *assumes* that the function of any legitimately elected official is to represent the primary interests of his or her constituents. In practice, this means advocating for the material interests of a region, key social groups, or industry sectors. Speaking generally, interests are clear and relatively few in number. Unlike the diverse and evolving nature of individual opinions, they are concrete and stable over time. This makes them ideally suited for the "labor-saving device" of representative government, a device intended to free citizens from the "burden" of public affairs.

The biggest problem with representative government, however, is not that it makes interests rather than opinions the stuff of politics. That, of course, is bad enough from Arendt's perspective. Interest group politics encourages citizens to privilege private or sectional interests over the common good—to become "corrupt" in the classical republican sense of the word. However, representative government also encourages us to view politics as a zero-sum game, one in which the advancement of our group's interests comes at the expense of the sectional interests of others. A cynical and strategic view of what goes on in the public sphere results, and politics devolves into a kind of war by other means. The symbiotic relationship of representative government and interest group politics thus makes it difficult if not impossible to view political action as the tangible expression of public freedom, let alone the vehicle of "public happiness."

In addition to contributing to the corruption of citizens, representative government is guilty of what is, in Arendt's eyes, a much greater sin. If representatives are bound by the instructions of their constituents, they will be no more than "glorified messenger boys" or, at best, "hired experts" who, like lawyers, are "specialists in representing the interests of their clients." Such mandate-bound representation indicates that a "decision on the very dignity of the political realm itself" has already been made. The electorate assumes, in classically "corrupt" fashion, that their private business is far more urgent in nature than the "government of affairs" ever could be. If, on the other hand, the representatives are "understood to become for a limited time the appointed rulers of those who elected them," then representation effectively means that "the voters surrender their own power, albeit voluntarily."[118] The distinction between rulers and ruled—a distinction republicanism wished to abolish—returns with a vengeance, as public affairs are controlled by an elite that constitutes what Arendt calls a "de facto oligarchy." Once more, Arendt writes, "the business of government has become the privilege of the few."[119]

Remarks such as these seem to confirm the impression that Arendt is a "participatory democrat" of the leveling sort. Apparently, what she *really* objects to in representative government is less the recourse to representative institutions (a structural necessity in large republics) than the effective re-constitution of a political elite. This new elite consists of a class of professional politicians who, nurtured by the party system, stand over and *above* the people, monopolizing both political power and the public realm. True, unlike the aristocratic elites of pre-modern times, the political elite born of representative government can lay legitimate claim to having "sprung from the people." Yet nowhere has this new elite "enabled the people *qua* people to make their entrance into political life." The result is that the relationship between "the few, who among themselves constitute a public space, and the many, who spend their lives outside it and in obscurity, has remained unchanged."[120]

The impression that Arendt thinks *any* elite in the political sphere marks a return to hierarchy and the hated ruler/ruled distinction is, however, mistaken. Directly following the passage just cited, Arendt writes:

> From the viewpoint of revolution and the survival of the revolutionary spirit, the trouble does not lie in the factual rise of a new elite: it is not the revolutionary spirit but the democratic mentality of an egalitarian society that tends to deny the obvious inability and conspicuous lack of interest of large parts of the population in political matters as such. *The trouble lies in the lack of public spaces to which the people at large would have entrance and from which an elite could be selected, or rather, where it could select itself.* The trouble, in other words, is that politics has become a profession and a career, and that the 'elite' therefore is being chosen according to standards and criteria [such as salesmanship] which are themselves profoundly un-political.[121]

If there *were* "public spaces to which the people at large" had access, then

> the joys of public happiness and the responsibilities for public business would...become the share of those few from all walks of life who have a taste for public freedom and cannot be 'happy' without it. Politically, they are the best...[122]

Does Arendt here stand revealed? Not, to be sure, as a participatory democrat, but rather as an elitist in republican garb? A political thinker removed from the popular sympathies of Machiavelli and Rousseau and ultimately closer in spirit to Aristotle and the "rule of the best"? Those skeptical of her treatment of the "social question" will no doubt be inclined to answer in the affirmative.

Arendt's "elitism" has long been a target of critics of her work. In addition to the remarks just cited, such critics point to her treatment of heroic political action in THC and her intellectual debt to such anti-egalitarian figures as Nietzsche and Heidegger.[123] For this reason, it's important to be clear about what she is saying—and what she is *not* saying—in OR. Her critique of representative government dovetails with her more limited criticism of the US Constitution insofar as the emphasis in both is on *the lack of accessible public spaces of debate and deliberation for ordinary citizens.* In the United States, such spaces once existed in the form of the townships. And in Europe, they have emerged, albeit episodically, in the form of the revolutionary council system. However, the triumph of representative government in conjunction with the party system produces a structure with two primary characteristics. First, access to public spaces of debate, deliberation, and decision is restricted to an elite of representatives; second, professional politicians with decidedly un-political gifts (salesmanship, deal-making ability) are rewarded, while ordinary citizens who possess authentically political talents (for persuasion, judgment, and joint action) are excluded. It is the latter group, not the former, who—in Arendt's estimation—are *politically speaking* "the best."

The qualification "politically speaking" is crucial. Arendt is *not* saying that such citizens are "the best" in the ancient Greek sense of constituting an *aristoi* of the "best and the beautiful." Nor does she use this phrase in Christian-Aristotelian fashion, the better to

designate a virtuous minority who supposedly possess ethical character in combination with a superior degree of moral wisdom.
Rather, she uses it to refer to those citizens "from all walks of life"
(and, one might add, all levels of formal education) who display the
most interest in, responsibility for, and commitment to public affairs
and the maintenance of public liberty. These are, *politically speaking*,
"the best" and "it is the task of good government and the sign of a
well-ordered republic to assure them of their rightful place in the
public realm."[124]

The one area in which the charge of "elitism" has some plausibility
is found in Arendt's preference for *quality* of participation over *quantity*.
While it is hard to think of a canonical political theorist who valued
the *bios politikos* as much as she did, Arendt never labored under the illusion that this was a life for everyone. She did not think that mandat-
ing participation at the electoral or any other level would bring about
a freer or more authentically political culture. Given her experience
with totalitarianism, it is not surprising that she thinks the freedom
to be left alone—to *not* participate—is a liberty we must protect at
all costs, even though it is not (from her point of view) the only or
most important freedom. The point of preserving the "revolutionary
spirit" is not to underwrite participation for the sake of participation; nor is it to dragoon people into public displays of patriotism or
party fealty. Rather, it is to preserve the taste for public freedom and
self-government in a world where "government of the people, by the
people, and for the people" has been progressively stripped of content
and reduced to little more than an edifying cliché.

Arendt's enthusiasm for the council system should be read in light
of the above considerations. Even though she thinks the emergence
of the council system in disparate revolutionary moments provides
us with a glimpse of a possible "alternative model of the state," she
hardly privileges the preservation of revolutionary spontaneity and
spirit *over* the constitutional creation of durable institutions. Admittedly, she sometimes gives this impression, as when she observes
that—"paradoxical as it may sound"—it was "under the impact of
the Revolution that the Revolutionary spirit in America began to
wither away, and it was the Constitution itself, this greatest achievement of the American people, which eventually cheated them of
their proudest possession."[125]

As previously noted, her primary point in this regard is that the Constitution's failure to incorporate accessible public spaces into its ingenious "system of power" shifted, in principle, all power to the people *in their private capacity* without providing them with the space to act "in their capacity as citizens." This failure produced corruption in the form of a citizen body habitually inclined to privilege particular over general interests. It also produced a system of representative government predicated on the hegemony of interest group politics (on the one hand) and the revival of the distinction between rulers and ruled (on the other).

Arendt's critique of the devolution of constitutional government and representative democracy is thus hardly a critique of constitutions *as such*. However, an increasingly influential strand of "left Arendtian" thought has shrugged off her constitutional commitments, the better to focus on those historical episodes of popular action through which a people manifests itself not just as an actor in the revolutionary drama, but as *a democratic people*. On this view, democracy is less a form of government than it is a series of "moments" of popular action directed against elites and the hierarchical distribution of power and wealth.[126] It follows that the "constitutionalization of democracy" is tantamount to its neutering and poses a grave threat to political freedom, popular agency, and democracy as such.[127]

Obviously, anyone who thinks (as Arendt does) that "revolution on the one hand, and constitution and foundation on the other, are like correlative conjunctions" could scarcely hold such a view.[128] Like the American founders and republican forebears such as Machiavelli, Arendt was too concerned with the creation of durable institutions to fall prey to a vision of the revolutionary spirit that severed the poetry of spontaneous action from the prose of institutional life. While critical of constitutionalism in its most familiar iteration (namely, as a theory of limited government predicated upon the primacy of civil rights and negative liberty), she nevertheless saw the creation of a space for freedom as inseparable from the constitutional foundation of a new form of government. The "correlative conjunction" of revolution and constitution reminds us that the point of revolutionary action is not *politique pour la politique* but rather the erection of a "new house where freedom can dwell" for generations to come.

This last point brings us to the question of what some have called the "autonomy of the political" in Arendt's thought. Arendt's abiding concern to distinguish the political from the social, action from production, and political from civil rights has led some to view her as a kind of left-wing counterpart to Carl Schmitt. Schmitt's *The Concept of the Political* (1932) sought to recapture the specificity of the political in a world where it was usually subsumed under economic, legal, or ethical categories. Notoriously, he set about this project by invoking the distinction between friend and enemy. Schmitt thought this distinction could serve as an effective criterion whereby "the political" could be clearly distinguished from any other sphere of life (economic, ethical, aesthetic, social). With the deployment of this category, the political sphere emerged as a zone of real or potential conflict between nation-states. For Schmitt, then, the autonomy of the political was manifest in the irreducible possibility of enmity between two states or between large groups representing divergent "ways of life." This possibility remained in play, Schmitt argued, no matter how persistently liberalism and liberal ideology tried to replace the *political* vocabulary of battle, war, combat, etc. with the "depoliticized" concepts of (economic) competition and (ethical) debate.

Arendt's rigorous distinctions between political action and power (on the one hand) and violence and strength or force (on the other) clearly mark her distance from Schmitt's concept of the political. Yet her Schmitt-like insistence on recovering the specificity or autonomy of the political has troubled many readers. After all, they reason, if we are not to confuse the political realm with the social, economic, administrative, or ethical realms, what possible *content* is left for politics beyond the antagonistic? As her friend Mary McCarthy put it to her at the 1972 Toronto conference: "If all questions of economics, human welfare, busing, anything that touches the social sphere are to be excluded from the political scene, then I am mystified. I am left with war and speeches."[129]

In Chapter 3 I outlined how Arendt, in reply to a similar query from Richard Bernstein, suggested that many of the issues confronting us have a "double face," one social, the other political. The first "face" usually points to the governmental delivery of certain goods (health care, adequate housing), while the second raises questions about the type of community the political association wants to be (liberal versus republican; libertarian versus social democratic; egalitarian versus meritocratic).

To be sure, this is a partial and not entirely satisfying answer to the question "what else is there?" Here, I would like to suggest that, from an Arendtian perspective, the most important content of politics is to be found in matters that are tied to the creation, preservation, and "augmentation" of a constitution. If, as Arendt suggests, "the *raison d'être* of politics is freedom," then it stands to reason that preserving the health and integrity of the laws and institutions that articulate *our* space of freedom should be our foremost *political* concern. That this is by no means a "content-less" project (a version of *politique pour la politique*) is illustrated by the rapid decline of American political institutions in the twenty-first century, a decline due mainly to growing civic corruption and the cynical bending of American democracy to serve the oligarchic interests of the extraordinarily wealthy. "Care for the world" in the Arendtian sense entails care for the *public* world and the very legal-institutional architecture that sustains and supports it. As demonstrated by recent history, the American Constitution is not a machine that "runs by itself," nor is it a machine capable of preserving itself in the face of corruption, indifference, and widespread ignorance about the nature and structure of liberal constitutional democracy.

The constitutional focus suggests another source of content for Arendtian politics. Just as many social issues have a "double face," so too do many rights and due process claims. Despite the somewhat deprecating attitude she takes toward civil (as opposed to political) rights in OR, there can be no doubt that Arendt is a supporter of equal civil rights. The struggle for equal rights for blacks, women, and gay people in the United States can be viewed as *political* in the Arendtian sense insofar as in each of these cases there is a clear constitutional referent. The question "who is to be afforded full civil and political rights?" is a question about equal citizenship and about membership in the political association. As such, it goes to the civic and constitutional heart of the republican idea.

Finally, Arendt's idea of "care for the world" suggests a need to actively monitor and support not just our public-political institutions, but also what Arendt calls "the human artifice." This is the artificial world that stands between man and nature, a world that is currently under severe threat from the ecological crises created by pollution and climate change. "Care for the world" entails taking up the fight against those forces that would render cities uninhabitable and the "material bases" of polities across the globe unsustainable. In this regard, it is hardly implausible to suggest that present and future ecological crises might well create refugee crises of gigantic proportions. If, as Arendt suggested in OT, the interwar refugee crisis was among the factors that contributed to the decline of the nation-state and the rise of totalitarianism, then the prospect of tens of millions of ecological refugees—added to the millions of political and economic refugees who already exist—should make us fear for the future of constitutional democracy. The emergence of anti-immigrant nationalist regimes in Europe, Asia, and the Americas already point to the possible return of "dark times."

IV Power, promising, and authority

In the Anglo-American tradition it has long been second nature to identify constitutional government with limited government. We assume that the American founders were concerned, above all, with the protection of civil liberties by means of the constitutional limits they imposed on state power. However, as Arendt points out, once the colonists declared independence from the British Crown, "the main question for them certainly was not how to limit power, but how to establish it, not how to limit government but how to found a new one."[130] Immediately after the Declaration, it was the "fever of constitution-making" in all thirteen colonies that prevented a power vacuum from developing and that established "new centers of power" to take the place of the rejected power of King and parliament. Having enjoyed a relatively high degree of autonomy and (for the most part) the blessings of mild government under the Crown, the colonists were already quite familiar with the necessary "safeguards of civil liberty" and individual rights. What they needed to discover, however, was how to create an institutional framework that would result in the constitution and generation of power. The founders' awareness of their own relative ignorance on this score accounts for the almost comical ransacking of ancient and modern "political science" we find in their writings.

The eighteenth-century author who had the most influence on the framers in this regard was, of course, Montesquieu. We typically credit Montesquieu's *Spirit of the Laws* for teaching the framers about the need for a separation and balance of powers, the better to counteract governmental overreach and protect individual liberties. Arendt agrees that "the main subject of Montesquieu's great work was indeed the 'constitution of political freedom.'" However, against the standard interpretation of this phrase, she asserts that the word "constitution" hardly has the connotation of "being a negative, a limitation and negation of power." On the contrary, "the word meant... that the 'grand temple of federal liberty' must be based on the foundation of the correct distribution of power."[131] Montesquieu's real lesson, according to Arendt, is that *freedom and power belong together*. This, and not the advantages of the so-called mixed regime, is why we "find his name invoked in practically all debates on constitution."[132]

The framers realized that the *constitutio libertatis* demanded the construction of a system of power. They turned to Montesquieu because he had shown how

> power can be stopped *and still kept intact* only by power, so that the separation of powers not only provides a guarantee against the monopolization of power by one part of the government, but actually provides a kind of mechanism, built into the very heart of government, through which new power is constantly generated.[133]

This is, of course, an unorthodox reading of Montesquieu. It is based largely upon Arendt's interpretation of a single sentence in which Montesquieu (in chapter XI of *The Spirit of the Laws*) advises that "power must arrest power" if *abuse* of power is to be prevented and power itself is to be kept intact.[134]

This might seem a slim reed on which to base such a radical reinterpretation of Montesquieu's doctrine of the separation of powers. However, it finds support in the simple fact that the framers, in drafting the Constitution, were looking for a way to overcome the *weakness* of the colonial confederation that preceded the founding of the republic and the creation of the federal government. It was by grasping the *positive* content of Montesquieu's doctrine that the

framers were able to come up with what Arendt calls "the greatest American innovation in politics," namely, "the consistent abolition of *sovereignty* within the body of the republic."[135] The idea of the
sovereign nation-state—the seemingly inescapable European legacy
of the Treaty of Westphalia—is rejected in principle by the federal
structure of the new republic. The latter creates a multi-leveled and
decentered structure of political power, one in which "power arrests
power" without creating impotence.

Arendt's positive reading of the separation of powers doctrine is
lent further support by her suggestive reframing of the relationship between the American founding and the social contract tradition. This tradition is often identified with the idea of "government
with the consent of the governed"—that is, with the idea of an
agreement (explicit or tacit) between the individuals constituting
society and those who take charge of the government of public
affairs. The former "resign up their power" to their governors,
but with the stipulation that the latter govern in accordance with
known and public law and wield their power primarily to preserve
the "lives, liberties, and property" of the governed. Should the
governors betray their side of the bargain by arbitrarily infringing
upon the rights of individuals, the "contract" is broken and the
governed are effectively returned to a pre-civil "state of nature."
They are then entitled to create a new agreement with a different
set of governors. These (it is hoped) will not abuse the power they
have been entrusted with by society.

This, in generic form, is what is usually understood by a "social
contract" theory of government and legitimate political power. There
are different iterations of this theory in seventeenth- and eighteenth-
century political thought. Its most prominent representatives—Hobbes,
Locke, Rousseau, and Kant—dispute the exact nature of the agreement
in question, with some (Hobbes and Rousseau) even questioning
whether there is or ought to be anything like a *contract* between governors and governed.[136] Nevertheless, it is entirely plausible to interpret
the American Revolution and subsequent ratification of the Constitution along the lines suggested by social contract theory, particularly if
we stick to Locke's version. King George III breaks the implicit contract (or "trust") he had with the colonists, demanding taxation without representation. As a result of this "lawless" breach, the power of

constituting a government that faithfully protects the "lives, liberties, and properties" of the colonists reverts to them. The Constitution and the Bill of Rights create the terms of agreement between the people and its new government, with the conditions for the legitimate exercise of political power explicitly spelled out.

Within the social contract tradition it is common to draw a distinction between the "horizontal" contract or pact of association that forms a society out of aggregated individuals and the "vertical" contract between a society so formed and its government. In the "government with consent of the governed" model, it is clearly the latter type of contract that takes pride of place. Society either gives its consent (in which case the government exercises political power legitimately) or withdraws it due to serial governmental abuses. This distribution of emphasis structures Locke's *Second Treatise of Government*, the bulk of which is devoted to setting out when and how consent has been given (either tacitly or explicitly) by the governed; and when and how a government can be said to have abused its trust, deploying "power without right" in tyrannical fashion.

Given her distaste for the ruler/ruled distinction, it is not surprising that Arendt views the "vertical" contract negatively and the "horizontal" contract positively. The "mutual [or horizontal] contract by which people bind themselves together in order to form a community" is, according to Arendt, "based on reciprocity and presupposes equality." Its actual content "is a promise, and its result is indeed a 'society' or 'cosociation' in the old Roman sense of *societas*, which means alliance." Such an alliance, she writes, "gathers together the isolated strength of the allied partners and binds them into a new power structure by virtue of 'free and sincere promises.'"

However, when it comes to the "vertical" contract between a society and its rulers, "we deal with a fictitious, aboriginal act on the side of each member, by virtue of which he gives up his isolated strength and power to constitute a new government." The result is that "far from gaining a new power, and possibly more than he had before, he resigns his power such as it is, and far from binding himself through promises, he merely expresses his 'consent' to be ruled by the government."[137] From the standpoint of the individual, "it is obvious that he gains as much power by the system of mutual promises as he loses by his consent to a monopoly of power in the ruler."

And, while those who "covenant and combine themselves together" consciously transcend their isolation "by virtue of reciprocation," it is clear that individuals who simply consent to a governing power find that it is "precisely their isolation which is safeguarded and protected."[138]

These passages contain echoes of Marx's critique of bourgeois constitutionalism in "On the Jewish Question" and Tocqueville's analysis of the pathology of *individualisme* in *Democracy in America*. However, in contrast to both Marx and Tocqueville, Arendt's emphasis is not upon the broad phenomenon of social atomization. Rather, she wants us to see that the mutual contract "where power is constituted by means of promise" actually contains "*in nuce* both the *republican principle* according to which power resides in the people…and the *federal principle*…according to which constituted political bodies can combine and enter into lasting alliances without losing their identity."[139] Yet, if this indeed is the case, it is difficult to see how the individualizing idiom of "contract" facilitates the recognition of either principle. Indeed, neither principle looms large in the social contract tradition, the possible exception of Kant's political writings notwithstanding.

Where, then, if not in the political theories of the day did the colonists discover the power of promising? According to Arendt, it was

> No theory, theological or political or philosophical, but their own decision to leave the old world behind and to venture forth into an enterprise of their own [that] led into a sequence of acts and occurrences in which they would have perished, had they not turned their minds to the matter long and intensely enough to discover, almost by inadvertence, the elementary grammar of political action and its more complicated syntax, whose rules determine the rise and fall of human power…What they discovered…was no theory of social contract in either of its two forms, but rather the few elementary truths on which this theory rests.[140]

In other words, behind the discovery of the power of mutual promises lay an experience first expressed in the Mayflower Compact and subsequently expressed in virtually all the colonists' political arrangements, up through and including the Declaration of

Independence and the Constitution. This experience was that of a diverse group of individuals who recognized that their chances for success hinged upon their ability to act together for the sake of a common enterprise. It was this capacity for joint action that they articulated in terms of a system of mutual pledges to one another. Thus, while *action* could be initiated by an individual or by a group of individuals with disparate motivations, the *establishment of a new and lasting community* required a public and formal commitment on the part of each potential member to jointly carry through the task at hand, no matter what obstacles might be encountered along the way.

The power of such mutual promising, then, was something the colonists were familiar with long before the Revolution. They knew that, while power can be *created* by simply acting together, it can be *kept in existence* only by "binding and promising, combining and covenanting" for the future. Their victory over England, so astonishing to the Old World, was much less a surprise in the New. After all, the colonists had "a hundred and fifty years of covenant-making behind them" and they were quite aware of the power these agreements created. Through a system of mutual promises, they had successfully created "a country that was [politically] articulated from top to bottom—from provinces or states down to cities and districts, townships, villages, and counties—into duly constituted bodies... designed 'for increase'"—that is, for the generation of the political power required for these bodies to endure.[141] The success of the colonists, then, was due in no small part to their discovery of what Arendt refers to as "the grammar of action" and the "syntax of power":

> The grammar of action: that action is the only human faculty that demands a plurality of men; and the syntax of power: that power is the only human attribute which applies solely to the worldly in-between space by which men are mutually related, combine in the act of foundation by virtue of the making and keeping of promises, which, in the realm of politics, *may well be the highest human faculty.*[142]

What does Arendt mean by this compressed formulation? First, that the basic structure of action is *joint action* (or "acting in concert") and that therefore plurality is the *sine qua non* of political action. Second, that such joint action produces *power*—a fact clearly on display in the 1986 "people power" movement against Ferdinand Marcos in the Philippines and in the 1989 revolutions against communist domination in Eastern Europe. Third, that such power is not a commodity seized nor a quality possessed by an individual or group (it is not the same as *strength*); rather, it comes into being through the creation of a worldly in-between or *public* space. Fourth, that such power can be preserved and augmented only if the plurality of agents who produce it make use of promising—that is, of their faculty for stabilizing the future. Fifth, that it is through the making and keeping of promises that action and power are durably combined, and that this combination comes to fruition in the establishment or creation of a new public-political realm. Sixth, that, in the realm of politics, the capacity to make and keep promises "may well be the highest human faculty" because it is through this capacity that words and deeds lose their otherwise ephemeral ("futile") character and become lasting objects of communal memory. By "stabilizing the future" promising makes common memory possible, thereby providing human existence with a depth it would otherwise lack.

Arendt's treatment of promising as a political faculty par excellence is tremendously suggestive. However, it leaves unanswered the question of why, given the centrality of mutual pledges to the American colonial and revolutionary experience, Jefferson and others were wont to frame the revolutionary project in familiar Lockean "government by the consent of the governed" terms. As with the issue of public versus private happiness, Arendt suggests that it was a certain lack of clarity that led Jefferson to employ the language of the "consent of the governed" at the beginning of the Declaration of Independence, only to fall back upon the language of mutual pledges (of "our Lives, our Fortunes, and our sacred Honor") at its end:

> Jefferson could speak of the consent of the people from which governments 'derive their just powers' in the same Declaration which he closes on the principle of mutual pledges, and neither he nor anybody else ever became aware of the simple and elementary difference between 'consent' and mutual promise, or between the two types of contract theory.[143]

Arendt thinks that Jefferson's failure to distinguish these different types of contract theory can be traced back to "the lack of conceptual clarity and precision with respect to existing realities" that has been "the curse of Western history ever since…the men of action and the men of thought parted company and thinking began to emancipate itself altogether from reality, and especially from political factuality and experience."[144] As she had in her analysis of the reasons for the persistent privileging of a negative "freedom from politics" over a more positive "freedom for politics," Arendt here blames the Western tradition of political philosophy for contributing to the oblivion of a quintessentially political phenomenon: the power of promising. The result is that the self-understanding of the American revolutionary project changes from the republican one of the *constitutio libertatis* to the liberal one of limiting the power of government.

****

The "new beginnings" represented by the French and American revolutions clearly required new understandings of political freedom, power, and authority. However,

> just as the old [negative] concept of liberty…came to exert a strong influence on the interpretation of the new experience of freedom, so the old understanding of power and authority… almost automatically led the new experience of power to be channeled into concepts which had just been vacated.[145]

Traditionally, power was understood as sovereign power, the authority or legitimacy of which was understood to be grounded upon a transcendent source, such as God or the hierarchical order of Nature. The revolutions, on the other hand, had generated a radically different kind of *power*: the power produced by mutual promises and diverse equals acting together for the sake of a joint enterprise. Similarly, the new republics represented a radical break with the past and the kind of *authority* that had been predicated upon tradition, "natural" hierarchy, or the divine right of kings. Yet, despite these radical differences, we find the "men of the revolutions" almost immediately lapsing back into the rhetoric of sovereign power and "natural" or God-given authority. Why is this the case?

One obvious explanation—at least in the case of the French Revolution—is that the thinking of the revolutionaries was predetermined by the very regime-form they had overthrown. In an absolute monarchy of the French type, the will of the sovereign represented God's will on earth. As such, it laid claim to be the source of all legitimate power as well as the justice or legality of all law. With the overthrow of the monarchy, nothing seemed more "natural" than to put the sovereignty of the nation in the place just vacated by the sovereignty of the king.[146] This was the thinking behind Abbé Sieyès' famous distinction between the *pouvoir constituant* and the *pouvoir constitué*, which made the will of the nation the source of all law and, as such, effectively above the law. Like the will of the king, the will of the nation could do no wrong: it was the fountain from which justice and legitimacy sprang. Here, we return to the logic of the general will, which Rousseau quite consistently exempted from any preset limitation by "so-called" fundamental laws.[147]

But while the basic move of substituting the will of the nation for the will of the king may have solved the question of the law's legitimacy, it by no means solved the problem of the law's *authority*—that is, its possible permanence and stability. By reducing law and justice to emanations of the national will, Sieyès and Rousseau deprived the law of the "sacred" character it needed so that citizens might venerate it and their new institutions for generations to come. Rousseau himself was acutely aware of the problem. He had gone so far to argue that, in order to put the law above men and thereby establish its lasting validity, "one would actually need gods."[148] This is one reason why semi-divine founder-figures like Lycurgus and Moses play such a central role in Rousseau's political thought. Only such an "immortal legislator" could possibly endow a set of laws and institutions with the aura of sanctity necessary for the stability and durability of a new republic. Robespierre's rather desperate attempt to salvage the French situation through his cult of the Supreme Being only underlined the authority deficit suffered by revolutionary laws and institutions.[149]

Like their French counterparts, the American revolutionaries knew that they had to "establish a new source of law and a new system of power." However, they were unburdened by any tradition of absolute monarchy and enjoyed the benefits of the "mild government" that followed the English constitutional settlement of 1688. As a result, the American Framers were never tempted to "derive law and power from the same origin." As Arendt notes,

> the seat of power to them was the people, but the source of law was to become the Constitution, a written document, an endurable objective thing, which, to be sure, one could approach from many different angles...but which nevertheless was never a subjective state of mind, like the will.[150]

These advantages notwithstanding, the Americans nevertheless found themselves confronting what Arendt refers to as "the problem of an absolute": the seemingly unavoidable need for something more than compacts, covenants, or promises that would "bestow upon the affairs of men that measure of stability without which they would be unable to build a world for their posterity."[151] The "problem of an absolute" thus arose less from the need to put some new absolute in the place of the absolute power of the king than from the fact that *secularization*—the modern separation of the political and religious realms—

> inevitably posed the problem of how to found and constitute a new authority without which the secular realm, far from acquiring a new dignity of its own, would have lost even the derivative importance it had held under the auspices of the church.[152]

For the American founders, the problem of authority took the form of "the so-called 'higher law'" which, it was hoped, "would give sanction to positive, posited law."[153] Arendt sums up the conundrum faced by the "men of revolution" on both sides of the Atlantic:

> No doubt, the laws owed their factual existence to the power of the people and their representatives in the legislatures; but these men could not at the same time represent that higher source from which these laws had to be derived in order to be authoritative and valid for all, the majorities and the minorities, the

present and future generations. Hence, the very task of laying down a new law for the land, which was to incorporate for future generations the 'higher law' that bestows validity on all man-made laws, brought to the fore, in America no less than France, the need for an absolute, and the only reason why this need did not lead the men of the American Revolution into the same absurdities into which it led those of the French Revolution…was that the former distinguished clearly and unequivocally between the origin of power, which springs from below, the 'grass roots' of the people, and the source of law, whose seat is 'above,' in some higher and transcendent region.[154]

The appeal to a "higher" or "natural" law—and, ultimately, to a higher legislator—seemed the only possible solution for such eminently practical men as John Adams and Thomas Jefferson. The former felt that worship of a Supreme Being ("the great legislator of the universe") was essential to the stability of the republic and its laws, while the latter famously appealed to "the laws of nature and nature's God" in the Declaration of Independence. It was thus the American and not the French Revolution which demonstrated that, while the need for stability and a clear source of legal validity were great, it was actually "the need for an immortal legislator [that] was the most urgent." Arendt concludes by stating that

> it was precisely the revolutions, their crisis and emergency, which drove the very 'enlightened' men of the eighteenth century to plead for some religious sanction at the very moment they were about to emancipate the secular realm from the influences of the churches and to separate politics and religion once and for all.[155]

The paradox is all the more pronounced when we recall that the ancient Greeks and Romans were in no way perplexed by "the problem of an absolute." As Arendt correctly observes, neither the Greek *nomos* nor the Roman *lex* were thought to be of divine origin, nor were the Greek or Roman concepts of legislation dependent upon divine inspiration.[156] The very word *nomos* means "conventional" or man-made, and while the Greek lawgiver frequently came from outside the *polis*, he was by no means "above" it. Indeed, the whole idea of a legislator "outside and above his own laws" would have struck both the Greeks and the Romans as anti-political. "It was not the sign of a god but the characteristic of a tyrant to impose on the people laws by which he himself would not be bound."[157] This raises an obvious question: why were the secular revolutionaries of the eighteenth century unable to settle for a similarly this-worldly understanding of the ultimate ground of legal validity and political authority?

Arendt's answer to this question builds upon arguments first laid out in her 1958 essay "What is Authority?" In that essay she frames *authoritarian* government as a non-coercive hierarchical relationship, one clearly distinct not only from the so-called "authoritarian" regimes of today (China, Russia) but also from the egalitarian order of *persuasion* exemplified by Greek democracy and the anti-egalitarian order of *coercion* typified by the rule of a tyrant or slave master. According to Arendt, in a genuinely "authoritarian" form of government, authority and power flow from the top down. The legitimacy of the hierarchical relationship binding each rank to those above and below it is recognized by all. It is for this reason, Arendt suggests, that nature of authoritarian government is perhaps best conveyed by the image of a pyramid:

> The pyramid is indeed a particularly fitting image for a governmental structure whose source of authority lies outside itself, but whose seat of power is located at the top, from which authority and power are filtered down to the base in such a way that each successive layer possesses some authority, but less than the one above it, and where, precisely because of this careful filtering process, all layers from top to bottom are not only firmly integrated into the whole but are interrelated like converging rays whose common focal point is the top of the pyramid as well as the transcending source of authority above it.[158]

Strictly speaking, this pyramidal image "can only be used for the Christian type of authoritarian rule as it developed under the constant influence of the Church in the Middle Ages," in which the focal point at the top of the pyramid was the papally approved monarch and the "transcending source of authority" God himself. For the

Romans, who invented the idea of *auctoritatis* in the first place, the pyramidal image must be inverted. The source of authority was not located in some transcendent beyond, but rather in the *past*, in the foundation of the city of Rome and in the greatness of the ancestors.[159] The Greeks, who knew only the egalitarian order of persuasion *or* the inegalitarian order of coercion, had no conceptual space for the idea of a non-coercive hierarchical relation, even though both Plato and Aristotle struggled mightily to introduce something like the idea of authority into the political discourse of the Greeks.

In Plato, this attempt takes the form of an otherworldly realm of "ideas" that—in an analogy with the image of the final product envisioned by the craftsman with the "eyes of the mind"—are able to serve as transcendent standards for the judgment and direction of human behavior. "Truth," in the distinctively Platonic sense of an intelligible order of Being capable of providing such behavioral "yardsticks," *compels the mind* without any need for threats or physical force. The patent trouble with such coercion through reason, however, is that only the few are subject to it: the unphilosophical many who constitute the bulk of the polity remain mired in the sensible here and now. Forever trapped in the cave of illusory appearances and "mere" opinion, they are ignorant of true reality's immutable nature and therefore have no possibility of grasping the standards that can be rationally derived from it. Plato's solution to this formidable difficulty is to propagate a myth about judgment in the hereafter, a myth specifically designed to bring the insufficiently rational *hoi polloi* to heel. The Myth of Er that concludes the *Republic* is the nothing less than the first myth of hell—a myth crafted solely for political reasons.[160]

It is no exaggeration to state that Plato's appeal to transcendent standards (on the one hand) and a myth of hell (on the other) enormously impacted the development of Christian dogma. Indeed, in Arendt's telling, the Church effectively synthesized the Platonic appeal to transcendent standards with the Roman emphasis upon a foundational historical event (in the Church's case, the birth of Jesus). The Church is thus the institution in which the Platonic brand of transcendent authority is married to the Roman brand of historical authority. Moreover, it is through the Church that these two forms of authority come to be understood as dependent upon one another.

The Christian conjoining of transcendent standards to a foundational moment thus provides the depth background of the "problem of an absolute" as it appeared to the generally secular men of the eighteenth-century revolutions. While it is true that "the whole problem of an absolute which would bestow validity upon positive, man-made laws" was partly an inheritance of absolutism, it is important to recall that absolutism in Europe was itself a relatively recent phenomenon in the eighteenth century. It was heir to what Arendt calls

> those long centuries when no secular realm existed in the occident that was not ultimately rooted in the sanction given to it by the Church, and when therefore *secular laws were understood as the mundane expression of a divinely ordered law*.[161]

In other words, the modern monarchical tradition, its long-established emancipation from papal authority notwithstanding, preserved and transmitted an essentially theological approach to the problems of the legitimacy of authority and the validity of law.

While they came to repudiate the institution of monarchy root and branch, the revolutionaries of the eighteenth century still found themselves unable to conceive the validity of law—or the durability of a foundation—without reference to something eternal. There *had* to be an absolute above history and politics, one beyond the vicissitudes of time and chance. The sheer contingency of the radical beginning they had made thus proved too much for even "the men of the revolutions." Like virtually all Western political thinkers before them, they retreated from the "abyss of freedom" to the false security provided by an absolute (God, Natural Law, Natural Rights) safely above the realm of human affairs.

But even this is not the end of the story. "It is of even greater importance and impact," Arendt writes, "that the very word 'law' had assumed an altogether different meaning" throughout these long centuries when no secular realm existed.[162] For the Romans, *lex* was not a pre-political activity; rather, legislation established relations between citizens and—later—between the Roman people and the citizens of cities they had defeated. The laws were thus "more than the means to re-establish peace; they were treaties and agreements with which a new alliance, a new unity, was constituted."[163] In other words, the Romans were convinced that former enemies could become partners by means of *lex*. A notable echo of this understanding is found in the very first chapter of Montesquieu's *Spirit of the Laws*, where he defines "law" as the *rapport* or relation between different entities.[164] Yet Montesquieu is the exception. In the intervening centuries, the basic sense of the word "law" changed from that of a *relation* to that of a *commandment*:

> The model in whose image Western mankind construed the quintessence of laws, even those whose Roman origin was beyond doubt…was itself not Roman at all; it was Hebrew in origin and represented by the divine Commandments of the Decalogue. And the model did not change when in the seventeenth and eighteenth centuries natural law stepped into the place of the divinity—into the place, that is, which once had been held by the Hebrew God who was a lawmaker because he was the Maker of the Universe, a place which then had been occupied by Christ, the visible representative and bodily incarnation of God on earth, from whom the vicars of Christ, the Roman popes and bishops as well as the kings who followed them, had derived their authority, until finally the rebellious Protestants turned to Hebrew laws and covenants and to the figure of Christ himself.[165]

Indeed, the model did not change when, in the seventeenth and eighteenth centuries, "natural law stepped into the place of divinity." As Arendt succinctly puts it, "the trouble with natural law was precisely that it had no author" and therefore stood in need of divine sanction for it to become binding for men.[166] Without such sanction, laws of nature would be universally compelling, but only because they were inescapable and all-determining, like the law of gravity. In order to "be a source of authority and bestow validity upon man-made laws," one had to add to "the laws of nature" the phrase "and nature's God," precisely as Jefferson had done in the Preamble to the Declaration of Independence.

An even more striking example of the appeal to a transcendent ground for earthly law and authority is found in the Preamble's assertion that "We hold these truths to be self-evident, that all men are created equal, that they are endowed by their Creator with certain unalienable rights, that among these are Life, Liberty, and the pursuit of Happiness." Jefferson's words, according to Arendt,

> combine in a historically unique manner the basis of agreement between those who have embarked upon revolution, an agreement necessarily relative because related to those who enter it, with an absolute, namely with a truth that needs no agreements since, because of its self-evidence, it *compels without argumentative demonstration or political persuasion.*[167]

Self-evident truths are pre-rational truths. While they inform reason, they are not the product of rational argumentation or demonstration, and they brook no disagreement. They are "in a sense no less compelling than 'despotic power' and no less absolute than the revealed truths of religion or the axiomatic verities of mathematics."[168] Yet, despite the quasi-Euclidean pretensions of Jefferson's assertion, he must have been dimly aware of the fact that the laws of a political community are different from the theorems of geometry— otherwise, Arendt argues, he would not have written "we hold these truths to be self-evident" but simply "these truths *are* self-evident."[169] Regardless, Jefferson clearly wants us to understand that these truths have been vouchsafed to us by "the Laws of Nature and Nature's God." It follows that those who would dispute them are not only less than rational, but also in some sense less than "natural" and certainly less than godly. Considered as a speech act, then, the Declaration is a magnificent example of initiatory action put into words. But rather than putting its faith in the freedom of human action and the power of mutual promises, it rhetorically appeals to a concept of right ostensibly divine in origin, the better to assert its own authority and overcome the contingency built into every beginning.

****

The American founders' turn to quasi-religious language and expedients resulted from a mix of practical and theoretical considerations. On the one hand, there was the fear that a polity shorn of popular belief in a "future state of rewards and punishments" would create a world without fixed moral limits, one in which murder might be considered "as indifferent as shooting plover, and the extermination of the Rohilla nation as innocent as the swallowing of mites on a morsel of cheese" (Adams).[170] On the other, there were the conceptions of law and authority handed down from the Hebraic-Christian tradition, conceptions that made it well-nigh impossible to think the validity of law or the legitimacy of authority without the appeal to a "higher law," one ultimately grounded in commandments handed down by "the great legislator of the universe."

True, the settlers of America had discovered the power of promising and joint action when, in the course of confronting the new continent's "uncharted wildness and frightened by the chartless darkness of the human heart" they constituted themselves into new bodies politic, mutually binding themselves into "an enterprise for which no other bond existed." By this act alone they made a "new beginning in the very midst of the history of Western mankind," albeit one that came at the price of interrupting what Arendt calls "the original unity of Atlantic civilization."[171] The price of separation and isolation, Arendt suggests, might well have been worth it if this "political release" from the Old World was accompanied by a liberation from the intellectual and conceptual framework of the Western tradition. This was a framework that consistently distorted or covered over such fundamental political phenomena as human plurality, freedom, action, power, and authority. The fact that the "men of the American revolution" remained stuck within this conceptual framework meant that they "were no more capable of articulating theoretically the colonial experience of the tremendous strength inherent in mutual promises than they were ready to admit...the intimate relationship between 'happiness' and [political] action."[172]

This failure of the American theoretical imagination might well have spelled doom in the face of what Arendt calls "the onslaught of modernity." She uses this phrase to refer to "the loss of religious sanction for the political realm," a loss which she—like Nietzsche and Weber before her—considers an "accomplished fact."[173] If the late modern survival of America's constitutional regime hinged upon belief in a divine legislator, judgment in the hereafter, and a dogmatically asserted natural rights philosophy, then things did not look especially promising: the "disenchantment of the world"

(Weber) had made rational belief in each of these items literally incredible. What saved the American republic from experiencing a crisis of legitimacy as severe as that suffered by European regimes was the fact that, in America, it was the Roman model of authority that came to predominate. Or, as Arendt puts it, "what saved the American Revolution from this fate [the loss of authority that accompanied a decline in religious belief] was neither 'nature's God' nor self-evident truth, but the act of foundation itself."[174] It was the historical act of foundation embodied in the Constitution, rather than some otherworldly "absolute," that became the object of veneration. As Arendt writes:

> The great measure of success the American founders could book for themselves, the simple fact that their revolution succeeded where all others were to fail, namely, in founding a new body politic stable enough to survive the onslaught of centuries to come, one is tempted to think, was decided the very moment when the Constitution began to be 'worshipped,' even though it had hardly begun to operate. And since it was in this respect that the American Revolution was most conspicuously different from all other revolutions that were to follow, one is tempted to conclude that it was the *authority which the act of foundation carried within itself*, rather than belief in an immortal Legislator, or the promises of reward and the threats of punishment in a 'future state,' or even the doubtful self-evidence of the truths enumerated in the preamble to the Declaration of Independence, that assured stability for the new republic.[175]

And she continues:

> This authority, to be sure, is entirely different from the absolute which the men of the revolutions so desperately sought to introduce as the source of validity of their laws and the fountain of legitimacy for the new government. Here again, it was ultimately the great Roman model that asserted itself almost automatically and almost blindly in the minds of those who, in all deliberate consciousness, had turned to Roman history and Romans political institutions to prepare themselves for their own task.[176]

V Conclusion: self-assertion and self-grounding

No doubt some readers will find Arendt's appeal to Constitution "worship" and the authority of the American founding as more than problematic. What, after all, distinguishes the "sacredness" of the founding from the crypto-religious appeal to "natural rights" and natural law? Doesn't she wind up substituting one (neo-Roman) absolute for another (Hebraic-Christian) one?

Such questions are bound to arise in a political-cultural context in which (in America, at least) it is common to find political and legal theorists mimicking the Church's basic approach by merging a Platonic appeal to transcendent authority with the Roman appeal to the authority of the foundational event itself. The Word, after all, did become flesh, and for many a cultural conservative the synthetic approach pioneered by the Church offers an easy way out of what some have called the "discourse of disenchantment." Contra avowedly secular thinkers such as Arendt, Habermas, and Rawls, these authors in effect argue that the German philosopher Karl Löwith and legal theorist Carl Schmitt were right when they suggested that virtually all modern political concepts are simply secularized versions of theological ones.[177] There is, it is claimed, no way around that fact that modernity and the modern revolutions have theological roots.

Arendt was fully aware of such arguments, just as she was aware of the founders' recourse to religious sanctions when it came to bolstering the authority of their new government. She was unconvinced by the arguments of thinkers like Löwith and Schmitt, and she thought that men like Adams and Jefferson had succumbed to the traditional framework out of practical fears (on the one hand) and a failure of theoretical imagination (on the other). The result was that the American revolutionary tradition never received a theoretical articulation in any way comparable to the one Marx had provided for the French Revolution. The consequences were nothing short of catastrophic. Theoretically speaking, the American failure of theoretical imagination—the inability of the founders and subsequent commentators to provide conceptual resources adequate to capture the power of promising, joint action, public freedom, and public happiness—left the field clear for the dominance of Marxist and neo-Marxist theories of revolution. Practically speaking, this

failure facilitated America's counter-revolutionary foreign policy
during the Cold War, a policy that led not only to the propping up
of Latin American dictatorships and the Vietnam war, but that also
constituted an effective betrayal of America's own revolutionary origins and tradition.

When Arendt suggests that "it was the authority which the act
of foundation carried within itself...that assured stability for the
new republic," she is suggesting a political version of the argument
Hans Blumenberg advanced in his mammoth refutation of Löwith
and Schmitt's "secularization thesis," *The Legitimacy of the Modern Age*
(1966).[178] In that work, Blumenberg argued that Löwith's thesis
that the modern idea of progress was merely Christian eschatology
secularized was wrong for a simple reason. Löwith had grounded
his argument by making nineteenth-century philosophies of history
(e.g. those of Hegel and Marx) the fount of the idea of progress. In
fact, Blumenberg argues, the predominant Enlightenment conception was one of *possible* (not "necessary") *progress* of the sort made
possible by the expansion of scientific-theoretical curiosity to a wide
array of phenomena.

From this perspective, nineteenth-century philosophies of history
aren't really "modern" at all. They hark back to questions framed
initially by medieval thinkers, for whom the ways of God and his
relationship to man were central concerns. With the emergence of
modern science and the Enlightenment, such questions are set aside
as the idea of progress is dissociated from providence and the deci-
pherment of God's mysterious ways. Modern humanity doesn't put
itself in the place of God so much as come to view itself as capable of
exploiting the *possibility* of progress through scientific-technological
discoveries and their practical applications. From the point of view
of the Enlightenment, what "legitimated" the modern age was not
some secularized version of providence, but *results*. Modernity did
not have to look to *Geist*, History, or anything else to justify man's
emergence from a theocentric cocoon. The concrete (but hardly
"necessary") progress created by its expanded theoretical and scientific curiosity was legitimation enough. The modern age is thus
singular in that it is *self-grounding*.

On *Revolution* is a work that is, in many respects, utterly different
from Blumenberg's magisterial account of the emergence of the

modern project. Her focus is on political theory and experience, whereas his is upon the transformation of theoretical curiosity as science and philosophy cross the threshold to the modern age. Arendt, moreover, is decidedly critical of the idea of progress, an idea which Blumenberg thinks can be (and historically was) separated from the very doctrines of inevitability she associates it with. Finally, in THC, Arendt gives a decidedly critical account of many of the very developments in early modern science and technology that Blumenberg celebrates. Nevertheless, when it comes to the issue of the *modernity* of revolution, the comparison is helpful.

For Arendt, the modernity of revolution is found in its character as a radical or absolute beginning, the "start of a completely new story." The French and American revolutions were not "revolutions back" to a pre-established order; nor were they divinely ordained, despite whatever musings men like Adams might have had about the "designs of Providence." They were the results of people acting together, acting in concert, in a realm defined by plurality and contingency. The French Revolution failed in the task of founding a durable set of institutions in which the "free play" of political participation would be guaranteed for generations. The American Revolution succeeded, but at the price of forgetting some if not all the experiences which had been central to its success. The one thing the Americans did not forget, however, was the *authority which the act of foundation carried within itself*. Like Blumenberg's modern age, Arendt's American Revolution grounds itself—as, she would argue, every authentic modern revolution, every radical beginning, must.

Summary

On Revolution has been called both Arendt's "theory of modern political action" and her "settling of accounts" with Marxist and liberal accounts of revolutionary events. Each of these characterizations is illuminating, but it is better to view OR as Arendt's fullest account of political action as *beginning* and as providing testimony to the fundamental role she assigns *constitutions* in her political thought. With respect to political action as beginning: OR stresses the basic discontinuity between the way "revolution" was used prior to the American and French revolutions and how the French and American

"men of the revolutions" both experienced the "pathos of novelty."
They knew that they were commencing a new story not simply by
repudiating monarchy, but by creating a *new form of government*: a public
realm that would enable the "free play" of political participation for
generations to come. With respect to the role of *constitutions* in the
modern revolutionary tradition: Arendt makes it clear that "under
modern conditions, the act of foundation is identical with the framing of a constitution"—that is, with the creation of a legally and
institutionally articulated structure that not only protects individual
rights, but that also creates a new *space of freedom* enabling citizens to
become "participators in the government of affairs."

Arendt's stress on the *positive* freedom of political participation,
combined with her description of "agonistic" action in THC, has
led many readers to discount or fail to notice the central role that
constitutions play in her thinking about revolution and the nature
of political action. This constitutional emphasis underlies her otherwise puzzling distinction between the *struggle to achieve liberation from
oppression* (through violent means) and the revolutionary event proper
(the constitution of a new form of government). In the case of the
American Revolution, then, the eight-year war with Britain was not
the *real* revolution. Rather, the real revolution was the drafting and
ratification of the US Constitution that occurred in 1787. The inability of the French "men of the revolution" to establish a lasting
constitution signaled the ultimate failure of the French Revolution
to establish a new republican form of government.

The tale Arendt tells of the success of the American Revolution
and the failure of the French Revolution is tied to her sense that
the French Revolution was prevented from accomplishing its primary task by the Jacobin focus on the question of poverty (the "Social Question"). Arendt thinks that poverty is a problem that can be
solved, if it can be solved at all, by technological innovation and
efficient administration. It cannot be solved "politically," i.e. by "expropriating the expropriators" through violent social revolution. The
French Revolution took the latter course and the conviction that all
real revolutions are social as well as political—that they transform
social structures as well as political ones—has become canonical.
This is due to Marx's theorization of the French Revolutionary experience (on the one hand) and the American failure to remember

and adequately conceptualize its own revolutionary tradition (on the other).

It is this last point—the forgetting of its own revolutionary tradition and experience—that accounts for the only *partial* success of the American Revolution. The establishment of a durable Constitution and viable public-political sphere did not prevent a shift away from concern with *public* happiness to an almost exclusive concern with private happiness (the happiness of the economically successful individual). The decline of public spirit, combined with this forgetting of public happiness, erases the *republican* character of the American Revolution. It makes us think that ours was a Lockean-liberal revolution, one whose primary goal was the creation of limited government and the protection of property.

Notes

1 Albrecht Wellmer, "Arendt on Revolution" in *The Cambridge Companion to Hannah Arendt*, ed. Dana Villa (New York: Cambridge University Press, 2000).
2 Arendt, OR, p. 18.
3 Arendt, OR, p. 18.
4 Arendt, OR, p. 254.
5 Arendt, OR, p. 116.
6 See Arendt's essay "On Violence" in Hannah Arendt, *Crises of the Republic* (New York: Harcourt Brace Jovanovitch, Publishers, 1972), especially pp. 113–118.
7 Arendt, OR, p. 24.
8 Arendt, OR, p. 9.
9 Arendt, OR, p. 9.
10 Arendt, OR, pp. 19–20.
11 See George Mosse, *The Fascist Revolution* (New York: Howard Fertig, 1999).
12 Arendt, OR, p. 11.
13 Arendt, OR, pp. 16–17.
14 Arendt, OR, p. 17.
15 Arendt, BPF, pp. 52, 73.
16 Arendt, BPF, pp. 52, 73.
17 Arendt, OR, p. 18.
18 Arendt, OR, p. 32, my emphasis.
19 Arendt, OR, pp. 34–35.
20 Jonathan Schell, Introduction to Arendt, OR, pp. xi–xxix.
21 Arendt, OR, p. 32.
22 Arendt, OR, p. 38.
23 Arendt, OR, p. 38.
24 Arendt, OR, p. 38.
25 Arendt, OR, p. 39.

26 Arendt, OR, p. 39.
27 Arendt. OR, p. 40.
28 Arendt, OR, p. 40.
29 Arendt, OR, p. 41.
30 Arendt, OR, p. 41.
31 Arendt, OR, p. 42.
32 Arendt, OR, p. 42.
33 Arendt, OR, p. 42. Cf. Arendt, BPF, 67–68.
34 Arendt, OR, p. 42.
35 Arendt, OR, p. 42.
36 Arendt, OR, p. 42, emphasis mine.
37 Arendt, OR, p. 43.
38 Arendt, OR, p. 43.
39 Arendt, OR, p. 44
40 Arendt, OR, p. 44
41 Arendt, OR, p. 49.
42 Arendt, OR, pp. 49–50.
43 Arendt, OR, p. 50.
44 Arendt, OR, p. 50.
45 Arendt, OR, p. 102.
46 Arendt, OR, p. 51.
47 Arendt, OR, p. 51.
48 Arendt, OR, p. 51.
49 Arendt, OR, p. 52.
50 Arendt, OR, pp. 52–53.
51 Arendt, OR, p. 53.
52 Arendt, OR, p. 53.
53 Arendt, OR, pp. 53–54.
54 Arendt, OR, p. 54.
55 Arendt, OR, p. 65.
56 Arendt, OR, p. 64.
57 Arendt, OR, p. 64.
58 Arendt, OR, p. 65.
59 Arendt, OR, pp. 65–66.
60 Arendt, OR, p. 70.
61 Arendt, OR, p. 66.
62 Arendt, OR, pp. 66–67.
63 Arendt, OR, p. 67.
64 See Jean-Jacques Rousseau, *Social Contrast*, bk. IV, chapters 1–2.
65 Arendt, OR, pp. 70–71.
66 Arendt, OR, p. 71.
67 Arendt, OR, p. 75.
68 Arendt, OR, p. 79.
69 Arendt, OR, p. 79.
70 Arendt, OR, p. 81.
71 Arendt, OR, p. 80.
72 Arendt, OR, p. 82.

73 Arendt, OR, p. 87.
74 Arendt, OR, p. 89.
75 Arendt, OR, pp. 87–88.
76 Arendt, OR, p. 91.
77 Arendt, THC, p. 50.
78 Arendt, "What Is Freedom?" BPF, p. 151.
79 Arendt, OR, p. 96.
80 Arendt, OR, p. 96.
81 Arendt, OR, p. 98.
82 Arendt, OR, p. 98.
83 Arendt, OR, p. 99, my emphases.
84 Arendt, OR, p. 99.
85 Arendt, OR, p. 100.
86 See Patrice Higonnet, *Goodness beyond Virtue* (Cambridge: Harvard University Press, 1998).
87 Arendt, OR, p. 104.
88 Arendt, OR, p. 58.
89 Arendt, OR, p. 109.
90 Arendt, OR, p. 111.
91 Arendt, OR, p. 115.
92 Arendt, OR, p. 116.
93 Arendt, OR, p. 116.
94 Arendt, OR, p. 116.
95 Arendt, OR, p. 117.
96 Arendt, OR, p. 117.
97 Arendt, OR, p. 116.
98 Arendt, OR, p. 117.
99 Cited by Arendt, OR, 118. My emphasis.
100 Arendt, OR, p. 118.
101 Arendt, OR, p. 118.
102 Arendt, OR, p. 118.
103 Arendt, OR, p. 119.
104 Arendt, OR, p. 123.
105 Arendt, OR, p. 126.
106 Arendt, OR, p. 125.
107 Arendt, OR, pp. 124–125.
108 Arendt, OR, p. 243.
109 Arendt, OR, p. 243.
110 Arendt, OR, p. 245.
111 Arendt, OR, p. 245.
112 Hannah Arendt, *Crises of the Republic* (New York: Harcourt Brace & Company), p. 175; Hannah Arendt, *Denktagebuch*, edited by Ursula Ludz and Ingeborg Nordmann (Munich: Piper, 2002), vol. 2, p. 713.
113 Arendt, OR, p. 217.
114 Arendt, OR, p. 219.

115 Arendt, THC, p. 57.
116 Arendt, BPF, p. 237.
117 See "Socrates" in Arendt, *The Promise of Politics*, pp. 5–39.
118 Arendt, OR, pp. 218–220.
119 Arendt, OR, pp. 218–220.
120 Arendt, OR, p. 269.
121 Arendt, OR, p. 269.
122 Arendt, OR, p. 279.
123 Sheldon Wolin, "Hannah Arendt: Democracy and the Political" in *Hannah Arendt: Critical Essays*, edited by Lewis P. Hinchman and Sandra K. Hinchman (Albany: State University of New York Press, 1994); Martin Jay, "The Political Existentialism of Hannah Arendt" in Jay, *Permanent Exiles* (New York: Columbia University Press, 1985); Hanna Pitkin, "Justice: On Relating the Public and the Private" in Hinchman, eds., *Hannah Arendt: Critical Essays*.
124 Arendt, OR, p. 279.
125 Arendt, OR, p. 231.
126 Sheldon Wolin, "Norm and Form: The Constitutionalizing of Democracy" in Wolin, *Fugitive Democracy and Other Essays*, edited by Nicholas Xenos (Princeton: Princeton University Press, 2016), pp. 77–99.
127 Wolin, "Norm and Form" in *Fugitive Democracy and Other Essays*.
128 Arendt, OR, p. 117.
129 Hannah Arendt, "On Hannah Arendt" in *Hannah Arendt: The Recovery of the Public World*, edited by Melvyn Hill (New York: St. Martin's Press, 1979), p. 316.
130 Arendt, OR, p. 139.
131 Arendt, OR, p. 141.
132 Arendt, OR, p. 141.
133 Arendt, OR, pp. 142–143.
134 Arendt, OR, p. 142.
135 Arendt, OR, p. 144 (my emphasis).
136 For Hobbes, the governed make a "free gift" of their power to the sovereign in order to escape a hellish "state of nature"; in Locke, there is no agreement per se but rather a trust relationship; in Rousseau, the magistrates are mere delegates of the people who can be replaced at any point; and in Kant, the contract functions in a clearly hypothetical, "as if" manner, the better to determine the boundaries of the legitimate exercise of political power.
137 Arendt, OR, p. 161.
138 Arendt, OR, p. 162.
139 Arendt, OR, p. 162 (my emphasis).
140 Arendt, OR, p. 164.
141 Arendt, OR, p. 167.
142 Arendt, OR, p. 167 (my emphasis).
143 Arendt, OR, p. 168.
144 Arendt, OR, p. 168.
145 Arendt, OR, p. 146.
146 Arendt, OR, p. 147.

147 Rousseau, *Social Contract*, Bk. II, chapter 12.
148 Rousseau quoted by Arendt, OR, p. 175.
149 Arendt, OR, p. 174.
150 Arendt, OR, p. 148.
151 Arendt, OR, p. 173.
152 Arendt, OR, p. 151.
153 Arendt, OR, p. 173.
154 Arendt, OR, p. 173.
155 Arendt, OR, pp. 174–175.
156 Arendt, OR, p. 177.
157 Arendt, OR, p. 177.
158 Arendt, BPF, p. 98.
159 Arendt, BPF, p. 98.
160 Arendt, BPF, p. 108.
161 Arendt, OR, p. 181.
162 Arendt, OR, p. 181.
163 Arendt, OR, p. 179.
164 Arendt, OR, p. 179.
165 Arendt, OR, p. 182.
166 Arendt, OR, p. 182.
167 Arendt, OR, p. 184.
168 Arendt, OR, p. 184.
169 Arendt, OR, p. 185.
170 Arendt, OR, p. 183.
171 Arendt, OR, p. 187.
172 Arendt, OR, p. 187.
173 Arendt, OR, p. 188.
174 Arendt, OR, p. 188.
175 Arendt, OR, p. 191.
176 Arendt, OR, p. 191.
177 See Karl Löwith, *Meaning in History* (Chicago: University of Chicago Press, 1957), and Carl Schmitt, *Political Theology*, translated by George Schwab (Chicago: University of Chicago Press, 2005).
178 Hans Blumenberg, *The Legitimacy of the Modern Age*, translated by Robert M. Wallace (Cambridge: MIT Press, 1983).

Further reading

J. Waldron, "Arendt's Constitutional Politics" in D. Villa (ed.), *The Cambridge Companion to Hannah Arendt* (New York: Cambridge University Press, 2000), pp. 201–219.
A. Wellmer, "Arendt on Revolution" in D. Villa (ed.), *The Cambridge Companion to Hannah Arendt* (New York: Cambridge University Press, 2000).

Six
Judging

I The place of judgment in Arendt's thought

Arendt's commentators and critics have often divided up her political thought into a set of discrete "theories." They see her oeuvre as comprising an unconventional theory of totalitarianism (OT), followed by a "Greek" theory political action (THC), a theory which is then modified by her contrarian "theory" of revolution in OR. This way of approaching her work is heuristically useful, but it distorts the nature of her contribution. It makes it appear that Arendt has a self-contained set of theoretical views on each of these topics, views that can be neatly encapsulated and then compared with competing theories of totalitarianism, political action, and revolution. The goal of this comparative exercise is to then offer a verdict on the historical correctness, conceptual adequacy, and contemporary relevance of each of her respective "theories."

Comparing what Arendt said on these topics with what other thinkers, canonical and contemporary, have written can be quite illuminating. And it can reveal unsuspected strengths as well as weaknesses. However, before undertaking such comparative exercises, it is important to remember that Arendt thought of herself *not* as a "political philosopher" but rather as a political thinker and "a kind of phenomenologist." This means that while her work is full of analyses, descriptions, and interpretations of various political, historical, and social phenomena, it is not easily reducible to a set of theoretical doctrines about specific issues or problems. Her penchant for making distinctions notwithstanding, she was not a systematic thinker, nor did she harbor any ambition to be one. The unsystematic quality of her work has provided her critics with a kind of standing invitation to reconstruct her "argument" on a particular issue or theme, the better to "refute" it.

Such reconstructions have their place. Overall, however, they tend to one-dimensionalize explorations that are critical, historical, and thematic in character. These explorations do indeed make arguments, but arguments that are laid out over many pages and that often have a decidedly experimental character. Rather than view Arendt as offering us a collection of discrete "theories," I think it is more productive to see her as advancing a set of interrelated reflections on key political and historical phenomena—about (for example) the nature of totalitarianism, the fundamental characteristics of political action, and the nature of political freedom. While unsystematic in comparison to the political philosophies of a Hobbes or a Rawls, these reflections can hardly be dismissed as "essayistic" in the pejorative sense. They are backed up by extensive historical documentation and interpretation, phenomenological analysis, and conceptual interrogation—all in support of clear, albeit often counterintuitive, theses. Moreover, Arendt's "critical and experimental" reflections present a fundamentally consistent and coherent view of politics and the public world.

One could, of course, collect Arendt's primary theses concerning the importance of human plurality, the phenomenal nature of the public realm, the initiatory nature of political action, etc., and put them in some sort of lexical or logical order. The assembled package could then be presented as "Hannah Arendt's political philosophy" or "theory of politics." Such a procedure has expository advantages, but one must not lose sight of the fact she was a "pearl diver" and not a system builder. What interested Arendt was the possibility of seeing political phenomena in new and fresh ways, unburdened by the distorting conceptual framework inherited from the Western philosophical and theological traditions. These traditions departed from the standpoint of *vita contemplativa* and (as a result) were inherently hostile to the "fragility, boundlessness, and unpredictability" that characterizes political action and the *bios politikos*.

Keeping these caveats in mind becomes even more important when we approach what is often referred to as Arendt's "theory of judgment." It is more important because, while judgment is a central theme in Arendt, she famously did not live to write the third part of her final work, the posthumously published *The Life of the Mind* (1978). That work was conceived as tripartite, with volume I devoted to the mental activity of thinking, and volume II to the activities of willing and judging. At the time of her death in 1975, only the sections on thinking and willing were complete. The section on judging remained completely unwritten. There are, of course, remarks about moral and political judgment scattered throughout Arendt's work, but nothing remotely comparable to the chapter on action in THC or the introductory discussion of "the meaning of revolution" in OR. Beyond this assortment of tantalizing passages (many in *Between Past and Future*), there exists a manuscript of lectures on Kant she gave at the New School in 1970, which was posthumously published in 1982 under the title *Lectures on Kant's Political Philosophy*. The subject of these lectures was Kant's "unwritten" political philosophy and the relation of Kant's conception of judgment to both the theory of politics and to the Western philosophical tradition.[1]

While the lectures are extremely suggestive, they do not, in my view, constitute Arendt's "theory of judgment." They *do* give us some important clues as to her *conception* of judgment, its nature and function in the public world. This is a minority position among her interpreters, many of whom have attempted to reconstruct "Arendt's theory of judgment" using the lectures as their *point de départ*.

The first and by far most successful of these attempts was by the editor of the *Lectures*, Ronald Beiner. His "Interpretive Essay" appended to the lectures remains required reading for any serious student of Arendt's thought. In addition to providing crucial background for her thinking about judgment, Beiner suggested that Arendt had not one but *two* theories of judgment: an early one oriented towards the judgment of the involved political actor, and a later one departing from the contemplative-retrospective standpoint of the impartial historian, poet, or "storyteller."[2] He also suggested that had Arendt lived to write the section on judgment for *The Life of the Mind*, it would have provided the solution to the "impasse" Arendt confronted at the conclusion of *Willing*.

What is this "impasse"? As I mentioned previously, the concluding chapter of *Willing* suggested that not only *philosophers* blanched at the idea of freedom as form of absolute beginning. The "men of the revolutions" shared their embarrassment, if not their sense of scandal. The "abyss of pure spontaneity" encountered in the moment of revolutionary beginning implied a caesura, a moment of sheer discontinuity that the "men of the revolutions" found disturbing and which they attempted to cover up by appealing not to the Bible, but to the foundation legend of Rome. As recounted by Virgil's *Aeneid*, the foundation of Rome was *not* something absolutely new; it was, rather, a "re-foundation" of the fallen city of Troy. The idea that foundation could be a *re-foundation* was, as Arendt puts it, "quite reassuring and consoling" to the "men of the revolutions" even though they should have been the first to affirm a power of spontaneously beginning.[3]

The "impasse" that appears at the conclusion of *Willing*, then, is the problem presented by the human capacity to spontaneously begin, a capacity that philosophers and the "men of the revolutions" viewed as threatening to reduce the realm of human affairs to a condition of unrelieved contingency and, ultimately, to meaninglessness. Judgment, in form of the historian or storyteller's retrospective view of the whole, evidently has the capacity to take the "meaningless" contingent event and—without recourse to God, metaphysics, or historical "necessity"—endow it with meaning, thus enabling us to escape from the conclusion that, as human beings, we are somehow doomed to freedom, contingency, and meaninglessness (the "absurd").

In this way, the faculty of judgment—the capacity to consider particulars *qua* particulars, albeit in light of a retrospective "whole"—can be said to concretely realize the "quest for meaning" that Arendt sees driving the "inner dialogue" of thought. It simultaneously affirms its own freedom as well as that of the words, deeds, and events it judges. On this reading, it is judgment that enables us to find meaning in the "spectacle" of historical words and deeds, a spectacle so many theologians and philosophers have deemed meaningful only insofar as it could be construed as animated by some greater-than-human purpose or endowed with some greater-than-human design.[4]

I should state up front that I don't agree with the "two theories" theory. Nor do I see the faculty of judgment as Arendt's way out of a self-constructed philosophical impasse. As I will argue below, the problem with the "two theories" theory is that it suggests Arendt abandoned her earlier concern with a worldly or involved form of judgment, preferring instead to focus on a contemplative or "disinterested" version of the same faculty whose primary purpose is to help us reconcile ourselves to reality and the human condition. This has the odd consequence of reading Arendt back into the very contemplative tradition she sought to escape from. Indeed, the more one reads her work as a response to the question of how we can reconcile ourselves to existence and the world, the more Arendt comes to resemble the very philosophers she so explicitly criticized.

This is not to say that Arendt was totally unconcerned with the problem Beiner identifies, that of existential reconciliation. *On Revolution's* closing invocation of the tragic wisdom of Silenus—"Not to be born prevails over all meaning uttered in words; by far the second-best for life, once it has appeared, is to go as swiftly as possible whence it came"—puts paid to that idea.[5] However, in the conclusion to *OR*, she clearly identifies her own response to the question of "what it was that enabled ordinary men, young and old, to bear life's burden" with that of the Sophocles' Theseus, the legendary founder of Athens. For both Theseus and Arendt, "it was the *polis*, the space of men's free deeds and living words, which could endow life with splendor."[6]

Thus, while Arendt did indeed desire to be "at home in the world," we need to be clear about the specific weight the words "in the world" carry in this phrase. Contrary to the drift of Theodor Adorno's famous remark about the barbarity of writing poetry after Auschwitz, the Holocaust did not swallow the possibility of worldly meaning or beauty. An immeasurable tragedy, it destroyed European Jewry—but it did not destroy the world. So long as the world (the "human artifice" that is also a "space of appearances") remained, so did the possibility of being at home in it—not just contemplatively, but *actively*. For Arendt, action, not contemplation, remains existentially supreme.

II Judging particulars: Eichmann in Jerusalem

The publication of *On Revolution* in 1963 was hardly noticed compared to the other book Arendt published that year, *Eichmann in Jerusalem: A Report on the Banality of Evil.* It is important to mark the description contained in the subtitle. Arendt intended the book to be a *report* of the 1961 trial of S.S. Lieutenant Colonel Adolf Eichmann that took place in Jerusalem from April 11 to August 1 (a verdict of guilty and a sentence of death by hanging was announced in mid-December of that year). Eichmann had been centrally involved in each of the key phases of Nazi policy toward the Jews, from that of forced emigration from the Reich (1938–1939); to deportation and concentration of Jews in specially created ghettoes in Poland and elsewhere after the beginning of the war (1939–1941); to, finally, extermination in the various "killing centers" in the east, including Auschwitz-Birkenau (late 1941–1944). After the war, he escaped to Argentina, where he was captured by Israeli agents in 1960 and smuggled back to Israel to stand trial for the mass murder of Jews and others.

Arendt, upon hearing of Eichmann's capture, contacted the then editor of *The New* Yorker, William Shawn, and proposed herself as a trial reporter for the magazine. Her offer accepted, she set off for Jerusalem, where she attended Eichmann's trial for a number of weeks. Upon return to the United States, she wrote up her "report," which was duly published by *The New Yorker* in five parts from February 16 to March 16, 1963. The articles were revised and published in book form later the same year.

It is difficult to convey to the newcomer to Arendt the intensity of the controversy the articles and book generated upon their publication. Suffice it to say it is a controversy which continues to this day. Arendt's criticism of the "stage management" by Israel's then prime minister, David Ben-Gurion, combined with her exposure of the facilitating role played by Nazi-assembled councils of "Jewish elders" (*Judenräte*) and her skepticism toward the prosecution's thesis of Eichmann's "all-inclusive" responsibility, led to her virtual excommunication from the American Jewish community. Such mainstream Jewish organization as the B'nai B'rith and the World Jewish Congress waged campaigns to de-legitimate the book, charging Arendt with sympathy for the perpetrator and contempt for the victims.[7] Thanks to their efforts and those of others, a legend about the book was born: Arendt was a self-hating Jew who had exculpated Eichmann and blamed the victims for their own destruction.

Of course, Arendt did nothing of the sort. She read the many pages of the Israeli police interrogation of Eichmann, attended the trial, and familiarized herself with the massive evidence against Eichmann (evidence often lost in a sea of documents presented by a prosecution team mistakenly bent on establishing Eichmann's comprehensive authority over every aspect of Nazi policy toward the Jews). Like the three-judge panel that conducted the trial, Arendt was convinced of Eichmann's guilt. He had indeed played an integral role in the mass murder of European Jews, even if he could not be said to have conceived the Final Solution (Hitler did) nor to have engineered it (an "honor" deserved by Heinrich Himmler and Eichmann's immediate commanding officer, Reinhard Heydrich). And—again like the judges—she thought he should hang for his crimes.

Yet Arendt did not think that Eichmann did what he did out of a deep-seated anti-Semitism or out of fanatical belief in the racial ideology of the Nazis. After studying the police transcript of Eichmann's interrogation (in which he repeatedly and unsuccessfully tried to minimize his involvement) and observing him "in the flesh" at his trial, Arendt came to the conclusion that the devil in the dock was in fact no devil, but a quite ordinary individual who had willingly participated in the perpetration of enormous evil. As she put it in the essay "Thinking and Moral Considerations" (1971):

> However monstrous the deeds were, the doer was neither monstrous nor demonic, and the only specific characteristic one could detect in his past as well as in his behavior during the trial and the preceding police examination was something entirely negative: it was not stupidity but a curious, quite authentic inability to think.[8]

As we shall see, it was Eichmann's "thoughtlessness"—his inability to see things from another's perspective or to transcend the clichés, stock phrases, and bureaucratese that shielded him from the reality of what he was in fact doing—that led Arendt to posit an internal link between thinking or reflection and moral judgment.

It was Eichmann's very ordinariness, combined with his apparent lack of any strong anti-Semitic feeling or other recognizably evil motivation, that led Arendt to coin the phrase "banality of evil." By this she meant

> no theory or doctrine but something quite factual, the phenomenon of evil deeds, committed on a gigantic scale, which could

not be traced to any particularity of wickedness, pathology, or ideological conviction in the doer, whose only personal distinction was perhaps an extraordinary shallowness.[9]

Since "the banality of evil" has long since entered the lexicon of editorial page writers and political commentators, it is important to note that Arendt never intended it to stand as a global characterization of *all* the perpetrators. She was aware that the Nazi machinery of destruction contained more than its fair share of ideologues, fanatical anti-Semites, and sadists. However, like other apparatuses designed to implement evil as policy in the twentieth century, this machinery depended upon the availability of large numbers of normal (that is, non-pathological and non-fanatical) individuals for its effective functioning.

The other thing important to note about "the banality of evil" is that it was, at the time, a novel concept "generated" (so to speak) by Eichmann's concrete particularity. Like other observers at the trial, Arendt had expected to see an unregenerate anti-Semite in the dock, someone who was well aware of the criminal nature of his deeds but who performed them nevertheless out of sheer ideological conviction. In other words, she assumed that Eichmann would be easily subsumable under the familiar rubric of "fanatical Nazi." Confronted by Eichmann in the flesh, however, she was forced to abandon this preconception and search for another concept that might illuminate more accurately the sort of evil performed by this particular individual.

The "banality of evil" is thus an instance of what Kant, in the *Critique of Judgment*, describes as "reflective judgment"—that is, an example of how judgment operates when the *particular* is given but a clear or ready-to-hand universal concept is lacking. If, as Kant asserts in the third *Critique*, "judgment in general is the ability to think the particular as contained under the universal," then the faculty of judgment appears to be little more than our faculty for subsuming an endless variety of concrete particulars and events under the appropriate general concept or principle (for example, the *concepts* of "man," "dog," "revolution," and "civil war"; the *principles* of honor, equality, fairness, etc.). But this definition of judgment as essentially the logical operation of subsuming particulars applies to cases where, as Kant says, "the universal...is given." In cases where "only the particular is given" it is no longer a question of descending from a ready-to-hand general concept to a particular instance, but of *ascending* from a given concrete particular to a *universal* that the judging agent must either *locate* (through an exercise of discernment that is anything but mechanical or deductive) or, if need be, *invent* (through the exercise of critical thinking and imagination).[10]

It should come as no surprise that Arendt, who considered many of the defining political events of the twentieth century to be unprecedented, should rely so heavily on the exercise of reflective judgment (in Kant's sense). Her dismissal of the idea that totalitarian regimes were merely twentieth-century instances of the age-old phenomena of tyranny; her rejection of the widely accepted framing of political action in terms of the means/end category; and her refusal to equate freedom with national sovereignty or individual autonomy are all examples of a mind unwilling to fall back on long-established prejudices and what she termed "pre-conceived categories." It must be stressed, however, that Arendt did not go to Jerusalem expecting to encounter a novel form of evil, the performance of which evidently did not rely upon recognizably wicked motivations. She expected to encounter a typical S.S. man, one who was fanatical in his ideological commitment and utterly convinced that the Jews were an "evil race"; one who was totally immune to the voice of conscience. What she found, instead, was a "new type of criminal" whose conduct had been crucial to the perpetration of a "new type of crime"—genocide, a term first coined by the Polish-Jewish law professor and refugee Raphael Lemkin in 1944.

In retrospect, it is easy to understand how the Nazi extermination of European Jewry constituted a "new type of crime." As Arendt noted in OT, terror and massacres are to be found throughout history. What is not to be found is a bureaucratically organized and systematically executed attempt to wipe an entire people off the face of the earth, not for anything they had done but simply because of who they were. This attempt, carried out by a totalitarian regime that had taken the reins of one of the most advanced nation-states of Europe, entailed an enormous amount of planning (the coordination of government ministries, military and paramilitary formations, and private industry, among others) and a huge commitment of resources, all in the middle of a two-front war. When we add to this what Arendt called "the industrial production of corpses" in extermination camps like Auschwitz-Birkenau (which, together with the "on site" massacres carried out by S.S. *Einsatzgruppen* and Wehrmacht troops, resulted in the death of roughly six million European Jews), further argument that this was unprecedented—a "new type of crime"—hardly seems necessary.

What *does* seem necessary to pursue is the idea that Eichmann and people like him constituted a "new type of criminal." What did Arendt mean by this phrase? We get a clue in the "Epilogue" to EJ:

> The trouble with Eichmann was precisely that so many were like him, and the many were neither perverted or sadistic; that they were, and still are, terribly and terrifyingly normal. From the viewpoint of our legal institutions and our moral standards of judgment, this normality was much more terrifying than all the atrocities put together, for it implied…that this new type of criminal, who is in actual fact *hostis generis humani* [enemy of the human race], commits his crimes under circumstances that make it well-nigh impossible for him to know or to feel that he is doing wrong.[11]

This passage contains two claims. The first, that Eichmann was normal, neither "perverted or sadistic," was one backed up by the Israeli psychologists who examined him before the trial. While this claim was vehemently challenged during the original controversy, the idea that there could be such a thing as a "normal" Nazi—that one need not be monstrous to perpetrate or be party to monstrous crimes—is more widely accepted today, thanks to historical works like Christopher Browning's *Ordinary Men.*[12] However, the second claim, that Eichmann and people like him committed their crimes under circumstances that made it "well-nigh impossible" to "know or feel" that they were doing wrong still elicits incredulity. Like the three judges in Jerusalem, we assume that this was impossible. Eichmann *must* have known that the duties he so efficiently per-formed were criminal and wrong, yet he did them anyways, with "will and intent." The idea that "an average, 'normal' person, nei-ther feeble-minded nor indoctrinated nor cynical could be perfectly incapable of telling right from wrong" in the case of a genocide simply sounds too far-fetched to be taken seriously. Yet that was the case, Arendt claims, with Eichmann and the "many others" like him. To not see this—to assume that "the defendant, like all 'normal persons,' must have been aware to the criminal nature of his acts"—is to miss what Arendt calls "the greatest moral and even legal challenge of the whole case."[13]

The moral and legal challenge is this: how do we judge perpetrators who lack what the law calls "criminal intent"? Who perform clearly criminal actions and yet are somehow unaware that what they are doing is wrong? To be clear, Arendt thinks they must be judged and judged as harshly as those who committed their crimes with will and intent. The "new type of criminal" is no mindless cog. Rather, he is part of a large organization, one that frames its tasks in bureaucratic language and which benefits from a broader social context of widespread self-deception and mendacity.[14] His role in the organization evidently relieves him of ever having to render judgment on the tasks he carries out, while the organization's place in a culture of self-deception (such as we find in the Germany of the *Nazizeit*) more or less guarantees the minimization of whatever moral qualms might arise.

After having achieved what was, for him, a good deal of professional success as the organizer of the forced emigration of Viennese Jews in 1938, Eichmann (by his own account) lost all joy in his work once he was informed by Heydrich (in June of 1941) of the proposed "Final Solution to the Jewish Question."[15] His conscience nagged him about "such a bloody solution," and he even went so far as to divert his first "shipment" of 25,000 Rhineland Jews and Gypsies from their designated destinations in Riga or Minsk to the Jewish ghetto created in Lodz, located in that part of conquered Poland the Nazis designated as the "General Government." Eichmann knew that if the 25,000 arrived at their originally assigned destinations, they would be immediately shot by the *Einsatzgruppen*; while if he sent them to Lodz, they would face overcrowding, disease, and possible starvation, but not immediate violent death. This was to be the first and last time he ever took initiative and deviated from orders (it wound up getting him in a good deal of trouble with the Nazi overseer of the Lodz ghetto). Arendt cites it as evidence of what she calls "an instinctive aversion to crime"—an aversion that completely dissipated once he saw the general enthusiasm for the Final Solution evinced by a "distinguished" group of undersecretaries of state at the infamous Wannsee Conference organized by Heydrich in January of 1942.

It was at this conference that Eichmann, acting as Heydrich's secretary, had what he called his "Pontius Pilate moment." If the undersecretaries from the Finance, Transport, Foreign, and other ministries thought "such a bloody solution through violence" was a good idea, who was he, Eichmann, to judge? After all, these men were uniformly better educated, higher not only in rank but also in terms of class and social status as well. They were, as Eichmann was well aware, his social betters. If they saw nothing wrong with the Final Solution, then there was evidently no reason for him to continue to be bothered by questions of conscience.

> What he [Eichmann] fervently believed in up to the end was success, the chief standard of 'good society' as he knew it... He did not need to 'close his ears to the voice of conscience'... not because he had none, but because conscience spoke with a 'respectable voice,' with the voice of respectable society around him.[16]

But even if this was the case—even if Eichmann's conscience had been lulled by what his superiors thought and approved of—mustn't he have been aware of voices from outside his immediate social and organizational matrix, voices that that made clear the wrongness of what he was doing?

In the course of planning the deportation of millions of Jews from ghettoes scattered across Europe, Eichmann dealt with the so-called "Jewish Elders" who comprised the Nazi-organized *Judenräte* (Jewish councils). Charged with maintaining order in the ghettoes and with compiling the lists of their fellow Jews who were scheduled to be deported to the death camps, these Jewish Elders met frequently with Eichmann to voice concerns and make complaints. However, they never objected to the nature of his duties or to his carrying out the new "radical" policy. This is less surprising than it might first appear, given the enormous power differential between Eichmann and the members of these councils. But their failure to protest the policy itself bolstered Eichmann's sense of the legitimacy of what he was doing.

Even those who weren't under Eichmann's direct authority—people like pastor Heinrich Grüber, who, along with a small group of like-minded protestant clergy, opposed Hitler on principle—did not question the overall policy. A much-anticipated witness for the prosecution at the trial in Jerusalem, Grüber had pleaded with Eichmann on behalf of Jewish WWI veterans who had been wounded or decorated for bravery, as well as on behalf of Jewish war widows. Grüber wished to persuade Eichmann that these groups were deserving of more humane treatment. The problem was that Jewish WWI veterans and widows were among the groups the Nazis themselves recognized as constituting exceptions to their overall policy. Thus, rather than pricking Eichmann's conscience, Grüber's intervention on behalf of these groups effectively conceded the legitimacy of the rule under which Eichmann operated. At the trial, Eichmann could truthfully claim that "nobody came to me and reproached me for anything in the performance of my duties. Not even Pastor Grüber claims to have done so."[17] This was a point even Grüber himself acknowledged, albeit with some embarrassment.

The quieting of Eichmann's conscience, the absence of voices from the "outside," and the cementing of his sense that there was nothing wrong or criminal in his conduct come to a head in the infamous episode of the deportation of Hungarian Jews in 1944. Hitler had lost patience with the lax Hungarian enforcement of Nazi Jewish policy and ordered Himmler and Eichmann to take care of the problem. By this time, it was clear to Himmler that Germany had lost the war. He was looking for a way to survive the collapse and to ingratiate himself with the victors. So, contrary to Hitler's wishes, Himmler ordered an effective shut-down of the Final Solution, in the hope that he could use Hungarian Jews as a bargaining chip in later negotiations with the soon to be victorious Allies. Eichmann was shocked by this action of Himmler's part and—quite out of character—disobeyed the orders of his superior and did his very best to insure that Hitler's wishes would be carried out. The result of his efforts was 147 trains carrying over 400,000 Hungarian Jews to the gas chambers at Auschwitz.

From Arendt's point of view, this episode—seen by the court as proof positive of Eichmann's fanatical Nazism and anti-Semitism—provides additional support to the claim that Eichmann was indeed representative of a "new type of criminal," one incapable of telling right from wrong when it came to the implementation of evil as policy. At the trial, Eichmann did not simply reiterate what the defendants at the Nuremburg trials had claimed, that he was "only following orders." Yes, he followed orders, but he also did his duty and was particularly cognizant of the imperative to be a law-abiding citizen. Moreover—and this is one of the more bizarre features of the whole case—Eichmann claimed during his police interrogation that he had "lived his whole life according to Kant's moral precepts, and especially according to a Kantian definition of duty."

As Arendt notes, "this was outrageous on the face of it," yet during the trial, under questioning by Judge Raveh, Eichmann was able to give a plausible account of his meaning: "I meant by my remark about Kant that the principle of my will must always be such that it can become the principle of general laws."[18] And, while Eichmann recognized that he had ceased to live his life according to Kantian moral principles once he was ordered to help carry out the Final Solution, there is a (warped) sense in which he never abandoned his "Kantianism." Rather than dismissing the Kantian formula outright, he had

> distorted it to read: Act as if the principle of your actions were the same as that of the legislator or of the law of the land—or, in Hans Frank's formulation of 'the categorical imperative in the Third Reich,' which Eichmann must have known: 'Act in such a way that the Führer, if he knew your action, would approve it.'[19]

This version accords with what Eichmann himself referred to as Kant "for the household use of the little man," a household use in which

> all that is left of Kant's spirit is the demand that a man do more than obey the law, that he go beyond the mere call of obedience and identify his own will with the principle behind the law— the source from which the law sprang.[20]

In Kant, as Arendt notes, this source is practical reason, whereas in Eichmann's household use, "it was the will of the Führer." The demand that an individual identify his own will with the source or principle behind the law was rendered almost redundant by the fact that the legal system of the Third Reich was based upon a command theory of law: the words of the Führer had the force of law.[21] As Theodor Maunz, a well-known expert on the constitutional law of the Third Reich, put it in 1943: "The command of the Führer…is the absolute center of the present legal order."[22]

To go against Hitler's wishes, as Himmler had done in ordering the drawing-down of the Final Solution in 1944, was therefore not merely to disobey an order: it was to disobey a *law*. Arendt argues that Eichmann's palpable sense of scandal at Himmler's actions flowed not from any sense of betrayal of National Socialist ideology, nor even from the fact that Himmler had dared disobey an order from Hitler. Himmler had, in fact, *broken the law*: if anyone was a criminal, he was. Like the soldier who, relying upon his previous experience of lawfulness, recognizes a "black flag" with the warning "prohibited!" flying over a clearly criminal order, so Eichmann saw a "black flag"—not over Hitler's command (itself an embodiment of lawfulness), but over Himmler's "criminal" countermand.[23] However tempted the individual might be to extricate himself from the apparatus of mass killing (and Eichmann repeatedly insisted during his trial he would have welcomed the opportunity to do so), he had to resist this temptation and *follow the law*.

At his trial, Eichmann recognized that his actions—perfectly lawful in the context of the Third Reich—were, in fact, "crimes legalized by the state." Despite the initial lack of enthusiasm for the "bloody solution through violence" he testified to in court, Eichmann was able to adapt himself with surprising ease to his new duties, carrying them out with zeal and meticulousness. The same ability showed itself during his trial in Jerusalem. He now adapted himself to the standards and perspective of Israeli law. "Of course" he had aided and abetted "the annihilation of the Jews," an event that he now described as "one of the greatest crimes in the history of Humanity."[24] He pleaded "not guilty in the sense of the indictment" to each of the counts against him *not* because he denied what he did or that he had "acted on purpose." Rather, he did so because the indictment claimed he did what he did "out of base motives and in full knowledge of the criminal nature of his deeds."[25]

The point here is that there is a plausible case to be made that Eichmann didn't act out of base motives (such as fanatical anti-Semitism) or "in full knowledge" of the criminal nature of his conduct.[26] For a man like Eichmann, one hardly given to reflection, the shape of law and morality were fluid and dependent upon the context in which he found himself. Arendt thinks Eichmann's "shallowness" in this regard was truly exceptional. However, a similar adaptability and lack of reflection is to be found in the many non-sadistic, non-fanatical individuals who obeyed the law and performed their duties as functionaries or enforcers in the Soviet camp system, the apartheid regime of South Africa, and the many Latin American military dictatorships propped up by the United States during the Cold War. While there may not be a "little bit of Eichmann in each one of us" (an interpretation of the "banality of evil" that Arendt loathed), his peculiar brand of thoughtlessness and lack of independent judgment are probably more widespread than we care to admit. As J. S. Mill put it in a famous passage from On Liberty:

> For in proportion to a man's want of confidence in his own solitary judgment does he usually repose, with implicit trust, on the infallibility of "the world" in general. And the world, to each individual, means that part of which he comes in contact: his party, his sect, his church, his class of society; the man may be called…almost liberal and large-minded to whom it means anything so comprehensive as his own country or age…Nor is his own faith shaken by his being aware that other ages, countries, sects, churches, classes and parties have thought, and even now think, the exact reverse. He devolves upon his own world the responsibility of being in the right.[27]

Arendt does not herself appeal to Mill in this regard (she identified his liberalism with an ideology of progress she completely rejected). She *does*, however, appeal to Kant, whose essay "An Answer to the Question: What Is Enlightenment?" (1784) in many respects prefigured Mill's argument for freedom of thought and expression in On Liberty. Like Mill, Kant emphasized just how common it is to let others do our thinking for us. While his citation of "laziness and cowardice" as the chief obstacles to thinking for oneself (*Selbstdenken*) is a bit at odds with Mill's indictment of majority public opinion in the mid-nineteenth century, the overall message is much the same: "Have courage to use your own understanding!"[28] That Arendt fundamentally endorses this message is made abundantly clear in her Kant lectures as well as her Lessing essay, both of which emphasize the tie between the spirit of criticism and *Selbstdenken*.[29]

The courage required to make one's own judgments can be a remarkably rare commodity, especially in those "emergency situations" where "everybody is swept away unthinkingly by what everybody else does and believes in."[30] Nevertheless, in a case like Eichmann's—where the defendant has committed crimes legalized by the regime and (thus) did not recognize his conduct as criminal at the time—we still insist that human beings be capable of telling right from wrong "even when all they have to guide them is their own judgment." But here we must recognize that both Kant and Mill actually understated the depth of the problem. It is not simply inertia or "immaturity" that has to be dealt with. Rather, it is a historical context in which the beliefs that once set limits to human behavior have been emptied of their content, transformed first into mere social conventions (or *mores*) and later into sets of "values" that are themselves as exchangeable as any other commodity. The oft-made claim that the whole "totalitarian business" could have been avoided if only Europeans had remained true to their "traditional values" rings hollow for reasons Arendt underlined in her response to a question posed by her friend and colleague Hans Jonas in Toronto:

> If you go through such a situation [as totalitarianism] the first thing you know is the following: you *never* know how somebody will act. You have the surprise of your life! This goes throughout all layers of society and it goes throughout various distinctions between men. And if you want to make a generalization then you could say that those who were still very firmly convinced of the so-called old values were the first to be ready to change their old values for a new set of values, provided they were given one. And I am afraid of this, because I think that whenever you give anybody a new set of values…you can immediately exchange it.

And the only thing the guy gets used to is having a "bannister" and a set of values, no matter.[31]

The point is driven home in Arendt's "Postscript" to EJ. "We know," she writes, "that the few who were 'arrogant' enough to trust only their own judgment were by no means identical with those persons who continued to abide by the old values, or who were guided by religious belief." Confronted by an utterly unprecedented situation, "those few who were still able to tell right from wrong" had only their own faculty of judgment to fall back upon: "There were no rules to be abided by, under which the particular cases with which they were confronted could be subsumed. *They had to decide each instance as it arose, because no rules existed for the unprecedented.*"[32] What distinguished these relative few was their trust in their own faculty of judgment and their ability to recognize an unprecedented situation, one in which the old verities lacked all moral (as opposed to social) content. The speed with which the Nazis were able to effectively convert the commandment "thou shalt not kill" into "thou shalt kill" in a country as overwhelmingly Christian as Germany illustrates just how empty and eminently exchangeable the old rules and values had become.

III Thinking and judging: Socrates and Kant

The truth was that neither faith, education, or the "respectability" enjoyed by the middle and upper classes prevented the great majority of Germans from succumbing to Hitler. But was there anything, aside from a certain "arrogance," that characterized the few who did not? In "Thinking and Moral Considerations," Arendt gives us a partial answer to this question.

"Thinking and Moral Considerations" (TMC) is a key text in Arendt's *oeuvre* because it provides a bridge between her earlier work on the *vita activa* and her later (never fully completed) work on mental activities, activities we are prone to associate with the *vita contemplativa*. As Arendt makes plain in "Thinking and Moral Considerations," however, her interest in thinking as an activity did not arise out of a long-suppressed desire to return to philosophy proper and the calm of the *bios theoretikos*. Rather, what spurred her in this direction was the concrete phenomenon of Eichmann's *thoughtlessness* encountered at the trial in Jerusalem. It was his "total absence of thinking" that attracted her interest, and which led her to the following questions:

> Is evil-doing, not just the sins of omission but the sins of commission, possible in the absence of not merely 'base motives' (as the law calls it) but of any motives at all, any particular prompting of interest of volition? Is wickedness, however we may define it…not a necessary condition for evil-doing? *Is our ability to judge, to tell right from wrong, beautiful from ugly, dependent upon our faculty of thought? Do the inability to think and a disastrous failure of what we commonly call conscience coincide?*[33]

Such questions prompted Arendt to wonder whether the activity of thinking—the "habit of examining and reflecting upon whatever comes to pass"—could "be of such a nature that it 'conditions' men against evil-doing?" At first glance, this thesis hardly seems to go against the grain of the Western tradition of philosophical thought. After all, from Plato and Aristotle forward, this tradition has posited an intimate connection between philosophical reason and the attainment of moral truth (or knowledge).

Yet Arendt is by no means simply echoing a well-worn nostrum of the Western tradition. In TMC she takes great pains to point out just how *unlike* cognition or logical reasoning the process of thinking (or reflection) actually is. In thinking, we withdraw from the world of appearances and reflect on "invisibles" that we mentally re-present to ourselves. The "soundless dialogue" between me and myself that takes place when I am thinking something over is *not* like the mental operations we perform in order to solve technical-practical problems, or to add to an existing body of knowledge. Rather, it issues from a perplexity that strikes us only when we *stop* acting, working, or problem-solving. Then and only then is a given phenomenon removed from its place in the instrumental hierarchy of our various projects and allowed to become, as we say, thought-provoking. Thinking or reflection is, in Arendt's characterization, a "resultless enterprise," one that will always appear to be "out of order" from the perspective of the actor or fabricator. *Contra* Plato and Aristotle, it is not a special form of reasoning, nor is it a faculty of knowledge available only to the few.

This last point is key to the fleshing out of Arendt's thesis. If thinking is to be morally and politically relevant—that is, if it is indeed somehow related to our capacity for judgment—then is has to be something we can require from not just a philosophically educated few but from *everyone*. As Arendt puts it,

> if the ability to tell right from wrong should have anything should have anything to do with this ability to think, then we must be able to 'demand' its exercise in every sane person no matter how erudite or ignorant, how intelligent or stupid he may prove to be.[34]

Thoughtlessness is not a function of stupidity or ignorance; rather, it is often simply a function of our being absorbed in (and distracted by) our daily activities. It is also a function of the misplaced confidence we have in the preconceived categories and customary rules we already possess, categories and rules we assume provide adequate guidelines for judgment no matter how unusual or unprecedented a given phenomenon or event might be.

It is at this juncture in her argument that Arendt attempts to illustrate her point by turning to a "model thinker": Socrates. Rather than viewing Socrates as the philosophical teacher par excellence, one who claims moral expertise and a knowledge of the ends of life that the many lack (but which a gifted few might possibly learn), Arendt sees him as a "citizen among citizens." He is, however, a citizen with an unconventional mission. He wants to slow the notoriously active Athenians down by stimulating perplexity about the basic moral terms (piety, courage, justice) that structure their common life. He wants, in other words, to make the Athenians stop and think. To do so he employs the method of questioning and cross-examination (*elenchus*), a method that does not trace the ascent from opinion (*doxa*) to truth, but rather is largely negative or dissolvent in character. Socratic questioning reveals the inner contradictions of his interlocutors' conventional views (thus "dissolving" them), replacing them not with "the truth" but with more questions about the nature of courage, piety, and justice. As Socrates states in the *Apology*, he has no positive doctrine, nor does he claim any teachable wisdom about how to lead a good or just life. He knows what he does not know and he leaves his audience with questions, not answers.

In order to highlight the negative or dissolvent character of the type of thinking enacted in the Socratic dialogues, Arendt focuses on three similes Socrates used to describe himself. In the *Apology* he calls himself a "gadfly," in the *Theaetetus* a "midwife," and in the *Meno* a "stinging fish." Socrates is a gadfly in that he

> knows how to arouse citizens who, without him, will 'sleep on undisturbed for the rest of their lives.' And what does he arouse them to? To thinking, to examining matters, an activity without which life, according to him, was not only not worth living but was not fully alive.

Second, Socrates is a midwife in that, while being "sterile" himself (he has no answers or doctrines to impart), he knows how to deliver the thoughts of others and show them the implications of their opinions. Like the traditional Greek midwife, he is also capable of deciding whether the "child" (the opinion) so delivered was "fit to live" or rather a "mere wind egg" that should be discarded. Since most if not all conventional views fall into the second category, the actual function of the Socratic midwife is to purge people of their unexamined opinions and prejudgments. The latter effectively prevent thinking because they suggest that we know what we do not know.[35] Third and finally, Socrates is a "stinging fish" or "electric ray" in that he "remains steadfast in his own perplexities, and, like the electric ray, paralyzes with them whoever he comes in contact with."[36]

Engaging one's fellow citizens in arguments that purge them of their conventional opinions and leave them only with questions may seem an odd way to "condition them against evil-doing." Indeed, many would probably object that if Socratic negativity undermines conventional belief and opinion without offering a positive (alternative) code of conduct, the final product will likely be the promotion of cynicism and possibly nihilism. One need look no further than Socrates' second most famous "student," Alcibiades, who evidently concluded that Athens' democratic values were basically rubbish and that limitless self-aggrandizement was the path to pursue.

Arendt by no means shies away from this objection. She goes out of her way to draw attention to the risk inherent not just in Socratic, but in *all* thinking:

What we commonly call nihilism—and are tempted to date historically, decry politically, and ascribe to thinkers who alleg-edly dared to think 'dangerous thoughts'—is actually a danger inherent in the thinking activity itself. There are no dangerous thoughts; thinking itself is dangerous, but nihilism is not its product.[37]

One may find oneself in agreement with Arendt's primary claim here—thinking does indeed undermine conventional opinion and is, in this sense, dangerous—but find her subsidiary claim uncon-vincing. What prevents nihilism from being the logical result of the otherwise "resultless" exercise of thinking? To this question, Arendt has a particularly sharp response:

All critical examinations must go through a state of at least hy-pothetically negating accepted opinions and "values" by finding out their implications and tacit assumptions, and in this sense nihilism may be seen as an ever-present danger of thinking. But this danger does not arise out of the Socratic conviction that an unexamined life is not worth living, but, on the contrary, out of the desire to find results which would make further thinking unnecessary. Thinking is equally dangerous to all creeds and, by itself, does not bring forth any new creed.[38]

Nihilism, in other words, takes the temporary suspension and critical interrogation of established values and reifies this suspension into a firm set of negative results. Nihilism is, in fact, a creed arrived at by means of the abstract negation of the current reigning table of values. Once these negative results have been arrived at, they will be used "as sleepily, with the same unthinking routine, as the old values." Indeed, the moment they are applied to the realm of human affairs, "it is as though they had never gone through the thinking process."[39] We see this dynamic at work in those of Socrates' students who, having witnessed the paradoxes resulting from the attempt to define (for example) what piety is, came to the conclusion that a life of impiety was the more logical and intellectually honest path to take. And we see it at work in Nietzsche's "immoralism," a teaching derived from turning Plato and the Platonic view of the good life

upside down. In both instances, a dogma is questioned only to produce a new dogma. The thinking process is cut short in the name of
creating a new table of values, one produced by the simple inversion
of the old.

The possibility of nihilism implicit in the negativity of thinking—a
possibility apparently realized by such "students" of Socrates as
Alcibiades—puts the conduct of the "non-thinking many" in a new
and strangely positive light. If questioning and reflection lead us first to
doubt and thence to cynicism about the "fixed moral points" of our society, then perhaps there is something positive to be said for dogmatic
belief and the unexamined life. This was the conclusion Tocqueville
came to in the second volume of his *Democracy in America*. The Americans,
Tocqueville observed, put great store in their own individual judgment.
However, the stability of their democracy and the relative moderation
of their individual lives was made possible by a network of dogmatic
(Christian) opinions that virtually no one questioned.[40]

Tocqueville's position has received a surprising degree of support
from contemporary sociologists and political scientists. However, as
Arendt reminds us, "non-thinking, which seems so recommendable
a state for political and moral affairs, also has its own dangers":

> By shielding people against the dangers of examination, it
> teaches them to hold fast to whatever the prescribed rules of
> conduct might be at a given time in a given society. What people
> then get used to is not so much the content of the rules, a close
> examination of which would always lead them into perplexity,
> as the possession of rules under which to subsume particulars.
> In other words, they get used to never making up their minds.
> If somebody then shows up who, for whatever reasons and pur-
> poses, wishes to abolish the old "values" or virtues, he will find
> it easy enough provided he offers a new code, and he will need
> no force or persuasion—no proof that the new values are better
> than the old ones—to establish it. The faster men held to the
> old code, the more eager they will be to assimilate themselves
> to the new one.[41]

We return here to the argument Arendt made in response to Hans
Jonas' suggestion that, in light of the horrors of the twentieth century,

our most pressing need is for the guidance once provided by traditional or "ultimate" values. From Arendt's point of view, the quest
for such "bannisters" ultimately reduces to a quest for something
that will render thinking and independent judgment moot when
it comes to questions of conscience and right conduct. Although
she does not cite him in this regard, Arendt's argument about the
exchangeability of new values for old and the habitual reliance upon
pregiven codes of conduct owes something to Nietzsche's insights
concerning the nature and origins of what he called the "formal
conscience" in *Beyond Good and Evil*:

> Inasmuch as at all times...there have been herds of men (clans,
> communities, tribes, peoples, states, churches) and always a
> great many people who obeyed, compared to the small num-
> ber of those commanding—considering, then, that nothing has
> been exercised and cultivated better and longer among men so
> far than *obedience*—it may fairly be assumed that the need for
> it is now innate in the average man, as a kind of *formal* con-
> science that commands "thou shalt unconditionally do some-
> thing, unconditionally not do something else," in short, "thou
> shalt." This need needs to satisfy itself and to fill its form with
> some content....It seizes upon things as a rude appetite...and
> accepts whatever is shouted into its ears by someone who issues
> commands—parents, teachers, laws, class prejudices, public
> opinion.[42]

Against the all too common reduction of conscience to the inter-
nalization of social mores or commands, Arendt suggests that we
all have the capacity to form an authentic (non-formal) conscience
since we are all capable of thinking. She sees the "two-in-one" of
consciousness as fully actualized in the thinking experience, where
it takes the form of a dialogue between me and myself. A person
given to thought or the habit of reflection will, over time, develop an
intimate relationship with this internal other, their "thinking partner." This partner constitutes a kind of second self, one whom, for
obvious reasons, we will want to remain on good terms with.

When, in the *Gorgias* (482), Socrates says that "it would be better
for me that my lyre or a chorus I directed should be out of tune and

loud with discord, and that multitudes of men should disagree with
me rather than that I, *being one*, should be out of harmony with myself
and contradict me," he is articulating the moral stance of someone who has, through reflection, fully developed his inner plurality.
"Conscience in the most general sense is...based on the fact that I
can be in agreement or disagreement with myself, and that means
that I not only appear to others but that I also appear to myself."[43]
When Socrates goes home, he knows that he will not be alone.[44]
And because of this, he knows that it would be far more painful for
him to be out of harmony with the self who is his thinking partner
than to suffer punishment at the hands of authorities who want to
implicate him in injustice. His conscientious avoidance of injustice
can thus be said to be, at least in part, a result of his experience of
thinking. This is a point Arendt generalizes with her suggestion that
the *secular conscience* is itself a by-product of the thinking activity and
the "two-in-one" of consciousness.[45]

While Arendt is adamant that the activity of thinking is neither
essentially cognitive nor practical in nature (it produces no knowledge; it provides no theories for the guidance of practice), she *does*
believe that it plays an important role in certain types of political
situations. In moments where "everybody is swept away unthinkingly by what everybody else does and believes in," the negative or
purging element of thinking provides a crucial service. By drawing
out the implications of the unexamined opinions enthusiastically
held by everybody else, it effectively destroys them—at least for the
individual who thinks them through.

This destruction through thinking has, in turn, a "liberating" effect on the faculty of judgment. Since judgment is the capacity to
"judge *particulars* without subsuming them under those general rules
which can be taught and learned until they grow into habits that
can be replaced by other habits and rules," the dissolution of such
general rules and categories in the course of the thinking process
enables the individual to grasp the particular (a policy, an order, a
law, or a regime) in its concrete reality, however shocking, evil, or
grotesque it may turn out to be. Thus, while "thinking deals with
invisibles" (i.e. with things that are absent which we re-present to
ourselves in the course of reflection) and judging "always concerns
particulars and things close at hand," the two faculties are in fact

interconnected. For if thinking—the "two-in-one of the soundless dialogue"—can be said to "actualize the difference in our identity," creating conscience as its by-product, then judging (which Arendt now characterizes as "the by-product of the liberating effect of thinking") can be said to *realize* thinking, making it "manifest in the world of appearances, where I am never alone and always much too busy to think."[46]

In "emergency situations" the judgment of the thinking individual leads to non-compliance and a conscious withdrawal from public life. Such non-participation constitutes "a kind of action" since it occurs against the backdrop of mass enthusiasm—the ready enlistment of the non-thinking many in what is, in fact, evil as policy. Arendt concludes her essay with a forceful declaration of the political and moral relevance of this most solitary of activities, thinking. "The manifestation of the wind of thought," she writes, "is no knowledge; it is the ability to tell right from wrong, beautiful from ugly. And this indeed may prevent catastrophes, at least for myself, in the rare moments when the chips are down."[47]

But what about less dire situations, situations where not everyone has been "swept away unthinkingly" and where making judgments in public is not suicidal? How, in other words, should we view the relationship between thinking and judgment in less extreme political circumstances? That is, in circumstances where the public realm has not been transformed into a "desert" by a dictator or squeezed out of existence by ideology and terror? What then?

Here, we find ourselves back in the arena of debate and deliberation, however restricted that arena might be. To be in such an arena is to take one's place as a "citizen among citizens." This condition would appear at first glance to preclude the "stop and think"—the withdrawal from all doing—that Arendt sees as the necessary precondition for thinking. Political and moral judgment in the public realm seem to be less matters for reflection and conscience than matters demanding what Aristotle called practical wisdom (phronēsis). For Aristotle, practical wisdom is the capacity to "deliberate well about what is good," about "the sort of thing that contributes to the good life in general." As such, practical wisdom is clearly different from pure or theoretical sciences (like physics or mathematics) and from the technical art or expertise exercised by craftsmen. Phronēsis is not a science or form of theoretical wisdom because it concerns "matters of action"—that is, it concerns things that could always be other than they are. And it is not an art because applied technical knowledge concerns matters of production that are "generically different" from matters involving human action in the ethical and political realms.[48] According to Aristotle, the man of practical wisdom is someone like Pericles who, on the basis of his ethical character, experience, self-control, general education, and good judgment is able to do the right thing at the right time.

Aristotle's invocation of Pericles as the exemplary man of practical wisdom reveals a problem that neo-Aristotelian advocates of practical wisdom like Hans-Georg Gadamer and Alastair McIntyre are wont to gloss over. For while Pericles was, technically, a citizen among citizens in the Athenian democracy, it is clear that he owed his position of power and influence to qualities that, if not unique, are certainly rare, and rarer still in combination. Pericles is a virtuoso of practical wisdom, an elite political actor who, like Winston Churchill, had the benefit of aristocratic background, education, and political connections. This background helped mold his "uncorruptible" character and provided the basis for development of the persuasive skills necessary to become a leader of the Athenian democracy. Unsurprisingly, those who take a *phronimos* like Pericles as their model tend to view judgment as a faculty possessed by a statesman-like few, an elite of virtue and character.

This fact gives us a clue as to why Arendt chose to frame her thinking about moral and political judgment in Kantian rather than Aristotelian terms.[49] Her turn to Kant is counterintuitive, if only because Kant conceived *moral* judgment as a straightforward logical operation by which any individual "rational being" measures a particular personal maxim of action (for example, getting out of personal difficulties by making false promises) against the standard or general rule given by the Categorical Imperative. Can the particular maxim in question be consistently universalized, or can it not?[50] The turn to Kant appears even more counterintuitive when we stop to consider a fact Arendt actually foregrounds in her Kant lectures. While it's plausible to say that Kant had a philosophy of history, he certainly didn't have anything like a worked out political philosophy. Arendt's turn to Kant and his conception of "judgments of taste" in the third *Critique* has therefore struck more than a few of her readers as perplexing, especially given the ethical-political resources readily available in Aristotle's treatment of judgment in book VI of the *Nicomachean Ethics*.

Why does Arendt turn to Kant and the third *Critique*? First, there is Kant's commitment to equality and his insistence that we all have the faculty of judgment and the capacity to form reflective judgments— this despite the fact that we often fail to make use of this faculty and that many of us have come to view *abstention from judgment* as a positive virtue. Second, Arendt turns to Kant because, even though the third *Critique* does not address any of the traditional topics of political philosophy (justice, the nature of political regimes, constitutions), it is concerned throughout with commonly shared *appearances* and the judgment of *particulars* (this is beautiful, this is ugly, etc.). Third, she turns to Kant's third *Critique* because his conception of judgments of taste is, despite our first impression, not subjective but (in fact) deeply intersubjective in nature.

While, for Kant, valid *cognitive* judgments are made possible by the individual's possession of the faculty of understanding (a faculty which organizes our otherwise chaotic "manifold" of sense impressions by means of such "built-in" cognitive categories as substance and causality) and valid *moral* judgments are made possible by our possession of pure practical reason (a faculty that provides rational beings with the idea of a universally valid moral law, one independent of the promptings of either interest or desire), the validity of *taste* judgments can be established only by *persuading* our judging peers that *this* particular painting is beautiful or ugly, or *this* particular historical event is morally uplifting or degrading. In other words, judgments of taste are redeemed intersubjectively, by a process of "woo[ing] the consent of everyone else" rather than by means of empirical demonstration or compelling logical argument.[51] They are, as Arendt puts it, matters of *opinion*, whereas cognitive and moral judgments (which *can* be established through empirical demonstration and/or logical argument) are matters of truth or correctness.

One may be inclined to grant Arendt's general point here. Neither the truths revealed by scientific investigation nor the "moral law" laid down by pure practical reason are matters suited to rhetorical persuasion and public debate. But most will still find it odd to associate taste judgments with intersubjectivity or anything approximating a claim to general validity. Yet this is precisely what Arendt, following Kant's analysis in the third *Critique*, does. In order to understand her line of reasoning, we need to attend to a cluster of concepts Kant develops in his analysis of judgments of taste. These are: communicability, common sense (*sensus communis*), the notion of an "enlarged mentality," disinterestedness, and imagination.

In his 1793 essay "On the Common Saying: 'This May be True in Theory, but Does Not Apply in Practice,'" Kant makes the seemingly off-hand observation that "it is a natural vocation of man to communicate with his fellows, especially in matters affecting mankind as a whole."[52] This concern with communication and sociability, so notable by its absence from Kant's epistemological and ethical writings, can be traced back not only to "What Is Enlightenment?" (1784) but also to his "pre-critical" period (especially his "Observations on the Sense of the Beautiful and the Sublime" from 1764). In the "Enlightenment" essay, Kant asserts the central importance of the "public use of one's reason" (as exercised by a "man of learning" addressing "the entire reading public") in bringing about enlightenment. In the much earlier "Observations," he sees fit to include the parable of "Carazan's Dream"—a parable which recounts a selfish man's horror at being condemned by the "angel of death" to an eternity of isolation without any future possibility of communication with his fellow men.[53] Not only is communication a "natural vocation" of man for Kant; it is also the distinguishing mark of his humanity and (in the form of "the public use of one's reason") *the* precondition of enlightenment.

According to Kant, the communicability of a sensation is the precondition for effective exercise of our faculty of judgment, and this communicability is itself predicated upon our sharing a "common sense" (*sensus communis*) of the world with our judging peers.[54] It is easy to see why this must be the case. Unless we assume the existence of a common sense that broadly aligns our experience of the world with that of others (they smell what we smell, see what we see, hear what we hear, etc.), we have no basis for the expectation that our peers will find a particular sensation agreeable or disagreeable, let alone that they will be able to share in our experience of a work of art. It is precisely the decay of such a "common feeling for the world" that leads many of us to assume, *contra* Kant, that sensation *lacks* communicability and that judgments of taste are therefore irreducibly personal or subjective in nature. The widespread belief that the faculty of taste is entirely subjective is reflected in our cognate view of the faculty of opinion. For many, to say "that's *your* opinion" is tantamount to saying "that's your *subjective* view of the matter"—it may be valid for you, but there's no reason why it could or should be valid for me.

Arendt fastens onto Kant's analysis of judgments of taste precisely because Kant thought such judgments *do* make a claim to our assent:

> The power of judgment rests on a potential agreement with others, and the thinking process which is active in judging something is not, like the thought process of pure reasoning, a dialogue between me and myself, but finds itself always and primarily, even if I am quite alone in making up my mind, in an anticipated communication with others with whom I know I must finally come to some agreement. From this potential agreement judgment derives its specific validity.[55]

For example, if I offer the judgment that a certain picture or poem is especially beautiful, I do so with the expectation that you will agree with me. If for some reason you don't, I will proceed to offer arguments as to *why* I think the picture or poem in question is beautiful in the way I have claimed it to be. You may be persuaded by my arguments, or you may offer counterarguments challenging my judgment (the picture is conventional, the poem *jejune*, etc.). The crucial point here is that taste judgments, while hardly demonstrable, are not "merely subjective" either. They make a claim to an exemplary or *general* form of validity that others *ought* to recognize, but in fact may not.[56] As Arendt puts it in her Kant lectures: "In matters of 'taste' I never judge only for myself, for the act of judging always implies a commitment to communicate my judgment; that is, judgment is rendered with a view to persuading others of its validity."[57] Judging that lacks the commitment to communicate and persuade is in fact a contradiction in terms, since it yields a relativism (or indifference) of the "you prefer pea soup, I prefer champagne" variety.

The giving of arguments aimed at persuasion marks the formation of political opinions and taste judgments as *rational* processes, even though neither can be said to give us *truth*. As Arendt notes in OR, "opinion and judgment obviously belong among the faculties of reason, but the point of the matter is that these two, politically most important, rational faculties had been almost entirely neglected by the tradition of political as well philosophical thought."[58] (This statement should dispose of the canard that Arendt was some sort of irrationalist or "political existentialist" once and for all.) Yet one need not be a moral objectivist to charge that Arendt carries her polemic against ostensibly compelling "philosophical truths" in the moral and political realms too far. It has been urged, notably by Jürgen Habermas, that we should view the outcome of argumentative processes conducted on the basis of reciprocity, sincerity, and verified fact as *true*. The fundamental idea is that we still need to be able to distinguish between the "true" consensual outcomes of open debate and deliberation (in which relevant arguments have been fully canvassed and the "force of the better argument" allowed to win out) and the "opinions" that provide, at best, the starting points for such argumentation.

It is important to note that, in directing this critical point specifically against Arendt, Habermasians like Albrecht Wellmer shift the locus of argumentation away from a public realm inhabited by diverse citizens to something more like a community of inquirers disputing the proper definition of a problem, the appropriate theory to apply, and the relative weight that should be accorded different types of evidence.[59] Post-empiricist philosophy of science, drawing on the work of Thomas Kuhn, has emphasized the "political" aspects of such inquires, rightly noting that appealing to the facts alone will not resolve disputes in disciplines where the specification of what constitutes appropriate and verifiable factual evidence is itself a contentious and theory-laden exercise. Within a disciplinary matrix, it makes sense to view the current scholarly or scientific consensus as *true*, but only if we remind ourselves that truth here is a matter of what the pragmatist philosopher John Dewey referred to as "warranted assertability." It is always subject to revision and correction within the ongoing process of scholarly or scientific inquiry.

Arendt resists this analogy. However, she insists on distinguishing matters of truth from matters of opinion *not* because she is somehow loath to acknowledge the place of rational argumentation or factual evidence in political argument—quite the contrary. Arendt insists on the distinction because she is aware of how heavily the Western philosophical and theological traditions have relied on the idea that there is one and only one "correct" answer to fundamental moral and political questions. A not insubstantial part of her political thought is devoted to reminding us of just how strong a hold this form of monism has on our imaginations. Platonism may have been abandoned long ago as a strictly *philosophical* doctrine, but Platonic prejudices of the monist sort live on and continue to distort our idea of political debate and deliberation. To hold out "truth" as the goal of political and moral argument is to tap into the deep wells of residual Platonism that remain in our culture, thanks in no small part to Christian theology. Better, in Arendt's view, to reserve "truth" for matters of established fact (e.g. in 1914 Germany invaded Belgium, and not the other way round) or for the rationally demonstrable propositions of mathematics, logic, geometry, etc. than to muddy the waters once again by holding out "truth" as the proper *telos* or object of consensus aimed at by political or moral argument.[60]

But isn't the claim of a "judgment of taste" to *general* validity ultimately equivalent to the claim that it is *true*? Arendt disagrees:

> Judgment is endowed with a certain specific validity but is never universally valid. Its claims to validity can never extend further than the others in whose place the judging person has put himself for his considerations. Judgment, Kant says, is valid "for every single judging person," but the emphasis in the sentence is on "judging"; it is not valid for those who do not judge or for those who are not members of the public realm where the objects of judgment appear….Culture and politics…belong together because it is not knowledge or truth which is at stake, but rather judgment and decision, the judicious exchange of opinion about the sphere of public life and the common world, and…what kinds of things are fit to appear in it.[61]

Aesthetic or political judgment thus makes an implicit claim to *general* validity among a *specific* group of judging peers. It is valid for *me* and it should be valid for *them* as well, provided they exercise *their* faculty of judgment and inhabit the same world of appearances as I do. Taste and political judgments therefore have a horizonal dimension that rationally true propositions (like $2 + 2 = 4$) or factually true statements (like "in 1914, Germany invaded Belgium") do not. But while political and taste judgments address themselves to a specific audience of judging peers (fellow citizens, the reading public, lovers of culture, etc.), they can plausibly stake a claim to *general* validity only if they have been previously purged of arbitrary elements of the kind introduced by personal idiosyncrasy. Otherwise, the philistine charge of "that's *your* opinion" may well have some bite.

How is it possible for us purge our judgments of idiosyncrasies and thus avoid mistaking "subjective and private conditions for objective ones"? In §40 of the third *Critique*, Kant argues that the way we do this is by comparing our judgment "not so much with the actual as rather with the merely possible judgments of others," thus putting ourselves "in the position of everyone else, merely by abstracting from the limitations that happen to attach to our own judging."[62] Indeed, for Kant to "think from the standpoint of everyone else" is (along with "think for oneself" and "think consistently") one of the chief maxims of "common human understanding." Someone who follows this maxim possesses what Kant calls an "enlarged mentality" or a "broadened way of thought" (*eine erweiterte Denkungsart*), a characterization Arendt seizes upon in order to depict the "representative" character of opinion formation. In a passage I cited earlier, Arendt writes:

> Political thought is representative. I form an opinion by considering a given issue from different viewpoints, by making present to my mind the standpoints of those who are absent; that is, I represent them. This process of representation does not blindly adopt the actual views of those who stand somewhere else…this is neither a question of empathy, as though I tried to be or feel like somebody else, nor of counting noses and joining a majority, but of *being and thinking in my own identity* where actually I am not. The more people's standpoints I have present in my mind while I am pondering a given issue…the stronger will be my capacity for representative thinking and the more valid my final conclusions, my opinion. (It is this capacity for an 'enlarged

mentality' that enables men to judge; as such, it was discovered by Kant...though he did not recognize the political and moral implications of his discovery).[63]

Representative thinking—the cultivation of an "enlarged mentality" by "training one's imagination to go visiting"[64]—is thus the key to transcending the subjective and the idiosyncratic, whether in forming a political opinion or in rendering a judgment of taste in the cultural sphere.

But while the capacity to "think from the standpoint of everyone else" may well be crucial to redeeming judgment's claim to a general (or "exemplary") validity, Arendt's transfer of Kant's notion of an "enlarged mentality" to the political realm presents certain difficulties. First, there is the problem posed by representative thinking's need for detachment. Impartiality (Kant's "disinterestedness") may well be practicable in historical and aesthetic judgments, but it is hard to see how this form of critical distance is to be achieved in the press of political events and passions. More troublingly, Arendt's description of the role that "enlarged mentality" plays in opinion formation can be read in such a way that the question of *actual* communication with my fellow citizens is rendered moot. If political thinking is "representative" in the manner Arendt describes, then it may appear that I am more reliant upon the nimbleness of my own imagination than upon any concrete acquaintance with the actual views of others. That assumption, in turn, could lead me to believe that I have a more "enlarged" way of thinking than I in fact do.

Both difficulties can be lessened if, following Beiner's suggestion, we view Arendt as having not one but two "theories" of judgment, the first based on the experience of the political actor and the second on the more detached or contemplative experience of the historian or poet. In her essay "The Concept of History" Arendt herself emphasizes the impartiality of Herodotus and Homer. The former wants to do justice to the deeds of both Greeks and Persians, and the latter the words and deeds of both Achaeans and Trojans.[65] The impartiality of historical or poetic judgment—*sine ira et studio*, as Tacitus says—has no relation to positivistic "neutrality" or the split between facts and values. Rather, it follows from the historian or poet's desire to remember and give due appreciation to great or extraordinary words and deeds. Without the poet or historian, such words and deeds are ephemeral. Their existence goes unremembered and their meaning goes unredeemed. The illumination they cast on the human condition—on our worldly, mortal existence—is lost forever.

Temporal distance—the historian or poet's removal from the immediate context of action—is the precondition of his or her appreciation of "great" words and deeds on both sides of a struggle. The relevance of this point to any worthwhile political history—a genre littered with apologia of one sort or another—is obvious. The role that imagination and representative thinking play in the work of a historian or poet is equally obvious: to be incapable of representing the viewpoints of plural actors is to be incapable of writing either good history or good epic poetry. In short, by moving judgment from the involved perspective of the political actor to the contemplative perspective of the historian or poet, we radically diminish the problem posed by the ideal of impartiality. In addition, we avoid the possible perversion of representative thinking through a subjective overestimation of our capacity to adequately imagine the perspectives of others.

This is not to say that the contemplative standpoint of the historian or poet makes these issues disappear. Rather, it is to say that this standpoint makes the attainment of impartial judgment through the deployment of perspectival imagination more plausible and less paradoxical. This is one of the strengths of Beiner's "two theories" suggestion. Another is that judgment from the standpoint of the political actor can be separated off and treated under the more actor-friendly rubric of Aristotle's phronēsis or practical wisdom—something Arendt herself suggests in the essay "The Crisis in Culture."[66] The "two theories" theory, in other words, rests on the entirely plausible suggestion that, when it came to the judgment of the political spectator (the historian or poet), Arendt was a Kantian; while when it came to the judgment of the political actor, she was a de facto Aristotelian. Finally, the "two theories" theory also helps us to make sense of one of Kant's more peculiar assertions about the nature and significance of judgment, an assertion Arendt evidently endorses.

In the third part of his "Theory and Practice" essay, Kant addresses Moses Mendelssohn's view that, while man as an individual may progress, mankind fluctuates "between fixed limits," maintaining more or less the same level or morality, religion, virtue, vice, happiness, and misery.[67] Kant thinks that such a view is bound to produce a sense of meaninglessness and despair, or "melancholy haphazardness" (*trostlose Ungefähr*):

> It is a sight fit for a god to watch a virtuous man grappling with adversity and evil temptations and yet managing to hold out against them. But it is a sight quite unfit not so much for a god, but even the most ordinary, though honest man, to see the human race advancing over a period of time towards virtue, and then quickly relapsing the whole way back into vice and misery. It may perhaps be moving and instructive to watch such a drama for a while; but the curtain must eventually descend. For in the long run, it becomes a farce. And even if the actors do not tire of it—for they are fools—the spectator does...[68]

One way out of meaninglessness and despair produced by the "spectacle" of human history is to presume that *nature* has a purpose of its own, utilizing man's selfish inclinations in order to fully develop the species' potential talents and capacities. The development of knowledge, technology, and culture—brought about not through any human intention but rather through a "ruse of nature" that makes use of man's "unsocial sociability"—would contribute to the spread of trade and republican civil constitutions and (ultimately) to the creation of a law-governed federation of nations.[69] This philosophical postulation of historical progress achieved under nature's providential guidance is the heart of Kant's "Idea for a Universal History with a Cosmopolitan Purpose" (1784).

However, according to Kant, there is another way of redeeming the spectacle, one that is less reliant upon man's "unsocial sociability" and the questionable presupposition of a providential "ruse of nature." That is to note the enthusiasm and moral uplift experienced by "disinterested" (i.e. uninvolved) spectators to such grand historical spectacles as the French Revolution—a spectacle whose very bloodiness marked it clearly as immoral (Kant's moral philosophy strictly prohibiting the use of violence and other immoral means for the achievement of moral ends). In a well-known footnote from *The Conflict of the Faculties* (1798) Kant writes:

> This event [the Revolution] consists neither in momentous deeds nor misdeeds committed by men whereby what was great among men is made small or what was small is made great, nor in ancient splendid political structures which vanish as if by magic while others come forth in their place as if from the depths of the earth. No, nothing of the sort. It is simply the *mode of thinking of the spectators which reveals itself publicly* in this game of great transformations, and manifests such a general yet disinterested sympathy for the players on one side against those on the other...This mode of thinking demonstrates a *character of the human race at large and all at once*; owing to its disinterestedness, a moral character of humanity, at least in its predisposition, a character which not only permits people to hope for progress toward the better, but is already itself progress insofar as its capacity is sufficient for the present.[70]

In the hearts of such disinterested spectators one finds a "wishful participation that borders closely on enthusiasm"—a sympathy that, according to Kant, "can have no other cause than a moral predisposition of the human race."[71] Kant is making the counterintuitive claim that the *meaning or significance* of the Revolution is not to be found in the words or deeds of the actors in the drama. It is, rather, to be found in the spectators' judgment of the event—specifically, in the response "bordering on enthusiasm" which evidently attests to the presence of a moral predisposition in mankind.

This passage from Kant provides warrant for Arendt's assimilation of political judgment to his conception of taste judgment, deploying as it does many of the same notions—distance, disinterestedness, phenomenality—that serve to define that conception. Not only that. Its clear distinction between the involved standpoint of the actor and the disinterested standpoint of the spectator provides support for Beiner's contention that there are in fact two theories of judgment in Arendt, with the second or spectator-oriented theory taking pride of place. And, just as Kant suggests that the redemption of meaning from the "melancholy haphazardness" of worldly events is reserved for the spectator, so, Beiner argues, Arendt gives precedence to the contemplative standpoint of the judging historian or poet. It is *their* judgment, and not that of the actors in the drama, that determines the meaning of words, deeds, and events in the realm of human affairs. In support of this claim, he cites the following passage from Arendt's *Lectures*:

> We...are inclined to think that in order to judge a spectacle you must first have the spectacle—that the spectator is secondary to the actor; we tend to forget that no one in his right mind would ever put on a spectacle without being sure of have spectators to watch it. Kant is convinced that the world without man would be a desert, and a world without man means for him: without spectators.[72]

Now, the priority of the judging spectator certainly makes sense within Kant's framework, but does it in Arendt's? Does Arendt see a fundamental discontinuity between the judgment of the political actor and that of the "disinterested" or impartial spectator? I think the answer to this question must be no. Of course, there is a difference between the political judgment of an engaged actor and the retrospective judgment of the historian or poet. But stipulating a deep discontinuity between these two types of judgment and privileging the latter has the ironic effect of reading Arendt back into the very contemplative tradition she was trying to escape.

Judgment is the other side of action for Arendt and (I would argue) the two are never fully separate. A political actor like Pericles *performs* his words and deeds upon a public stage, in front of the Athenian assembly. He exercises *his* judgment and practical wisdom in offering his advice to the *demos*, and they in turn judge the merits of his speech. They are either persuaded by what he has to say or not. In the Athenian democracy, citizens are both actors and spectators: voting members of the assembly and judges of the persuasive speech and policies of leading actors such as Pericles. The actor always stands in need of an audience; otherwise, his words and deeds will fail to gain public ("objective") reality and their meaning will never be actualized, let alone remembered. The important point here, of course, is that the actor is not an author-fabricator who exerts full control over the meaning of his words and deeds. He speaks and acts, to be sure, but it is his judging audience that ultimately determines the meaning and status of his words and deeds. And, of course, there is no guarantee that his audience will *agree* about the meaning, persuasiveness, or status of his words. Does Pericles' Funeral Oration, for example, provide an accurate or persuasive account of the greatness of Athens? Has he fulfilled his duty to those who have fallen in action? The audience decides—judges—whether what they have heard is inspiring and visionary or overblown and rhetorical.

The same is true of that other audience to the "spectacle" of the Funeral Oration, the many readers of Thucydides' *History* since the Renaissance. While the speech long ago took its place as a canonical piece of political rhetoric, one that has inspired appreciators of Athenian culture as diverse as Hegel and Nietzsche, there is no set interpretation of its meaning or significance. Is the Funeral Oration, with its allusion to the monuments Athens has created attesting to the help it has given to its friends and the harm it has inflicted upon its enemies, edifying or terrifying? One's answer to this question will depend on one's attitude to two seemingly contradictory realities: Athens' democracy and Athens' empire. The more we focus on the democracy and the "way of life" Pericles praises, the more likely we are to find the Oration edifying. But the more we focus on the root of Athens' greatness and beauty—her empire and the riches it brings—the more likely we are to find it, if not exactly terrifying, at least deeply troubling.

It is not surprising, then, that modern-day readers of Thucydides are even less united in their judgment of Pericles' words and deeds than were his contemporaries. The point in the present context is that historical judgment does not stand on some Olympian height, self-contained and final. The moment it is rendered it immediately becomes part of a broader conflict of interpretations, an *agon* of competing viewpoints on the same words, deeds, and events. Not only does political action depend upon judgment from the very beginning: the very meaning it engenders is forever "in process," subject to debate, deliberation, and radical reinterpretation from a variety of standpoints.

Thus, while there certainly is a concrete difference between the actor and the spectator, it turns out that—for Arendt—the two are more deeply intertwined that the "two theories" theory can possibly allow. There is, in other words, a real continuity between action and judgment, actor and spectator. This continuity has a variety of iterations, and the meaning it produces is far less stable than the monumentality of Periclean discourse, or the "self-evidence" of the truths in the American Declaration of Independence, would lead us believe. Indeed, few of us today are likely to be persuaded of the "general validity" of Kant's judgment on the significance of the French Revolution. In hindsight, this judgment seems idiosyncratic, a function of Kant's desire to have it both ways. On the one hand, he wants to morally condemn the violence of the Revolution; on the other, he wants to convey the human importance of the morally edifying effect it had on his generation. Here, as elsewhere, judgment redeems meaning, but the meaning it redeems is not a package, delivered intact once and for all. The agonistic dimension of political action is mirrored in the agon of judgment and interpretation, an agon that plays out even in the realm of the "disinterested" spectator.

I'd like to suggest that Arendt's Kant lectures are best read not as propounding her "theory of judgment," but rather as supplementing the diverse set of reflections on judgment we find laid out in her earlier work. As we have seen, Arendt considers judgment in a number of different contexts. There is, first, the judgment of the engaged citizen or political actor that we encounter in THC and OR. Second, there is independent judgment (*Selbstdenken*) of the critical citizen or thinker we encounter in her essays on Socrates and Lessing. Third, there is the radicalized version of independent judgment exercised by conscientious individuals in "emergency situations where everyone else is swept away" in TMC. And fourth, there is the "disinterested" judgment exercised by the historian or poet who considers words, deeds, and events from the relative safety of geographical or temporal distance.

The citizen, the critic, the conscientious individual, and the poet or historian are all exemplars of the activity of judgment. While some features of judging as an activity are, in principle, common to them all, others clearly are not. Obviously, "thinking in the place of everyone else" is of little use in situations where "everyone else is carried away." And, while distance and disinterestedness are often crucial to putting things in perspective and judging them properly, they can also create an illusion of objectivity where the prejudices of the "judging spectator" are still quite active. (The contemplative prejudices of the philosopher, for example, find ample expression in

Kant's "disinterested" judgment of the French Revolution.) Finally, and perhaps most importantly, while all publicly made judgments can be said to implicitly or explicitly "woo the assent" of one's judging peers, successful persuasion or the achievement of consensus can hardly be held out as the standard of a judgment's validity.

The "banality of evil" is a case in point. Like many others in attendance, Arendt went to Eichmann's trial in Jerusalem expecting to come face to face with a true believer in Nazi ideology and Aryan supremacy. Instead, she found herself confronted by an extraordinarily ordinary individual, a man incapable of expressing himself except in clichés and bureaucratese. It was clear to her that Eichmann's reliance upon clichés and stock phrases went well beyond what she calls the "socially recognized function" of protecting us against the otherwise unrelenting claim on our thinking attention "that all events and facts make by virtue of their existence."[73] In the case of Eichmann, the protection from reality afforded by "conventional, standardized codes of expression" was so complete that he "clearly knew of no such claim at all." Thus insulated from the standpoint of the victims and the criminal nature of Nazi Jewish policy, he could go about his duties secure in the knowledge that his conscience would trouble him only if he failed to perform his duties with the requisite zeal and attention to detail.

Confronted by Eichmann in the flesh, Arendt knew that the preconceived categories she and others had brought to trial were inadequate. Eichmann's very ordinariness made her question whether ideology was as central to totalitarian regimes as she previously thought. Indeed, it even made her question whether there was such a thing as "radical evil." In a famous exchange of letters with Gershom Scholem in the journal *Encounter*, she defended the idea of the banality of evil, which Scholem had dismissed as a mere "catchword" compared to the more "profound" conception of radical evil found in OT. "You are quite right," Arendt writes,

> I changed my mind and no longer speak of 'radical evil'...It is indeed my opinion now that evil is never 'radical,' that it is only extreme, and that it possesses neither depth nor any demonic dimension. It can overgrow and lay waste the whole world precisely because it spreads like a fungus on the surface.[74]

The encounter with Eichmann was evidently so jarring that it compelled Arendt to rethink the nature of political evil.

In attempting to explain her concept of radical evil to Jaspers in her letter of March 4, 1951, Arendt had written

> the Western tradition is suffering from the preconception that the most evil things human beings can do arise from the vice of selfishness. Yet we know that the greatest evils or radical evil has nothing to do anymore with such humanly understandable, sinful motives.

The concept of "the banality of evil"—which Arendt describes as coming to her "willy-nilly" in the course of her encounter with Eichmann—actually extends this strand of thought. "The most evil things human beings can do" can, in fact, be performed in the absence of any "wicked" motivations whatsoever. Concepts such as sinfulness, selfishness, fanaticism, and hatred do little to illuminate the quality of Eichmann's evil and the thoughtlessness—the absence of reflection and lack of moral imagination—that lay at its root. This is not to say Eichmann was an unthinking bureaucratic automaton. Rather, it is to say that his case demonstrates how the problem of *evil as policy* in the twentieth and twenty-first centuries can scarcely be grasped in terms of the conceptual resources provided by our tradition.

The point with respect to how we should view Arendt's broader conception of judgment is this. Confronted by a manifestly shallow individual for whom the more obvious concepts (fanatical Nazi, vicious anti-Semite, sadistic SS man) seemed patently wrong, Arendt did not deductively subsume the particular under a ready-to-hand universal. Instead, she performed what Kant described as the characteristic operation of reflective judgment: she *ascended* from the concreteness of the particular—Eichmann in the flesh—to a *new* concept (the banality of evil). This operation obviously depended on insight, imagination, and intellectual mobility. EJ is the logical consequence of this judgment. It sets out the evidence and arguments Arendt thought might woo the assent of her readers and establish the "general validity" of her judgment. Many of Arendt's readers were and still are unpersuaded, albeit for reasons that often have little to do with the central arguments of the book. Yet the fact that her judgment was and is controversial hardly means that is idiosyncratic or unsupported by rational argument and historical evidence. Judgments are indeed made in anticipated communication with others, but their validity does not stand or fall with their actual success in *winning* universal assent. If it did, independent thought and judgment would have to give way to rhetorical appeals that cater to the established prejudices of the audience or reading public. Such appeals, after all, are far more likely to emerge victorious.

Summary

In this chapter we have seen how, thanks to her reportage at the Eichmann trial, *judgment* came to occupy a central place in Arendt's thinking. The fact that Eichmann "in the flesh" did not conform to any of the preconceptions Arendt and others had of an S.S. Lieutenant Colonel forced her to "ascend" from the particular (Eichmann) to a "universal" that she was the first to conceive and articulate: the "banality of evil." This exercise of what Kant termed "reflective" judgment led Arendt to address the relationship of *thinking* to moral and political judgment. With the "thoughtless" Eichmann in mind, she wondered in TMC whether our ability to judge, to tell right from wrong and beautiful from ugly, was dependent upon our faculty of thought. If this was in fact the case, then an inability to think and "a disastrous failure of what we commonly call conscience" might well coincide.

In TMC, Arendt looks for a "model thinker" to help her answer these questions. Her model, Socrates, is a "citizen among citizens" who uses dissolvent rationality to rid his interlocutors of their prejudices and preconceptions when it comes to giving accounts of justice, courage, and piety. While this critical use of reason questions regnant mores and creedal morality, it does not see its task as that of providing a new (positive) code of conduct. Rather, Arendt views Socrates as trying to wake his interlocutors up, to make them see the perplexities lurking in their understanding of the moral terminology they so routinely and thoughtlessly apply.

Thinking—the habit of reflection—takes the form of an inner dialogue I have with myself. Following a statement of Socrates in the *Gorgias*, Arendt suggests that the desire to maintain good relations with one's other self (or thinking partner) lies at the root of the development of a non-religious form of conscience. The fundamental idea is that thinking, by actualizing the two-in-one through the habit of reflection, creates conscience as its by-product. Moreover, the ability to judge particulars (this is beautiful, this is ugly, this is right, this is wrong) is itself a by-product of the liberating effect of thinking—the fact that thinking dissolves prejudices and preconceptions, preparing one for the active exercise of moral and aesthetic judgment.

Kant's conception of "judgments of taste" in the third *Critique* gave Arendt the tools to deepen and extend her thinking about judgment. Unlike his presentation of moral judgment (which, in the form of the Categorical Imperative, subsumed particular practical maxims under the form of universal rules), Kant's conception of taste judgment addressed particulars as particulars. This turn to Kant's aesthetic theory on the topic of judgment has perplexed many of Arendt's readers. However, it makes eminent sense if we view it in terms of her overall conception of judgment. Whether exercised by the engaged citizen, the man or woman of conscience navigating dark times, the immortalizing poet, or the temporally distanced historian, judgment must always be attuned to the particular—to specific actions, events, words, and deeds—if it is to make these phenomena meaningful rather than reduce them to fodder for our prejudices and our preconceived categories.

Notes

1 Hannah Arendt, *Lectures on Kant's Political Philosophy*, edited and with an Interpretive Essay by Ronald Beiner (Chicago: University of Chicago Press, 1982). Hereafter cited as LKPP.
2 Ronald Beiner, "Interpretive Essay" in Arendt, LKPP, pp. 91–92.
3 Arendt, LM, Vol. II, pp. 210–211.
4 Arendt treats this possibility quite skeptically in her chapter on Hegel in LM, II, pp. 39–51.
5 Sophocles, *Oedipus at Colunus*, line 1410.
6 Arendt, OR, p. 273.
7 Young-Bruehl, pp. 339–343.
8 Hannah Arendt, "Thinking and Moral Considerations" in Arendt, *Responsibility and Judgment*, edited by Jerome Kohn (New York: Schocken Books, 2003), p. 159. Hereafter cited as TMC.
9 Arendt, TMC, p. 159.

10 Immanuel Kant, *Critique of Judgment*, translated by James Creed Meredith (Oxford: Oxford University Press, 1911), p. 18.

11 Hannah Arendt, *Eichmann in Jerusalem: A Report on the Banality of Evil* (New York: Penguin Books, 2006), p. 276. Hereafter cited EJ.

12 Christopher Browning, *Ordinary Men* (New York: Harper, 1998).

13 Arendt, *EJ*, p. 26.

14 Arendt, *EJ*, p. 52.

15 Arendt, *EJ*, pp. 83–84.

16 Arendt, *EJ*, p. 126.

17 Arendt, *EJ*, p. 131.

18 Arendt, *EJ*, p. 136.

19 Arendt, *EJ*, p. 136.

20 Arendt, *EJ*, pp. 136–137.

21 Arendt, *EJ*, p. 148.

22 Arendt, *EJ*, p. 24.

23 Arendt, *EJ*, p. 148.

24 Arendt, *EJ*, p. 22.

25 Arendt, *EJ*, p. 25.

26 I say "plausible" because there is evidence that Eichmann was more genuinely anti-Semitic than Arendt acknowledges. See Bettina Stangneth, *Eichmann before Jerusalem* (New York: Knopf, 2014). What Arendt downplays Stangneth overplays—the truth most likely lies in the middle.

27 J.S. Mill, *On Liberty* (New York: Penguin Books, 1985), pp. 77–78.

28 Immanuel Kant, *Kant's Political Writings*, edited by Hans Reiss (New York: Cambridge University Press, 1970), p. 54.

29 Arendt, *LKPP*, pp. 32–33; Arendt, *MDT*, pp. 8–10.

30 Arendt, *TMC*, p. 188.

31 Arendt, "On Hannah Arendt" in Hill, ed., p. 314.

32 Arendt, *EJ*, 295, my emphasis.

33 Arendt, *TMC*, p. 160, my emphasis.

34 Arendt, *TMC*, p. 164.

35 Arendt, *TMC*, p. 174.

36 Arendt, *TMC*, p. 175.

37 Arendt, *TMC*, p. 177.

38 Arendt, *TMC*, pp. 177–178.

39 Arendt, *TMC*, p. 177.

40 Tocqueville, *Democracy in America*, vol. 2, Bk. 1, chapters 4–5.

41 Arendt, *TMC*, p. 178.

42 Friedrich Nietzsche, *Beyond Good and Evil*, translated by Walter Kaufmann (New York: Vintage Books, 1989), p. 110 (sec. 199).

43 Arendt, *Promise of Politics*, p. 21.

44 Arendt, *LM*, I, p. 188.

45 Arendt, *TMC*, p. 189.

46 Arendt, *TMC*, p. 189.

47 Arendt, *TMC*, p. 189.

48 Aristotle, *Nicomachean Ethics*, translated by Martin Ostwald (Indianapolis: Bobbs-Merrill Co., 1962), 1140a–b.

49 For Arendt's own discussion of *phronesis* see *LM*, II, pp. 59–62.

50 Immanuel Kant, *Groundwork of the Metaphysics of Morals*, translated by H. J. Paton (NewYork: Harper & Row, 1964), pp. 70–71.
51 Arendt, BPF, p. 219.
52 Kant, *PoliticalWritings*, pp. 85–86.
53 Kant, *PoliticalWritings*, p. 55; Arendt, LKPP, pp. 11–12.
54 Kant, *Critique of Judgment*, §39–40.
55 Arendt, BPF, p. 217.
56 Kant, *Critique of Judgment*, §22.
57 Arendt, LKPP, pp. 119–120.
58 Arendt, OR 221.
59 Albrecht Wellmer, "Hannah Arendt on Judgment: The Unwritten Doctrine of Reason" in Wellmer, *Endgames*, translated by David Midgley (Cambridge: MIT Press, 1998), pp. 300–301.
60 It's in this (anti-Platonic) regard that Arendt's focus on *plurality of opinions* can be said to share an underlying impulse with the otherwise quite distinct forms of pluralism advocated by Berlin and Rawls.
61 Arendt, BPF, pp. 217, 219–220.
62 Kant, *Critique of Judgment*, §40.
63 Arendt, BPF, 237.
64 Arendt, LM, II, p. 278.
65 Arendt, BPF, p. 51.
66 Arendt, BPF, p. 218.
67 Kant, *PoliticalWritings*, p. 88.
68 Kant, *PoliticalWritings*, p. 88.
69 Kant, *PoliticalWritings*, pp. 44–47.
70 Kant, quoted in Arendt, LKPP, p. 45 (my emphases).
71 Kant, quoted in Arendt, LKPP, p. 45.
72 Arendt, LKPP, pp. 61–62.
73 Arendt, TMC, p. 4. My emphasis.
74 Hannah Arendt, *The JewishWritings*, edited by Jerome Kohn and Ron H. Feldman (New York: Schocken Books, 2007), pp. 470–471.

Further reading

R. Beiner, "Interpretive Essay" in Hannah Arendt, *Lectures on Kant's Political Philosophy*, R. Beiner (ed.) (Chicago: University of Chicago Press, 1982), pp. 89–156.
M. Passerin d'Entrevcs, *The Political Philosophy of Hannah Arendt* (New York: Routledge, 1994).

Seven
Thinking and willing

I Thinking as a mental activity

Arendt commences the two volumes of *The Life of the Mind* by recalling her surprise upon discovering Eichmann's "manifest shallowness" at his trial in Jerusalem. Eichmann's thoughtlessness led her to wonder whether "the activity of thinking as such, the habit of examining whatever happens to come to pass or to attract attention…could… be among the conditions that make men abstain from evil-doing or even 'condition' them against it?"[1] This question, combined with Arendt's previous emphasis on how thinking dissolves prejudices and "liberates" the faculty of judgment, might lead one to expect that *Thinking* (the first volume of LM) will take the form of an extended appreciation of the moral and political role thinking plays— or can play—in the realm of human affairs. But in *Thinking* Arendt is not interested in what she previously termed "side effects." Her subject in the first volume is the activity of thinking as such, an activity we undertake only when we cease all doing and withdraw, however briefly, from the "world of appearances" in order to reflect, to engage in "soundless dialogue" with ourselves. She is interested, in other words, in thinking considered as a *mental activity*. The capacity for thought is a faculty we all possess and, together with the faculties of willing and judging, is constitutive of the "life of the mind."

Viewed in these terms, *The Life of the Mind* appears to be a kind of contemplative bookend to *The Human Condition*. THC confronted what Arendt called the "problem of Action" and the difficulties caused by the effacement of the distinction between it and the other activities comprising the *vita activa*. Arendt presented this effacement as born of the contemplative focus of both Greek philosophy and early Christian theology. This "onto-theological tradition" (to use Heidegger's phrase) turned its back on the realm of contingent events, actions, and appearances the better to behold (contemplate) a cosmic or divine order available only to intellectual intuition and the "eyes of the mind." Nevertheless, the first-time reader of LM might assume that Arendt has seen fit to forgive the Western philosophical-theological tradition its sins in this regard. She appears to be turning from political theory to philosophy proper, the better to perform a probing exploration of the *vita contemplativa* itself.

The problem with this assumption is that *contemplation*—as construed by Plato, Aristotle, and medieval theology—is not an *activity* but a *passivity*. One beholds "the Truth" only in complete stillness, when all other activity, mental as well as physical, has ceased. From the standpoint of this contemplative stillness, the different activities that compose the *vita activa* appear more alike than different, interchangeable examples of the "unquiet" that characterizes all worldly affairs and activities. The crucial point in the present context is that, for Plato and Aristotle, the *activity* of thinking served only to open the "eyes of the mind," thus preparing the philosopher for his vision of the true order of Being. Thinking was subsequently identified with the practice of meditation by medieval theology. Once again, it served as a propaedeutic for the receptive passivity of contemplation.[2] Anyone who, like Arendt, wants to consider the mental faculties of thinking, willing, and judging as *activities* will soon discover that the contemplative tradition obscures or denatures the constituent parts of the life of the mind almost as much as it had those of the *vita activa*.

The distortion introduced by the contemplative tradition into the consideration of our mental life is highlighted by a "curious sentence that Cicero ascribed to Cato" which Arendt uses in her conclusion to THC: "Never is he more active than when he does nothing, never is he less alone than when he is by himself."[3] Coming at the end of a book praising the *bios politikos*, this is indeed a "curious sentence." It focuses our attention on the inner dialogue that occurs when we think, on the *active* quality of the "soundless dialogue between me and myself." The commencement of this thinking dialogue is of course contingent upon the temporary cessation of our daily activities and behaviors. The phrase "stop and think" has a deeper significance than we are wont to attribute to it. But the relative immobility of the thinking individual who has "ceased all doing" hardly indicates the passive receptivity prized by the contemplative tradition. Rather, this immobility reflects our absorption in the activity of thinking itself. Hence, Arendt's question: "What are we 'doing' when we do nothing but think?"

To aid her in answering this question, Arendt finds herself turning once again to the model provided by Socrates, of whom it was once reported that he stood stock still for twenty-four hours, lost in thought. In that instance, the "winds of thought" (what Heidegger refers to as "the storm of thought") had descended upon Socrates in an unusually dramatic fashion, inducing a day-long paralysis in which he was totally absorbed by his own perplexities, questions, and trains of thought.

A hint of the intensity of Socrates' inner dialogue may be found in the relentlessness of his questioning in the dialogues he has with others. Arendt is not being rhetorical when, in the Kant lectures, she describes these dialogues as public demonstrations of the power of dissolvent or negative thinking. What Socrates does is to "make *public*, in discourse, the thinking process—the dialogue that soundlessly goes on within me, between me and myself; he *performed* in the marketplace the way the flute-player performed at a banquet. It is sheer performance, sheer activity."[4] Socrates "performs" thinking by repeatedly asking his interlocutors questions in the form of *what do you mean when you say*...? Such questions "infect" them with the perplexity Socrates himself feels when he reflects upon the meaning of concepts such as courage, piety, friendship, justice, and knowledge. These are all words whose meanings seem straightforward yet are anything but. His questioning works by "unfreezing" concepts that have become "frozen" through everyday use. The point of such questioning is not, or not simply, to alert his interlocutors to logical inconsistencies in the accounts or definitions they offer. It is, rather, to wake them up. From Socrates' perspective, the unexamined life is like the life of a sleepwalker.

Left at this, the Socratic answer to the question "what makes us think?" would seem to be our latent desire to be fully awake, to avoid "sleeping to the end of our days." But if thinking in the Socratic sense does not produce knowledge, nor provide us with usable practical wisdom, what beyond an enhanced sense our own being alive *does* it provide? What motivates Socrates to move the "soundless dialogue" of thinking out onto center stage?

Arendt's description in "Thinking and Moral Considerations" (TMC) of how the habit of reflection actualizes the two-in-one of consciousness, creating a "thinking partner" which ultimately develops into the voice of conscience, might lead one to conclude that—were it not for this morally significant "by-product"—the activity of thinking would take its place among other, different but perhaps equally worthwhile, activities we perform for their own sake. If we bracket the development of conscience and focus strictly on the *activity* of thinking, then it seems plausible to claim that Socratic thinking is a *complement* to life, but not that it is the *sine qua non* of a fully human or realized life. Other activities we perform for their own sake, such as playing a musical instrument or engaging in sport, could plausibly be said to provide a similar degree of life-enhancement and wakefulness. Arendt herself made the case for restoring dignity to the *bios politikos* precisely on the grounds that the performance of political action—the "sharing of words and deeds"—was crucial to leading a fully human life.[5]

Making sense of the Socratic answer to the question "what makes us think?" is facilitated, I think, if we first look at two alternative answers Arendt considers in LM. The first is Plato's and is found in a short passage from the *Theaetetus*. In the course of a discussion about the relativity of sense perceptions, Theaetetus admits he has been left "wondering" at various puzzles Socrates has reminded him of in the course of their conversation. Plato's Socrates responds by complimenting him on this wondering:

> For this is chiefly the passion (*pathos*) of the philosopher, to wonder (*thaumazein*). There is no other beginning and principle (*archē*) of philosophy than this one. And I think he [namely Hesiod] was not a bad genealogist when he made Iris [the Rainbow, the messenger of the gods] the daughter of Thaumas [the Wonderer].[6]

Arendt glosses this passage by telling us Plato is appropriating a word Homer often used to describe the wonder-struck beholding "usually reserved for men to whom a god appears." Such wonder is something suffered, not acted. It is a *pathos* in the literal sense.

In appropriating Homer's term, Plato is, in effect, asserting that philosophical thinking begins in admiring wonder, rather than per-plexity or puzzlement.[7] What is the object of this admiring won-der? Not the beauty of worldly appearances nor the glory of human words and deeds, as it was for Homer and other "pre-philosophic" Greeks. It was, rather, the harmonious order found behind "the sum total of things in the world." These "things," constituting the to-tality of the world available to our senses, conceal this order while simultaneously giving us hints of its existence. As the pre-Socratic philosopher Anaxagoras put it, "For the appearances are a glimpse of the non-revealed."[8] Thus, philosophy begins "with an awareness of this invisible harmonious order of the *kosmos*, which is manifest in the midst of the familiar visibilities as though these had become transparent."[9] The order of nature—*physis*—constitutes a non-visible harmony, one that is, in the words of Heraclitus, "better than the visible."

Arendt relies here upon the testimony of the pre-Socratics be-cause, as she admits, "Plato himself does not specify what his ad-miring wonder is directed at" (even though the *Republic's* cave parable gives us a pretty good idea). Be that as it may, it is clear the admiring wonder that strikes the philosopher concerns no particular thing or entity in the world but is rather "aroused by the whole, which, in contrast to the sum total of entities, is never manifest."[10] Since Parmenides, the name philosophers have given this "invisible im-perceptible whole implicitly manifest in all that appears" has been Being. "Wonder at Being" is the root of philosophy and the answer Plato gives to the question "what makes us think?" The philosopher is someone who not only experiences but *endures* the pathos of won-der. He is, so to speak, an "expert in wondering."[11]

In the course of the Christian era, such "admiring wonder" comes to be restricted to the glory of God and his works. With the rise of rationalist philosophy in the seventeenth century, this change led to wonder being directed not at "the whole" but rather at the fact that there was something rather than nothing. This question, first asked by Leibniz, was "solved" by means of the "God of the philosophers," the logically necessary first cause of nature and all its laws. From Leibniz, Arendt traces a philosophic trajectory that progressively strips Plato's answer to the question of "what makes us think?" of the qualities of admiration and affirmation it originally possessed. With the "death of God" in the nineteenth century, Leibniz's question—"why is there something rather than nothing?"—is revealed to lack any positive answer whatever.

Instead of Being, nothingness now comes to the fore. Wonder at Being gives way to puzzlement over the apparently contingent fact of existence, a puzzlement clearly present in Heidegger's rephrasing of Leibniz's question as "why is there *anything at all* rather than nothing?" The late Heidegger's linking of thinking to thanking—of *denken* to *danken*—can be seen as an attempt to recapture some trace of Platonic wonder.[12] However, Sartrean nausea at the opaqueness of sheer existence—at the "naked thereness of the factually given" that "no thought has ever succeeded in reaching"—provides a more fitting conclusion to the Platonic metaphysical arc.[13] Thinking is no longer the path to true Being as it was for Parmenides and Plato. Instead, the possibility of reconciling thought with reality evaporates in the face of the "meaningless thereness" of entities in the world. Affirmation, confirmation, and admiration of reality give way to profound alienation from it.

From "Plato's answer and its echoes" Arendt turns to the "Roman answer" to the question of what makes us think. This is the answer of the Stoics. It is not wonder at Being but rather the desire to escape the harshness of a worldly reality that has lost its luster. The Stoic answer builds on the fact that the activity of thinking always involves an at least momentary withdrawal from the world, a withdrawal during which we make present what is absent by means of memory and our faculty of representation. We re-present an absent reality to ourselves, the better to reflect upon it. For the Stoics, and for Epictetus in particular, the emphasis in thinking's ability to present what is absent "shifts from reflection to imagination." The goal of thinking is no longer to distance ourselves from our everyday involvements, the better to create a "thinking space" in which we can reflect upon some phenomenon, concept, or event. It is, rather, to employ our imaginations in order to make reality disappear altogether. As Arendt puts it, "if thinking is normally the faculty of making present what is absent, the Epictetian faculty of 'dealing with impressions aright' consists in conjuring away and making absent what actually is present."[14]

For Epictetus, "dealing with impressions aright" meant using our imagination to focus on our perceptions (or "impressions") of things rather than on the things themselves. I focus on the act of seeing rather than upon the object seen, with the result that the original object "loses its impact upon me." Arendt illustrates this by means of the familiar phenomenological distinction between the (real, objective) tree which exists outside of me and the "seen tree" I experience as conscious perception. By focusing on the "seen tree," I deprive the external tree of its realness, creating an alternative (phenomenological) reality comprised of the perceptual contents of my consciousness. Thus, the "trick discovered by Stoic philosophy" is to deploy the mind in a such a manner that "reality cannot touch its owner *even when he has not withdrawn from it*."[15] To take only the most notorious example: I may be roasting inside the "brazen bull" of the tyrant Phalaris, but as long as I realize that the painful sensations I feel are contents of my consciousness and that *this* and nothing else constitutes their reality, I am able to rise above the external reality of my torture.

It is doubtful whether any Stoic actually believed one could be happy inside the Phalaric bull, but the general point is clear: thinking does indeed have the capacity to make things seem unreal. Not only can I perform the "trick" of Epictetus and bracket external reality. I can also, following Cicero's suggestion in the "Scipio's Dream" section of his *Republic*, bracket my own situated standpoint and imaginatively take up one that is outside not just the immediate "world of appearances" but also my life and even history. The further out in space and time one projects this imaginary standpoint, the more trivial worldly events, fame, fortune, and misfortune seem. For a Stoic like Cicero, philosophical thinking provides the successful man of the world who has unexpectedly been brought low with the consolation that "in relation to the universe, the earth is but a dot" and "in relation to the immensity of time, centuries are but moments."[16] From a perspective so distant from the present it hardly matters what men do.

The Platonic and Stoic answers to the question "what makes us think?" could hardly appear more different. One emphasizes wonder at Being and is characterized by an affirmative response to reality (albeit one outside the "cave" of appearances), while the other emphasizes the human desire to escape reality by means of a retreat to the "inner citadel" of consciousness. Yet different though they may be—one admiring and idealistic, the other negative and emphatically practical—they are, at a deeper level, linked. Each is an example of the "alienation from the world" Arendt had analyzed at length in THC. In that volume, she had focused on the roots of modern world alienation in the new science and the rise of capitalism. In LM the focus shifts to philosophical antecedents in the classical world, with an emphasis upon the way the *activity of thinking as such* has a way of taking us "out of the world," either to that *other* (intelligible) world behind the veil of the visible one, or to the shelter of an alternate reality imagined by consciousness. Even though the Platonic answer begins in *admiring* wonder, there is never any suggestion that the everyday reality we share with our peers—the "realm of appearances" constituted by human plurality and diverse perspectives—is itself worthy of admiration or confirmation. All of this is in sharpest contrast to pre-philosophical Greek thought, which assumed that it was the realm of appearances as such—the world of "great words and deeds" performed by heroic actors—that provoked a thinking yet poetic response of admiration, affirmation, and confirmation.

The possibility that the world alienation expressed in these classical examples might be lessened as we move into the modern age is dashed by Descartes' response to the discoveries of the new science founded by Galileo and Copernicus. According to Arendt, what Cartesian doubt shows is that "it is precisely the thinking activity—the experiences of the thinking ego—that gives rise to doubt of the world's reality and my own."[17] The complete bracketing of the world given by our senses logically entailed doubt as to our own bodily reality. The inescapable conclusion seemed to be that the only thing the thinking ego could be sure of—the only thing that could plausibly provide a firm ground for knowledge—was its own thinking experience.

In Arendt's telling, this inward turn, compelled by destruction of the illusion that truth revealed itself, gave rise to a wide array of philosophical subjectivisms ranging from Descartes' *res cogitans* and Berkeley's phenomenalism to Husserl's transcendental ego and Heidegger's analytic of *Dasein*. All these approaches gave pride of place to what is, in effect, a reality-constituting ego.[18] Arendt's focus on how philosophy invariably winds up radicalizing the thinking ego's withdrawal from the world prompts George Kateb to describe LM as the locus classicus of "Arendt's war on philosophical thinking."[19] By consistently privileging of the solitary experience of the thinking ego, Western philosophical thought reveals its hostility not just to the effects but to the *fact* of human plurality. This privileging leads to a radical devaluation of the intersubjectively constituted world, the reality of which is confirmed by means of our shared "common sense." The predictable fruit of such thoroughgoing devaluation is either some version of a "two worlds" theory (in which the real, true, or noumenal world is posited as lurking behind the appearances of the phenomenal one) or some form of epistemological cum ontological subjectivism.

Does Socrates' answer to the question "what makes us think?" avoid Arendt's indictment of *philosophical* thinking? For the most part, yes, but it should first be noted that in LM, Arendt fails to give us a completely integrated account of his answer. Her *point de départ* is the perplexity Socrates experienced and which he attempted to share with others. Plato's answer to the question of "what makes us think?"—wonder at Being—was clearly inspired by those moments where Socrates, completely motionless and absorbed in his own thoughts, appeared overcome by speechless wonder.[20] Yet, as I noted earlier, what appeared to Plato as the paradigm of contemplative stillness was, in fact, an example of what happened when the "storm of thought"—the pathos of enduring perplexity—overtook the "purest thinker of the West."

Socrates' paralysis masked an intense inner dialogue, one provoked not by stunned wonder at Being but by questions generated by both concepts and practices. Our misplaced confidence that we can provide complete and definitive accounts about what courage, piety, justice, and virtue *mean* flows from our everyday use of, and familiarity with, such words. But when these concepts are "unfrozen" by means of questioning and cross-examination, the solidity of our accounts dissolves and we find ourselves left with nothing but perplexities. It is crucial to see that such perplexities mirror Socrates' own. "Socrates taught nothing; he never knew the answers to the questions he asked...Had he known what courage, justice, piety, etc. were, he would no longer have had the urge to exam- ine them, i.e., to think about them."[21] For Arendt, the sincerity of Socrates' professions of ignorance is manifest in the aporetic nature of the dialogues themselves. If she is right in claiming that the di- alogues reveal Socrates *performing* the activity of thinking in public, then Plato's identification of Socratic paralysis with stunned wonder appears to be simply wrong. To invoke Cato once again, "never is he [Socrates] more active than when he does nothing, never is he less alone than when he is by himself."

In the *Theaetetus*, Plato's Socrates describes thinking as "a discourse that the mind carries on with itself about any subject it is consid- ering...when the mind is thinking it is simply talking to itself, ask- ing questions and answering them," while in the *Sophist*, the Eleatic Stranger describes thinking as "the inward dialogue carried on by the mind with itself."[22] These are the descriptions upon which Arendt bases her own characterization of thinking as the "soundless dia- logue between me and myself." The point here is that while *contem- plation* aims at complete stillness and self-containedness—at an *escape* from both worldly distractions and the fact of human plurality— *thinking* delivers the individual over completely to his or her *inner* plurality. "Nothing perhaps indicates more strongly that man exists *essentially* in the plural," Arendt writes,

> than that his solitude actualizes his merely being conscious of himself...into a duality during the thinking activity. It is this *du- ality* of myself with myself that makes thinking a true activity, in which I am both the one who asks and the one who answers.[23]

The significance of Socrates, then, is that he discovered this "two- in-one" as the "essence of thought."[24] By revealing just how much the activity of thought rests upon our inner plurality, Socrates also reveals how it is possible for this solitary activity to become at least partly externalized in its public performance with others. "Discourse" and "plurality" are the bridges that connect the inner dialogue of thought with the aporetic dialogues performed in the marketplace. And, like the dialogues Socrates performs in public, our thinking dialogue with ourselves addresses not just such big un- answerable questions as "what is the meaning of existence?" but a broad range of perplexities that appear the moment we liberate ourselves from the prejudices and false certainties contained in everyday discourse. If it is true that LM "wages war" on philosophical thinking because of its propensity to reify the experience of the thinking ego—a reification that produces "metaphysical fallacies" such as the "two worlds" theory and various forms of subjectivisim—then it is tempting to make a distinction between such thinking and Socratic or "ordinary" thinking. This second type of thinking is provoked not by shocked wonder at Being but by an episodic yet deep perplexity about the meaning and logic of basic moral concepts and practices.

To dub the latter type of thinking "ordinary" is, perhaps, a disservice to the hardly ordinary Socrates. Nevertheless, making this distinction helps us to see the enormous difference between a form of thinking that aims at discovering the ultimate nature of reality and a form of reflection stimulated by perplexities of a decidedly less cosmic or totalizing sort. We have seen how, in TMC, Arendt deploys the Socratic paradigm in order to establish the relationship between such ordinary thinking or reflection and the development of conscience. We've also seen why Arendt expresses strong skepticism about the presumed advantages of creedal belief and the avoidance of reflection. It is clear, then, that the notion of an "ordinary" form of thinking—one that follows the basic Socratic model of "thinking things through"—plays a central role in *Arendt's* thinking about morals and politics.[25] Yet, when it comes to articulating the fundamental difference between the Platonic and Socratic answers to the question of *what* makes us think, this distinction between two broad types of thinking gets us only so far. Its utility is limited because it suggests that the Socratic answer to the question is guided by the *moral* imperative of avoiding injustice.

There is indeed a link between Socrates' moral integrity and his intellectual integrity.[26] However, giving pride of place to the former inevitably results in the instrumentalization of the latter. Thinking becomes an auxiliary to, rather than the root of, Socratic or "secular" conscience. And that is pretty much the opposite of the relationship Arendt has in mind when, in both TMC and LM, she describes how the activity of thinking gives rise to the "two-in-one," to an inner plurality which is capable of generating conscience as its "by-product."

If the desire to avoid injustice is *not* the Socratic answer to the question "what makes us think?" then what is? Answering this question returns us to Socrates' assertion in the *Apology* (38a) that an unexamined life is not worth living. Why is it not worth living? Because without self-reflection, we risk becoming accomplices to, or even perpetrators of, evil, like Eichmann? Or because without reflection, we fail to develop our full potential and thus fail to perfect ourselves or our souls? The answer is neither. An unexamined life would not be worth living for Arendt's Socrates because "a life deprived of thought would be meaningless, even though thought will never make men wise or give them answers to thought's own questions."[27]

For Arendt, the meaning of Socratic thinking "lay in the activity itself" and not in any presumed end product. Socrates "did the examining for examining's sake, not for the sake of knowledge." His uniqueness lies in "this concentration on thinking itself, regardless of results." There is "no ulterior motive or ulterior purpose for the whole enterprise. An unexamined life is not worth living. That's all there is to it."[28] Thinking "accompanies life and *is itself the de-materialized quintessence of being alive.*"[29] It focuses on concepts such as justice, happiness, courage, and virtue because we rely upon these concepts to articulate "the meaning of whatever happens in life and occurs to us while we are alive."[30] "To think and to be fully alive are the same" because thinking engages us most directly in the destruction, creation, and perpetual re-articulation of conceptual meaning. "Thinking must always begin afresh" because otherwise the concepts we work over in the thinking process become frozen once again. They lapse back into preconceived categories, categories we exchange thoughtlessly, like so many worn-out coins.

Thinking, then, is not concerned with discovering truth or realizing man's nature as a "rational animal." It is an activity driven by the human quest for meaning, a quest prompted by the ultimate unanswerableness of the questions Socrates poses to his interlocutors and that reason is apt to pose to itself. The philosophical life as led by Socrates is thus a life driven by love of a wisdom that is forever beyond its grasp. Not only does it know what it does not know; it also has a pretty good idea of what *cannot* be known and expresses gratitude for this limitation. For if we *could* know the nature of beauty, justice, virtue, etc., there would no longer be any need to think about them. The quest for meaning would resolve itself into a series of set questions and "correct" answers, somewhat along the lines of Aquinas' *Summa Theologica*.

The restless and erotic character of Socratic thinking is thus fundamentally at odds with the stillness prized by the contemplative tradition, a stillness that supposedly leads to communion with the truth of Being, God, or Nature. Arendt's Socrates, like her Lessing, is a figure who is entirely glad that he *doesn't* possess the Truth.[31] It is precisely this *lack* that gives both Socrates and thinking itself its erotic character, and that insures "the unending discourse among men will never cease so long as there are men at all."[32] When Socrates tells his jury that he is untroubled by the thought of death because death is either annihilation or a passage "to some other place" where it becomes possible for him to question and cross-examine long-dead figures like Orpheus and Homer, he expresses a love of the sheer *activity* of thinking that is rare in the Western tradition.[33] What matters are not the supposed results of philosophical inquiry (which philosophers from Plato through Hegel have identified as metaphysical truths revealed by reason), but the active and the open-ended nature of the questioning itself. Not for nothing did Heidegger dub Socrates, the philosopher who never wrote anything, the "purest thinker of the West."

The negative or destructive quality of Socratic thinking suggests a link to Kant, whom Moses Mendelssohn called the *Alles-Zermalmer* (the "all-destroyer") because he demonstrated the impossibility of valid knowledge concerning the "ultimate" questions pursued by metaphysics. Arendt pursues this link in her Kant lectures. The most obvious similarity is the critical character of both Socratic and Kantian thinking. Socrates' "midwifery" in Athens consisted in "emptying his partners of all unfounded beliefs and 'wind eggs'—the mere fantasies that filled their minds."[34] Similarly, Kant identified his own program, as well as that of the Enlightenment more generally, with the destruction of dogma and prejudice, whether of a religious or rationalist variety. The plea he offers in "What is Enlightenment?" for the uncensored (public) use of one's reason is a direct descendent of Socrates' ultimately ill-fated dialogical practice. However, there is a distinct difference between the presuppositions and aims of the two critical projects. Whereas Socrates knew what he did not know and *seemed* to have a good idea of what cannot be known, the project of Kant's Critique of Pure Reason is to establish, once and for all, the demonstrable limits to human reason and knowledge.

Kant begins the first Critique by stating

> human reason has this peculiar fate that in one species of its knowledge it is burdened by questions which, as prescribed by the very nature of reason itself, it is not able to ignore, but which, as transcending all its power, it is also not able to answer.[35]

Arendt glosses this statement as "our mind is not capable of certain and verifiable knowledge regarding matters and questions that it can help thinking about."[36] For Kant, the questions human reason was thus "burdened" by were questions concerning the existence of God, the freedom (or unfreedom) of the will, and the immortality of the soul. Steering a middle course between overly optimistic rationalist claims regarding the extent of our "a priori" or purely rational knowledge and the deflationary skepticism born of Hume's empiricism, Kant saw the Critique as a "tribunal" charged with answering the question "what and how much can the understanding and reason know apart from all experience?"[37]

Divorced from all experience, *reason* can deliver only analytic judgments (judgments in which the predicate is definitionally part of the subject) of the type found in such completely formal sciences as logic and geometry. However, divorced from experience, the *understanding* can deliver what Kant calls synthetic a priori judgments (judgments in which the predicate is *not* contained definitionally in the subject). An example of that latter type of judgment is "all events have a cause." Kant suggests that our faculty of understanding is able to deliver such a priori knowledge of the way the world is because the human mind operates with such "built-in" categories as substance, causality, unity, and totality. Along with what Kant calls the "forms of intuition," space and time, these categories bring order to the otherwise chaotic "manifold" delivered by our sense impressions (or "representations"). If we focus on the "conditions of possibility" required for objective knowledge of the phenomenal world, Kant claims, we are compelled to assume that the categories and forms of intuition are inherent features of the mind's cognitive equipment. Otherwise, we couldn't possibly have the coherent and sequential experience of the world that we do, let alone the verifiable knowledge provided by sciences like Newtonian physics.

As for direct knowledge of things *beyond* our experience of the phenomenal world, neither the formal constructions of the human mind (the products of pure reason) nor the categories bringing order and unity to the "manifold" of sense impressions (the "operating system," so to speak, of the understanding) are capable of providing it. The answer to the questions as to whether God truly existed, our will was really free, and our souls actually immortal remained forever beyond our grasp—as did all knowledge of the "things in themselves" we assume to exist behind the appearances given us in our sense-based experience of the phenomenal world. Pure reason's attempts to grasp an ultimate reality beyond experience (thereby providing *answers* to the questions concerning God, freedom, and immortality) delivered nothing but the epistemologically unfounded "gropings" of scholastic-rationalist metaphysics. Such at least was the verdict of Kant's "tribunal" in the first *Critique*.

The execution of Kant's critical project hinges upon the distinction he makes between reason (*Vernunft*) and understanding (*Verstand*). The former refers to our faculty for systematic thought and logical inference, while the latter refers to the cognitive categories that organize our representations into coherent (knowable) experience. Both faculties are spontaneous and "a priori" in the sense that neither is determined by experience. Reason operates independently of experience (hence its proclivity to overestimate its own powers), while understanding makes our objective experience of the phenomenal world possible, thanks to the cognitive structuring provided by its categories.

In the "Introduction" to LM Arendt tells us that Kant's distinction will be crucial to her investigation of thinking as an activity, as well as to her attempt to answer the question "what makes us think?" However, while accepting the standard translation of *Vernunft* as "reason," she translates *Verstand* as "intellect." This is unorthodox, but it makes a certain amount of sense given Arendt's use of the word "understanding" in previous books and essays. In these earlier writings, "understanding" consistently denotes the effort to *comprehend and interpret* an event or phenomenon. In LM Arendt informs us that the distinction between reason and intellect coincides with "a distinction between two altogether different mental activities, thinking and knowing, and two altogether different concerns, meaning, in the first category, and cognition, in the second."[38] This claim is even more unorthodox than her translation, and it requires a bit of explaining.

Arendt cites a remark Kant once made in a discussion about Plato: "It is by no means unusual, upon comparing the thoughts which an author has expressed in regard to his subject…to find that we understand him better than he has understood himself."[39] Taking this as her cue, she suggests that when Kant stated (in the preface to the *Critique*) that he had "found it necessary to deny knowledge, in order to make room for faith" he actually misconstrued the nature and significance of his accomplishment.[40] True, he had placed the "ultimate" questions of God, freedom, and immortality beyond the reach of the cognitive powers of both reason and the understanding. But he also acknowledged our ineliminable (practical and existential) interest in these questions, pointing out how it is part of reason's make-up to be drawn to them. From Arendt's perspective, then, Kant had not really denied knowledge in order to make room for faith. Rather, what he really did was to separate *knowledge* from *thinking*, i.e. from reason understood as reflection. It turns out that

> the great obstacle that reason (*Vernunft*) puts in its own way arises from the side of intellect (*Verstand*) and the entirely justified criteria it has established for its own purposes, that is, for quenching our thirst, and meeting our need, for knowledge and cognition.[41]

Arendt here anticipates a theme that runs throughout *Thinking*, namely, that Western philosophy repeatedly and mistakenly subjects the reflective activity of reason to criteria that are more appropriate to the cognitive search for knowledge. Indeed, she goes so far as to state that the "reason why neither Kant nor his successors ever paid much attention to thinking as an activity" is that "they were demanding the kind of results and applying the kind of criteria for certainty and evidence that are the results and the criteria of cognition."[42] However, if it is true that "thinking and reason are justified in transcending the limitations of cognition and the intellect"—and Arendt thinks that Kant's first *Critique* justifies such transcendence when it comes to the unanswerable questions of God, freedom, and immorality—then "the assumption must be that thinking and reason are not concerned with what the intellect is concerned with." This is the case no matter how often philosophy misconstrues itself as a "science" devoted to providing rationally demonstrable answers to such patently unanswerable questions. What Kant called "the need of reason" is thus "not inspired by the quest for truth, but by the quest for *meaning*." And, as Arendt insists against the accumulated weight of the Western onto-theological tradition, "*truth and meaning are not the same.*"[43]

If we combine Arendt's interpretation of Kant's "need of reason" with her account of the Socratic answer to the question "what makes us think?" we are in a better position to appreciate her alignment with the most famous "dismantlers" of metaphysics, Nietzsche and Heidegger. However, unlike Nietzsche's "philosophizing with a hammer" or Heidegger's "destruction" (*Abbau*) of the onto-theological tradition, Arendt's project in LM is not primarily negative, not even with regard to that most dubious of sciences, metaphysics.[44] On the one hand, the main fallacies of the Western philosophical tradition—that idea there is a "true world" behind appearances; that Being has the character of constant or unchanging presence; that meaning should be interpreted on the model of truth—had to be exposed. On the other, one can't simply sweep the rubble of this tradition aside, if only because traditional concepts and categories continue to have such a profound and distorting impact on our views of the *vita activa* and life of the mind. The impact of this distortion notwithstanding, it turns out that it is the "professional thinkers" themselves—the metaphysical system builders from Plato to Hegel—who have provided us with our most important "clues" to the nature of thinking as an activity. As Arendt puts it:

> None of the systems, none of the doctrines transmitted to us by the great thinkers may be convincing or even plausible to modern readers; but none of them...is arbitrary and none can be simply dismissed as sheer nonsense. On the contrary, the metaphysical fallacies contain the only clues we have to what thinking means to those who engage in it—something of great importance today and about which, oddly enough, there exist few direct utterances.[45]

This is not—or not just—a case of flawed testimony being better than none. Rather, in LM, Arendt repeatedly draws our attention to how characteristic features of thinking as an activity are given powerful albeit distorted expression by canonical philosophers. Thus, the "two worlds" theory—whether in its Platonic, Christian, or Kantian form—testifies not just to thinking's necessary *withdrawal* from everyday activities and the world of appearances, but also to its focus upon "invisibles." The latter are "essences" created through the "de-sensing" operations our faculties of memory and representation perform upon concrete worldly phenomena.[46] Thinking is thus an invisible activity that deals with invisibles, with thought things (concepts) that are clearly different in nature from the phenomenal particulars we encounter in the world. This, so to speak, is the "truth" of Platonism and all subsequent idealisms. Indeed, it is the very invisibility of thought and its objects that leads us to posit the distinction between essence and existence, a distinction whose reification provides the ground for all "two-world" metaphysical doctrines.

The interpretation of Being as "constant presence" by Parmenides and Plato—hegemonic, as Heidegger pointed out, for the entire Western tradition[47]—is likewise based upon the reification of a phenomenon first encountered in the activity of thinking. This is the thinking ego's feeling of being removed not just from the surrounding world of appearances, but from all worldly and existential temporality as well. Medieval philosophers tried to capture the experience of the atemporality of thought by means of the notion of the "standing now" (*nunc stans*). The point in the present context is that the thinking ego's sensation of being removed from both the world and time is phenomenologically grounded in the activity of thinking itself. Arendt underscores the seemingly isolated character of the "now" of thinking by citing a remark made by the poet and critic Paul Valéry: *tantôt je pense et tantôt je suis* ("sometimes I think and sometimes I am"). Valéry's remark echoes, to a degree, the Cartesian ego's doubts about external reality even as it undercuts the logic of the *cogito*. A disjunction ("and sometimes") is substituted for a deduction (*ergo sum*). The overall effect, however, is to focus our attention even more intently upon the apparently situationless character of thinking as an activity. Thinking seems to be not just "worldless" but *homeless* as well. For the greater part of the tradition, this very home-lessness has been singled out as one of the primary advantages of the philosophical life. Describing the superiority of the *bios theoretikos* in the *Protrepticus*, Aristotle observes that this is a way of life that needs "neither implements nor special places for [its] trade; wherever on earth somebody devotes himself to thinking, he will attain the truth everywhere as though it were present."[48]

If, then, instead of asking "*what* makes us think?" we were to ask, "*where* are we when we think?" the answer would seem to be *every-where*. Thinking, unlike acting, is an activity that is tied to no par-ticular city or country (a fact of some importance to Aristotle, who, bearing the fate of Socrates in mind, chose to flee Athens in 322 BCE rather "allow the Athenians to sin twice against philosophy"). It is an activity whose "objects" are not entities in the world but rather the de-sensed "thought things" (concepts, representations, memories) that can be summoned "from any distance in time or space" into the thinking ego's presence "with a velocity greater than light's."[49] How-ever, looked at from the perspective of the world of appearances that it has left behind, this "everywhere" of the thinking ego seems more like a *nowhere*. That would make the question "where are we when we think?" a non sequitur—unless, of course, we opt once again for a "two worlds" theory in which mind had the capacity to inhabit an intelligible realm that lies somewhere beyond the sensible one.[50]

Great anti-Platonist that she was, we can hardly expect *Arendt* to employ such a strategy in order to answer the question of "where are we when we think?" Yet Arendt never abandons her conviction that every human activity, the activity of thinking included, has its proper location. So what is the site of this most solitary and un-worldly of human activities, thinking?

Answering this query becomes easier once we realize that we are taking the spatial metaphor a bit too literally. We make a mistake if we think the "where" in the question "where are we when we think?" refers to a place on the map or to a realm that our minds can inhabit, but not our bodies. Thinking as a mental activity is not spatially fixed, but neither is it "everywhere" or "nowhere." It has a *location*, but this location is *temporal*, not spatial. The answer to the question "where are we when we think?" is in the "gap" between past and future.

In the "Preface" to the essays collected in *Between Past and Future* (1968), Arendt cites a short parable by Franz Kafka, titled simply "He":

> He has two antagonists: the first presses him from behind, from the origin. The second blocks the road ahead. He gives battle to both. To be sure, the first supports him in his fight with the second, for he wants to push him forward, and in the same way the second supports him in his fight with the first, since he drives him back. But it is only theoretically so. For it is not only the two antagonists who are there, but he himself as well, and who really knows his intentions? His dream, though, is that some time in an unguarded moment—and this would require a night darker than any night has ever been yet—he will jump out of the fighting line and be promoted, on account of his experience in fighting, to the position of umpire over his antagonists in their fight with each other.[51]

In LM Arendt returns to "Kafka's time parable" in the hope "of finding out where the thinking ego is located in time and whether its relentless activity can be temporally determined."[52] In her interpretation, the parable is a description of the "time sensation of the thinking ego." This is not a sensation we experience in everyday life, where our daily business establishes a continuity between the projects we started yesterday and the things we hope to finish tomorrow.[53] Rather, it is a sensation we experience in reflection, but only in those moments "when we are not entirely absorbed by the absent non-visibles we are thinking about but begin to direct our attention onto the activity itself"—that is, when we find ourselves reflecting upon our own thinking process.[54]

For the reflecting ego, "past and future are equally present because they are equally absent from our sense." The past is absent in the sense that it seems to "lie behind us," while the future is something that seems to "approach from ahead."[55] The existence of these two absences is testified to by the "nowness" of the present moment of thought. From the standpoint of the contemplative tradition, this "now" appears as one of total stillness and quiet. But, as Kafka's parable helps us to see, it is actually the site of a battle "where the forces of past and future clash with each other." Inserted into the temporal flow, the sheer presence of "He" (man) breaks up the time continuum into the tenses of past, present, and future, while his finitude transforms the no-longer of the past and the not-yet of the future into antagonists—of each other and of himself.[56] The insertion of man thus "produces a rupture," a battleground which, "by being defended in both directions," establishes the present as a kind of island or in-between assaulted from both sides. This temporal in-between—the present as battleground—is Kafka's metaphor "for man's home on earth."[57] Man

> lives in this in-between, and what he calls the present is a life-long fight against the dead weight of the past, driving him forward with hope, and the fear of a future (whose only certainty is death), driving him backward toward 'the quiet of the past' with nostalgia for and remembrance of the only reality he can be sure of.[58]

The "time sensation" of the thinking ego—the present—is thus an in-between or gap that opens "only in reflection, whose subject matter is what is absent—either what has already disappeared or what has not yet appeared."[59] Reflection "draws these absent 'regions' into the mind's presence" and, seen from this angle, the activity of thinking "can be understood as a fight against time itself."[60] In other words, it is only in reflection that the past and future appear as distinct entities, pressing the thinking ego forward from behind and driving him back from ahead. So situated, the thinking ego confronts its antagonists as relentless destroyers of the small gap of "non-time" it has created through the activity of reflection. It is this temporal "space"—the "standing now" of the present—that reflection establishes and defends as its own.

Given the constant struggle necessary to preserve a small space of non-time against the ceaseless pressure of past and future, what could be more natural than for the thinking ego than to imagine itself "jumping out of the fighting line" and being "promoted...to the position of umpire over the fight of his antagonists with each other"? What is this, Arendt asks rhetorically, other than the "old dream of Western metaphysics"? The dream of philosophers from Parmenides to Hegel of a timeless region, of an "eternal presence" lying "beyond human clocks and calendars altogether," the region, precisely, of thought?[61] And what is the traditional desire of the philosopher to view things *sub specie aeternitatis* other than an expression of the Pythagorean conviction that "the best" are not those who participate in the competition for fame, glory, and honors but rather those who come as "disinterested spectators" in order to judge the spectacle itself?

In passages like these, in which she links the besieged present of the thinking ego to what Heidegger called the "metaphysics of presence" underlying the Western tradition as a whole, it might appear that Arendt is extending her "war on philosophical thinking" to the activity of thinking as such. This impression is mistaken. Like Heidegger and Nietzsche, she thinks the metaphysical pretension to a standpoint beyond time and chance is the height of bad faith and the consummate expression of an ultimately indefensible world alienation. However, unlike them, she thinks that the "old dream of Western metaphysics" contains a kernel (but only a kernel) of truth. Rejecting the "chasm" (*chōrismos*) Plato and Christianity posited between Being and Becoming does not entail that we deny the reality of the present and embrace Heraclitean flux.[62] Kafka's parable, it turns out, provides an "x-ray" not only of the dream of metaphysics, but of the situation-location of thought itself.

Arendt comes up with a novel way of illustrating what she means by constructing a parallelogram of forces. In her diagram, two vectors—one emanating from an infinite past and the other from an equally infinite future—converge, at a right angle, on the present. They converge at an angle for the simple reason that if they met head-on they would cancel each other out. The "resultant" of these two vectors representing the forces of the past and future is a diagonal originating from the point where they meet: the present. The diagonal is meant to represent thought trains originating in the present—the point at which "He" stands. These shoot off, at a forty-five degree angle, toward infinity. Arendt comments:

> The advantage of this image is that the region of thought would no longer have to be situated beyond and above the world and human time; the fighter would no longer have to jump out of the fighting line in order to find the quiet and the stillness necessary for thinking. "He" would recognize that "his" fighting

has not been in vain, since the battleground itself supplies the region where "he" can rest when "he" is exhausted. In other words, the location of the thinking ego in time would be the in-between of past and future, the present, this mysterious and slippery now, a mere gap in time, towards which nevertheless the more solid tenses of past and future are directed insofar as they denote that which is no more and that which is not yet. That they *are* at all, they obviously owe to man, who has inserted himself between them and established his presence there.[63]

With respect to the resultant that diagrammatically represents thought trains emanating from the present, Arendt remarks

> this diagonal force, whose origin is known, whose direction is determined by past and future, but which exerts its force toward an undetermined end as though it could reach out into infinity, seems to me a perfect metaphor for the activity of thought.[64]

Perfect or not, what the metaphor illustrates is the *temporally situated nature of thought*, a situatedness which is irreducible yet which provides the conditions of possibility for thinking's present—for the ability of thought to seemingly suspend the inexorable flow of time. The diagonal remains firmly "bound to and in the present— an entirely human present though it is fully actualized only in the thinking process and lasts no longer than this process lasts."[65] It is "the quiet of the Now in the time-pressed, time-tossed experience of man," the "quiet in the center of a storm which, though totally unlike the storm, *still belongs to it*."[66] This is the "standing now" of thought, the moment the medieval philosophers reified into the *nunc aeternitatis*, a "model and metaphor for divine eternity."[67]

But, as Kafka's parable and Arendt's gloss upon it reveal, it is certainly *not* eternal. The "present that endures" for as long as thinking lasts is not a suspension of time, let alone the *transcendence* of time. As Arendt observes,

> such an interpretation shrouds our whole mental life in an aura of mysticism and strangely overlooks the *very ordinariness of the experience itself*. The constitution of an 'enduring present' is

'the habitual, normal, banal act of our intellect' [Bergson], performed in every kind of reflection, whether its subject matter
is ordinary day-to-day occurrences or whether the attention is
focused on things forever invisible and outside the sphere of
human power.[68]

Nor does this situated present, the "location" of thinking, have anything genuinely *spatial* about it. The "seeming spatiality of a temporal
phenomenon is an error," one caused by metaphors that leads us to
habitually express duration as extension and thus to view the past as
lying behind the "thinking space" of the present, just as the future
seemingly lies ahead of it.[69] Nor, finally, is the present created by
thinking something that can be inherited or handed down by tradition. "Each new generation," Arendt writes, "every new human being, as he becomes conscious of being inserted between an infinite
past and an infinite future, must discover and ploddingly pave anew
the path of thought."[70]

This is, of course, what Arendt herself did—although by no means
"ploddingly." When in the "Preface" to BPF, she invokes Kafka's parable, she does so not in order to mount a critique of Western philosophical thought, metaphysical or otherwise. She invokes it, rather,
as a description of the situation of thought at a time when "the past
has no longer casts its light on the present." The parable serves as an
introduction to the eight "exercises in political thought" that comprise BPF, exercises that she describes as "critical and experimental"
in nature. When Arendt asks her Socratic "what is?" questions in
essays like "What Is Authority?" and "What Is Freedom?," her intention is not to provide definitive or pseudo-definitive answers delivered *sub specie aeternitatis*. It is, rather, to loosen the soil of thought, to
provoke us to reflect upon political concepts like freedom, authority,
power, and action that we think we know well and that we assume
harbor few if any perplexities.

The concepts Arendt interrogates in BPF and other works are, obviously, not selected arbitrarily. They form the center of situationally
influenced exercises that are designed to rid us of certain hard and
fast preconceptions, much in the spirit of Socratic midwifery. They
consist of thought trains and arguments Arendt invites us to consider, question, and use (or not use) when it comes to our own

thinking about politics and historical events. As "exercises in political thought," they are closer to philosophical thinking than to the "ordinary" thinking of the conscientious individual or citizen. However, unlike philosophical thinking, they are intensely worldly in character. They focus us on not just the concepts, but on the *experiences* that underlie them.

Arendt's *political* thinking thus focuses on a realm of experience, a dimension of reality, that philosophers have habitually devalued: the public realm—the space of appearances, opinions, and action. Not for nothing does LM begin with a series of chapters on "the world's phenomenal nature" and "the value of the surface." It is these things, Arendt argues, together with the fact of human plurality itself, that should be the objects of our wonder and provoke ever-renewed thinking.[71] By reifying the present moment of reflection into the constant presence of an eternal or cosmic order, the Western philosophical tradition has denied not only thought's temporal situatedness; it has also denied the meaning born of human plurality and of words and deeds performed in the public realm. The conclusion of *Thinking* returns us to the opening themes of THC: immortality versus eternity, worldliness versus otherworldliness, *amor mundi* versus *amor Dei* and the salvation of the soul as the "one thing needful."

II Willing and the "abyss of freedom"

Like *Thinking*, *Willing* addresses a component part of the "life of the mind" from a perspective that is at once phenomenological and critical. As in volume I, Arendt turns to canonical thinkers for clues about the nature of a mental activity and the faculty or capacity that underlies it. However, unlike the faculty of Reason, which philosophers have generally apotheosized, the faculty of Will is one they have often denied. "An uncomfortably large number of great philosophers," Arendt writes, "who never doubted the existence of Reason or mind held that the Will is nothing but an illusion."[72] The reason for this skepticism is that few philosophers could accept the idea of a human faculty that possessed the power to rise above all chains of causal necessity—a power, as Kant said in the Third Antinomy, "of spontaneously beginning a new series of successive series or states."[73] Moreover, those who *did* acknowledge the Will's existence tended to obscure the "actual experiences of the willing ego" by means of "doctrines and theories" that are, as Arendt drily puts it, "not necessarily interested in 'saving the phenomena.'"[74]

Compounding these difficulties is the fact that "the faculty of the Will was unknown to Greek antiquity." It was only discovered as a result of experiences "about which we hear next to nothing before the first century of the Christian era."[75] Since we tend to view human faculties as part of our nature, as given and "coeval with the appearance of man as such," Arendt's claim about the historicity of the Will may strike some as outlandish. Yet, as Gilbert Ryle pointed out, "Plato and Aristotle never mentioned [volitions] in their frequent and elaborate discussions of the nature of the soul and the springs of conduct." Ryle himself saw this fact as one small piece of evidence for the view that the Will was a "mere illusion of consciousness," a kind of ghost in the machine born during the Christian era in order to validate our pretensions to being a special kind of self-moving animal.[76] And indeed, in Plato's *Republic*, it is Reason that commands the other parts of the soul (spirit and desire) with no aid from a separate volitional faculty. Likewise, Aristotle makes no mention of the Will and broadly follows the Platonic schema. Reason for him is the part of the soul that is "the natural judge and ruler" while desires are blind and in need of discipline and command.[77]

Yet, despite his silence regarding a distinct volitional faculty, Aristotle (according to Arendt) "laid the foundations" for later philosophy's generally skeptical attitude toward the Will. In book VII of the *Metaphysics* he makes an important distinction between things that necessarily are as opposed to things that are contingent, a distinction he frames ontologically in terms of the difference between *substance* (the underlying or essential substrate of a thing) and its non-essential or accidental attributes (color, smell, taste, etc.). The higher ontological status of the substantial and necessary is taken for granted, not just by Aristotle but by virtually the entire Western philosophical tradition as well. One obvious consequence of this is that the realm of human affairs is relegated to a lower, less dignified and important, ontological status. What, after all, could be more contingent and "accidental" than the events and actions constituting this realm?

However, there was a type of human activity that Aristotle thought escaped from this relegation to the realm of the accidental and

"merely" contingent. Unlike the unpredictable and ephemeral results of action (*praxis*), the products of fabrication (*poiēsis*) were predictable and durable. Moreover, these products clearly do not just
appear out of thin air. They pre-exist in the shape of the matter or
material at hand (their "material cause") and the form or idea the
craftsman imposes upon it (their "formal cause"). A bowl, for example, can be said to exist potentially in the ingot of bronze before
it is actualized by a craftsman who fabricates it in accordance with
his pre-existing idea of its form.

Like his distinction between the necessary and the contingent,
Aristotle's conception of things existing *potentially* before their productive "actualization" is fraught with consequences for philosophical
thought about the Will. As Arendt points out, "the view that everything
real must be preceded by a potentiality as one of its causes implicitly
denies the future as an authentic tense." From Aristotle's teleological standpoint, the only difference between natural products (the oak
"produced" by the acorn) and man-made ones (the bowl fashioned
by the craftsman) is that between "potentialities that *necessarily* grow
into actualities and those that may or may not be actualized."[78]

Viewed through this optic, the future "is nothing but a consequence of the past." Under these circumstances, "any notion of
the Will as an organ for the future…was entirely superfluous."[79]
It is therefore not surprising that (in the words Etienne Gilson),
"Aristotle speaks neither of liberty nor of free will…the term itself
is lacking."[80] However, in the *Nicomachean Ethics* Aristotle does draw
our attention to a faculty for free and deliberate *choice* between two
possible courses of conduct.[81] This faculty, which Aristotle called
proairesis, is, in Arendt's view, the only real "forerunner" to the Will to
be found in Greek thought. Yet the faculty identified by Aristotle is
hardly synonymous with the capacity for spontaneous beginning or
genuine novelty. *Proairesis* is, rather, the human capacity to *decide* between two possible courses of conduct, courses that are *pregiven* to the
agent. He knows what his alternatives are and he must deliberate and
choose between them. The traditional concept of the Will as a *liberum
arbitrium* (or freedom of choice) is obviously derived from *proairesis*.[82]

The absence of anything like a volitional faculty for spontaneous beginning in the moral philosophy of both Plato and Aristotle
becomes less perplexing when we remember the cyclical nature of

antiquity's concept of time. Patterned after the cycles of the seasons and the motions of the stars, this was a concept of time "where indeed every end is a beginning and every beginning an end." And, just as in the ever-recurring cycles of nature, so too in the realm of human affairs, where it was thought that nothing radically new ever happens—a view that allowed Thucydides to claim that his History would have great practical utility since the basic situations and conflicts recounted there were bound to recur in more or less the same form. Even the pre-philosophic Greek praise of greatness and the extraordinary, which seems to run counter to such a conception, actually presupposes it. Homer's "circling years" form the backdrop against which story unfolds and heroic deeds recounted.[83]

According to Arendt, the recognition of a separate mental faculty, the Will, that was the seat not just of deliberate choice but of the freedom to begin something genuinely new hinged upon three transformations brought about by the advent of Christianity. First, the conceptual possibility of spontaneous beginning depended upon the replacement of antiquity's cyclical time concept by Christianity's rectilinear one. "The story that begins with Adam's expulsion from Paradise and end's with Christ's death and resurrection is a story of unique, unrepeatable events," and it was this fact that made it possible for genuine novelty to be conceived.[84] Second, the idea that man was made in the image of a Creator God strongly implied that he too possessed something like a power to spontaneously begin, to rise above the "eternal recurrence" that confined all of God's other creatures. Third, whereas freedom had previously been identified with an objective state of being—the free being enjoyed by citizens of ancient democracies and republics—it was now identified with the believer's inward state of *consciousness*. With the decline of citizenship and political freedom in the ancient world, the "I can" of the citizen who acts in concert with his peers was replaced by the "I will" of the solitary believer struggling to conform to the teachings of Jesus.

"The Old [Mosaic] Law said: thou shalt do; the New Law says: thou shalt will."[85] It was this "experience of an imperative demanding *voluntary* submission" that "led to the discovery of the Will"—that is, to the discovery of a faculty of *inner* freedom "by virtue of which, regardless of necessity or compulsion, [the individual] can say 'Yes' or 'No,' agree or disagree with what is factually given, including [even] his own self and his existence."[86] Yet the discovery of this faculty was, paradoxically, made possible by the experience of its relative impotence rather than its power, by the "I-will-and-*cannot*" manifest in the pathos of St. Paul's declaration "For to will is present with me; but how to perform that which is good I find not." As Augustine was to recognize, what first appears as nothing short of "monstrous"— that we are endowed with a faculty whose very nature it is "partly to will, partly to nill"—is in fact the precondition of its actuality. "For the will commands that there be a will, it commands not something else but itself...Were the will entire, it would not even command itself to be, because it would already be."[87]

The first chapter of *Willing*, "The Philosophers and the Will," only sketches these transformations and their profound implications for "a history of the Will." (Arendt treats the relevant Christian theological texts—Paul, Augustine, Aquinas, and Scotus—at length in the second and third chapters.) This preliminary and cursory treatment allows Arendt to skip ahead to the modern age, where—given the advances made possible by the new science's more "willful" approach to Nature and the ascendency of the idea of Progress—one expects to find philosophers affirming the Will's *power* rather than its self-divided weakness. Yet, during the early modern period (up through and including the Enlightenment) this is not what we find at all. In fact,

> So strong was the suspicion of the willing faculty, so sharp the reluctance to grant human beings, unprotected by any divine Providence or guidance, absolute power over their own destinies and thus burden them with a formidable responsibility for things whose very existence would depend exclusively on themselves, so great, in Kant's words, was the embarrassment of "speculative reason in dealing with the question of the freedom of the will...[namely with] a power of *spontaneously* beginning a series of successive things or states"...that it was not till the last stage of the modern age that the Will began to be substituted for Reason as man's highest mental faculty.[88]

It was only in the first flush of post-Kantian speculation that the Will usurped the place of Reason in the philosophical hierarchy of mental faculties. In this regard, Arendt cites Schiller ("there is no other power in man but his Will"), Schopenhauer (the Being behind appearances, the "thing in itself," is Will), Schelling ("In the final and highest instance there is no other Being than Will"), and Hegel.[89] The seeming apotheosis of the Will in Nietzsche's philosophy is precisely that— seeming. In fact, Arendt argues, Nietzsche's doctrine of the Eternal Return signifies nothing less than "an explicit reversion to the cyclical time concept of antiquity," the modernity of which is apparent in "the pathetic tone in which it is expressed."[90] Finally, Heidegger—whose early philosophy in *Being and Time* emphasized *Dasein*'s future-oriented care for its own being—came, in his later philosophy, to view modernity's technological nihilism as rooted in the domination of the Will. His work after the famous *Kehre* (turning) is thus animated throughout by what Arendt calls the "will not-to-will."[91]

As for the early modern period from Hobbes to Kant—a period supposedly marked by different versions of "voluntarism"—Arendt claims it was characterized by three oft-reiterated objections to the Will. The first, given archetypal expression in the work of both Hobbes and Spinoza, was that the Will was a mere illusion, a "phantasm" born of consciousness' very structure. Men "believe themselves to be free, simply because they are conscious of their actions, and unconscious of the causes whereby those actions are determined."[92] For Hobbes and Spinoza, the Will and its freedom are subjectively *felt*. However, objectively speaking, the actions of men are as determined by chains of efficient causation every bit as necessary and sufficient as those determining the motion of a thrown stone or a spinning top.

The second reason for early modern philosophy's distrust of the Will had to do with its "inevitable connection with Freedom." As Augustine had pointed out long before, the notion of an "unfree will" is a contradiction in terms: "If I must necessarily will, why need I speak of will at all?....Our will would not be will unless it were in our power. Because it is in our power it is free."[93] Over a millennium later, Descartes amplifies Augustine's point:

> I am conscious of a will so extended as to be subject to no limits...It is a free will alone...which I find to be so great in me that I can conceive no other idea to be more great; it is...this will that causes me to know that...I bear the image and similitude of God.[94]

Yet, if the Will exists and is indeed as free as Augustine and Descartes maintain, its freedom transcends the sort of "moral causality" Kant attributed to it. Not only is the Will so conceived outside the "mechanism of nature." It is effectively *lawless* in its power of sheer spontaneity.

The third broad objection modern philosophers lodged against the Will was that a free volitional faculty could not but operate under the "curse of contingency." If the mark of a free Will was that it could as easily leave an action undone as perform it, then everything that flowed from it—abstentions as well as actions—was irreducibly contingent. Considered from the standpoint of a thinking ego that desired to commune with "things necessary and everlasting," the Will's domain—that of human actions and affairs—appeared as a realm of unrelieved contingency and ultimate meaninglessness. For centuries, Christian philosophy had kept this threat at bay by means of the idea of divine Providence. However, with the rise of the modern age and its concomitant de-Christianization and secularization, "men of thought" were "more radically and more mercilessly" exposed to the contingency of all things human than they had ever been before.[95] The problem of freedom was thus incorporated into the "haphazardness of history," a haphazardness that could be transcended only by means of the *ersatz* Providence offered by secular philosophies of history such as Hegel's.

Behind these archetypal philosophical objections to the Will looms the specter of an *absolute* beginning. Such an idea could obviously not arise within the framework established by antiquity's cyclical time concept, nor within the Greek philosophical interpretation of Being as a pure or constant presence. The Biblical account of creation, however, widely disseminated the idea of an absolute beginning. This is an idea which Arendt thinks resonated with the experience of the willing ego, forever devising new projects, but which—viewed from the perspective of the thinking ego—bordered on incoherence. How, after all, could one possibly navigate the transition from Nothing to Something?[96] The only escape from the contradiction between the metaphysical presuppositions of Greek philosophy and the dogmas of Christian faith was redeployment of the old Aristotelian distinction between potentiality and actuality. This strategy enabled medieval thinkers like Thomas Aquinas to reconcile the particular and contingent (the domain of the Will) with the universal and the necessary (the objects of the Intellect).

This escape route was, apparently, closed once and for all by the assault of the "new science" upon teleological explanation and by Kant's presentation of the stark and irresolvable conflict between the logic of efficient causation and the possibility that human beings possessed a "power of *spontaneously* beginning a series of successive things or states."[97] It was only with the retrospective glance of Hegel's "owl of Minerva" that events which previously appeared as either totally contingent (and therefore meaningless) or physically-psychologically determined (and therefore unfree) could be meaningfully woven into the story of man's growing consciousness of his own freedom. According to Hegel, the ideal principle of freedom gradually realized itself through the historical development of rational laws, institutions, and constitutional arrangements—laws, institutions, and arrangements which humanity would ultimately recognize as full and adequate expressions of its own free nature.[98] Human freedom is thus the "end of history" in two senses for Hegel. First, it is the goal implicit in the whole dialectical process of history, the principle that drives the whole process of development forward. Second, it is the "end of history" in the sense that is only at the end of the journey that we become fully conscious of the fact that freedom was the driving principle and that it has (finally) achieved its full actualization in the (post-historical) present.

Hegel famously described the task of philosophy to be the elimination of the contingent. His philosophy of history distinguishes the necessary from the contingent in history by making full use of the Aristotle's teleological categories of *potentiality* and *actualization*. Freedom is thus made into the fruit of (historical) necessity—the necessity underlying all teleological development. At other moments in her work Arendt presents this Hegelian thought as an unbearable paradox, one whose influence on political theory and practice has been entirely destructive. However, in LM she is, if not sympathetic to Hegel's idea, at least more appreciative of its phenomenological grounding in human temporality and memory. After all, Arendt writes,

> in the perspective of memory, that is, looked at retrospectively, a freely performed act loses its air of contingency under the

impact of now being an accomplished fact, of having become
part and parcel of the reality in which we live. The impact of reality is overwhelming to the point that we are unable to 'think
it away'; the act appears to us now in the guise of necessity, a necessity that is by no means a mere delusion of consciousness.[99]

For support, she cites the philosopher Henri Bergson: "By virtue
of its sheer factuality, reality throws its shadow behind it into an
infinitely distant past; thus it appears to have existed in the mode of
potentiality in advance of its own actualization."[100]

This "reality effect" is felt most strongly by thinking ego who, in
reflection on the present, turns to memory and projects lines of narrative continuity back onto the past, the better to facilitate its own
quest for meaning. All thinking is a kind of after-thought (*nach-denken*).
It is this fact more than any other that underlies our impression of
the apparent inevitability of historical events. However, seen from
the future-oriented perspective of the willing ego, "it is not freedom
but necessity that appears as a delusion of consciousness."[101]

Arendt calls Bergson's insight "both elementary and highly significant." Yet despite its plausibility it seems not to have played any
role in "the endless discussions of necessity versus freedom." If it
had—that is, if more philosophers had been willing to acknowledge
the illusory quality of the shadow cast by the sheer factuality of the
present—it is possible that Duns Scotus, "the lonely defender of the
primacy of the Will over the Intellect," would have been less lonely
in his affirmation of an all-pervasive contingency. In the event, the
"original [philosophical] bias against contingency, particularity, and
Will—and the predominance accorded to necessity, universality, and
Intellect—survived the challenge deep into the modern age."[102] Like
the religious and medieval philosophy that preceded it, secular and
modern philosophy "found many different ways of assimilating the
Will, the organ of freedom and the future, to the older order of
things."[103]

Arendt thus finds herself in profound agreement with Bergson's
observation that "most philosophers…are unable…to conceive of
radical novelty and unpredictability."[104] Incompatible with both the
idea of divine Providence and the law of causality, the Will's freedom can be *assumed* on the basis of our inner experience, but it can

never be proved. Moreover, it is not only the shadow cast by the factuality of the present that makes a power of spontaneously beginning appear illusory. Our entire "outward experience" in the world of appearances evidently confirms the fact that "we seldom start a new series." Bergson himself noted that "free acts are exceptional." This accords with what Arendt asserted in THC. For the most part, especially in mass societies, human behavior is statistically predictable and decidedly unoriginal in nature. Yet the extraordinary does (occasionally) happen in the midst of the ordinary, a "miracle" that interrupts the routines of daily life and the automatism of our biological and social existence.[105]

The philosophers' disinclination to acknowledge the interruptive character of creative or initiatory action leads Arendt to conclude that "we can no more trust the men of thought to arrive at a fair estimate of the Will than we could trust them to arrive at a fair estimate of the body."[106] But the antagonism of the thinking ego to the Will is of a different order than the antagonism between mind and body. What we are dealing with, according to Arendt, is a clash "between two mental activities that seem unable to coexist."[107] What is the root of this incompatibility?

Forming a volition entails focusing our attention on a future project. Like thinking, the activity of willing depends upon our ability to withdraw from the world, at least for short periods of time. Moreover, both willing and thinking operate by making present to our minds things that are actually absent. However, whereas thinking draws into its "enduring present" what either is or at least was, willing stretches out into a future where "no such certainties exist."[108] The future is the dimension of the unknown and the uncertain, and our "psychic apparatus" (the soul or self as distinguished from the mind) is equipped to deal with what approaches from this "region of the unknown" by means of expectation, "whose chief modes are hope and fear."[109] And, as Arendt notes, "every hope carries within itself a fear, and every fear cures itself by turning to the corresponding hope."[110]

The result is a profound difference in what Arendt calls the "tonality" of willing and thinking. The latter withdraws to the reflective standpoint of an "enduring present," and this withdrawal from the realm of appearance and the cares of the world contains the promise of a contemplative serenity. Willing, on the other hand, not only "relates to the world of appearances in which its project is to be realized," it occurs in the face of anxiety-producing uncertainty. Stretching itself out toward the future, the willing ego desires nothing more than the achievement of its projected goal. This achievement would bring release from the tension that is constitutive of the act of willing. The "normal mood" of the willing ego is one of impatience (for the securing of the goal) and disquiet (in the face of an unknowable future). This "worrying disquiet" is overcome only by action and by confidence in our ability to perform what the will wills.

Willing is thus characterized by three things the thinking ego wishes to escape: contingency, uncertainty, and tension. Recognizing the Will as a "power of spontaneously beginning" would be tantamount to acknowledging an "abyss of freedom" that could not be bridged by Aristotelian/Hegelian ideas of potentialities that actualize themselves through natural or historical development. Making this acknowledgement was not something the philosophers (or "men of thought") were inclined to do. But neither, Arendt argues, were "men of action" such as those who led the American Revolution inclined to embrace such a power or such a freedom.

In the concluding chapter of LM Arendt recounts the founders' desire to bridge the "abyss of nothingness" that their revolutionary interruption—their radical beginning—had inserted into history. In her telling, they turned to the Old Testament and the *Aeneid* in the hope that these foundation legends "might tell them how to solve the problem of beginning—a problem because beginning's very nature is to carry in itself an element of complete arbitrariness."[111] To avoid the appearance of groundlessness, these secular and enlightened men invoked a natural or divine order behind events. And to avoid the appearance of discontinuity and arbitrariness, they appealed to the Roman idea that every foundation is in fact a re-foundation. "The abyss of pure spontaneity," Arendt writes, "was covered up by the device, typical of the Occidental tradition (...) of understanding the new as an improved re-statement of the old."[112] Like the philosophers but in a different way, the "men of action" quailed in the face of the "abyss" that their absolutely unprecedented action had opened.

III Conclusion

The reader of *Willing* could well come away with the impression that in it Arendt reveals herself as a voluntarist. The contrast between her critical analysis of early modern philosophical objections to the Will and her positive presentations of Augustine (the "first philosopher of the Will"), Scotus (who upheld the "primacy of the Will"), and Bergson evidently confirms such an assessment.

While understandable, this impression is nevertheless mistaken. Although Arendt affirms a power of spontaneous beginning, she makes no attempt to *ground* this power in the Will or any other faculty we each possess *qua* individual human subjects. She concludes *Willing* by once again citing Augustine ("That there be a beginning man was created") and telling us that "the very capacity for beginning is rooted in *natality*, and by no means in creativity, not in a gift but in the fact that human beings, new men, again and again appear in the world by virtue of birth."[113]

This statement is in perfect accord with the skepticism she expressed in THC about the very idea of a "human nature" and with her overarching emphasis on the "human conditions" of plurality and mortality. The power of spontaneously beginning is not a faculty that we, as *individual subjects*, possess thanks to God or Nature. Rather, it is a power that we, as plural and finite beings, embody by virtue of our coming into the world, a world already inhabited by others. Another way of putting this is to say that freedom was never a *problem* for Hannah Arendt. It was, rather, an indisputable phenomenological reality encountered in the realm that is most associated with, and defined by, the fact of human plurality: "The field where freedom has always been known, not as a problem, to be sure, but as a fact of everyday life, is the political realm."[114] The will to deny this freedom and this reality had been one of the most powerful animating forces of the Western philosophical and theological traditions. This denial continues to permeate our culture, deepening our alienation from the world at a moment in history when care for it was never more imperative.

Summary

Arendt's final work, *The Life of the Mind*, was originally conceived as an investigation of thinking, willing, and judging as mental activities.

The third part, on judgment, was left unwritten at the time of her death but the volumes on Thinking and Willing were in sufficiently complete form to be published posthumously.

Thinking picks up were Arendt's reflections on Eichmann (in Eichmann in Jerusalem) and Socrates (in "Thinking and Moral Considerations") left off. However, the focus on the activity of thinking as such entails a step back from the suggestive connections Arendt made between our capacity for thought and the development of conscience. When treated as a mental activity, the question shifts from "what are the possible moral implications of thinking?" to "where are we when we think?"—what is the peculiar (non-) time and (non-) space we inhabit when lost in reflection? Answering these questions demands a phenomenology of thinking parallel to the one of action given in THC. However, unlike action, thinking is an "invisible activity"—a silent dialogue between me and myself—that deals not with anything visible and present but with "invisibles" that take the form of concepts and memories our imagination "re-presents" to us.

Arendt suggests that the best phenomenological evidence for the nature of this activity may be found in the texts of the Western philosophical canon, even though she believes that these "professional thinkers" were more interested in the supposed results of thinking (metaphysical or moral truths) than with the activity itself. They were inclined to frame the withdrawal from worldly activity that thinking demands as a complete turning away from the flux of this world to an eternal realm of ideal forms or true Being. Thus, while the great philosophers of the Western canon give us clues about the nature of thinking, their own desire to transcend the world of appearances led them to interpret thinking as a contemplative exercise, one far removed from the activity of "passionate thinking" Heidegger attributed to Socrates. In sum, the great philosophers instrumentalized thinking by presenting it as a path to Truth. In so doing they further encouraged alienation from the world. Rescuing thinking as reflection on the events, concepts, and opinions that shape our experience of this world thus demands that we make a distinction between ordinary thinking (the habit of reflection on whatever comes to pass) and the philosophical or metaphysical thinking practiced by the "professional thinkers." Moreover, it demands that we recognize that location of thinking is defined temporally. The thinking ego does not occupy a "pure present" outside of time, but rather a small gap of non-time between past and future.

If the philosophers distort the activity of thinking by interpreting it in contemplative terms, they habitually deny the reality of the Will as our capacity to spontaneously begin. The philosophical preference for necessity over contingency, "substance" over "accident," and Being over appearance leads to doctrines of teleological, mechanical, and historical causation, all of which present the human capacity to freely begin as an illusion. This preference for necessity over contingency is so deeply set into our philosophical and theological traditions that it led even the eighteenth-century "men of revolution" to deny the radical novelty of their own enormous and utterly unprecedented achievement.

Notes

1 Arendt, LM, p. 5.
2 Arendt, LM, p. 6.
3 Arendt, THC, p. 325.
4 Arendt, LKPP, p. 37.
5 Arendt, THC, p. 176.
6 Plato, Theaetetus, 155d, quoted in Arendt, LM, I, p. 142.
7 Arendt, LM, I, p. 143.
8 Quoted in Arendt, LM, I, p. 143.
9 Arendt, LM, I, p. 143.
10 Arendt, LM, I, p. 144.
11 Arendt, "Socrates" in Promise of Politics, pp. 34–35.
12 Arendt, LM, I, p. 150. See also LM, II, p. 185.
13 Arendt, LM, I, p. 147.
14 Arendt, LM, I, p. 155.
15 Arendt, LM, I, p. 156.
16 Arendt, LM, I, p. 160.
17 Arendt, LM, I, p. 49.
18 Arendt, LM, I, pp. 48–52.
19 Kateb, Hannah Arendt, p. 195.
20 Arendt, Promise of Politics, p. 33.
21 Arendt, LKPP, p. 37.
22 Plato, Theaetetus, 189e–190a; Sophist, 263e.
23 Arendt, LM, I, p. 185.
24 Arendt, LM, I, p. 185.
25 Arendt, Promise of Politics, p. 13.
26 See Dana Villa, Socratic Citizenship (Princeton: Princeton University Press, 2001).
27 Arendt, LM, I, p. 178.

28 Arendt, LKPP, p. 37.
29 Arendt, LM, I, 191. My emphases.
30 Arendt, LM, I, p. 178.
31 Arendt adds Jaspers to this list: see LM, II, p. 22.
32 Arendt, MDT, p. 27.
33 Plato, "The Apology of Socrates" in Plato, Collected Dialogues, edited by Edith
    Hamilton and Huntington Cairns (Princeton: Princeton University Press, 1989),
    40d–41d.
34 Arendt, LKPP, p. 37.
35 Kant, Critique of Pure Reason, Avii.
36 Arendt, LM, I, p. 14.
37 Kant, Critique of Pure Reason, Axvii.
38 Arendt, LM, I, p. 14.
39 Kant quoted by Arendt, LM, I, p. 63.
40 Kant, Critique of Pure Reason, Bxxx.
41 Arendt, LM, I, p. 15.
42 Arendt, LM, I, p. 15.
43 Arendt, LM, I, p. 15.
44 She actually makes a point of stating that "the dismantling process itself is not
    destructive" (LM, I, p. 212).
45 Arendt, LM, I, p. 12.
46 Arendt, LM, I, p. 199.
47 See especially Heidegger, Introduction to Metaphysics (New Haven: Yale University
    Press, 1959).
48 Aristotle quoted by Arendt, LM, I, p. 200.
49 Arendt, LM, I, p. 200.
50 Arendt, LM, I, p. 200.
51 Kafka cited in Arendt, BPF, p. 7.
52 Arendt, LM, I, p. 202.
53 Arendt, LM, I., p. 205.
54 Arendt, LM, I, pp. 202–203.
55 Arendt, LM, I, p. 203.
56 Arendt, LM, I., p. 203.
57 Arendt, LM, I, p. 205.
58 Arendt, LM, I, p. 205.
59 Arendt, LM, I, p. 206.
60 Arendt, LM, I, p. 206.
61 Arendt, LM, I, p. 207.
62 Martin Heidegger, An Introduction to Metaphysics, p. 106.
63 Arendt, LM, I, p. 208.
64 Arendt, LM, I, p. 209.
65 Arendt, LM, I, p. 209.
66 Arendt, LM, I, p. 209. My emphasis.
67 Arendt, LM, I. p. 210.
68 Arendt, LM, II, p. 12. My emphasis.
69 Arendt, LM, II, p. 13.
70 Arendt, LM, I, p. 210.

71 Arendt, "Socrates," in Promise of Politics, pp. 38–39.
72 Arendt, LM, II, p. 13.
73 Kant, Critique of Pure Reason, B476.
74 Arendt, LM, II, p. 3.
75 Arendt, LM, II, p. 3.
76 Ryle quoted in Arendt, LM, II, p. 4.
77 Aristotle, Protrepikos, quoted by Arendt, LM, II, 58.
78 Arendt, LM, II, p. 15.
79 Arendt, LM, II, p. 15.
80 Arendt, LM, II, p. 16.
81 Aristotle, Nicomachean Ethics, 1135b.
82 Arendt, LM, II, p. 29.
83 Arendt, LM, II, p. 17.
84 Arendt, LM, II, p. 18.
85 Arendt, LM, II, p. 68
86 Arendt, LM, II, p. 68.
87 Augustine, Confessions, bk VIII, ch. 8.
88 Arendt, LM, II, pp. 19–20.
89 Arendt, LM, II, p. 20.
90 Arendt, LM, II, p. 21.
91 Arendt, LM, II, p. 22.
92 Spinoza, quoted by Arendt, LM, II, p. 23.
93 Augustine, De Libero Arbitrio, quoted by Arendt, LM, II, p. 26.
94 Descartes, Meditation IV in Meditations, quoted by Arendt, LM, II, p. 26.
95 Arendt, LM, II. P. 28.
96 Arendt, LM, II. P. 30.
97 Kant, Critique of Pure Reason, B476.
98 G. W. F. Hegel, Philosophy of History, translated by J. Sibree (New York: Dover Publications, 1956), pp. 18–19.
99 Arendt, LM, II, p. 30.
100 Bergson quoted in Arendt, LM, II, p. 31.
101 Arendt, LM, II. p. 31.
102 Arendt, LM, II, p. 32.
103 Arendt, LM, II, p. 32.
104 Arendt, LM, II, p. 32.
105 Arendt, THC, pp. 246–247.
106 Arendt, LM, II, p. 34.
107 Arendt, LM, II, p. 35.
108 Arendt, LM, II, p. 35.
109 Arendt, LM, II, p. 35.
110 Arendt, LM, II. p. 35.
111 Arendt, LM, II, p. 207.
112 Arendt, LM, II, p. 216.
113 Arendt, LM, II. p. 217.
114 Arendt, BPF, p. 144.

Further reading

A. Heller, "Hannah Arendt on the *vita contemplativa*" in G. T. Kaplan and C. S. Kessler (eds.), *Hannah Arendt: Thinking, Judging, Freedom* (London: Allen and Unwin, 1989), pp. 144–159.

J. Taminiaux, *The Thracian Maid and the Professional Thinker: Arendt and Heidegger* (Albany: SUNY Press, 1997).

E. Young-Bruehl, "Reading Hannah Arendt's *The Life of the Mind*" in Young-Bruehl, *Mind and the Body Politic* (New York: Routledge, 1988).

Eight
Legacy

Arendt was famous at the time of her death in 1975 but it took twenty years for the full extent of her achievement to be appreciated. Early studies of her thought, such as Margaret Canovan's first book (1974) and George Kateb's *Hannah Arendt: Politics, Conscience, Evil* (1984), did much to set the stage, as did Elisabeth Young-Bruehl's biography, *Hannah Arendt: For Love of the World* (1982). But recognition as a canonical figure in political theory and a truly wide audience within the academy eluded her until the 1990s. Before that decade many still thought of her as a public intellectual or "Cold War" thinker. As late as 1988 the political theorist Thomas Pangle could write that Arendt "cannot be called a scholar," stating that she "was too much a journalist and even a café intellectual"—presumably because she had published in *The New Yorker* and *The New York Review of Books*.[1] The socialist-leaning left in the American academy viewed her warily, while her work went largely ignored in the *marxisant* intellectual culture of post-war France. Despite achieving a certain amount of popularity among self-proclaimed "participatory democrats" in the 1960s, the rise of such social movements as feminism, environmentalism, and gay rights in the 1970s apparently left Arendt's specifically political concerns behind.

What accounts for the sudden upsurge of interest in Arendt's work in the 1990s? Such questions are difficult to answer. One could point to events like the collapse of the Soviet Union and dissolution of the eastern bloc in 1989, or the bloody breakup of the former Yugoslavia in the early 1990s. The fall of communism in Czechoslovakia, Poland, and East Germany certainly had their

"Arendtian" moments of "people power," with leading figures such as the Polish dissident Adam Michnik citing Arendt's influence on his own thinking. In Paris the so-called *nouveaux philosophes* publicized Solzhenitsyn's account of the Soviet gulag in the mid-to-late 1970s, thereby helping to dislodge Marxism from its dominant position among French intellectuals.

Arendt's analysis of the inner workings of totalitarianism certainly spoke to democratizing tendencies in the eastern bloc, just as her analysis of the camps as the "central institutions" of both Nazi and Soviet totalitarianism seemed prescient in light of Solzhenitsyn. But these factors, important as they are, hardly account for the dramatic upsurge of interest in Arendt's work in north and south America, Germany, Japan, England, France, Italy, and Australia during the 1990s.

It is difficult to make generalizations about the underlying reasons for Arendt's growing influence in the post-communist world. One can, however, point to the removal of two obstacles blocking wider appreciation of her thought. First, the fall of communism helped bury the (false) image of Arendt as "Cold Warrior." Second, the end of 1960s helped remove the perception of her as an *eminence grise* among student radicals. The fading of these two (contradictory) aspects of her public image allowed Arendt's work to be read without ideological preconceptions. Her extraordinarily original *oeuvre* could (finally) be read on its own terms. It turned out that she had incisive things to say not just about totalitarian evil or participatory politics, but also about the public sphere, political freedom, the legacy of republicanism, the anti-democratic character of much of the Western tradition, and the civic corruption produced by an unfettered capitalism.

Not only that. Once the images of Arendt as a fifties-style Cold Warrior or sixties-style participatory democrat dissolved it became possible to recover her deep intellectual roots in the German philosophical tradition. While her debts to such figures as Jaspers, Heidegger, Kant, and Nietzsche had been noted before, they had rarely been explored in any depth. Once this exploration commenced, interest in her work rapidly moved beyond the narrow disciplinary confines of political theory and political science.

Arendt is now read in virtually all fields in the humanities. Scholars in philosophy, literature, history, religion, and cultural studies routinely cite and critically engage with her work. In 2006, the year of her centenary, conferences in her honor were held in Paris, Berlin, Italy, Scandinavia, the United States, south America, Israel, and Turkey. There is a journal, *Arendt Studies*, devoted to her work, and a team of German and American scholars is in the process of preparing a critical scholarly edition of her writings. Last, but by no means least, the rise of proto-totalitarian populist movements in America, Brazil, and Europe in the 2010s has given the appropriation of Arendt's thought inside and outside the academy an added urgency.

What aspects of her work, then, have been especially influential over the past few decades?

First, her analysis of the elements that helped make totalitarianism possible in the mid-twentieth century has proven of more than historical value, as such critical observers of the contemporary scene like Timothy Snyder and Masha Gessen have shown. Sad to say, "totalitarian fiction" appears to be alive and well, even in the liberal democracies that once considered themselves immune.

Second, Arendt's idea of the "banality of evil" has spurred Holocaust and genocide studies to undertake ever more fine-grained psychological, sociological, and historical studies of perpetrators across cultures. While the idea remains controversial, there can be little doubt that it has complicated our sense of what leads ordinary individuals to participate in the worst of crimes. To be sure, there were and are plenty of ideologically motivated ethnic nationalists, racists, and anti-Semites in the world. However, any real or potential realization of their ideologically driven projects ultimately relies upon the enlistment of many thousands of "normal" individuals. It is only with the cooperation of the "good family man"—the individual who wants to keep his job and put food on the table—that it becomes concretely possible to carry out "evil as policy."

Third, Arendt's idea of the public realm in THC has proven remarkably valuable as a critical conceptual tool, even for those who do not agree with her "agonistic" (Greek-inspired) version. Jürgen Habermas' *Structural Transformation of the Public Sphere* (1963), the book that laid the foundation for much of his subsequent theorizing, is in many respects a critical dialogue with Arendt, with Habermas urging a more argument-focused version of the public sphere as an alternative to the "space of appearances" model delineated by Arendt.

Richard Sennett's influential *The Fall of Public Man* (1974) is a work of similarly Arendtian inspiration, one that takes the distinction between the public and private self seriously in its critical exploration of the historical roots of the politics of authenticity. Finally, the "middle" work of Michel Foucault (e.g. *Discipline and Punish*) can be read as a genealogy of our contemporary dystopian or "disciplinary" public sphere. This is a public sphere that serves the purposes of surveillance and normalization rather than facilitating of debate, deliberation, and decision on matters of public concern. The Italian philosopher Giorgio Agamben has been particularly adept at drawing out connections between Arendt and Foucault.

Fourth, Arendt's retrieval of the republican tradition in OR came at a time when many historians were beginning to question conventional liberal interpretations of the American and French Revolutions. It inspired theoretical works like J. G. A. Pocock's *The Machiavellian Moment* (1975) and, more recently, has served as a critical foil for Phillip Pettit's *Republicanism* (1997). Communitarian theorists such as Michael Sandel and Charles Taylor also owe Arendt a small debt of gratitude for the critique of liberalism she mounts in that book. A more extensive debt of gratitude is owed by members of the so-called "Berkeley School" of political theory such as Sheldon Wolin and Hanna Pitkin. These theorists have criticized Arendt from the left but are similarly reliant upon elements of her republican critique of liberalism.

Fifth, Arendt's account of political action in THC has proven remarkably suggestive. Her focus on *praxis* as *praxis*—on political action as debate, deliberation, decision, and acting together—yielded not only a classic critique of the Marxian "work model of action." It also provided the basis for a thorough-going critique of the Western tradition of political philosophy. In recent times, it has provided inspiration for both deliberative democrats and "radical democratic" proponents of agonistic forms of political action. The fact that Arendt's conception of action serves as a touchstone for these two antagonistic strands of contemporary political theory gives some idea of its richness and suggestiveness. Additionally, Arendt's framing of action as initiatory performance on a public stage has generated intense interest in cultural studies, where "performativity" has been fruitfully explored as a crucial dimension of identity-formation and social action.

Sixth, Arendt's critique of the anti-political elements contained in the Western tradition of political thought has provided an interpretive angle that has yet to be fully exploited. This is the dimension of Arendt's thought that owes most to the examples of Nietzsche and Heidegger, each of whom undertook their own depth critiques of the Western philosophical and metaphysical traditions. Arendt's *political* concerns are, as I remarked above, the polar opposite of Nietzsche's aristocratism and Heidegger's reactionary conception of community. Nevertheless, her reading of the tradition, like her "pearl diving," owes much to both thinkers. It is hard to imagine her undertaking a project of such depth and ambition without their example.

Seventh, Arendt's notion of the "rise of the social" has produced a surprisingly diverse set of offspring. The extension of economic categories of thought and administrative modes of action to virtually all spheres of life has served as the *point de départ* for Habermas' notion of the "colonization of the lifeworld" (in his *Theory of Communicative Action*) as well as for such diverse diagnoses of the contemporary "withdrawal of the political" as Sheldon Wolin's (in *Politics and Vision*) and Philippe Lacoue-Labarthe's and Jean-Luc Nancy's (in their *Retreat of the Political*). And, while Habermas for one cast his argument primarily in Weberian terms (as the unconstrained "growth of subsystems of purposive-rational action"), there can be little doubt as to where the original critical inspiration lies.

Finally, Arendt's emphasis on the reality of "what is seen and heard by all" (Aristotle) and the perspectival constitution of the public world has provided a critical check on the more subjectivist tendencies of contemporary identity politics.

Identity politics has been at the center of gender and critical race studies for the past few decades, and it is not uncommon to find scholars in these fields equating it with politics *simpliciter*. This, I think, is a mistake. Arendt's emphasis upon the objectivity of the public world as well as its perspectival constitution serves as a useful corrective to the tendency to accord the category of identity unquestioned priority in all matters political. Of course, class, race, and gender identity are an irreducible part of our contemporary politics, and it would be wrong to minimize them in the name of an ostensibly "universal" category of citizenship that has yet to be concretely achieved. However, equal rights and freedoms are constitutional (i.e. *public*) ideals, ideals that all struggles for recognition, justice, and equal access presuppose. It is one virtue of Hannah Arendt's political thought to remind us of this fact, and to remind us that success in these struggles is dependent upon grasping the imperative to actively preserve and augment the "world"—the constitutionally articulated "space of freedom"—in which these ideals originally took shape.

Note

1 Thomas Pangle, *The Spirit of Modern Republicanism* (Chicago: University of Chicago Press, 1988), p. 49.

Index